Discoveries in the
Economics of Aging

A National Bureau
of Economic Research
Conference Report

Discoveries in the Economics of Aging

Edited by **David A. Wise**

The University of Chicago Press

Chicago and London

DAVID A. WISE is the John F. Stambaugh Professor of Political
Economy at the Kennedy School of Government at Harvard
University. He is the area director of Health and Retirement Programs
and director of the Program on the Economics of Aging at the
National Bureau of Economic Research.

The University of Chicago Press, Chicago 60637
The University of Chicago Press, Ltd., London
© 2014 by the National Bureau of Economic Research
All rights reserved. Published 2014.
Printed in the United States of America

23 22 21 20 19 18 17 16 15 14   1 2 3 4 5

ISBN-13: 978-0-226-14609-6 (cloth)
ISBN-13: 978-0-226-14612-6 (e-book)
DOI: 10.7208/chicago/9780226146126.001.0001

Library of Congress Cataloging-in-Publication Data

Discoveries in the economics of aging / edited by David A. Wise.
        pages cm— (A National Bureau of Economic Research
    conference report)
    "This volume consists of papers presented at a conference held in
    Carefree, Arizona, in May 2013."—Preface.
        ISBN 978-0-226-14609-6 (cloth : alkaline paper)—ISBN 978-0-
    226-14612-6 (e-book) 1. Older people—Economic conditions—
    Research—Congresses. 2. Older people—Health and hygiene—
    Research—Congresses. 3. Well-being—Economic aspects—
    Congresses. 4. Economics—Research—Congresses. I. Wise,
    David A., editor. II. Series: National Bureau of Economic
    Research conference report.
      HQ1061.D5595 2014
      305.26—dc23
                                                        2013040454
⊚ This paper meets the requirements of ANSI/NISO Z39.48-1992
(Permanence of Paper).

Relation of the Directors to the
Work and Publications of the
National Bureau of Economic Research

1. The object of the NBER is to ascertain and present to the economics profession, and to the public more generally, important economic facts and their interpretation in a scientific manner without policy recommendations. The Board of Directors is charged with the responsibility of ensuring that the work of the NBER is carried on in strict conformity with this object.

2. The President shall establish an internal review process to ensure that book manuscripts proposed for publication DO NOT contain policy recommendations. This shall apply both to the proceedings of conferences and to manuscripts by a single author or by one or more co-authors but shall not apply to authors of comments at NBER conferences who are not NBER affiliates.

3. No book manuscript reporting research shall be published by the NBER until the President has sent to each member of the Board a notice that a manuscript is recommended for publication and that in the President's opinion it is suitable for publication in accordance with the above principles of the NBER. Such notification will include a table of contents and an abstract or summary of the manuscript's content, a list of contributors if applicable, and a response form for use by Directors who desire a copy of the manuscript for review. Each manuscript shall contain a summary drawing attention to the nature and treatment of the problem studied and the main conclusions reached.

4. No volume shall be published until forty-five days have elapsed from the above notification of intention to publish it. During this period a copy shall be sent to any Director requesting it, and if any Director objects to publication on the grounds that the manuscript contains policy recommendations, the objection will be presented to the author(s) or editor(s). In case of dispute, all members of the Board shall be notified, and the President shall appoint an ad hoc committee of the Board to decide the matter; thirty days additional shall be granted for this purpose.

5. The President shall present annually to the Board a report describing the internal manuscript review process, any objections made by Directors before publication or by anyone after publication, any disputes about such matters, and how they were handled.

6. Publications of the NBER issued for informational purposes concerning the work of the Bureau, or issued to inform the public of the activities at the Bureau, including but not limited to the NBER Digest and Reporter, shall be consistent with the object stated in paragraph 1. They shall contain a specific disclaimer noting that they have not passed through the review procedures required in this resolution. The Executive Committee of the Board is charged with the review of all such publications from time to time.

7. NBER working papers and manuscripts distributed on the Bureau's web site are not deemed to be publications for the purpose of this resolution, but they shall be consistent with the object stated in paragraph 1. Working papers shall contain a specific disclaimer noting that they have not passed through the review procedures required in this resolution. The NBER's web site shall contain a similar disclaimer. The President shall establish an internal review process to ensure that the working papers and the web site do not contain policy recommendations, and shall report annually to the Board on this process and any concerns raised in connection with it.

8. Unless otherwise determined by the Board or exempted by the terms of paragraphs 6 and 7, a copy of this resolution shall be printed in each NBER publication as described in paragraph 2 above.

Contents

Preface

This volume consists of papers presented at a conference held in Carefree, Arizona, in May 2013. Most of the research was conducted as part of the Program on the Economics of Aging at the National Bureau of Economic Research. The majority of the work was sponsored by the US Department of Health and Human Services, through the National Institute on Aging grants P01-AG005842 and P30-AG012810 to the National Bureau of Economic Research. Any other funding sources are noted in the individual papers.

Any opinions expressed in this volume are those of the respective authors and do not necessarily reflect the views of the National Bureau of Economic Research or the sponsoring organizations.

Introduction

David A. Wise and Richard Woodbury

The long-anticipated aging of the baby boom generation across the threshold of eligibility for Social Security and Medicare has arrived. The 76 million Americans making up the baby boom generation are currently between ages forty-eight and sixty-seven, and their initiation of retirement benefits is accelerating. The societal impact of aging baby boomers is compounded by longer life expectancies, which have risen continually over many decades. The implications of these demographic trends are extensive and significant, yet they are just one part of the rapidly changing landscape of aging in the United States and around the world.

The changing landscape includes a number of long-term trends, such as increased saving in 401(k)-type retirement plans, rising health care costs and, as noted, age demographics. It also includes unanticipated pressures, such as volatility in financial and housing markets, and strained macro-economic conditions. The impact of the financial crisis and its continuing ramifications have emerged as key concerns, adding to the fiscal challenges of government, and complicating people's financial planning for later life. Research in the economics of aging seeks to understand the health and financial well-being of people as they age, and how well-being is affected by this changing landscape.

This is the fifteenth in a series of National Bureau of Economic Research (NBER) volumes synthesizing analyses of economics of aging research.

David A. Wise is the John F. Stambaugh Professor of Political Economy at the Kennedy School of Government at Harvard University. He is the area director of Health and Retirement Programs and director of the Program on the Economics of Aging at the National Bureau of Economic Research. Richard Woodbury is a senior administrator with the Program on the Economics of Aging at the National Bureau of Economic Research.

For acknowledgments, sources of research support, and disclosure of the authors' material financial relationships, if any, please see http://www.nber.org/chapters/c12961.ack.

The previous volumes in this NBER series are *The Economics of Aging, Issues in the Economics of Aging, Topics in the Economics of Aging, Studies in the Economics of Aging, Advances in the Economics of Aging, Inquiries in the Economics of Aging, Frontiers in the Economics of Aging, Themes in the Economics of Aging, Perspectives on the Economics of Aging, Analyses in the Economics of Aging, Developments in the Economics of Aging, Research Findings in the Economics of Aging, Explorations in the Economics of Aging* and *Investigations in the Economics of Aging.*

The goal is to bring together studies that are at the forefront of research in the field. The volumes are not intended to cover the entire area of economics of aging research, but rather to highlight cutting edge research projects that together contribute to a more comprehensive understanding of health and economic well-being as people age. Many of the studies are components of longer-term research themes of the NBER program on aging, and an attempt is made to place these new studies in the context of our larger agenda. Through fifteen volumes, the large majority of this research has been funded by the National Institute on Aging, which has made a long-term commitment to advancing the economics of aging field.

A particular focus of the research reported in this volume deals with health, and its relationship to financial well-being. Why is health so important? First, health is perhaps the most essential aspect of what constitutes well-being as we age. As people live longer, it is important whether those increased years of life are characterized by poor health and functional disability, or by good health and functional independence. Second, health affects one's ability to work at older ages, and is strongly associated with financial well-being. And third, health has societal implications, such as for labor markets, government finances, and health care costs.

In past work, we developed a structural framework for studying health and disability, which we summarize in figure I.1. This framework includes key factors that influence health (the "determinants" in the left section of the figure), the multiple dimensions through which health is measured or characterized (the "characteristics" in the center section of the figure), and some important implications of health (the "consequences" in the right section of the figure).

While the arrows in figure I.1 suggest a unidirectional flow from determinants to characteristics to consequences, much of the research reported in this volume suggests more complicated interactions between variables. For example, health may affect work and retirement decisions at older ages. But whether someone retires may also affect their health. Also emphasized in the volume is the potential for interventions and policy changes to improve health and well-being, using approaches that may be implemented throughout this system of health-related interactions.

The first three chapters of the volume deal with health measurement and health trends. They fit largely within the center section of the figure I.1 framework. Chapter 1 looks at trends in morbidity. Chapter 2 looks at the

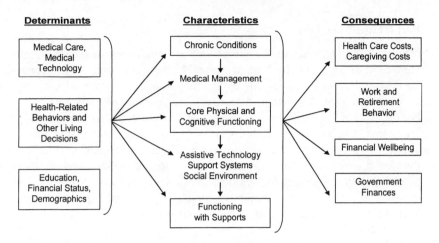

Fig. I.1   A framework for studying health and disability

lifetime risk of nursing home use. Chapter 3 analyzes the differences between various indices of health that have been used for research.

Chapters 4 and 5 look at the relationships and causal interactions between health and financial circumstances. As noted, these relationships are complex, as economic circumstances affect health, as health affects economic circumstances, and as both aspects of well-being interact continually over the life course. In the framework of figure I.1, financial circumstances are explicitly included as both determinants and consequences of health. Chapter 4 explores the extent to which better health and better financial circumstances are related to each other in the latter years of people's lives. Chapter 5 focuses on the causal relationships between health and economic well-being, and how they begin from early childhood.

The next four chapters in the volume consider how other aspects of people's lives affect their health. They fit best in the left sections of figure I.1, on the determinants of health. Chapter 6 looks at whether retirement improves or harms health. Chapter 7 looks at spousal effects on health. Chapter 8 looks at the effects of living with grandchildren. And chapter 9 looks at how aging affects optimism, uncertainty, and potential cognitive decline.

The last three chapters in the volume look at the potential for innovations, interventions, and public policies to improve health and financial well-being. Chapter 10 analyzes an experimental intervention to reduce anemia in a low-income region of the world. Chapter 11 looks at the uneven dissemination of medical advances. Chapter 12 looks at how the availability of a Roth 401(k) option has affected saving in employer-sponsored retirement plans.

The remainder of this introduction provides an overview of the studies contained in the volume, relying to a significant extent on the authors' own language to summarize their work.

Part I: Health and Disability

Continuing increases in life expectancy are one factor in the changing landscape of aging in the United States. Using data from the National Center for Health Statistics, life expectancy at age sixty-two is currently about twenty years for men and twenty-three years for women. The number of years of life expectancy has increased by about a year every decade for at least the last four decades. Longer life is valuable to people, but it is even more valuable if the additional years lived are in good health. For the public sector as well, the consequences of longer lives depend on their quality. Medical spending for healthy seniors is modest, while spending for individuals with severely disabilities is much greater. Part I of the volume looks at trends in health impairments, as well as evaluating alternative measurements of health.

In chapter 1, David M. Cutler, Kaushik Ghosh, and Mary Beth Landrum present "Evidence for Significant Compression of Morbidity in the Elderly US Population." The question of whether morbidity is being compressed into the period just before death has been at the center of health debates in the United States for some time. If morbidity is being compressed into the period just before death, the impacts of population aging are not as severe as if additional life involves many years of expensive care.

Empirical evidence on trends in morbidity is unclear. Some studies suggest that morbidity is being compressed into the period just before death, while others believe that the period of disabled life is expanding or that the evidence is more mixed. There are three reasons for this disagreement. First, there is not a single definition of morbidity. Some studies look at whether people report specific chronic conditions, which have increased over time, while other studies look at functioning. Second, it is often difficult to link health to the stage of life of the individual. If people are reporting more chronic disease, is that in the period just before the end of life, in which case the additional disease does not encompass many years? Or is the disease occurring in periods of time far from the end of life, in which case it represents many years of poor health? To answer this question one needs data on quality of life matched to time until death, and most cross-section data sources do not have such a link. Third, the data samples that tend to be used often focus on a particular subset of the population; for example, the noninstitutionalized. Since there are changes in the residential location of the elderly population over time, focusing on population subsets can give biased results.

Chapter 1 examines the issue of compression of morbidity, addressing these three concerns. The primary data source is the Medicare Current Beneficiary Survey (MCBS). The study analyzes health trends, linked to death records, for a representative sample of the entire elderly population between 1991 and 2009. The data are used in two ways. First, the authors examine trends in various measures of morbidity by time until death. They consider a number of different metrics: the presence of disease; whether the person reports activities of daily living (ADL) or instrumental activities of daily living (IADL) disability; and various summary measure of functioning that draw together nineteen different dimensions of health. They show trends overall and by time until death.

As is well known, the MCBS data from the 1990s and 2000s show a reduction in the share of elderly people who report ADL or IADL limitations. A first result of this study is that this reduction in disability is most marked among those with many years until death. Health status in the year or two just prior to death has been relatively constant over time; in contrast, health measured three or more years before death has improved measurably. In chapter 1, these changes are translated into years of disability-free life expectancy and years of disabled life expectancy. The authors find that disability-free life expectancy is increasing over time, while disabled life expectancy is falling.

For a typical person age sixty-five, life expectancy increased by 0.7 years between 1992 and 2005. Disability-free life expectancy increased by 1.6 years; disabled life expectancy fell by 0.9 years. The reduction in disabled life expectancy and the increase in disability-free life expectancy were found for both genders and for nonwhites as well as whites. Hence, morbidity is being compressed into the period just before death.

A major question raised by these results is why this occurred. How much of this trend is a result of medical care versus other social and environmental factors? The results do not speak to this issue, but they give us a metric for analyzing the impact of changes that have occurred.

In their discussion of chapter 1, Daniel McFadden and Wei Xie highlight the significant differences between trends in disease prevalence and trends in functional morbidity. For many disease categories, for example, they show increases in disease prevalence, based on analysis of Medicare claims data from 1999 to 2010. When combined with the results from chapter 1, the implication is a sharp drop in the proportion of people with diagnosed diseases who also have functional morbidity. It is an open question, according to the discussants, whether this results from improved coping skills and functional aids, or improved and earlier diagnosis and treatment, or more aggressive disease coding that makes people with a diagnosed condition less sick on average. The discussants suggest further research on whether the measured increase in disease prevalence is a result of actual disease increases or more aggressive diagnosis, and further research on how people are managing their health conditions.

In chapter 2, Michael D. Hurd, Pierre-Carl Michaud, and Susann Rohwedder analyze "The Lifetime Risk of Nursing Home Use." The risk of spending for long-term care is one of the most important risks faced by older households. However, finding data to estimate the risk has been difficult because of the necessity of following individuals over long periods of time. The study in chapter 2 is based on ten waves of data from the Health and Retirement Study (HRS), following individual respondents for up to two decades. The data are used to assess the lifetime distribution of stays in nursing homes and, by consequence, the long-term care risk of nursing home use faced by households.

While the HRS only samples from the noninstitutionalized population at baseline, participants continue to be followed in subsequent survey waves, even if they move to a nursing home. As a result, after several waves of responses, the nursing home residence rates in the HRS sample closely reflect the residence rates in the population as a whole. In addition to the interviews with primary respondents in the sample, HRS data include proxy interviews, usually with a spouse or other close relative, for those unable to participate in a given interview wave. In addition, and particularly important for this study, the HRS data contain "exit interviews" with a proxy after the death of a primary respondent. The exit interviews allow investigators to estimate lifetime risk of a nursing home stay both nonparametrically and with a flexible transition model that simulates nursing home histories.

Similar results are found using both analytic approaches. Specifically, the authors find that a fifty-year-old has a 53 to 59 percent chance of ever staying in a nursing home in their lifetime. This likelihood is considerably higher than the risk reported in previous literature. Conditional on entering a nursing home, the average number of nights spent in a nursing home over the lifetime is just over a year (370 days). Of course, the 370-day average hides considerable variation in nursing home use across the population, including the extremely long stays of some individuals.

The study also looks at how sociodemographic factors affect the lifetime risk of using a nursing home. The results of this part of the analysis highlight two competing influences: first, the risk of entering a nursing home at any given age and second, the risk of dying younger as a result of poor health. Both relate to sociodemographic characteristics. For example, smokers have a higher risk of entering a nursing home at any age than nonsmokers. But since they also die younger than nonsmokers, on average, their lifetime exposure to nursing home risk is reduced. Combining both influences, the study finds that being female, white, and a nonsmoker are associated with higher lifetime risk, because average life expectancy is longer, and because nursing home use rises at older ages.

In his discussion of chapter 2, David Cutler proposes two extensions to the analysis for future study. First, he suggests differentiating between short- and long-term nursing home stays, which differ in both purpose and financing. Short stays are typically used to recover from acute events, and are generally covered by Medicare. Long stays are associated with frailty or severe and worsening impairment, such as from Alzheimer's disease, Parkinson's disease, and other degenerative impairments. Payment for these stays generally comes from individuals, their family, or Medicaid. Second,

Cutler suggests further exploration on the various substitutes for nursing home care. For example, inpatient rehabilitation services offer an alternative to skilled nursing facilities for shorter-term recovery, and assisted living is an alternative to nursing homes for long-term care.

Chapter 3 is "A Comparison of Different Measures of Health and Their Relation to Labor Force Transitions at Older Ages," authored by Arie Kapteyn and Erik Meijer. Health can be characterized by a large number of indicators. For many analytic purposes, it is desirable to integrate multiple indicators into a single health index. A number of health indexes have been proposed in the literature, varying in statistical methodology and in the breadth of variables used to construct the index. Since different health indexes may be used for different purposes, there is no need to settle on any one preferred index. What matters is the statistical property of the index, what aspects of health are being described by the index, and how the index relates to economic behavior and outcomes.

Health indexes can be constructed using a number of different approaches. The simplest approach is to simply ask people to rate their own health on an ordinal scale. A second, more involved approach relates such self-reports to other explanatory variables, such as health conditions or difficulties with activities of daily living. Regressions can be used to weight the explanatory variables in the construction of the health index. A third approach considers health to be a latent construct for which a number of indicators exist; and the indicators can then be used to estimate the underlying latent variable. The study in chapter 3 compares these approaches.

The data are from the eleven countries that are in both waves 1 and 2 of the Survey of Health, Ageing and Retirement in Europe (SHARE). The traditional health measure is self-reported general health (SRH), which has five categories: excellent, very good, good, fair, and poor. SRH generally correlates strongly with objective measures of health. It is a short and easy question, and is widely available in many data sets. This makes it a useful measure for many purposes. However, it is also a crude measure, and it appears to be incomparable across countries without corrections. Hence, for comparing health across countries, it is not very suitable.

Three other health indices are considered in the chapter, all of which draw on a larger number of explanatory health variables. Their potential advantages over SRH are continuous values, greater reliability, and improved comparability across countries. The authors label these indices as MKA, PVW, and Jue, referring to the investigators who constructed them. A goal of the study is to describe the theoretical and empirical differences between these indices, so that researchers who want to include a measure of health in their analyses can make an informed choice as to which index is most appropriate, and so that readers can interpret differences between results from papers that use different indices.

The most important difference between the indices is in the choice of variables that are included in their construction. Among the explanatory variables used to construct one or another of the indices are mobility limitations, ADLs, IADLs, self-reported health, physical attributes like grip strength and body mass index, specific health conditions, pain, and health care utilization. Indices may also draw on variables that may be correlated with health, such as gender, age, living with spouse or partner, household size, education, and net worth. The chapter helps to understand the uses of these various indices for different research applications.

In his discussion of chapter 3, Steven F. Venti elaborates on the issues that complicate the construction of health indices; and particularly those that can be applied in a cross-national research context. The discussion covers three considerations in developing a health index. The first is the choice of a statistical model that translates available health measures into a single index. The second is the choice of health measures to include in the construction. The third is how to account for country-specific reporting bias. Cross-national variation in respondent reported health measures may arise from genuine differences in health, or from the way that residents of each country answer questions. The challenge, Venti emphasizes, is distinguishing between genuine health effects and reporting bias.

Part II: Health and Financial Well-Being

The studies in part II of the volume analyze relationships and causal interactions between health and financial circumstances. In chapter 4, James M. Poterba, Steven F. Venti and I look at "The Nexus of Social Security Benefits, Health, and Wealth at Death." Our study focuses on the drawdown of assets between the first year an individual is observed in the Asset and Health Dynamics Among the Oldest Old (AHEAD) data (1995) and the last year that individual is observed before death. We relate the drawdown of assets over this period to an individual's health, Social Security benefits, and other annuity benefits. By considering income from Social Security and defined benefit (DB) pensions jointly with changes in asset stocks, we develop a more complete picture of the financial resources available to the elderly. We are also interested in the association between health status and these other variables.

We find that a significant fraction of people approach the end of life with few financial assets and no home equity, relying almost entirely on Social Security benefits for support. Whether people reach late life with positive nonannuity wealth depends importantly on health, which is quite persistent over the lifetime. People in poor health in old age have a higher-than-average probability of having experienced low earnings while in the labor force, which puts them at greater risk of having low Social Security benefits in retirement. While the progressivity of the Social Security benefit formula provides a safety net to support low-wage workers in retirement, a noticeable fraction of people, especially those in single-person households, still have income below the poverty level in their last years of life. Many of these individuals have few assets to draw on to supplement their income, and are in poor health.

In addition to confirming the strong relationship between health and financial well-being in later life, our results also show that higher Social Security income and higher defined benefit pension benefits are strongly "protective" of nonannuity assets. Those with larger income flows from Social Security and defined benefit pensions are less likely to exhaust their nonannuitized assets.

While these are our general conclusions, it is difficult to summarize the drawdown of assets in any simple way; there is enormous variation across people. Because many individuals were observed in 1995 with relatively low levels of nonannuity assets, the median percent drawdown is sometimes quite large even though the dollar amount of drawdown is small. People who remained single and married persons predeceased by a spouse experienced median asset reductions of 30 to 50 percent between 1995 and the last year observed before their death. The reductions for persons whose spouse out-lived them were much smaller.

In his discussion of chapter 4, Jonathan Skinner suggests that further work on consumption at older ages will be important to understanding more fully asset trends in later life. Poor health, Skinner agrees, is central to declines in wealth. He references previous work suggesting that mean levels of out-of-pocket expenditures in the last five years of life are remarkably large. His suggestion for future research is to focus in more detail on the components of consumption that are most likely to be variable near death.

In chapter 5, Till Stowasser, Florian Heiss, Daniel McFadden, and Joachim Winter report on "Understanding the SES Gradient in Health Among the Elderly: The Role of Childhood Circumstances." They introduce their study as the classic "chicken and egg" problem. We know that people with high socioeconomic status (SES) tend to be in better health and live longer than their economically disadvantaged counterparts—but we are not sure which came first. Do economic resources determine health (hypothesis A)? Or does health influence economic success (hypothesis B)? Or are both health and wealth dependent on some third unaccounted factor (hypothesis C)?

The traditional view that causality flows from SES to health is especially common among epidemiologists. Often cited causal pathways are the affordability of health services, better health knowledge and lifestyles among the higher educated, environmental hazards associated with poorly paying occupations and low-income living conditions, or the mere psychological burden that comes with a life of constant economic struggle. Economists were among the first to argue that causality may also work its way from health to economic outcomes. For example, physical frailty is likely to have adverse effects on educational attainment, occupational productivity and, consequently, the accumulation of wealth. In addition to these direct causal pathways, the observed correlation between health and financial well-being is, at least in part, likely caused by factors that jointly affect both. Family circumstances in childhood, for example, may have an influence on both health and financial well-being later in life.

While many past studies have explored these relationships, the research in chapter 5 draws on the increasing availability of retrospective life-history data within large panel studies. These data innovations are relevant, because of the potential long-term influences of early life circumstances on health and financial well-being at older ages. First, by incorporating longer health histories, one can construct a more realistic model of health dynamics. Second, to the extent that retrospective data also covers information on family backgrounds and parental SES, it will be possible to study factors that may jointly influence both health and wealth. Third, controlling for both historic and contemporary variables may elucidate when the association between SES and health is established.

The results confirm that childhood health has lasting predictive power for adult health. The study also uncovers strong gender differences in the intertemporal transmission of SES and health. While the link between SES and functional as well as mental health among men appears to be established later in life, the gradient among women seems to originate from childhood.

In his discussion of chapter 5, Robert J. Willis provides additional insights both on this study and on the studies that preceded it. An original 2003 study was controversial, because it suggested noncausation from SES to health, a finding that Willis emphasizes was narrowly applicable to a particular sample of quite elderly people who were largely retired and covered by Medicare. A 2012 follow-up study used a larger sample, a longer period of observation, and a wider age range, and the findings suggested that any of the three causal pathways were possible. Willis interprets the findings from this chapter as reinforcing that multidimensional conclusion, noting that any causal account of the determinants of the SES-health gradient is likely to be very complex, with room for feedback loops involving causation running in multiple directions.

Part III: Determinants of Health

The studies in part III of the volume consider other determinants of health, including retirement, marriage, living with grandchildren, and life expectations.

In chapter 6, Axel Börsch-Supan and Morten Schuth consider "Early Retirement, Mental Health, and Social Networks." Early retirement is popular in Europe, as it is in other parts of the world. It is widely viewed as a social achievement that increases personal well-being, particularly among employees who suffer from work-related health problems. First introduced in the 1970s and 1980s, generous early retirement provisions in most European countries were instituted with minimal actuarial adjustments. In response to financial pressures, the costs of early retirement have come under increased scrutiny, leading to reforms in many European countries since the 1990s.

The question addressed in this study is whether early retirement actually improves well-being. An immediate benefit from early retirement is the receipt of income support without the necessity to continue working, enabling individuals to enjoy more leisure. Moreover, early retirement relieves workers who feel constrained in their place of work, whether due to stressful job conditions or to work-impeding health problems. For such individuals, early retirement should manifest itself in an improvement of well-being and, potentially, also health. On the other hand, early retirement might also be harmful, because individuals who stop working may lose social connections, or a sense of purpose in life. This might, in turn, decrease subjective well-being and mental health.

Research on the causal impact of early retirement on health is complicated by the fact that survey measures of well-being, cognition, and health may suffer from justification bias. That is, early retirees may report worse health in order to justify their early exit from the workforce. Moreover, early retirement is not an exogenous outcome; it is related to health. The aim of the study in chapter 6 is to disentangle these relationships.

The analysis takes advantage of innovative social network data in wave 4 of the Survey of Health Ageing and Retirement in Europe (SHARE). SHARE wave 4 includes a name generator that identifies people with whom the respondent "discuss things that are important to them," such as "good or bad things that happen to you, problems you are having, or important concerns you may have."

The study finds a significant erosion of social networks after retirement. Retirement in general and early retirement in particular, reduces the size of the social network, and in particular the number of friends and other non-family interpersonal contacts. Put differently, social contacts are a side effect of employment that keeps workers mentally agile. The study presents evidence that early retirement has negative effects on people's social networks which, in turn, accelerates cognitive aging.

In her discussion of chapter 6, Elaine Kelly highlights the challenge of evaluating causation in this type of investigation. Importantly, the timing of retirement may be determined by both current and expected future health and cognition. This makes it especially difficult to analyze how retirement causally affects future health and cognition. Similar difficulties in estimation arise from the interactions between social networks, the timing of retirement, and cognition. Kelly discusses potential identification strategies to address these analytic challenges. She also suggests further research on how these connections vary across the characteristics of individuals as a way to better understand the mechanisms through which retirement, cognition, and social networks interrelate.

In chapter 7, "Spousal Health Effects: The Role of Selection," James Banks, Elaine Kelly, and James P. Smith look at the tendency for people to choose a spouse with similar characteristics as themselves. For example, if healthy people marry healthy people, unhealthy people marry unhealthy people, and the health of a spouse affects one's own health, then partner selection will exacerbate health inequalities in a population.

Health histories of partners may matter for at least three reasons. First, individuals may select their partners based in part on their partner's health history and current health status. Second, partner selection may depend on factors such as education and health behaviors (smoking, drinking, and exercise), which are correlated with current and future health. Third, couples typically share a common lifestyle and household environment, leading to more closely correlated health outcomes over time.

Chapter 7 explores these issues in the context of England and the United States. The investigators find a strong and positive association in family background variables including education of partners and their parents. Adult health behaviors such as smoking, drinking, and exercise are more positively associated in England compared to the United States. Childhood health indicators are also positively associated across partners. In general, these correlations are more positive for first than for subsequent partnerships. Especially for women, poor childhood health is associated with future marital disruptions in both countries.

The study explores in greater depth the pre- and postpartnership smoking behavior of couples. The results indicate that smokers are much more likely to partner with smokers and nonsmokers with nonsmokers; and this relationship is far stronger in England compared to the United States. In the United States, the influence of a partner's smoking behavior on one's own smoking behavior is asymmetric. Men's premarriage smoking behavior influences his female partner's postmarriage smoking behavior. But women's premarriage smoking behavior does not appear to influence their male partner's postmarital smoking. These influences are much more symmetric across genders in England.

In his discussion of chapter 7, Amitabh Chandra relates the study to some well-publicized prior work by Nicholas Christakis on "Mortality after the Hospitalization of a Spouse." That research suggested that having a sick spouse was bad for a partner's health, increasing their mortality risk. Drawing on the results from chapter 7, Amitabh notes that some of this relationship is likely explained by partner selection, rather than entirely by the causal effects of bad health across spousal partners.

In chapter 8, Angus Deaton and Arthur A. Stone present "Grandpa and the Snapper: The Well-Being of the Elderly who live with Children." This study lies at the intersection of two literatures, one on whether children bring well-being to those who live with them, and one on the living arrangements of the elderly. Whether or not children make their parents' life better is an old question that remains unsettled. Some even suggest a more complicated relationship in which both are true: parents of children gaining more happiness and more enjoyment, as well as more stress and more worry.

The literature on the living arrangements of the elderly in the United States argues that the elderly value their ability to live independently. Those who are living with children under eighteen, therefore, are more likely to be doing so because of low income or poor health. On the other hand, outside of the United States and other rich countries, it is common for the elderly to live in multigenerational families. Where this is the case, there is less reason to believe that there is negative selection into living with children among the elderly. In such places, we should observe something closer to the direct effects of living with children.

This study analyzes two large data sets collected by Gallup, one for the United States, the Gallup-Healthways Well-Being Index, and one for 161 countries around the world, the Gallup World Poll. They include measures of life evaluation as well as a range of emotional well-being measures. They also have the advantage of using identical questions in all locations. These advantages are offset by incomplete information on living arrangements. In particular, we have information on one respondent from each household, and know only whether or not there is a child at home, not the relationship of the respondent to that child.

The study finds that elderly Americans who live with people under age eighteen have lower life evaluations than those who do not. They also experience worse emotional outcomes, including less happiness and enjoyment, and more stress, worry, and anger. In part, these negative outcomes come from selection into living with a child, especially selection on poor health, which is associated with worse outcomes irrespective of living conditions. Yet even with controls, the elderly who live with children do worse. This is in sharp contrast to younger adults who live with children, likely their own, whose life evaluation is no different in the presence of the child once background conditions are controlled for. Parents, like elders, have enhanced negative emotions in the presence of a child, but unlike elders, also have enhanced positive emotions.

In parts of the world where fertility rates are higher, the elderly do not appear to have lower life evaluations when they live with children; such living arrangements are more usual, and the selection into them is less negative. They also share with younger adults the enhanced positive and negative emotions that come with children.

In his discussion of chapter 8, David Laibson emphasizes that the relationships between living with children and life satisfaction need not be causal. He makes the case that selection probably lies behind the results of the study. Laibson discusses four kinds of selection that may be relevant. The first is adverse selection on the characteristics of older adults: "Grandpa is disabled so he's going to move in with us so we can take better care of him." The second is adverse selection on the characteristics of the middle generation: "We need to move in with Grandpa, since we can no longer afford to live independently." The third is advantageous selection on the characteristics of older adults: "Grandpa is rich and has invited us to move in with him." The fourth is advantageous selection on the characteristics of the middle generation: "We have decided to ask Grandpa to move in with us since we are doing so well." Laibson describes how the results of the study are consistent with these theories of selection, including the differences between developed and developing countries.

In chapter 9, Gábor Kézdi and Robert J. Willis explore "Expectations, Aging, and Cognitive Decline." They use data from the Health and Retirement Study (HRS) to document general patterns in expectations in various domains with respect to aging and to investigate the potential role of cognitive decline in those patterns. They focus on two aspects of expectations: optimism and uncertainty. People who assign higher probabilities to events with positive consequences are considered more optimistic. People who respond to survey questions with "don't know" or "50 percent" are considered more uncertain. The measures are based on subjective beliefs about stock market returns one year in the future, the chance of a future economic depression, whether tomorrow will be a sunny day, whether one's income will keep up with inflation, job loss, and survival to a specific age.

Aging appears to decrease optimism and increase uncertainty. Optimism with respect to stock market expectations, expectations that income will keep up with inflation, and expectations of sunshine the next day all decline strongly with age. The increase in uncertainty is less robust and depends on the measure of uncertainty.

Aging could have these effects for several reasons. The authors speculate that cognitive decline associated with aging may affect an individual's view of the world and their ability to process information about the world, causing a person to overstate the likelihood of negative events and to hold less precise probabilistic beliefs. Another possibility is that the increase in the awareness of mortality that accompanies aging leads to decreased attention to events that are farther in the future, or to the relevance of particular types of economic events.

In his discussion of chapter 9, John B. Shoven notes the emphasis of the chapter on how cognition changes as an individual person ages. He suggests that an interesting question for future research might disentangle the effect of individual aging on cognition (which this chapter addresses), the selection effect (the fact that healthier people live longer, causing cross-sectional measures of cognition by age to differ from longitudinal measures of cognition by age), and the cohort effect (the fact that the cognitive health of a person at any given age may be improving over time, as is the case with other aspects of health). Shoven also notes the complexity in interpreting responses from the HRS survey. For example, answering "I don't know" to a question about

Dow Jones Industrial stocks might actually be more likely from someone with excellent cognition, whereas someone with reduced cognition might guess at an answer.

Part IV: Interventions to Improve Health and Well-Being

The studies in part IV of the volume explore the potential for innovations, interventions, and public policy to improve health and financial well-being.

Chapter 10, by Abhijit Banerjee, Sharon Barnhardt, and Esther Duflo, looks at "Nutrition, Iron Deficiency Anemia, and the Demand for Iron-Fortified Salt: Evidence from an Experiment in Rural Bihar." Iron deficiency anemia (IDA) is frequent among the poor worldwide. For children, IDA is associated with slower physical and cognitive development with potentially long-lasting effects. For adults, IDA may lower energy, productivity, and physical performance, and accelerate cognitive declines at older ages. Severe anemia during pregnancy can lead to low birth weight and child mortality.

While IDA can be prevented with the appropriate supplement or food fortification, these programs often do not reach the poorest. Providing supplements to a large population, particularly pregnant women, is a standard policy in many countries. However, it faces two problems. The first is that it relies on public health infrastructure and local providers that are difficult to monitor. The second is that individuals often do not comply with the protocol. A second approach is to add iron to foods that are a regular part of the local diet. Fortification is a compelling solution in locations where households regularly purchase packaged foods that can be fortified centrally during mass production. These channels do not effectively reach low-income populations in remote locations, however, because such populations do not buy as much processed grain.

The experiment described in chapter 10 explores an alternative approach, which is to subsidize salt that is fortified with iron and iodine, known as double-fortified salt (DFS). The chapter describes first steps and preliminary analysis of baseline data, from a large scale randomized controlled trial in 400 villages in Bihar. The baseline survey strongly suggests the need for an intervention to fight anemia. The study finds that 53 percent of women age 15–49 have hemoglobin levels under 12 g/dL and 21 percent of men have a hemoglobin level under 13, the rough cutoffs for anemia. A large majority of households (94 percent) purchase iodized salt, which makes an intervention to provide DFS potentially promising.

The baseline survey indicated that anemia is prevalent, and may be both caused by and a cause of poverty: households with low expenditure per capita and with low diversity in their diet are more likely to have an anemic member. Anemic individuals are weaker, sicker, and perform worse on cognitive tests than nonanemic individuals. Finding a way to solve this issue on a large scale is important for policy, and would also give us an opportunity for the first time to reliably measure the impact of a plausible instrument to fight IDA on health and economic outcomes.

The chapter also presents results from a small-scale experiment to assess willingness-to-pay for double-fortified salt using randomly assigned discount vouchers. The results show that the take-up of DFS falls quickly with price. At a price point of 45 percent of the retail price of DFS sold in major Indian metros, the take-up of DFS is 30 percent in private stores. The study also assesses the impact on purchase behavior of three separate information campaigns, though no differential impact was found among them, and the effects were small when used without price incentives.

In his discussion of chapter 10, Amitabh Chandra places this study in the broader context of human behavior, asking, "Why do people not always make decisions that are in their best economic interest?" After referencing a range of other research findings in which behavior appears to counter people's best interests, Chandra introduces a theory about how differences between people may affect such behavior. He notes, in particular, differences in time and hassle costs among people with more and less stress and complexity in their lives; differences in the side effects of treatment across individuals; and differences in the benefits of certain behaviors, conditional on those side effects.

In chapter 11, Amitabh Chandra, David Malenka, and Jonathan Skinner analyze "The Diffusion of New Medical Technology: The Case of Drug-Eluting Stents." Their focus is on the wide variation across hospitals and geographic regions in the diffusion, using drug-eluting stents as an illustrative case study. Drug-eluting stents are a commonly used approach to treating the narrowing of coronary arteries.

Before 2003, only bare metal stents were available to cardiologists seeking to perform revascularization for blockages in the heart. These cylindrical wire meshes were designed to keep arteries from narrowing. Yet bare metal stents were also subject to restenosis, or a renarrowing of the artery, leading to restricted blood flow. In April of 2003, the Food and Drug Administration (FDA) approved the use of coated antiproliferative drug-eluting stents, designed to reduce restenosis. In the same month, Medicare allowed for a higher reimbursement for drug-eluting stents to cover their higher cost. Adoption of the new technology was rapid; by December 2003 more than 65 percent of all stent placements in the Medicare population were drug eluting rather than bare metal stents. Yet different hospitals exhibited very different diffusion rates. In the bottom quintile of diffusion, drug-eluting stents comprised just 33 percent of total stents for the year following FDA approval, while in the top quintile the equivalent was 83 percent. The study in chapter 11 analyzes why some hospitals adopt drug-eluting stents earlier than others.

There are a variety of suggested explanations. One is profitability. Drug-eluting stents may not by themselves be more profitable than previous treatments, but they could confer a competitive advantage to hospitals seeking to charge insurance companies and employers higher prices for high-quality care. A second explanation is based on provider expertise; the possibility that higher quality hospitals are the first to adopt drug-eluting stents, because they have better knowledge about technological advances. A third hypothesis stresses knowledge spillovers; diffusion based on area norms or copycat behavior. A final hypothesis is that producers allocate drug-eluting stents to those hospitals whose patients are most likely to benefit from them.

The hypothesis most consistent with the empirical findings is that better quality hospitals adopt technology quicker. There is also suggestive evidence that hospitals whose patients are most likely to benefit from technology are quicker to adopt it. There is no support for models of competition, knowledge spillovers, or profit motivations.

The authors note that rapid adoption of new technologies is not always welfare improving. For example, drug-eluting stents were subsequently found to have more risks than previously understood in the early months of their introduction. So in this case, and likely others, there do not appear to be large welfare costs associated with the uneven diffusion rates.

In his discussion of chapter 11, Jay Bhattacharya elaborates on the biological function of stents, and on the prevention and treatment of heart disease more generally. He also describes the historical dissemination of drug-eluting stents from their first patent in 1997 through their testing, FDA approval, and dissemination over the subsequent fifteen years. Bhattacharya also reiterates the dual implications of early adoption of new technologies: providing the benefits of the new treatment, on the one hand, but serving as test subjects for the development of new technology, on the other.

In chapter 12, John Beshears, James J. Choi, David Laibson, and Brigitte C. Madrian explore "Who Uses the Roth 401(k), and How Do They Use It?" Beginning in 2006, employers sponsoring a 401(k) plan were allowed to offer a Roth option in their plans. Like contributions to a Roth individual retirement account (IRA), employee contributions to a Roth 401(k) or 403(b) are not deductible from current taxable income, but withdrawals of principal, interest, and capital gains in retirement are tax free. Roth contributions are advantageous to households whose current marginal tax rate is lower than their marginal tax rate in retirement. If households understand this fact, then we would expect younger employees to be more likely to allocate contributions to the Roth. Employees with transitorily low income would also be expected to utilize the Roth 401(k). If households are uncertain about whether their marginal tax rate will be higher or lower in retirement, they may wish to hedge this risk by contributing to both Roth and before-tax accounts in their 401(k).

Chapter 12 describes the characteristics of employees who take advantage of the Roth 401(k) options. The study uses administrative 401(k) plan data from twelve companies that introduced a Roth 401(k) option between 2006 and 2010. The results suggest somewhat limited use of Roth 401(k) contributions to date. One year after the Roth was introduced at these companies, just 8.6 percent of 401(k) participants had a positive balance in their Roth account, only 5.4 percent of contributions were to Roth accounts, and Roth balances made up only 1.8 percent of total 401(k) balances at these companies. Roth contributions were more significant for those who chose to make them. Conditional on having a positive Roth contribution rate, 66 percent of employee contributions go to the Roth. Consistent with the existence of a tax diversification motive, 55 percent of employees who contribute to the Roth also contribute to another 401(k) account.

The low usage of the Roth 401(k) may reflect an active preference against the Roth, but it can also be partially explained if employees who enrolled in the 401(k) when the Roth was unavailable failed to update their 401(k) elections in response to the introduction of the Roth. Supporting the importance of the passivity channel, the study finds that 19 percent of 401(k) participants who were hired after the Roth's introduction had a positive balance in the Roth after one year, while only 8 percent of 401(k) participants hired before the Roth's introduction had a positive balance.

The young are more likely to use the Roth and to allocate a larger fraction of their contributions to it. This correlation could be consistent with a rational response to the Roth's tax incentives, since Roth contributions are advantageous to those whose current marginal tax rate is lower than the marginal tax rate at which those contributions will later be withdrawn. Roth usage declines with age, is less likely among women, and only weakly correlated with salary and tenure once one controls for other employee characteristics.

In his discussion of chapter 12, James M. Poterba focuses on the complexities of comparing tax rates while employed with anticipated tax rates at retirement, thereby complicating the choice between traditional and Roth contributions. He describes individual uncertainties, such as one's future earnings or the age a person will retire. He describes the complexities of tax laws, such as interactions with the Earned Income Tax Credit while working, or the tax treatment of Social Security benefits when retired. There is also uncertainty in what reforms may be enacted to future tax policies. In response to the long-term fiscal gap in the federal budget, for example, one solution might raise tax rates to close the gap, another might broaden the tax base while retaining or even lowering rates, and a third might implement a value added tax that could also lower income tax rates.

As a future research project, Poterba suggests analyzing the behavior of individuals who contribute at the legal contribution limit of $17,500. These participants are an interesting subsample, because their only option for increasing the effective set-aside for retirement is by shifting to the Roth option. Thus they may have more incentive to use the Roth option than savers who are below the contribution limit.

I

Health and Disability

1

Evidence for Significant Compression of Morbidity in the Elderly US Population

David M. Cutler, Kaushik Ghosh, and Mary Beth Landrum

Older Americans are living longer. Life expectancy at age sixty-five has increased about two years in the past two decades. But are we living healthier? This issue is vital for health policy and economic reasons. Longer life is valuable to people, but it is even more valuable if the additional years lived are in good health. For the public sector as well, the consequences of longer lives depend on their quality. Medical spending for healthy seniors is modest; spending for the severely disabled is much greater. Thus, if morbidity is being compressed into the period just before death, the impacts of population aging are not as severe as if additional life involves many years of expensive care.

This question of whether morbidity is being compressed into the period just before death has been at the center of health debates in the United States for some time. Fries (1980) first put forward the argument that the United States was undergoing a compression of morbidity. His work was provocative, and others took different views. Gruenberg (1977) argued that reduced disease mortality would extend unhealthy life, while Manton (1982) posited a dynamic equilibrium where both morbidity and mortality are fall-

David M. Cutler is the Otto Eckstein Professor of Applied Economics at Harvard University and a research associate of the National Bureau of Economic Research. Kaushik Ghosh is a research specialist at the National Bureau of Economic Research, where he has worked extensively with the Medicare Data, National Health Surveys, and National Health Expenditure Accounts. He received a PhD in economics from Clark University in Massachusetts. Mary Beth Landrum is professor of health care policy, with a specialty in biostatistics, in the Department of Health Care Policy at Harvard Medical School.

We are grateful to the National Institute on Aging for research support (P01-AG005842) and to Dan McFadden for helpful comments. For acknowledgments, sources of research support, and disclosure of the authors' material financial relationships, if any, please see http://www .nber.org/chapters/c12966.ack.

ing, leading to indeterminate impacts on disability-free and disabled life expectancy.

Empirical evidence on trends in morbidity is also unclear. Some authors argue that morbidity is being compressed into the period just before death (Cai and Lubitz 2007; Manton, Gu, and Lowrimore 2008), while others believe that the period of disabled life is expanding (Crimmins and Beltrán-Sánchez 2010) or that the evidence is more mixed (Crimmins et al. 2009).

There are three reasons for this disagreement. First, there is not a single definition of morbidity. Some studies look at whether people report specific chronic conditions, which have increased over time, while other studies look at functioning. As a result, studies differ in the morbidity trends they incorporate.

Second, it is often difficult to link health to the stage of life of the individual. If people are reporting more chronic disease, is that in the period just before the end of life, in which case the additional disease does not encompass many years? Or is the disease occurring in periods of time far from the end of life, in which case it represents many years of poor health? To answer this question, one needs data on quality of life matched to time until death. Most cross-section data sources do not have such a link, however, and thus they need to make assumptions about the disease process to generate lifetime disease-prevalence estimates. These assumptions can have large impacts on the results.

Third, the data samples that tend to be used often focus on a particular subset of the population; for example, the noninstitutionalized. Since there are changes in the residential location of the elderly population over time, focusing on population subsets can give biased results.

In this chapter, we examine the issue of compression of morbidity, addressing these three concerns. Our primary data source is the Medicare Current Beneficiary Survey, or (MCBS). We have MCBS data for a representative sample of the entire elderly population between 1991 and 2009. The sample sizes are large, over 10,000 individuals annually. Further, the MCBS data have been linked to death records through 2008, and hence all deaths can be matched. Importantly, this includes deaths that occur after the person has left the survey. Thus, we can form morbidity measures by time until death for a large, representative share of the elderly population.

We use these data in two ways. First, we examine trends in various measures of morbidity by time until death. We consider a number of different metrics: the presence of disease, whether the person reports activities of daily living (ADL) or instrumental activities of daily living (IADL) disability, and various summary measures of functioning that draw together nineteen different dimensions of health (Cutler and Landrum 2012). We show trends overall and by time until death.

As is well known, the MCBS data from the 1990s and 2000s show a reduction in the share of elderly people who report ADL or IADL limitations (Freedman et al. 2004, 2013). Our first result is that this reduction in disability is most marked among those with many years until death. Health status in the year or two just prior to death has been relatively constant over time; in contrast, health measured three or more years before death has improved measurably.

We then translate these changes into disability-free life expectancy and disabled life expectancy. We show that disability-free life expectancy is increasing over time, while disabled life expectancy is falling. For a typical person age sixty-five, life expectancy increased by 0.7 years between 1992 and 2005. Disability-free life expectancy increased by 1.6 years; disabled life expectancy fell by 0.9 years. The reduction in disabled life expectancy and increase in disability-free life expectancy is true for both genders and for nonwhites as well as whites. Hence, morbidity is being compressed into the period just before death.

The chapter is structured as follows. We begin in the next section by defining the compression of morbidity and showing how disability and mortality changes jointly affect disability-free and disabled life expectancy. The second section describes the data we use. The third section presents simple trends in health status by time until death. The fourth section calculates disabled and disability-free life expectancy. The last section concludes.

1.1 The Compression of Morbidity

The question we wish to examine is whether morbidity has been compressed into the period just before death, or whether it is accounting for a greater part of the life of elderly individuals. While this goal is clear, the empirical implementation needs a more precise definition. We consider two definitions of a compression of morbidity. One definition, dating back to Fries (1980), is whether the life table is "rectangularizing"—that is, whether disabled life expectancy is falling over time. A second definition is more modest: the share of remaining life that is nondisabled is increasing over time. Note that in this latter formulation, disabled life expectancy may be increasing as well, just not as rapidly as nondisabled life expectancy.

In situations where only morbidity or mortality is changing, these two measures will always move together. In situations where both mortality and morbidity are changing, however, trends in the two measures of compression of morbidity may be different.

To see this, consider a simple example presented in table 1.1 The first column depicts a person who lives for five years, the first three of which are without disability, and the fourth and fifth are with a disability. To be concrete, suppose that the person has heart disease in the fourth year and develops chronic obstructive pulmonary disease in the fifth, which results in death six months later. The specific diseases do not matter, but as is typical in the data, we reflect disability as occurring progressively over life and generally do not consider recovery.

Table 1.1   **Impact of mortality and morbidity on disabled and disability-free life expectancy**

Year	Baseline	Morbidity decline	Mortality decline	Morbidity and mortality decline
1	ND	ND	ND	ND
2	ND	ND	ND	ND
3	ND	ND	ND	ND
4	D	**ND**	D	**ND**
5	D	D	D	D
6				
	—	—	**D**	**D**
Life expectancy	4.5	4.5	5.5	5.5
Nondisabled life expectancy	3.0	4.0	3.0	4.0
Disabled life expectancy	1.5	0.5	2.5	1.5
Share of life expectancy that is nondisabled	67%	89%	55%	73%

Notes: ND is nondisabled and D is disabled. The table shows a hypothetical population and the impact of changes in mortality and morbidity. Morbidity changes alone increase nondisabled life, and mortality changes alone increase disabled life. Mortality and morbidity changes together extend disability-free life and have an ambiguous effect on disabled life.

In forming life tables, people who die during a year are assumed to die halfway through the year. Thus, the baseline life expectancy[1] is 4.5 years, of which the first 3.0 years is disability-free and the latter 1.5 years is disabled.

Now imagine that morbidity declines (column [2]). To be specific, suppose that because of improved medical treatment of cardiac risk factors, the person does not suffer a coronary event in the fourth year and thus is not disabled in that year. In year 5, however, the person still suffers lung disease and dies. As the last rows show, overall life expectancy is unchanged, but disability-free life expectancy has increased to 4.0 years and disabled life expectancy has fallen to 0.5 years. By either definition, disability has been compressed into the period before the end of life.

The third column shows the impact of a reduction in mortality. We imagine that the medical system gets better at treating the combination of heart disease and lung disease, and thus the person survives an additional year with both conditions, albeit they are still disabled. Total life expectancy has increased by one year in this example, all of which is associated with disability. Further, the share of life that is disabled has increased. Thus, there is an expansion of disability by either measure. Note that in this example, the person is still better off; it is just that the disabled part of life has increased.

The final column shows a combination of disability reductions (the per-

---

1. We refer to life expectancy even though this is a life table for a single person. It is easier to show the point this way than to consider a population distribution.

son does not suffer the coronary event) and mortality reductions (the person survives an additional year with lung disease). Life expectancy has increased by one year, relative to the baseline. The increase is entirely in disability-free life; disabled life starts one year later but ends one year later. In this scenario, whether morbidity has been compressed depends on the definition employed: disabled life expectancy has not declined, but a greater share of life is spent in the nondisabled state.

In general, the impact of combined morbidity and mortality changes on disability-free and disabled life expectancy depends on how rapid each change is and when in the course of life it occurs. All of this we need to evaluate empirically.

1.2 Medicare Current Beneficiary Data

Our primary data source is the Medicare Current Beneficiary Survey (MCBS). The MCBS, sponsored by the Centers for Medicare and Medicaid Services (CMS), is a nationally representative survey of aged, disabled, and institutionalized Medicare beneficiaries that oversamples the very old (age eighty-five or older) and disabled Medicare beneficiaries. Since we are interested in health among the elderly, we restrict our sample to the population age sixty-five and older.

A number of surveys have measures of disability in the elderly population (Freedman et al. 2004), including the National Health Interview Study and the Health and Retirement Study. Still, the MCBS has a number of advantages relative to these other surveys. First, the sample size is large, about 10,000 to 18,000 people annually. In addition, the MCBS samples people regardless of whether they live in a household or a long-term care facility, or switch between the two during the course of the survey period. Third, the set of health questions is very broad, encompassing health in many domains. Fourth, and most importantly, individuals in the MCBS have been matched to death records. As a result, we can measure death for over 200,000 people, even after they have left the survey window. Death data are available through 2008.

The MCBS started as a longitudinal survey in 1991. In 1992 and 1993, the only supplemental individuals added were to replace people lost to attrition and to account for newly enrolled beneficiaries. Beginning in 1994, the MCBS began a transition to a rotating panel design, with a four-year sample inclusion. About one-third of the sample was rotated out in 1994, and new members were included in the sample. The remainder of the original sample was rotated out in subsequent years. We use all interviews that are available for each person from the start of the survey in 1991 through 2009. We ignore the panel structure of the MCBS interviews and treat each survey year as a repeated cross section that has been linked to mortality information.

The MCBS has two samples: a set of people who were enrolled for the entire year (the Access to Care sample) and a set of ever-enrolled beneficiaries (the Cost and Use sample). The latter differs from the former in including people who die during the year and new additions to the Medicare population. The primary data that we use are from the health status questionnaire administered in the fall survey, which defines the Access to Care sample. We thus use the Access to Care data. We compute time until death from the exact date at which the Access to Care survey was administered to the person.

The MCBS population becomes older and less white over time, as the elderly population changes demographically. We do not want to show trends that are influenced by these demographic changes. We thus adjust survey weights so that the MCBS population in each year matches the population in the year 2000 by age, gender, and race. All of our tabulations are weighted by these adjusted weights.

Recall that our death dates are available through 2008. For each individual interviewed in 1991–2007, therefore, we can determine if they died in the next twelve months or survived that period. Similarly, we can categorize individuals through 2006 as dying between twelve and twenty-four months or not, and individuals through 2005 as dying between twenty-four and thirty-six months or not. Death at thirty-six months or beyond is also known for the population through 2005.

Trends in the distribution of time until death are shown in figure 1.1 The share of the population that is within one year of death is about 5 percent on average. Reflecting the overall reduction in mortality, this share is declining over time (this will be true of the population 1–2 years from death and 2–3 years from death as well). Between 1991 and 2007, the decline is 1 percentage point, or 18 percent. Correspondingly, the share of the population that is three or more years from death increased by about 3 percentage points, also shown in figure 1.1.

The MCBS asks extensive health questions. The first set of health questions are about medical events the person has experienced. These include cardiovascular conditions (heart disease, stroke), diseases of the central nervous system (Alzheimer's disease, Parkinson's disease), musculoskeletal problems (arthritis, broken hip), pulmonary disease, and cancer. For purposes of disability assessment, we divide these diseases into four groups, based on their likely association with death and disability (Lunney et al. 2003). The first disease is cancer. Once past the acute phase of cancer treatment, people with cancer tend to have a reasonably high quality of life until the last few months of life, when health deteriorates markedly. The second group is permanently disabling conditions that get progressively worse. Alzheimer's disease, Parkinson's disease, and pulmonary disease fall into this category.[2] The third group is acute conditions for which recovery is possible but not assured. This includes heart disease, strokes, and hip fractures.

---

2. Congestive heart failure is natural to add to this list but is only asked about from 2003 on.

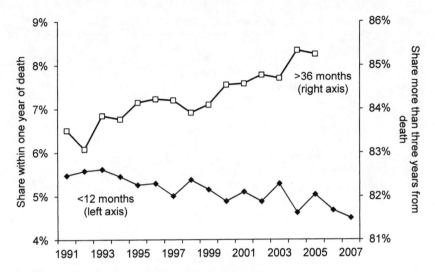

Fig. 1.1   Population distribution by time until death

Note: Data are from the Medicare Current Beneficiary Survey, 1991–2009, and are weighted to the population distribution in 2000 by age, sex, and race, as are all subsequent figures.

Finally, we group diabetes and arthritis as commonly disabling but generally nonfatal conditions.

Table 1.2 shows the prevalence of these conditions across all years of the survey, the annual percentage point change in the prevalence over time, and the disability rate conditional on having the disease (defined as whether the person reports an ADL or IADL limitation; see following). Nonfatal conditions are the most common. Over half of the elderly population reports a prior diagnosis of arthritis, the prevalence of which is increasing by 0.3 percentage points annually. Nearly one in five elderly people has diabetes. Acute conditions for which recovery is possible are the next most common, ranging in prevalence from 4 percent of the population (hip fracture) to 26 percent (ischemic heart disease). Perhaps owing to better prevention, the prevalence of both heart disease and heart attacks is declining over time. About 18 percent of the elderly population has a history of cancer, which is increasing over time. Degenerative diseases are relatively less common, though pulmonary disease affects about one-seventh of the elderly population. People with these conditions are extremely likely to report having an ADL or IADL impairment.

The MCBS also asks a number of questions about the impact of morbidity on a respondent's ability to function and perform basic tasks, shown in table 1.3. The first category of questions is about physical functioning, such as difficulty walking a reasonable distance (1/4 mile or 2–3 blocks) or carrying moderate-weight objects. Difficulty in these areas ranges from one-quarter to three-quarters of the elderly population.

Table 1.2   Medical event questions in the MCBS

Number	Ever told have . . .	Average prevalence (%)	Annual percentage point change (%)	Percent with ADL or IADL limitation (%)
1	Cancer	17.7	.13	50
	Chronic disabling conditions	19.5	.31	69
2	Alzheimer's disease	5.2	.12	91
3	Parkinson's disease	1.6	−.01	83
4	Pulmonary disease	14.0	.23	61
	Recoverable acute conditions	34	−.27	61
5	Acute myocardial infarction	13.9	−.07	59
6	Ischemic heart disease	25.6	−.32	59
7	Stroke	11.2	.04	71
8	Broken hip	4.1	−.08	77
	Nonfatal conditions	63.5	.45	52
9	Arthritis	56.5	.29	53
10	Diabetes	18.7	.52	58

Notes: Tabulations are from the MCBS Access to Care sample for 1991–2009 and use sample weights. The sample includes 251,872 observations.

The second and third categories are impairments in activities of daily living (ADL) such as bathing or dressing, and instrumental activities of daily living (IADL) such as doing light housework or managing money. Six questions are asked about each of the ADL and IADL limitations. Because limitations in these areas reflect more severe impairment, the share of the elderly population reporting difficulty in these areas is lower than the share reporting difficulty with functional limitations.

The final category is sensory impairments, including trouble seeing and hearing. In the case of vision, the difficulty also refers to correction such as glasses or contact lenses, and for hearing it is with hearing aid. The possible responses to the vision and hearing questions changed in 2002. Prior to 2002, the responses for each question were: *no trouble, a little trouble, and a lot of trouble.* Starting in 2002, a more severe category was added to each: *no usable vision* and *deaf.* After this change, more people reported less severe vision and hearing impairments—most likely, they judged themselves less severely disabled relative to the more severe categories now being offered as a response. The share of people reporting difficulty with vision and hearing each fell by 4 percentage points in 2002, far larger than in any other year.

To adjust for this, we create a counterfactual time series for difficulty with vision and hearing assuming that the trend in each variable in the year the survey changed was the same as the trend in the prior three years. We then extend this aggregate estimate back to 1991. At the individual level, we randomly choose individuals who reported that they had a little trouble seeing or hearing and recategorize their responses to having no trouble, to match

Table 1.3   **Health status questions in the MCBS, 1991–2009**

Number	Question	Prevalence (%)
	Functional limitation: Difficulty	
1	Stooping/crouching/kneeling	70
2	Lifting/carrying 10 pounds	39
3	Extending arms above shoulder	29
4	Writing/handling object	28
5	Walking ¼ mile or 2–3 blocks	47
	Activities of daily living: Reports difficulty doing the following activities by himself/herself because of a health or physical problem	
6	Bathing or showering	15
7	Going in or out of bed or chairs	15
8	Eating	5
9	Dressing	10
10	Walking	26
11	Using the toilet	8
	Instrumental activities of daily living: Reports difficulty doing the following activities by himself/herself because of a health or physical problem	
12	Using the telephone	10
13	Doing light housework (like washing dishes, straightening up, or light cleaning)	16
14	Doing heavy housework (like scrubbing floors or washing windows)	34
15	Preparing own meals	14
16	Shopping for personal items	18
17	Managing money (like keeping track of expenses or paying bills)	11
	Sensory problems	
18	Trouble seeing	32
19	Trouble hearing	38

Notes: Tabulations are from the MCBS Access to Care sample for 1991–2009 and use sample weights. Trouble seeing and hearing are adjusted to reflect questionnaire changes in 2002 and 2003. The sample includes 251,872 observations.

the adjusted aggregate totals. With these adjustments, about one-third of the elderly population reports vision and hearing impairments on average.

The health status questions are generally the same for the community population and the institutional population, with the exception that the institutionalized are not asked about three IADLs limitations—light housework, preparing meals, and heavy lifting. On average, 5 percent of people are in a nursing home. In order to utilize these questions, we assume that everyone in a nursing home has difficulty with these activities.[3]

3. With regard to the other IADLs, 61 percent of people living in institutions report difficulty using the telephone and 85 percent report difficulty shopping for personal items and managing money. Over 90 percent report difficulty with basic activities such as stooping, crouching or kneeling, or carrying a 10 lb. object (Cutler and Landrum 2011).

1.2.1 Summary Health Status Measures

The most common single measure of disability in the literature is any difficulty with ADL or IADLs. We follow this in our analysis and define disability as an ADL or IADL impairment.

While simple to implement, this measure lacks a rigorous theoretical foundation. Moreover, a binary measure does not capture heterogeneity in the population. For many purposes, we care about finer gradations in the distribution of health. There is a literature (e.g., Verbrugge and Jette 1994) arguing for a distinction between functional status (measures of specific physical functioning) and disability (the ability to engage in the activities typically expected of a person). Within this latter spirit, we examine the different dimensions of health among the elderly. In particular, we estimate a factor analytic model of the different domains of functioning and choose the number of domains that best summarize the data.

Formally, denote y_{ij} as the response to question j for individual i. Suppose there are J questions total ($J = 19$ in our setting). We imagine that these health states are a linear function of K different unobserved factors, denoted F_{ik}. We fit a factor analytic model of the form (e.g., Bartholomew 1987; Knol and Berger 1991):

$$(1) \qquad y_{ij} = \gamma_{0j} + \gamma_{1j}F_{i1} + \gamma_{2j}F_{i2} + \gamma_{3j}F_{i3} + \ldots + \gamma_{Kj}F_{iK},$$

where y_{ij} is a 0 or 1 outcome variable, γ_{0j} is a threshold parameter that accounts for varying prevalence of limitations in the population (for example, limitations climbing stairs are more common than limitations in bathing) and the γ_{kj}'s are factor loadings that describe the relationship between unobserved factor k and question j. Unobserved factors are assumed to follow a multivariate normal distribution. The latent variable model described by equation (1) is similar to the factor analyses and grade of membership models that have been previously used to describe dimensions of disability (Lamb 1996; Manton, Woodbury, and Tolley 1994; Manton, Stallard, and Corder 1998; Woodbury and Garson 1978).

We can fit this model provided $K < J$. Empirically, because the data tend to be highly correlated and we have nineteen dimensions of health, a small number of factors is associated with a wide range of variation in the data.

Table 1.4 shows the results of the factor analysis over the 1991–2009 time period. By the usual criterion of eigenvalues greater than 1, there are three significant factors. Together, these three account for 57 percent of the cumulative variation in the data. These three also have natural economic and demographic interpretations. We thus work with those three.

The predicted factor scores are positively correlated. Prior to rotation, the correlation between factors 1 and 2 is .501, between 1 and 3 is .246, and between 2 and 3 is .265. To aid in interpretation, we consider rotations of

Table 1.4   **Factor analysis for MCBS data**

	Eigenvalue	Proportion	Cumulative
1	7.978	0.420	0.420
2	1.779	0.094	0.514
3	1.122	0.059	0.573
4	0.872	0.046	0.619
5	0.851	0.045	0.663
6	0.809	0.043	0.706

Notes: The results are from factor analyses using the MCBS data for 1991–2009. The sample includes 251,872 observations.

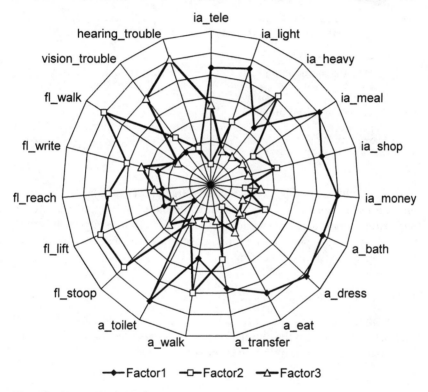

Fig. 1.2   Factor loadings
Note: The figure shows the factor loadings for the first three factors of the health status questions. Data are from the Medicare Current Beneficiary Survey, 1991–2009.

the factors that reduce the correlation between them. Specifically, we use an oblique rotation of the three factor scores (promax = 3).

Figure 1.2 shows a radar plot of the (rotated) factor scores. The first factor loads heavily on ADL and IADL limitations, including bathing, dressing, eating, managing money, and preparing meals. This is a very severely

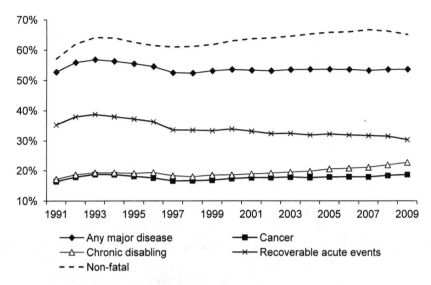

Fig. 1.3   Trends in disease prevalence

Note: Major diseases include cancer, chronic disabling conditions, and recoverable acute events. Specific conditions in the chronic disabling, recoverable acute event, and nonfatal condition categories are in table 1.2.

impaired population. The second factor is largely associated with functional limitations and related IADLs, including difficulty walking, lifting, stooping, reading, and doing heavy housework. This group is generally somewhat less impaired. The third factor is concentrated in sensory impairments, including both vision and hearing.

1.3 Trends in Health

Our goal is to examine health trends by time until death. We start with overall health trends in the population as a whole and then proceed to trends for the different subgroups by time until death.

1.3.1 Disease Prevalence

Disease prevalence is a first measure of health that we consider. Figure 1.3 shows the share of the elderly with the four categories of conditions over time: cancer, chronic degenerative diseases, recoverable acute conditions, and generally nonfatal conditions; individual trends are reported in table 1.2. There has been an increased prevalence of nonfatal disease over time, as more people report arthritis and diabetes. Major severe diseases as a whole have been relatively constant in prevalence. This constancy masks some differentiation by type of condition, however. Recoverable acute conditions have declined in prevalence over time, from about 40 percent of the

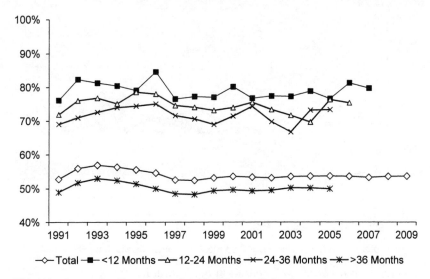

Fig. 1.4   Any major disease prevalence by time until death
Note: Major diseases include cancer, chronic disabling conditions, and recoverable acute conditions.

population in 1993 to about 30 percent in 2009. Chronic disabling conditions have increased (Alzheimer's and pulmonary disease), and cancer has been relatively constant.

We consider the major diseases as a group, since they are likely to have the biggest impact on health. Figure 1.4 shows the prevalence of any major disease by time until death. Since this figure is used repeatedly in the chapter, we describe it here in some detail. The second-to-the-lowest line of the figure is the overall prevalence of major conditions, analogous to the line in figure 1.3. Since this line is not conditioned on time until death, we can form this series through 2009. The upper line in the figure is the share of people within twelve months of death who have a major condition. That line extends through 2007, since we know twelve-month mortality for that group. The prevalence of major diseases is significantly greater in the population near death than in the overall population. About 80 percent of seniors near death have at least one major condition, and that share is relatively constant over time. The most common major disease in this group is heart disease (38 percent of the population, on average). Cancer affects about 25 percent of this population, as does Alzheimer's disease and pulmonary disease (chronic degenerative diseases) and heart attacks and stroke (recoverable acute conditions). Parkinson's disease has a lower prevalence (4 percent), as does hip fracture (9 percent).

The lines just below the top line are the prevalence rate for people 12–24 months from death and 24–36 months from death. For each line, we are

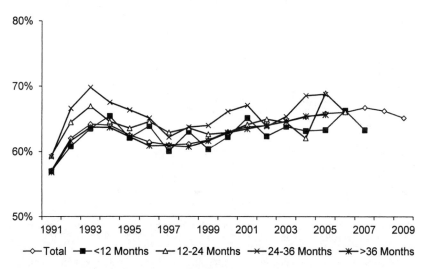

Fig. 1.5   Any minor disease prevalence by time until death
Note: Minor diseases include arthritis and diabetes.

restricted to data ending one year earlier, reflecting the fact that the mortality information is only available through 2008. The prevalence of major disease is slightly lower for these groups, but still high. In each case, the prevalence is 70–80 percent. As with the population within twelve months of death, major disease prevalence is not changing in the population 1–2 years and 2–3 years from death. The lowest line in the figure is the prevalence of major disease in people thirty-six or more months from death. This share is about 50 percent, and is flat after a rise and fall in the early to mid-1990s.

Figure 1.4 shows clearly that not only is major disease prevalence overall unchanged, but major disease prevalence is unchanged in each window of time until death. We return to lifetime disease-free years next.

The prevalence of minor diseases by time until death is shown in figure 1.5. There are five lines in the figure, but they are virtually indistinguishable. About 60–70 percent of elderly people have arthritis or diabetes, and that is independent of how close or far they are from death. Similarly, the prevalence of minor diseases increases over the years 2001 to 2009 for all groups.

1.3.2 Functional Limitations and Disability

We now proceed to functional limitations and ADL/IADL limitations, the latter of which is the most common metric of disability in the literature. Figure 1.6 shows the time series for any functional limitation, any ADL or IADL impairment, any ADL impairment, and any IADL impairment. The prevalence of functional limitations is high; about 60 percent of the elderly population reports some difficulty with the functional measures. ADL or

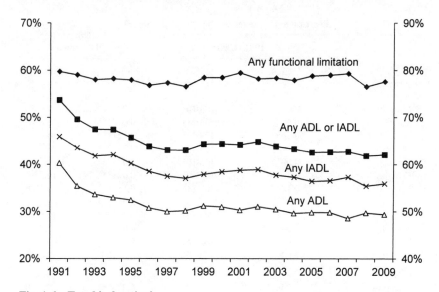

Fig. 1.6   Trend in functioning

Note: Specific questions used in functional limitations and ADL/IADL limitations are shown in table 1.2.

IADL impairment is lower but still high. Nearly half of the elderly population reports one or more ADL or IADL problems. Effectively, this means that about half of the life expectancy of the elderly is years lived with a disability.

Overall functional limitations are relatively constant over time, declining by 2.7 percent between 1991 and 2009. The prevalence of people with ADL or IADL impairments declined more dramatically, however. The overall reduction between 1991 and 2009 is 22 percent, with somewhat greater declines for ADL disability than IADL disability, but impressive declines in both. Most of the disability decline was in the 1991–1997 time period. Between 1997 and 2002, disability increased modestly, before declining again from 2005 to 2009.

Changes in disability may be influenced by demographic or disease factors. Although not the primary focus of our analysis, we consider this a little in understanding the change in disability over time. We start by relating disability in the early time periods of the sample (1991–1993) and the later time periods (2004–2006) to demographic and medical factors:

(2) $\text{Disability}_{it} = \text{Demog}_{it}\,\beta_{Dt} + \text{Clinical}_{it}\,\beta_{Ct} + \varepsilon_{it}.$

where i denotes individuals and t denotes the time period (1991–1993 or 2004–2006). Demographics include five-year age-sex dummy variables, a dummy variable for nonwhites, a dummy variable for being married, and a dummy variable for having a high school degree or more. The clinical

Table 1.5   **Regressions explaining disability**

	1991–1993		2004–2006	
	Coef.	**Std. Error**	**Coef.**	**Std. Error**
Demographics				
Male 70–74	0.018	(0.010)	0.002	(0.009)
Male 75–79	0.080***	(0.011)	0.048***	(0.010)
Male 80–84	0.166***	(0.013)	0.157***	(0.012)
Male 85	0.313***	(0.015)	0.283***	(0.014)
Female 65–69	0.093***	(0.010)	0.073***	(0.009)
Female 70–74	0.116***	(0.010)	0.094***	(0.009)
Female 75–79	0.176***	(0.011)	0.150***	(0.009)
Female 80–84	0.278***	(0.012)	0.247***	(0.010)
Female 85	0.381***	(0.012)	0.375***	(0.011)
Nonwhite	−0.0421***	(0.008)	0.016*	(0.007)
Married	−0.055***	(0.006)	−0.038***	(0.005)
> = High school	−0.077***	(0.005)	−0.091***	(0.005)
Conditions				
Alzheimer's	0.246***	(0.012)	0.323***	(0.010)
Parkinson's	0.212***	(0.019)	0.253***	(0.018)
Broken Hip	0.149***	(0.011)	0.188***	(0.012)
Stroke	0.187***	(0.008)	0.156***	(0.007)
Pulmonary	0.160***	(0.007)	0.163***	(0.006)
IHD	0.139***	(0.006)	0.068***	(0.006)
Diabetes	0.134***	(0.007)	0.130***	(0.006)
Arthritis	0.152***	(0.005)	0.139***	(0.005)
Cancer	0.063***	(0.007)	0.044***	(0.006)
Constant	0.205***	(0.010)	0.187***	(0.009)
N	31,374		38,880	
R^2	0.250		0.218	

Note: The table shows regressions for reporting an ADL or IADL impairment in either 1991–1993 (the first columns) or 2004–2006 (the second columns).

covariates include dummy variables for the conditions in table 1.2. Both the demographic and clinical covariates are strongly associated with disability (table 1.5). Older age is associated with higher disability, as being nonwhite, being single, and having less education. All of the clinical covariates are associated with higher disability rates, as we would expect.

We then perform an Oaxaca decomposition to understand how much of the reduction in disability can be explained by changes in the X's (for example, the population becoming better educated or less likely to have heart disease) versus changes in the impact of each demographic and clinical factor on disability. We do this as in equation (3):

$$(3) \qquad \Delta\text{Disability} \approx \{\Delta\text{Demog }\beta_{Dto} + \Delta\text{Clinical }\beta_{Cto}\} + \{\text{Demog}_{to}\,\Delta\beta_D + \text{Clinical}_{to}\,\Delta\beta_C\}$$

Table 1.6   **Impact of demographics and medical conditions on health**

Health change (percentage points)	Measure of health			
	Disability (%)	F1	F2	F3
Total change	−7.4	−.138	−.091	−.201
Effect of changes in Xs				
Demographics	−1.4	−.025	−.034	−.026
Condition prevalence	0.5	.008	.014	.010
Effect of changes in βs				
Conditions	−2.9	−.185	−.083	−.063
Demographics	−2.1	−.084	−.074	−.039
Constant	−1.8	.148	.090	−.093

Notes: The table is a decomposition of changes in the measure of health indicated in the columns. For each health measure, we estimate equations of the form $H_{it} = X_{it}\beta_t + \varepsilon_{it}$, for two time periods (1991–1993 and 2004–2006). The first row, total change, shows the percentage point change in H_{it} over time. The remaining rows show the predicted percentage point change in H_{it} resulting from changes in the X variables, decomposed into demographics and condition prevalence, and changes in the βs, decomposed into those for conditions, those for demographics, and the constant term.

where t_o denotes the initial time period and Δ indicates the changes over time. The first term on the right-hand side of equation (3) is the impact of changing demographics and clinical condition prevalence, holding constant their health impact, and the second term is the impact of changes in the relationship between clinical and demographic factors and disability, holding constant their prevalence. There is no i subscript because we use averages of each explanatory variable in the relevant time period.

Table 1.6 shows this decomposition. The first column uses disability as the health outcome measure. As the first row shows, the overall reduction in disability was 7.4 percentage points. The next two rows show the impact of changes in demographics and condition prevalence between 1991–1993 and 2004–2006 on disability. Demographic changes imply a modestly healthier population over time,[4] while the clinical conditions have become somewhat more prevalent. Overall, the contribution of changes in the explanatory factors is modest.

The next rows show that the bulk of the impact comes from changes in the severity of demographic and clinical risk factors. Conditions have become less disabling over time (see table 1.5)–especially heart disease and arthritis— and this lowers disability by 2.9 percentage points. Older age is less disabling than formerly, even given the clinical conditions we measure. This accounts for another 2.1 percentage points. Finally, the constant term, reflecting other

4. Recall that age, gender, and race changes have already been factored out, by reweighting the data to the population distribution in 2000. Thus, the demographic change is only marital status and education.

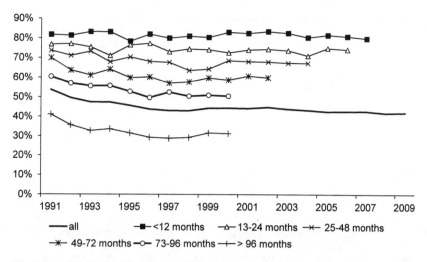

Fig. 1.7   ADL/IADL disability by time until death
Note: Specific ADL and IADL questions are defined in table 1.2.

factors not captured, shows a large decline in disability. The finding that conditions are less severely disabling than they were formerly motivates our focus on their relation to time until death, not on the incidence of conditions themselves.

Figure 1.7 shows the share of the population with an ADL or IADL limitation by time until death. Since disability defined in this way is the most common health metric in the literature, and it has fallen so much, this figure is in many ways the most crucial to understand population changes in health. Also for this reason, we decompose the change in disability by more periods of time: <12 months until death, 12–24 months until death, 25–48 months until death, 49–72 months until death, 73–96 months until death, and 97+ months until death.

Figure 1.7 shows clearly that the vast bulk of the reduction in disability is among people a few years away from death. Disability is high and has remained so for people within one year of death; about 80 percent of this population is disabled, and that has not changed over time. Indeed, more detailed analysis shows just how sick this population is. The average person in the last twelve months of life has 2.7 ADL limitations and 3.1 IADL limitations. Disability has declined marginally for those 12–24 months from death (2.8 percentage points over the period). Rather, the larger decline is for the population twenty-five or more months from death. Starting in the group three to four years from death, disability declines by 6 to 7 percentage points in each group.[5] Figure 1.8 shows this pattern graphically. The reduction in disability is greater the farther out from death one goes.

---

5. Each group is observed over a different time frame. However, since most of the disability decline occurred prior to the mid-1990s the differing observation windows has minimal effect.

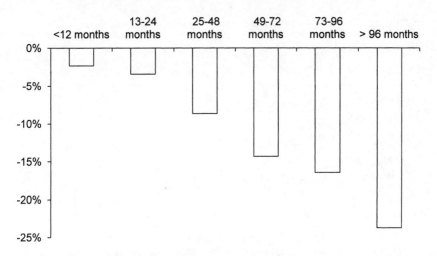

Fig. 1.8   Percent change in disability by time until death
Note: The data are based on figure 1.7 and represent changes from 1991 through 2000.

We can show the implications of these trends using a more formal analysis. Note that the average disability in the population can be expressed as the average of disability for people with different times until death, weighted by the share of people in that time-until-death category: $\text{Disability}_t = \Sigma_k \text{Share}_{kt} *$ Disability_{kt}, where k references the buckets of time until death. Then, the change in the disability rate is approximately equal to the change in the mortality rates, weighted by initial disability rates, and the change in disability rates, weighted by the population share with that time to live:

(4) $\Delta\text{Disability} \approx \Sigma_k \Delta\text{Share}_k \text{Disability}_{kto} + \Sigma_k \text{Share}_{kto} \Delta\text{Disability}_k.$

Table 1.7 shows the results of this decomposition. As the first row of the second column shows, disability declined by 6.3 percentage points. The next row shows the impact of mortality changes on the prevalence of disability. Because people are living longer, disability would have declined by 0.7 percentage points, even if all groups were just as disabled as in the early time period. The far bigger impact is of changes in disability for a given time until death. Disability declines particularly greatly for those two or more years from death. The decline is roughly similar in groups that far from death or longer. The largest share of disability decline occurred in the population eight or more years from death (almost 50 percent), though this group is about 60 percent of the population.

Given the importance of health trends by population subgroup, figure 1.9 shows the relationship between disability and time until death for different demographic groups, divided by gender (a and b), race (c and d), and education (e and f). The pattern in all cases is very similar. Disability declined only slightly near death, and much more the farther away from death one

Table 1.7   Decomposition of disability over time, by time until death

Measure	Disability change in group (%)	Decomposition of total change in disability (%)
Total change	—	−6.3
Effect of survival	—	−0.7
Change within time periods		
≤ 12 months	−0.4	−0.0
13–24 months	−3.7	−0.2
25–48 months	−10.0	−0.8
49–72 months	−9.4	−0.6
73–96 months	−12.3	−0.7
> 96 months	−15.9	−3.3

Notes: The first column shows the percent change in disability rate for people in each category of time until death. The change is taken from 1991–1993 to the latest three years available. The second column decomposes the total change in disability. The first row, total change, shows the percentage point change in disability over time from 1991–1993 to 1998–2000. The second row shows the change in disability resulting from changes in the share of people with different periods of time until death. The remaining rows show the change in disability resulting from changes in the disability rate in each time-until-death category.

gets. Indeed, even the magnitudes are similar. The decline in disability for those eight or more years from death is 20–25 percent in all cases. Thus, the results we find are quite robust across demographic groups.

Although functional status did not decline greatly in our data, we show the trend in functional limitations by time until death in figure 1.10. Almost everyone is functionally limited before death; in the last year of life, 95 percent of people have a functional limitation. This did not change greatly over time, however. Nor did it change meaningfully in any other population group.

1.3.3 Summary Measures of Health

We finally turn to our three summary measures of health, the factor scores from the factor analysis. We denote them F1, F2, and F3, corresponding to the three largest eigenvalues in table 1.4. We also identify them by the health measures that load on them most strongly: ADL and IADL limitations for F1, functional limitations for F2, and sensory impairments for F3. As is customary, we normalize each factor score to have a mean of 0 and a standard deviation of 1. A higher score indicates more "yes" answers to the impairments, and thus a greater level of sickness.

Figure 1.11 shows the trend in the three factor scores. All three decline over time. The greatest decline is for F3, the factor reflecting sensory impairments. The overall decline is approximately one-sixth of a standard deviation. F1, corresponding to ADL and IADL limitations declines the second largest, and F2, corresponding to functional limitations and related ADL and IADL limitations, declines the least.

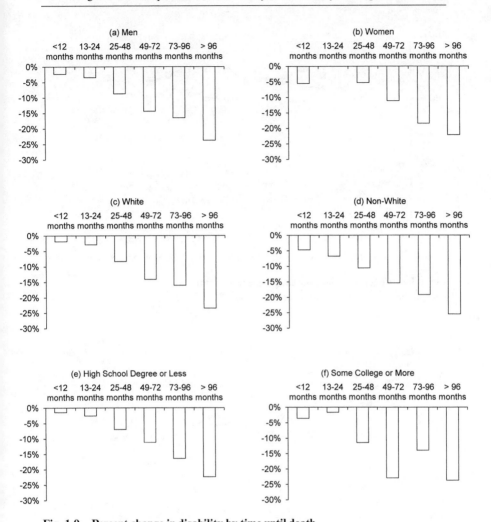

Fig. 1.9   Percent change in disability by time until death

Note: The data are for 1991–2000 and are based on data like those in figure 1.7.

Figure 1.12, in panels (a), (b), and (c), shows the changes for each factor score by time until death. Not surprisingly, there is enormous spread in the data. For those within 12 months of death, the average F1 score is about 1.5, the average F2 score is about 0.8, and the average F3 score is about 0.5. These decline somewhat as death moves away in time, but they remain high even for people 24–36 months from death. For that group, F1 and F2 are about 0.5.

Mirroring our results in the binary disability measure, the improvement in these health measures is particularly marked for those farther from death. Except for F3, these summary measures do not improve greatly for those in the three years prior to death. Rather, the vast bulk of the decline is in those

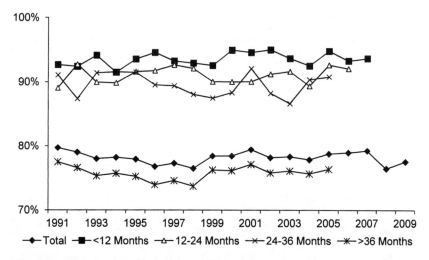

Fig. 1.10   Functional limitations by time until death
Note: Functional limitations are defined in table 1.2.

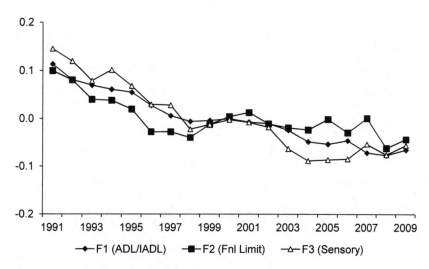

Fig. 1.11   Trend in factor scores
Note: F1, F2, and F3 are based on the factor analysis displayed in table 1.3.

with three or more years to live until dying. Sensory impairments, however, are declining in all groups, even those very close to death.

1.3.4 Summary

There are many measures of health, not all of which move in the same direction. As a result, there is no single conclusion we can draw. But there are some common trends that are important. Our major conclusion is that time spent in poor physical functioning is being increasingly compressed

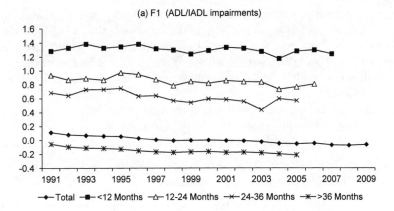

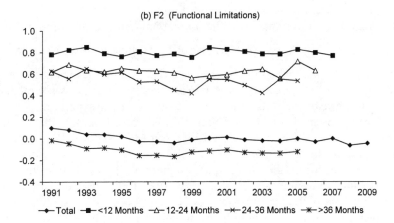

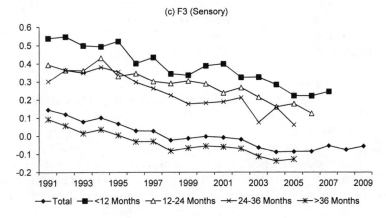

Fig. 1.12   Trend in factor scores by time until death

Note: F1, F2, and F3 are based on the factor analysis displayed in table 1.3.

into the period just before death. Limitations in very severe impairments such as ADLs or IADLs are falling for those not near the end of life, as are more severe functional limitations. Less severe functional limitations are constant, and overall disease prevalence is rising. People have more diseases than they used to, but the severe disablement that disease used to imply has been reduced.

The compression of morbidity into the period just before death means that disability-free life expectancy will be increasing. We explore changes in disability-free and disabled life expectancy quantitatively in the next section.

1.4   Disability-Adjusted Life Expectancy

Understanding the compression of morbidity is best done in the context of disability-adjusted survival. In this section, we turn our estimates of health changes into changes in disabled and disability-free life years. The starting point for our analysis is the standard measure of life expectancy:

(5) $LE(a) = \Sigma_s \{\Pr[\text{Survive } a + s \,|\, \text{Alive } a] + .5*\Pr[\text{Die at } a + s \,|\, \text{Alive } a]\}.$

Starting at age a, every (probabilistic) year that the average person survives adds one year to life expectancy. A person who dies in a year is assumed to live half the year, and thus adds half that amount to life expectancy.

Mortality is calculated by the National Center for Health Statistics and routinely published in the National Vital Statistics Reports. We use their data for mortality.

To account for disability, we modify equation (5). For those in the last year of life, we weight the half year they expect to live by the share of the people in that half year who are not disabled. As figure 1.8 shows, this is on average 20 percent. Similarly, we weight the years lived by those one year away from death, two years away from death, three years away from death, and more than three years away from death by the share of population in those intervals who are not disabled. Adding this up over all future ages yields disability-free life expectancy. Disabled life expectancy is the difference between total life expectancy and disability-free life expectancy.

We can form disability-free life expectancy and disabled life expectancy for any year in which we have mortality and disability data. To match our results, we estimate these values in two time periods: 1992 and 2005. The mortality data are from those exact years. The disability data are from 1991–1993 and 2003–2005. We present all of our calculations for a person age sixty-five in those years.

Relative to our earlier calculations, we make one additional refinement. Where earlier we showed disability rates on an age-adjusted basis, here we need to disaggregate disability by age. For example, about 45 percent of people who are thirty-six or more months from death in 1991–1993 have an ADL or IADL impairment. But that share is about 30 percent for the young-

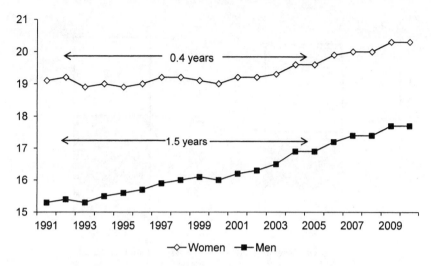

Fig. 1.13   Life expectancy at age sixty-five

Note: Data are from the National Center for Health Statistics.

est elderly and 80 percent for the oldest elderly. To account for this, we form an estimate of disability rates that is age specific. Rather than calculating means across single-year age by time-until-death cells, which would involve many small cells, we instead use regression analysis to smooth disability rates by age, and other demographic characteristics.

Specifically, we estimate a logistic regression model relating disability to age and its square, a dummy for females, and a dummy for nonwhite. We estimate this regression separately for 1991–1993 and 2003–2005 and for each category of time until death: < 12 months, 12–24 months, 24–36 months, and 36 months or more. We then predict the disability rates for each person and average the predictions across the relevant groups (e.g., single year of age). We match these to life tables in 1992 and 2005.

1.3.5 Results

We start with basic life expectancy calculations. Figure 1.13 shows the trend in life expectancy at age sixty-five, separately for men and women. Life expectancy is rising for both groups, but the increase is much greater for men than women. Between 1992 and 2005, life expectancy for a sixty-five-year-old male increased by 1.5 years, while life expectancy for a sixty-five-year-old woman increased by 0.4 years. Our life expectancy data differs from these calculations slightly, since the NCHS does not publish mortality tables beyond age 100. We thus assume everyone dies at that age. Effectively, this reduces our life expectancy increase by 0.2 years.

Figure 1.14 shows the trend in total life expectancy, disability-free life expectancy, and disabled life expectancy for the overall population at

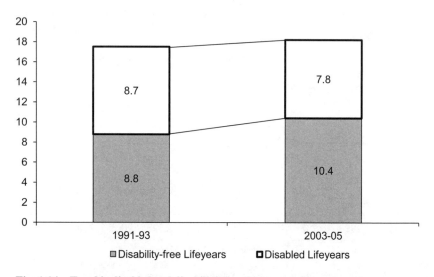

Fig. 1.14   Trend in disabled and disability-free life expectancy
Note: The figure combines life expectancy data from the NCHS with imputed disability rates by age and time until death.

age sixty-five. Table 1.8 shows specific numerical results. Life expectancy at age sixty-five was 17.5 years in 1992. This reflects the fact that about half the elderly population is disabled, and about half of those years were disabled.

Life expectancy increased by 0.7 years between 1992 and 2005. Because the fall in disability was so large, however, the increase in disability-free life expectancy was greater than the total increase in life expectancy—1.6 years in total. The residual was a reduction in disabled life expectancy of 0.9 years. Thus, both the metric of the change in disabled life expectancy as well as the share of life that is spent disability free, morbidity is being compressed into the time period just before death.

Figure 1.15 shows life expectancy, disability-free life expectancy, and disabled life expectancy by gender and race. In all four cases, the results are similar: overall life expectancy increased, and disability-free life expectancy increased by even more. As a result, disabled life expectancy fell in all cases. The decline in disabled life expectancy was greater for women than for men, but was similar by race.

In principle, we can estimate changes in life expectancy and disability-free life expectancy by education as well. In practice, while data on mortality by education are collected (since 1989), they are not routinely published.[6] In

---

6. Some authors have calculated life expectancy by education for particular years (e.g., Meara, Richards, and Cutler 2008), but they do not match the years we analyze for the other demographic groups.

Table 1.8 Changes in disabled and disability-free life expectancy at age sixty-five

Group	1991–1993			2003–2005			Change		
	Total	Disability free	Disabled	Total	Disability free	Disabled	Total	Disability free	Disabled
All	17.5	8.8	8.7	18.2	10.4	7.8	0.7	1.6	-0.9
Men	15.5	9.2	6.2	16.7	10.9	5.8	1.3	1.7	-0.4
Women	19.2	8.4	10.8	19.4	10.0	9.4	0.2	1.6	-1.4
White	17.6	9.0	8.6	18.3	10.6	7.7	0.7	1.6	-0.9
Nonwhite	15.8	7.0	8.9	16.7	8.8	7.9	0.9	1.8	-1.0

Notes: The table shows total life expectancy, disability-free life expectancy, and disabled life expectancy, in years. Disability is an indicator for the presence of an ADL or IADL limitation.

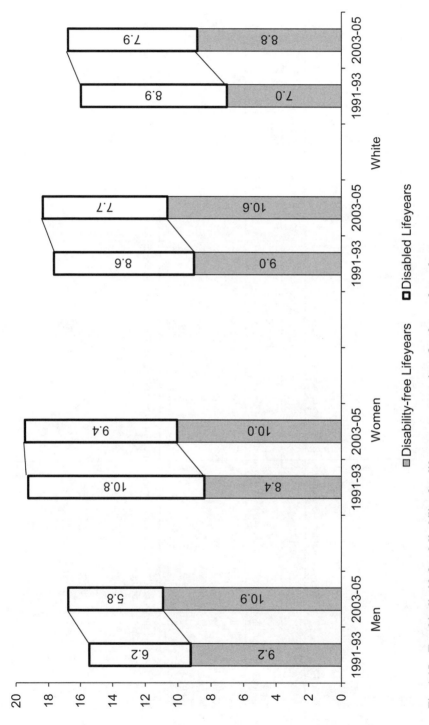

Fig. 1.15   Trend in disabled and disability-free life expectancy at sixty-five, by gender and race

Note: The figure combines life expectancy data from the NCHS with imputed disability rates by age and time until death.

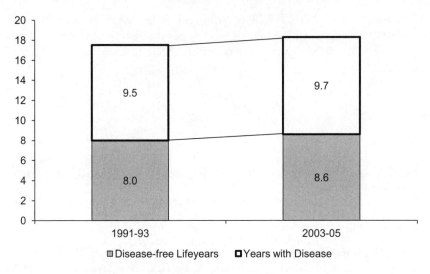

Fig. 1.16   Trend in disease-free life expectancy and life with disease
Note: The figure combines life expectancy data from the NCHS with imputed disease rates by age and time until death.

future work, we will construct relevant life tables from the micro data and calculate life expectancy by education.

Since so much of the literature has focused on disease-free survival, we have estimated disease-free survival trends as well. We focus on the major diseases in table 1.2, since they are the most consequential for health. Figure 1.16 shows the results. Disease-free survival increased over time, but so did life expectancy with disease. Of the total increase in life expectancy of 0.7 years, 0.6 years was associated with disease-free survival and 0.1 years was associated with additional life with major disease. The conclusion about the compression of morbidity thus depends on the definition used: the share of life that is disease free rose, but the length of life with major disease increased as well.

1.5   Conclusion

Our results show clearly that over the 1991–2009 period, disability has been compressed into the period just before death. Disability-free life expectancy rose, and disabled life expectancy declined. Thus, by either measure of compression of morbidity, morbidity is being compressed into the period just before death. Disease-free survival increased as well, although so did survival with a major disease.

The major question raised by our results is why this has occurred. How much of this trend is a result of medical care versus other social and environmental factors? Our results do not speak to this issue, but they give us a metric for analyzing the impact of changes that have occurred. We and others could usefully pursue the question about causality in subsequent research.

References

Bartholomew, D. J. 1987. *Latent Variable Models and Factor Analysis.* New York: Oxford University Press.

Cai, L., and James Lubitz. 2007. "Was There a Compression of Disability for Older Americans from 1992 to 2003?" *Demography* 44:479–95.

Crimmins, Eileen M., and Hiram Beltrán-Sánchez. 2010. "Mortality and Morbidity Trends: Is There Compression of Morbidity?" *Journal of Gerontology: Social Sciences* 66B (1): 75–86.

Crimmins, Eileen M., Mark D. Hayward, Aaron Hagedorn, Yasuhiko Saito, and Nicolas Brouard. 2009. "Changes in Disability-Free Life Expectancy for Americans 70 Years Old and Older." *Demography* 46 (3): 627–46.

Cutler, David M., and Mary Beth Landrum. 2012. "Dimensions of Health in the Elderly Population." In *Investigations in the Economics of Aging*, edited by David Wise, 179–201. Chicago: University of Chicago Press.

Freedman, Vicki A., Eileen Crimmins, Robert F. Schoeni, B. Spillman, H. Aykan, E. Kramarow, K. Land et al. 2004. "Resolving Inconsistencies in Trends in Old-Age Disability: Report from a Technical Working Group." *Demography* 41 (3): 417–41.

Freedman, Vicki A., Brenda C. Spillman, Patti M. Andreski, P. Andreski, J. Cornman, E. Crimmins, E Kramarow et al. 2013. "Trends in Late-Life Activity Limitations in the United States: An Update from Five National Surveys." *Demography* 50:661–71.

Fries, James F. 1980. "Aging, Natural Death, and the Compression of Morbidity." *New England Journal of Medicine* 303:1369–70.

Gruenberg, E. F. 1977. "The Failures of Success." *Milbank Memorial Fund Quarterly/Health and Society* 55:3–24.

Knol, D. L., and M. P. Berger. 1991. "Empirical Comparison Between Factor Analysis and Multidimensional Item Response Models." *Multivariate Behavioral Research* 26:457–77.

Lamb, V. L. 1996. "A Cross-National Study of Quality of Life Factors Associated with Patterns of Elderly Disablement." *Social Science and Medicine* 42 (3): 363–77.

Lunney, June R., Joanne Lynn, Daniel J. Foley, Steven Lipson, and Jack M. Guralnik. 2003. "Patterns of Functional Decline at the End of Life." *Journal of the American Medical Association* 289:2387–92.

Manton, Kenneth G. 1982. "Changing Concepts of Morbidity and Mortality in the Elderly Population." *Milbank Memorial Fund Quarterly/Health and Society* 60:183–244.

Manton, Kenneth G., X. Gu, and G. R. Lowrimore. 2008. "Cohort Changes in Active Life Expectancy in the U.S. Elderly Population: Experience from the 1982–2004 National Long-Term Care Survey." *Journals of Gerontology: Psychological Sciences & Social Sciences* 63B:S269–S281.

Manton, K. G., E. Stallard, and L. S. Corder. 1998. "The Dynamics of Dimensions of Age-Related Disability 1982 to 1994 in the U.S. Elderly Population." *J Gerontol A Biol Sci Med Sci* 53 (1): B59–70.

Manton, K. G., H. Woodbury, and D. Tolley. 1994. *Statistical Applications Using Fuzzy Sets.* New York: Wiley.

Meara, Ellen R., Seth Richards, and David Cutler. 2008. "The Gap Gets Bigger: Changes in Mortality and Life Expectancy, by Education, 1981–2000." *Health Affairs* 27 (2): 350–60.

Verbrugge, L. M., and A. M. Jette. 1994. "The Disablement Process." *Social Science Medicine* 38:1–14.

Woodbury, M., J. Clive, and A. Garson. 1978. "Mathematical Typology: A Grade of Membership Technique for Obtaining Disease Definition." *Computers and Biomedical Research* 11:277–98.

Comment   Daniel McFadden and Wei Xie

There is a plausible conjecture that morbidity should be expanding among seniors: risks from early, quick killers like heart attacks and strokes are falling, leaving the elderly more exposed to risk from slow, disabling "killers of last resort" like senile dementia. Improved treatments have increased survival times after onset of some potentially mortal conditions such as kidney disease, and people living with such diseases are prone to other complications. If health research dollars and medical advances are tilted toward acute conditions and their treatment, people may live longer, but do so with burdensome disabilities. The chapter "Evidence for Significant Compression of Morbidity in the Elderly US Population" by David Cutler, Kaushik Ghosh, and Mary Beth Landrum presents persuasive evidence that this conjecture is wrong. They make clever use of data from the Medicare Current Beneficiary Study (MCBS), linked to 2008 National Death Index data, and find that while disease prevalence is rising for key conditions, functional disabilities are falling, and overall, morbidity measured by disabilities that cause substantial functional limitations is falling as a portion of the total life span. In conclusion, medical science is not creating a population of zombies. We compliment the authors on this research, and in this comment will also complement it with tabulations from a 20 percent sample of Medicare claims records.

To understand the authors' results, it is useful to clarify what "morbidity" means. The correlated but distinct aspects in figure 1C.1 seem important.

Daniel McFadden is a Professor of the Graduate School of the University of California, Berkeley, the Presidential Professor of Health Economics at the University of Southern California, a 2000 Nobel Laureate in Economics, and a research associate of the National Bureau of Economic Research. Wei Xie is a graduate student in economics at the University of Southern California.

For acknowledgments, sources of research support, and disclosure of the authors' material financial relationships, if any, please see http://www.nber.org/chapters/c12967.ack.

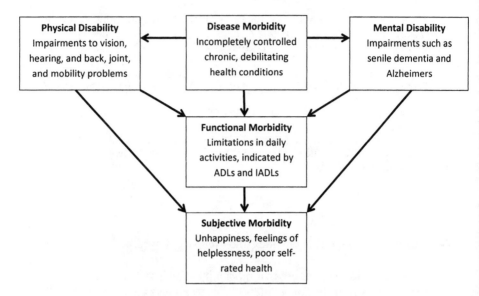

Fig. 1C.1   Physical disability, disease morbidity, and mental disability

Disease morbidity may contribute to physical and mental disabilities, and these impairments may contribute to functional and subjective morbidities. The authors conduct a factor analysis of nineteen questions on health limitations in the MCBS data, and identify three factors that among the aspects pictured roughly span functional morbidity and physical and mental disabilities. Their key finding is that their impairment factors, looking back one or more years before death, have been falling over time. This is despite an apparent increase in disease prevalence over time, particularly for controllable chronic diseases.

A leading interpretation is that with the assistance of medical science people are getting better at managing diseases and functioning without severe impairments. However, there are other possibilities. Figure 1C.2 shows health status over the life course, stylistically described in terms of "life force." The individual depicted has an onset of disease 1, from which she has a full recovery, and then has an onset of disease 2, which leads to a progressively disabling fall in life force and eventually to death. At some point disease 2 is diagnosed, and thereafter this person is observed as having disease 2 morbidity. When her life force falls below a threshold, she also has functional morbidity, indicated by ADL or IADL limitations. Now ask what factors could decrease functional morbidity or increase disease morbidity. Changes lowering functional morbidity include (a) lowering the threshold below which activities of daily living are limited; (b) changing the treatment of disease 2 in a way that slows the progress of the disease and the decline in life force more in its initial stages than in its late stages, pro-

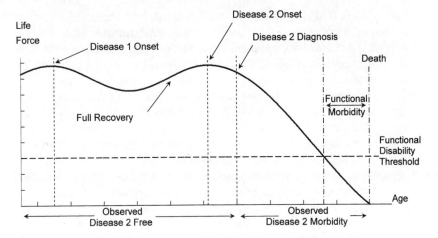

Fig. 1C.2   Disease and functional morbidities over the life course

longing the time during which life force is above the threshold level; and (c) lowering the incidence of disease 2 relative to quick killers that have short spells of morbidity. These changes are all real, so long as lowering the threshold reflects improvement in coping strategies (e.g., Internet grocery shopping for home delivery) rather than increasing reluctance to admit to functional disabilities. Changes that increase disease morbidity include (a) raising the relative risk of the disease (by lowing competing risks from quicker killers); (b) accelerating the diagnosis of the disease so that it is identified in an earlier stage; or (c) changing diagnostic coding so that the diagnosis includes people who have less virulent forms of the disease or are more resistant to it. Some of these changes may be apparent rather than real. A particular issue is that increased diagnostic testing, or upcoding that classifies less sick people as having a disease, could increase apparent disease morbidity without altering the real conditions that lead to functional morbidity; this is sometimes called a "Will Rogers effect" from his observation that migration between states can sometimes raise an average in both.

To complement the authors' analysis of disease prevalence using MCBS data, we have run tabulations from a 20 percent longitudinal sample of Medicare A and B claims from 1999 to 2010. We use Chronic Condition Warehouse (CCW) definitions of health conditions observed from ICD-9 diagnostic codes on claims.[1] To carry out the CCW coding of conditions, we restrict analysis to people age 67–95 with at least two years of full or nearly full enrollment in fee-for-service (ffS) Medicare coverage. This

---

1. For detailed information on the construction of the chronic conditions, see www.ccwdata .org/cs/groups/public/documents/document/ccw_conditioncategories2011.pdf .

selects out many dual-eligible, institutionalized, and Medicaid-qualified low-income people who are assigned to Medicare Advantage plans and do not have A/B claims for most conditions. For our analysis, we are left with 5,139,917 people in 2004, 4,831,246 in 2007, and 4,790,793 in 2010; the decline in the face of increasing overall Medicare enrollment by seniors reflects diversions from ffS to Medicaid and Medicare Advantage programs. The claims records contain no information on functional disabilities, biometric data, or self-rated health, so our analysis is limited to disease morbidity. Our tabulations do not account for drift in diagnostic practices, or drifts in the demographic mix of the Medicare ffS population other than age and sex, so they leave unanswered the question of whether observed drifts in prevalence are to some extent ecological or definitional.[2] We closely follow the authors in classifying diseases into *cancers* (prostate, breast, colorectal, lung), *chronic disabling conditions* (Alzheimer's, dementia, and related disorders, chronic obstructive pulmonary disease [COPD], chronic kidney disease, osteoporosis), *acute treatable diseases* (acute myocardial infarction [AMI], ischemic heart disease, stroke, and broken hip), and *nonfatal controllable conditions* (arthritis, diabetes, depression, glaucoma, hypertension, acquired hypothyroidism, anemia, asthma, hyperlipidemia).

Figures 1C.3, 1C.4, 1C.5, and 1C.6 present age-specific prevalence rates by gender for selected conditions for the years 2004, 2007, and 2010. Figure 1C.7 gives age-specific average counts of major (i.e., all except nonfatal controllable conditions) CCW conditions and of all CCW conditions. The cancers in figure 1C.3 show initially increasing prevalence with age, but eventually turn down as higher risk people are selected out of the population. There is relatively little drift, although breast and lung cancers for females show rising rates that may be attributable to rising smoking rates in the past in these age cohorts. Colorectal cancer shows a modest decline. In figure 1C.4 for chronic degenerative diseases, Alzheimer's and senile dementia and COPD show little drift, while osteoporosis and chronic kidney disease show significant increases over time. The acute treatable conditions in figure 1C.5 increase fairly sharply with age, and show very little drift over time except for falling prevalence of AMI and strokes. However, almost all the nonfatal, controllable conditions in figure 1C.6 show sharply increasing prevalence over time; the particularly strong drifts for diabetes, hypertension, and hyperlipidemia almost certainly are due in part to more aggressive diagnosis of these conditions conducted as part of implementing new, effective control therapies. Finally, figure 1C.7 shows that the numbers of major and total CCW conditions both rise with age, and drift up sharply over time for the

---

2. In general, Medicaid enrollees appear to be less healthy, and MA enrollees appear to be more healthy than the ffS population, so that drifts in enrollments are a factor in drifts in prevalence.

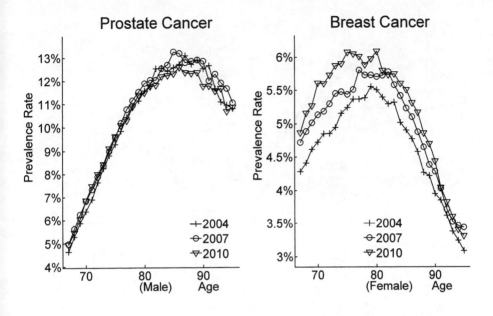

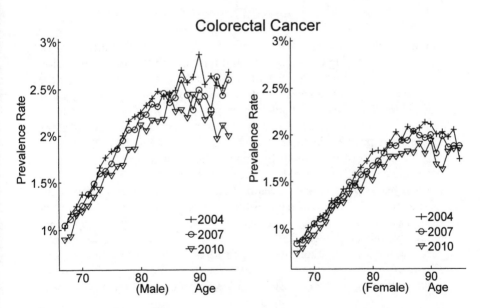

Fig. 1C.3   Cancer condition prevalence rates by year, age, and gender

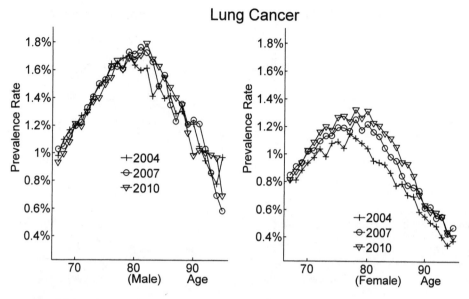

Fig. 1C.3   (Cont)

count of all conditions, and modestly over time for the count of major conditions. These figures agree with and reinforce the authors' conclusion that disease morbidity is rising, with AMI, stroke, and colorectal cancer the only significant exceptions, and age-specific prevalence is drifting up most sharply for nonfatal controllable conditions.

Next, we follow the authors and look at the prevalence of conditions in the years prior to death. The structure of the claims data allows us to take the cohort of individuals by gender who die in a given year and have a specific disease, and trace them back longitudinally to get disease prevalence in years up to the year of death.[3] Our findings are generally consistent with a story of improved therapies that increase survival times after onset of a disease, although they are also consistent with a story in which more aggressive diagnosis identifies people who are in earlier stages of the disease and are less sick. Our rates are age adjusted (to the 2010 age profile). Figure 1C.8 shows that cancer prevalence falls fairly sharply with years to death, reflecting the high mortality risk and hence short morbidity spells

3. Our death cohorts are not selected by cause of death, which may be attributed to multiple conditions, some of which may be opportunistic when the person has the disease that we are analyzing. These cohorts are also not adjusted for trends in comorbidities. There is some attrition in the sampled cohort as we look back, from people who were not enrolled in Medicare ffS plans throughout the look-back period; calculated look-back prevalence rates are for the subsample whose ffS data is sufficient for the CCW disease determination.

Alzheimer Disease and Related Disorders or Senile

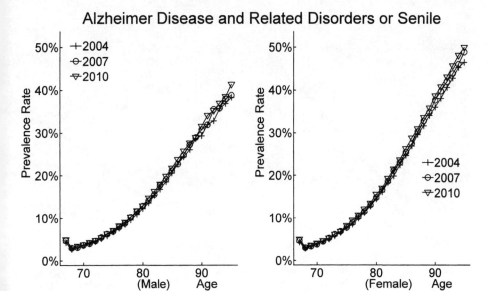

Chronic Obstructive Pulmonary

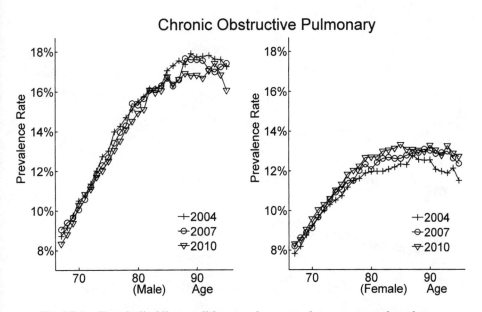

Fig. 1C.4 Chronic disabling condition prevalence rates by year, age, and gender

Chronic Kidney Disease

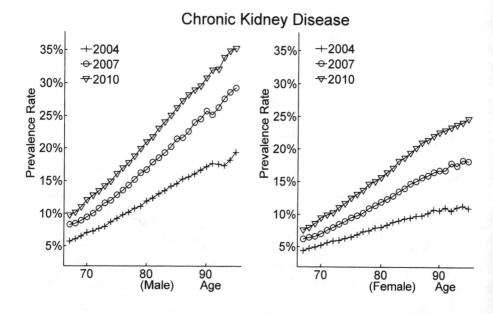

Osteoporosis

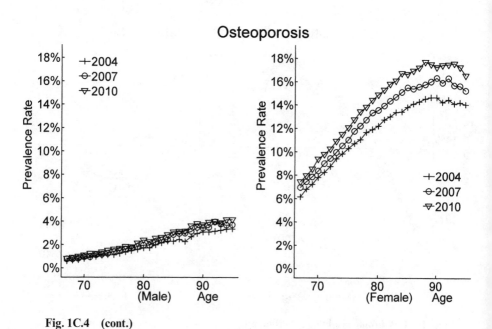

Fig. 1C.4 (cont.)

Acute Myocardial Infarction

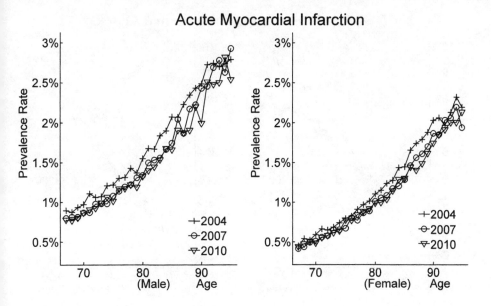

Ischemic Heart Disease

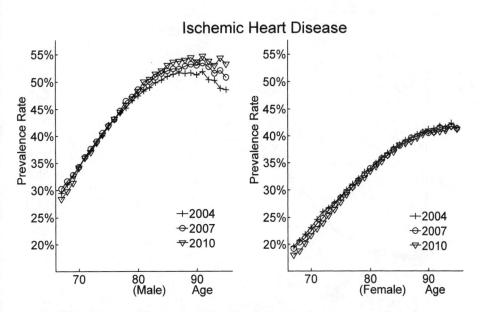

Fig. 1C.5   Recoverable acute condition prevalence rates by year, age, and gender

Stroke/Transient Ischemic Attack

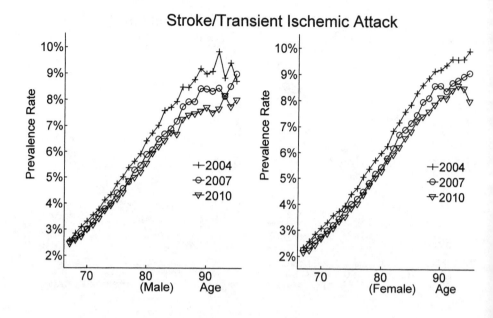

Hip/Pelvic Fracture

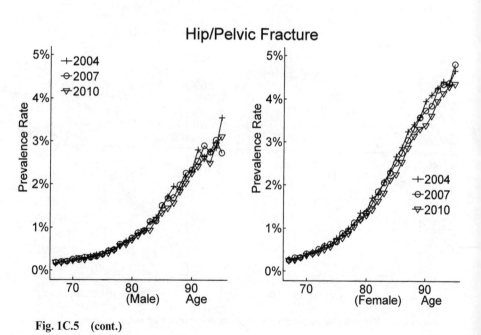

Fig. 1C.5   (cont.)

Rheumatoid Arthritis/Osteoarthritis

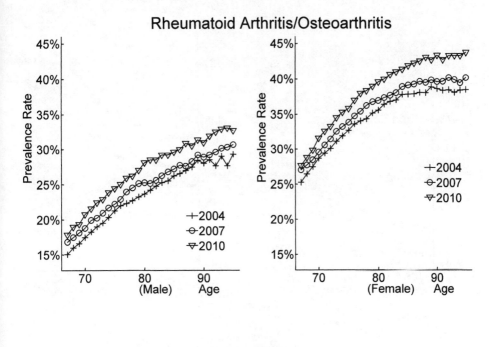

Diabetes

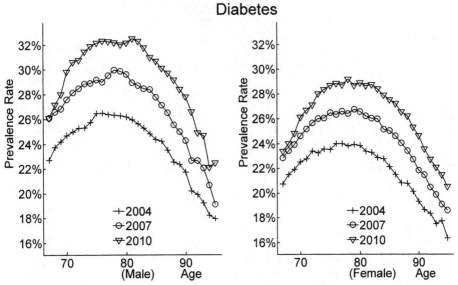

Fig. 1C.6   Nonfatal controllable condition prevalence rates by year, age, and gender

Depression

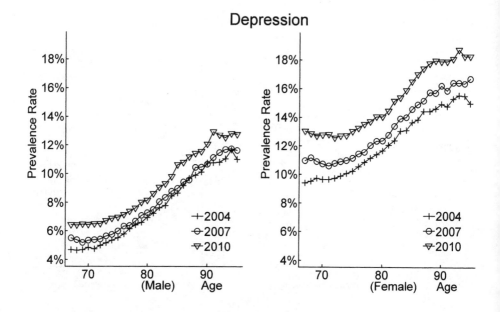

Glaucoma

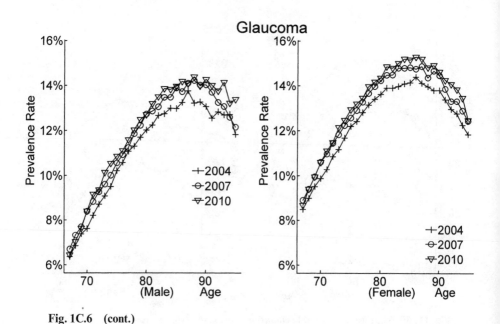

Fig. 1C.6   (cont.)

Hypertension

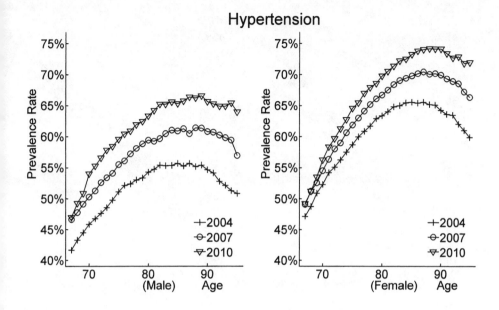

Acquired Hypothyroidism

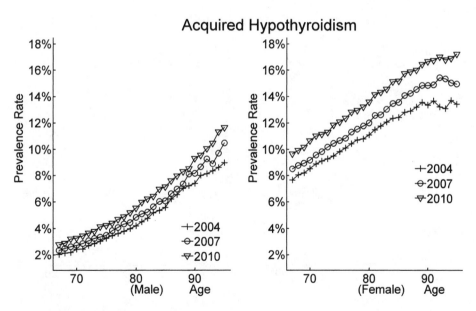

Fig. 1C.6   (cont.)

Anemia

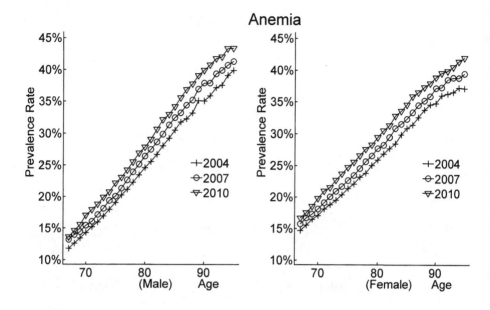

Asthma

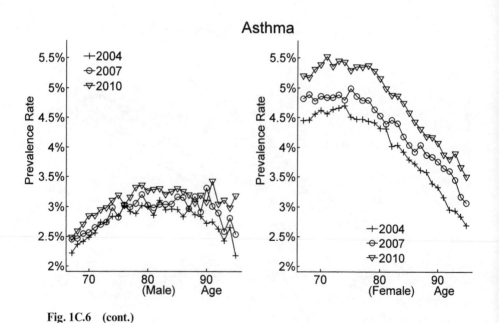

Fig. 1C.6   (cont.)

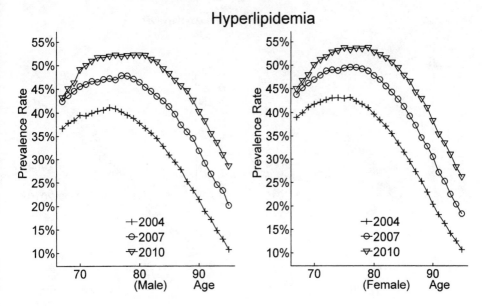

Fig. 1C.6   (cont.)

for these diseases. Both breast cancer and prostate cancer show modest upward drift over time in prevalence in each year before death, suggesting that therapies may be increasing survival times, but there is no evidence of this for colorectal and lung cancer. Figure 1C.9 shows upward drift in prevalence over time at each year prior to death for all the chronic degenerative diseases, again suggesting that therapies are prolonging survival. For the recoverable acute conditions shown in figure 1C.10, therapies appear to be prolonging survival with ischemic heart disease. Figure 1C.11 shows these curves for nonfatal, controllable conditions. For most of these conditions, we see a flattening of the prevalence gradients in the years before death, with sharp increases for diabetes, hypertension, and hyperlipidemia, conditions where new therapies have substantially improved disease control and the payoff to early diagnosis. Taken together, figures 1C.8, 1C.9, 1C.10, and 1C.11 show evidence of mild expansion of the duration of disease morbidity in the years before death. Combined with rising prevalence for many diseases, particularly in the nonfatal controllable category, these indicate a steady increase in the frequencies and durations of disease morbidities. Our disease-specific figures do not control for disease comorbidities. A more comprehensive analysis would have to look at the patterns of development of comorbidities, perhaps applying to the list of CCW conditions some dynamic version of the factor analysis that the authors have done for functional and other disabilities. Going further, it might be informative to estimate a dynamic multiple-indicator, multiple-cause model in which

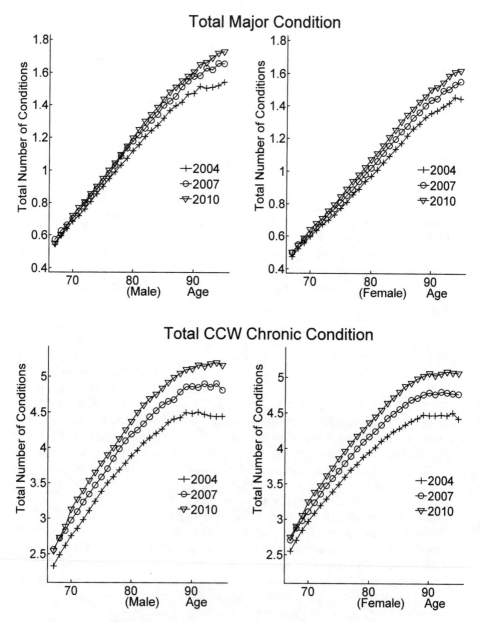

Fig. 1C.7   Counts of major and total CCW conditions by year, age, and gender

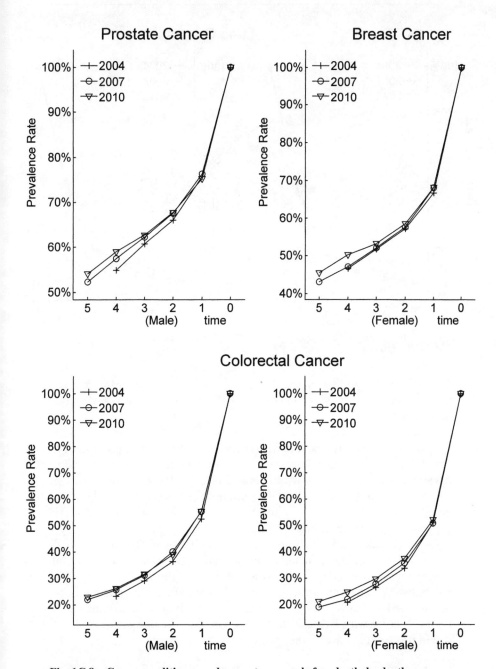

Fig. 1C.8   Cancer condition prevalence rates, years before death, by death year, and gender

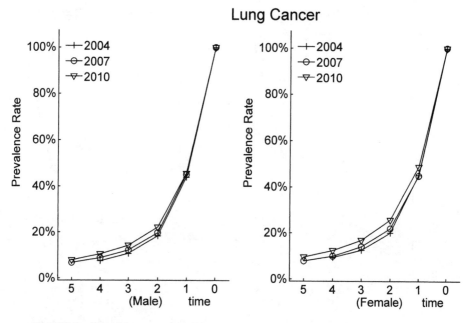

Fig. 1C.8   (cont.)

a list of CCW conditions and durations since onset map through a few life force factors to a list of functional limitations and physical and mental disabilities.

Finally, figure 1C.12 shows how numbers of total CCW conditions, and of major CCW conditions, vary with years before death; these give some evidence that disease comorbidity rates are rising. The curves show that people develop more conditions as death approaches, and these will frequently be causes of death. However, the curves are not very steep. We conclude that people can often live for quite a long time with multiple conditions, and still cope with the corresponding disabilities.

Given the lack of compression of disease morbidity, and the authors' finding of sharp compression in functional morbidity, there has to be a sharp fall in the proportion of people with disease morbidity who also have functional morbidity. Whether this is due to improved coping skills and functional aids, to improved and earlier diagnosis, or more aggressive coding that makes the pool of people with a disease less sick on average, is an open question. It would be useful to have further research on the following topics:

- Is coding of diseases drifting up over time, or is the apparent increase in disease prevalence really there? This might be tested by examining diseases with and without coding discretion, and by comparing CCW

Alzheimer Disease and Related Disorders or Senile Dementia

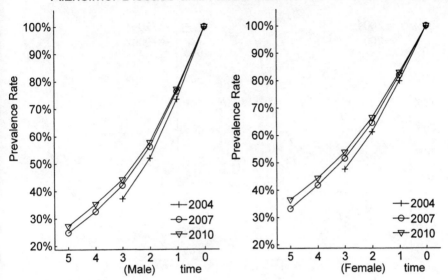

Chronic Obstructive Pulmonary Disease

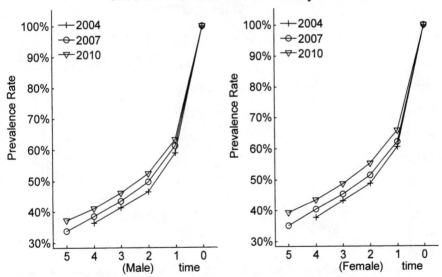

Fig. 1C.9   Chronic disabling condition prevalence rates, years before death, by death year, and gender

Chronic Kidney Disease

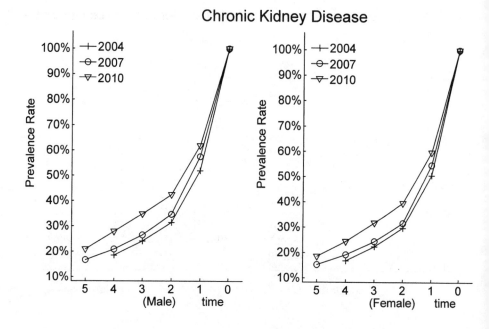

Osteoporosis

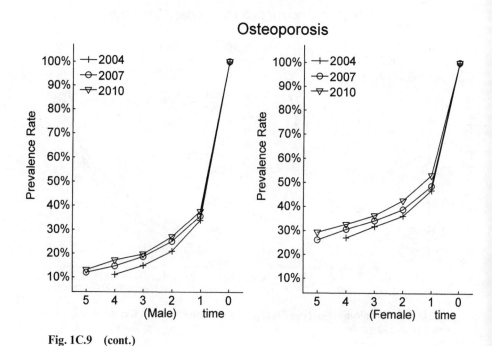

Fig. 1C.9   (cont.)

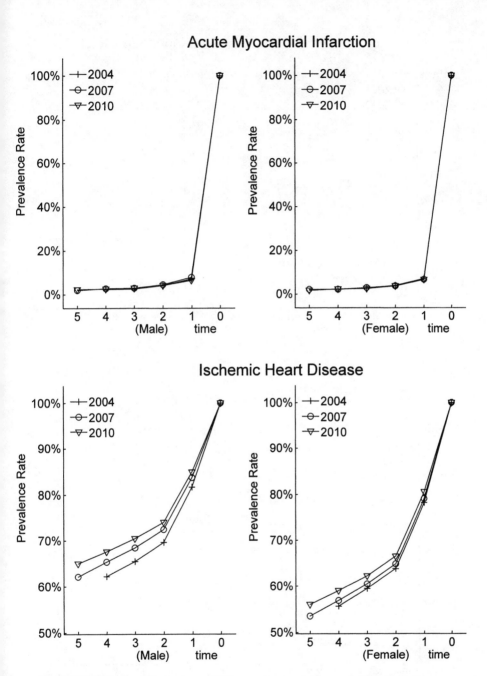

Fig. 1C.10   Recoverable acute condition prevalence rates, years before death, by death year, and gender

Stroke/Transient Ischemic Attack

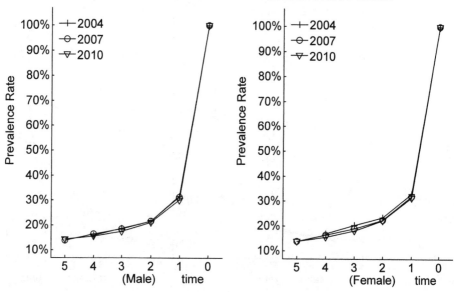

Hip/Pelvic Fracture

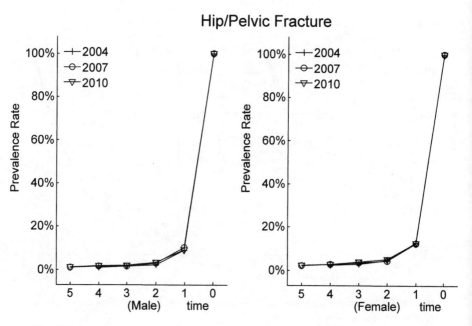

Fig. 1C.10   (cont)

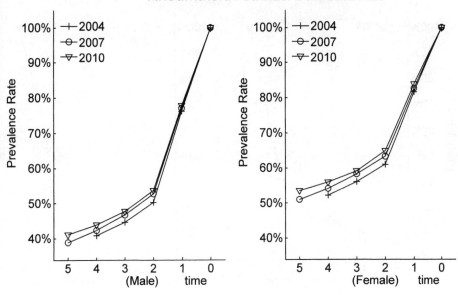

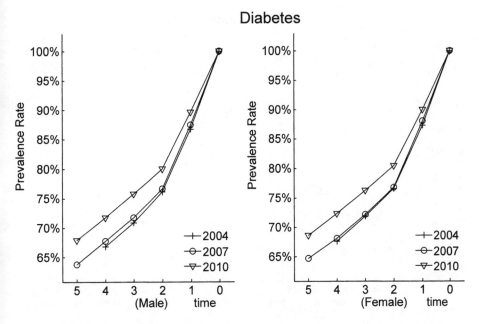

Fig. 1C.11   Nonfatal controllable condition prevalence rates, years before death, by
death year, and gender

Depression

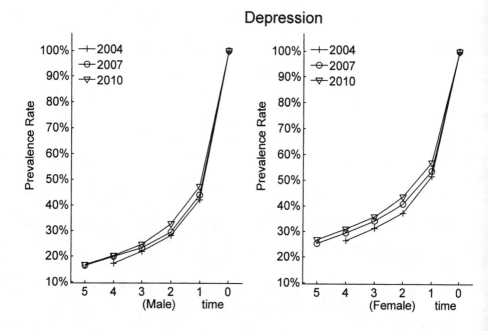

Glaucoma

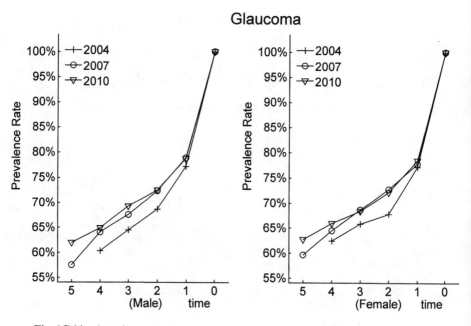

Fig. 1C.11   (cont.)

Hypertension

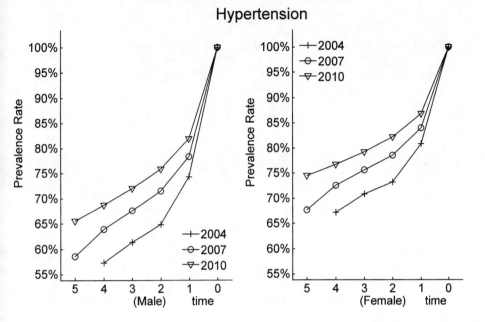

Acquired Hypothyroidism

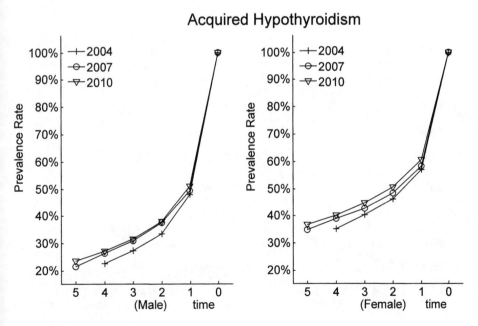

Fig. 1C.11 (cont.)

Anemia

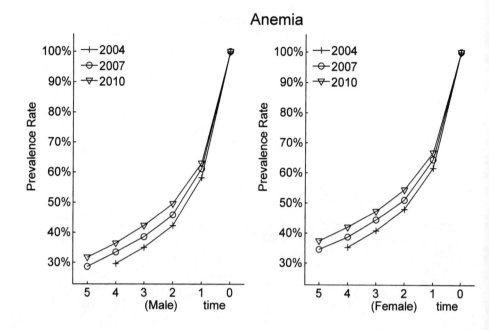

(Male)

(Female)

Asthma

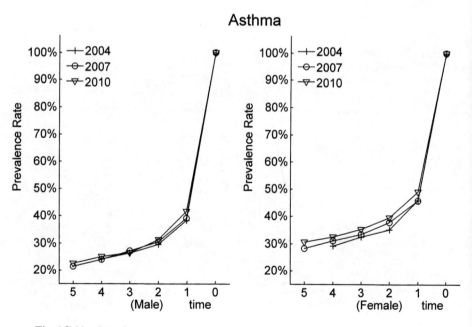

(Male)

(Female)

Fig. 1C.11   (cont.)

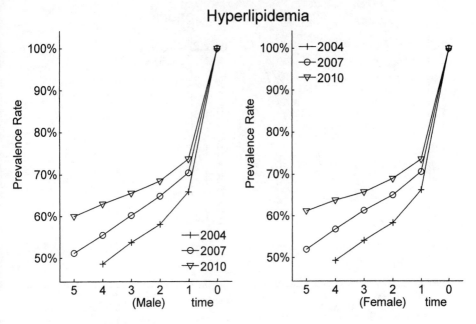

Fig. 1C.11   (cont.)

coding of conditions with clinical diagnoses in a sample of people with medical records, and by examining drifts in the scope and frequency of diagnostic tests.

- Are people really getting better in managing disabilities without reporting ADL and IADL limitations? This might be tested by studying the activities of people, and identifying coping strategies.
- Are subjective morbidity rates relatively stable, despite increased disease morbidity, as the "hedonic treadmill" would predict? This might be tested through use of some of the currently popular measures of happiness tabulated against levels of disease and functional morbidity.

Finally, we point out that while the authors' chapter does not dwell on policy implications, there are some important ones. First, if there is a tilt in NIH and commercial medical research toward innovation in acute care, it does not seem to be causing an explosion in disabled elderly. Specifically, apparently rising disease prevalence does not appear to be causing a lockstep increase in functional morbidity or prevalence of physical or mental disabilities. Second, both increasing disease morbidity and decreasing functional morbidity could be an artifact of progressively more aggressive diagnostic coding of conditions at earlier, more treatable stages. There is a

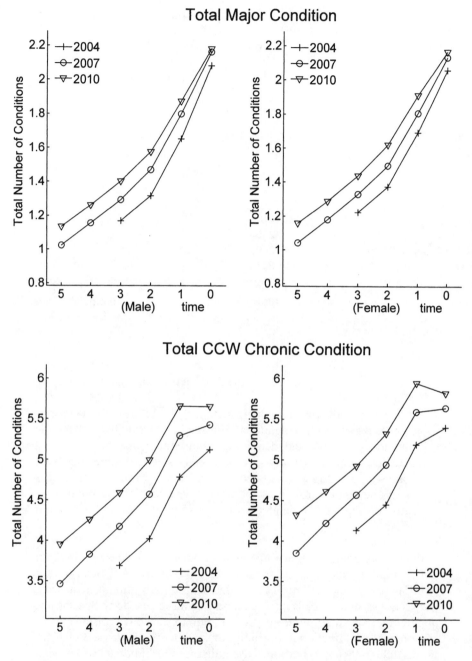

Fig. 1C.12   Counts of major and total CCW conditions, years before death, by death year, and gender

need for more time-consistent clinical data on disease onset and prevalence, and an analysis of the health consequences of early diagnosis, to determine how much of this drift is real, and what can be done to improve further the disability-free lives of people even if they are diagnosed and treated for a variety of diseases.

The Lifetime Risk of Nursing Home Use

Michael D. Hurd, Pierre-Carl Michaud, and
Susann Rohwedder

2.1 Introduction

The risk of spending for long-term care is one of the most important risks faced by older households because of the long right tail of days spent in nursing homes. However, finding data to estimate the risk has been difficult because of the necessity of following individuals over long periods of time. In this study, we use data from the Health and Retirement Study (HRS) to assess the lifetime distribution of stays in nursing homes and what these indicate for long-term care risks faced by households. While the HRS only samples from the noninstitutionalized population at baseline, the follow-up of this longitudinal survey includes all baseline respondents, in particular those who move to a nursing home. As a result, after several waves the HRS will also represent the nursing home population because of turnover in nursing homes: almost all those in nursing homes at baseline will have died and been replaced by persons initially residing in the community and represented by HRS respondents. We use 10 waves of the HRS including cohorts added after the original HRS cohort, those born in the years 1931–1941. Those

Michael D. Hurd is director of the Center for the Study of Aging, a senior principal researcher at RAND, a fellow of NETSPAR, and a research associate of the National Bureau of Economic Research. Pierre-Carl Michaud is professor of economics at the University of Québec at Montréal and an affiliated adjunct economist with RAND. Susann Rohwedder is associate director of the Center for the Study of Aging, a senior economist at RAND, and a research fellow of NETSPAR.

This research was supported by the National Institute on Aging, under grant 1R01AG041116. We thank Joanna Carroll for excellent programming assistance and David Boisclair for editorial assistance. Any remaining errors are our own. For acknowledgments, sources of research support, and disclosure of the authors' material financial relationships, if any, please see http://www.nber.org/chapters/c12970.ack.

additional cohorts were added in years following the initial interview of the HRS cohort in 1992. In addition to the core interviews we use data from the proxy interviews, usually with a spouse or other close relative, for those unable to participate in a given interview wave. Most importantly we use data from exit interviews that are conducted with a proxy after the death of a respondent. Our use of all waves of all relevant HRS cohorts as well as exit interviews allows us to estimate lifetime risk of a nursing home stay both nonparametrically and with a flexible transition model, which we use to simulate nursing home histories.

2.1.1 Prior Results

The types of studies that are most relevant to ours are those that estimate the lifetime chances of ever being in a nursing home (lifetime risk), those that estimate durations of stays in nursing homes, either conditional on a stay or unconditional, and those that estimate the lifetime duration in nursing homes. With respect to the first category, lifetime risk, the estimates range up to 55 percent (Arling, Hagan, and Buhaug 1992). A widely cited rate is 37 percent for those over the age of sixty-five (Kemper and Murtaugh 1991), and there are a number of other similar estimates.[1] A common finding is that lifetime risk is higher for women than for men, as for example, in Brown and Finkelstein (2008): 44 percent for women and 27 percent for men. As for durations of stay, there are often conditioning events that make comparisons across studies difficult. For example, Dick, Garber, and MaCurdy (1994) estimate the average length of stay to be twenty-one months conditional on entering. Arling, Hagan, and Buhaug (1992) estimate that on average individuals who have a nursing home stay will spend twenty-four months in a nursing home. Conditional on dying in a nursing home, the mean length of stay estimated over the seven waves of AHEAD data was fourteen months (Kelly et al. 2010). The average total time spent in nursing homes over a lifetime, counting multiple stays, was estimated to be 2.3 years in Liang et al. (1996). Regardless of the exact estimate, the duration of individual stays and of accumulated lifetime stays is substantial, putting individuals that must pay out of pocket at considerable financial risk.

2.2 Data

2.2.1 The HRS

Our analyses are based on data from the Health and Retirement Study (HRS). The HRS is a biennial longitudinal survey that covers a broad range of topics including income, work, assets, pension plans, health insurance,

---

1. See Cohen, Tell, and Wallack (1986), Dick, Garber, and MaCurdy (1994), and Spillman and Lubitz (2002).

disability, physical health and functioning, cognitive functioning, and health care expenditures. Its first wave was conducted in 1992. The target population was the cohorts born in 1931–1941, also called the original HRS cohort (Juster and Suzman 1995). Additional cohorts were added in 1993 of those born in 1923 or earlier (AHEAD cohort), in 1998 of those born between 1924 and 1930 (Children of the Depression Age [CODA] cohort), and of those born between 1942 and 1947 (War Babies), so that in 1998 the HRS represented the population of at least fifty-one years of age. New cohorts have subsequently been added every six years, including, in 2004, Early Baby Boomers born from 1948 to 1953, again making the HRS representative of the population age fifty-one or older.

Every cohort is sampled from the noninstitutionalized population at baseline so that the population residing in nursing homes is not represented. However, HRS makes extensive efforts to follow respondents after the baseline, including those who move into institutional settings such as nursing homes. Core interviews are conducted every two years. If a person is too frail or cognitively impaired to be interviewed, a proxy interview is conducted instead with a spouse or close relative. If a respondent dies between waves, HRS will attempt to conduct a so-called exit interview with a proxy informant, preferably someone who is knowledgeable about the family and financial situation and the circumstances preceding the person's death. Because nursing home stays are most prevalent among the frail, cognitively impaired, or those close to death, the information obtained in proxy and exit interviews is critical for assessing the prevalence and incidence of nursing home stays. If despite all efforts HRS cannot make contact with a respondent or any relative, the HRS conducts tracking efforts, with special emphasis on determining whether the respondent may have died. In these efforts HRS cross-checks data sources such as the Social Security Death Index and the National Death Index to ascertain whether the respondent has died.

Table 2.1 summarizes characteristics of the different cohorts included in the HRS. By the time wave 10 of the HRS was conducted in 2010, 14 percent of the oldest cohort was still alive, as was 79 percent of the youngest cohort. Vital status was unknown for few respondents in any wave. The HRS is quite successful in completing exit interviews with a proxy. For example, HRS gathered exit interviews for 96 percent of deceased respondents of the AHEAD cohort.

For all cohorts in the HRS, an analysis of nursing home stays will potentially suffer from either left censoring (do not observe nursing home spells prior to initial wave) or right censoring (do not follow until death so there could be spells beyond wave 10 in 2010). The importance of such censoring depends on the cohort and the initial age. For example, the subsample of AHEAD respondents who were age eighty-five at baseline in 1993 have all died by 2010. So there is no right censoring among this group of respondents, but there is considerable left censoring because no nursing home stays prior

Table 2.1   Cohorts included in the HRS defined by birth year

	AHEAD	CODA	HRS	War Babies	Early Baby Boomers
Birth years	1890–1923	1924–1930	1931–1941	1942–1947	1948–1953
Baseline interview	1993	1998	1992	1998	2004
Age at baseline	70 or older	68–74	51–61	51–56	51–56
Age in 2010 if still alive	87 or older	80–86	69–79	63–68	57–62
N	7,758	4,210	10,413	3,488	3,624
Overall status as of wave 10 (%)					
Alive and in survey as of wave 10	14.48	46.82	57.23	72.28	78.84
Dead with exit interview	76.48	39.33	23.07	9.86	4.47
Dead without exit interview	3.31	2.00	2.02	0.86	0.30
Alive, but no response to wave 10	2.23	7.17	8.39	11.47	14.40
Unknown, dropped from sample	3.51	4.68	9.30	5.53	1.99

Notes: AHEAD stands for Asset and Health Dynamics, the initial name of the 1993 survey. CODA stands for Children of the Depression.

to age eighty-five have been observed for these respondents. Conversely, with younger HRS respondents, there is very little left censoring but considerable right censoring, because by 2010 they are still in their early seventies and the majority of their nursing home stays will still be in the future and is not observed in the data. Both parametric and nonparametric analyses will address these issues.

2.2.2 Information on Nursing Home Stays in the HRS

The HRS collects the following information on respondents' nursing home stays in the core HRS interview:[2]

- whether the respondent was residing in a nursing home at the time of interview
  - if so, when the person moved to the nursing home (or if the person had stayed there continuously since the previous interview)
- whether the respondent had any (other) nursing home stay since the previous interview
  - if so, how many nursing home stays in total
    - if one stay, how many nights spent in nursing home
    - if more than one stay, how many nights in total spent in nursing home

The HRS also asks about the month and year of the nursing home entry and exit for up to three spells, which can be used to cross-check or complement the information on the total number of nights spent in the nursing home.

The exit interviews ask for the same information with reference to the time between the last interview the respondent completed and the respondent's time of death. We integrate the information obtained in the exit interviews into our key outcome measures:

Any nursing home stay in the previous two years. For respondents who participated in a particular wave t and in the immediately preceding wave $t - 1$ this variable takes the value one if the person was in the nursing home either any time between waves or is currently in a nursing home at wave t. For those respondents who died between the two waves, we use the information obtained from the exit interviews. If those indicate that the respondent was in a nursing home any time between the preceding wave $t - 1$ and the time of death, then this variable will take the value one in wave t. If someone missed one or more interviews this measure would cover a longer period. For most exit interviews the period covered averages about one year.

---

2. A respondent is asked about nursing home residence in the following way: "Are you living in a nursing home or other health care facility?" If a respondent asks for a definition, the following is read to him/her: "A nursing home or other health facility provides all of the following services for its residents: dispensing of medication, twenty-four-hour nursing assistance and supervision, personal assistance, and room and meals."

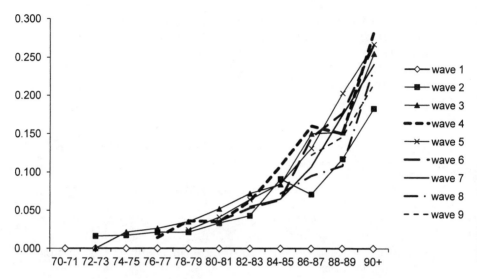

Fig. 2.1   **Prevalence of respondents being in nursing home at the time of interview, by age and wave: AHEAD cohort**

Number of nights spent in nursing home in the previous two years. The construction of this variable follows the same principle. It uses the information from the HRS core interview for all those respondents who survive, and the information from the exit interviews for those respondents who died between waves.

Lifetime measures of "any nursing home stay" and the "number of nights spent in a nursing home." These measures cumulate the survey information of any nursing home stay and the number of nights spent in a nursing home in the previous two years over all waves up to the last wave collected in the year 2010.

2.2.3 Population Representativeness with Respect to the Nursing Home Population

The HRS draws its baseline sample from the noninstitutionalized population, but then follows up with all respondents, including when they move to nursing homes. We want to establish how many waves it takes until the HRS survey reaches population representation with respect to the nursing home population. Figure 2.1 shows the fraction in nursing home residence by age for each wave of the AHEAD cohort. Because the AHEAD wave 1 sample is drawn from the community, nursing home stay prevalence upon entering the study is zero at all ages. By wave 2, substantial numbers are living in a nursing home; for example, 7.1 percent of those 86–87 years of age. Nonetheless, the curve for wave 2 mostly lies below the curves for later waves suggesting that after two years, nursing homes still had residents that

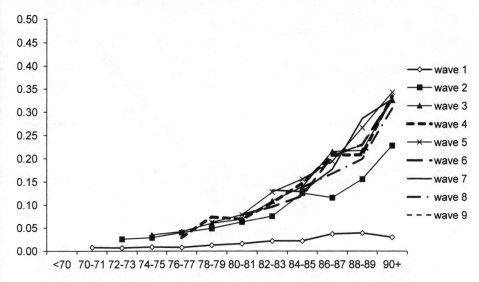

Fig. 2.2   Fraction with any nursing home stay in last two years, by age: AHEAD cohort (no exit interviews)

were not represented in the initial AHEAD wave. By wave 3 (1998) or five years after the baseline wave, the prevalence of residing in a nursing home was about the same as in later waves, leading us to surmise that by then, at least as far as prevalence is concerned, the AHEAD cohort was representative of the entire population, not just the community dwelling population.[3] Thus in addition to left and right censoring, nonparametric estimation of the risk of any stay must account for start-up, the fact that the initial waves did not represent adequately the nursing home population.

2.2.4 The Importance of the Exit Interviews for Assessing Lifetime Nursing Home Exposure

Some nursing home stays are short term, beginning and ending between waves. As a result, the measure of nursing home residence at the time of interview is not suitable for measuring lifetime exposure. Figure 2.2 adds exposure between waves. It shows, for example, that among those 86–87 years old in wave 2, 11.6 percent had nursing home exposure between wave 1 and wave 2 (including residence at wave 2) but just 7.1 percent were in residence (figure 2.1). This indicates the importance of shorter-term stays. The figure shows that by wave 3, nursing home exposure between waves was at about the same level as in later waves, again illustrating that the first two waves cannot be used to show nursing home exposure.

---

3. This statement cannot be true for the entire nursing home population; that is, those who survive for more than five years in a nursing home.

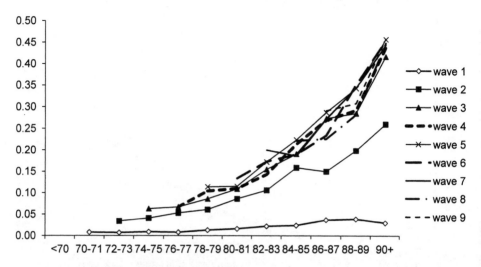

Fig. 2.3   Fraction with any nursing home stay in last two years, by age: AHEAD cohort (with exit interviews)

Because of the importance of relatively short-term stays, researchers will underestimate nursing home exposure if their estimates rely on interviews with respondents who are alive in each wave. Respondents who were living in the community in a wave, experienced a nursing home stay following that wave, and died before the succeeding wave would not be recorded as having a nursing home stay. In the exit interview, the proxy respondent is asked about nursing home stays since the previous interview. We find that including them increases substantially the estimate of nursing home exposure. Figure 2.3 illustrates their importance. Consider those 86–87 years old in wave 2. Adding those who were interviewed in wave 1 and would have been 86–87 years old in wave 2 had they survived shows that nursing home exposure in that larger group was 15 percent between waves 1 and 2, rather than 12 percent among survivors to wave 2 (figure 2.2). Thus the use of the exit interview increased nursing home exposure by 3.5 percentage points or 32 percent.

2.3 Age Prevalence of Nursing Home Stays and Lifetime Exposure

2.3.1 Age Prevalence of Nursing Home Stays and Nursing Home Use

In the calculations of the age prevalence, we exclude the first two waves of data for each cohort because of the lack of representation of the nursing home population as previously discussed. We pool all remaining waves and cohorts and apply respondent weights. Table 2.2 shows the age prevalence for two measures: the fraction residing in a nursing home at the time of interview and the fraction with any nursing home stay in the previous two

Table 2.2   Prevalence of nursing home stay by age[a]

| | All cohorts | | | | | |
| | Ns | | | Fraction | | |
Age of person including their wave of death	Live in nursing home at interview—CORE only	Nursing home stay, previous two years	Nursing home stay, previous two years—CORE only	Live in nursing home at interview—CORE only	Nursing home stay, previous two years	Nursing home stay, previous two years—CORE only
< 55	769	807	768	0.001	0.007	0.001
55–59	16,855	17,147	16,824	0.001	0.008	0.006
60–64	24,683	25,257	24,652	0.004	0.015	0.010
65–69	20,541	21,295	20,516	0.007	0.027	0.019
70–74	14,313	15,166	14,290	0.013	0.056	0.038
75–79	14,449	15,735	14,426	0.026	0.083	0.057
80–84	10,883	12,446	10,861	0.052	0.151	0.104
85–89	6,641	8,223	6,627	0.125	0.271	0.197
90–94	2,744	3,872	2,738	0.226	0.420	0.308
95 +	797	1,335	793	0.361	0.566	0.446
All	112,675	121,283	112,495	0.024	0.071	0.045

Source: Authors' calculations.

Notes: Data from all HRS cohorts used, except the cohort added in HRS 2010. For each cohort the first two waves are excluded in keeping with the previous finding that population representation of the population, including the nursing home population, is not achieved until the third wave. Age is set to age at death for those who died between waves and where this information was recorded in the exit interview. For all other observations, age is set to the average interview year by cohort minus the respondent's birth year. "Previous two years" refers to time since last interview, which for most respondents is approximately two years. "CORE only" excludes exit interviews. We used wave-specific respondent-level weights. For those in nursing homes or those who died between waves, the most recent nonzero weight is used to replace zero values or missing information in the respondent-level weights.

[a] At the time of the interview and in the previous two years, weighted.

years. For the latter we included a column incorporating the information from the exit interviews and one without ("core only") to highlight once again the much higher prevalence obtained when including the information from the exit interviews. The exit interviews capture the information of those respondents who died between waves that would otherwise be missed. Because nursing home stays are most prevalent toward the end of life, this is an important omission.

The fraction residing in a nursing home at the time of interview is low, less than 1 percent, at ages less than seventy. At ages seventy and older the fraction approximately doubles with every five-year age band up to age 90–94 when it reaches 23 percent. Among those surviving to age ninety-five and older, the fraction residing in a nursing home is 36 percent. The measure assessed at the time of the interview reflects just a moment in time, whereas the next column measures any nursing home stays that have occurred in the previous two years, and includes the exit interviews. At ages up to eighty-four the fraction with any nursing home stay in the previous two years is higher than the moment in time measure by a factor of three or more, reflecting the importance of short-term stays at relatively younger ages. At the oldest ages it is 20 percentage points higher than the moment in time measure. Among those 90–94 years old, 42 percent resided in a nursing home sometime in the previous two years, and among those age ninety-five or older, 57 percent did so. The final column has similar statistics but does not use the exit interviews. Overall the exposure to nursing homes is 2.6 percentage points lower, but at some ages the discrepancy is much greater: at ages 90–94 it is 11.2 percentage points lower.

Table 2.3 provides the average by age band of the total number of nights spent in a nursing home in the previous two years, again both with and without consideration of the exit interviews. For the number of nights the differences between the two columns are noticeable, but not particularly large. The explanation is that the exit interviews capture the information for those who died between waves for whom the period covered since the last interview is on average just one year and not two years as for the remainder of the sample.

Focusing on the column that incorporates the exit interviews, the total number of nights spent in a nursing home in the previous two years averaged over the entire sample (unconditional on nursing home stay) approximately doubles every five years between the ages of fifty-five and ninety-four, reaching 131 nights for those age ninety to ninety-four. Among those age ninety-five or older, the average number of nights in a nursing home is 203.

2.3.2 Lifetime Risk of a Nursing Home Stay

Using the long panel dimension of the HRS, we show in table 2.4 estimates of lifetime exposure obtained from the raw data without—for now—addressing the issue of left or right censoring. We start with the HRS cohort

Table 2.3   **Number of nights spent in nursing home, by age[a]**

	All cohorts			
	*N*s		Mean	
Age of person including their wave of death	Nights in nursing home, previous two years	Nights in nursing home, previous two years—CORE only	Nights in nursing home, previous two years	Nights in nursing home, previous two years—CORE only
< 55	807	768	0.64	0.52
55–59	17,139	16,818	0.84	0.72
60–64	25,236	24,643	2.45	1.74
65–69	21,265	20,501	4.13	3.53
70–74	15,139	14,273	8.63	6.75
75–79	15,676	14,395	15.74	12.55
80–84	12,358	10,812	33.59	26.89
85–89	8,111	6,557	67.03	58.32
90–94	3,784	2,685	130.55	117.26
95 +	1,311	780	202.97	204.47
All	120,826	112,232	16.37	12.04

Notes: Data from all HRS cohorts used, except the cohort added in HRS 2010. For each cohort the first two waves are excluded in keeping with the previous finding that population representation of the population, including the nursing home population, is not achieved until the third wave. Age is set to age at death for those who died between waves and where this information was recorded in the exit interview. For all other observations, age is set to the average interview year by cohort minus the respondent's birth year. "Previous two years" refers to time since last interview, which for most respondents is approximately two years. "CORE only" excludes exit interviews. We used wave-specific respondent-level weights. For those in nursing homes or those who died between waves, the most recent nonzero weight is used to replace zero values or missing information in the respondent-level weights.

[a]All cohorts, weighted.

born between 1931 and 1941 and observed from 1992 until 2010. In the youngest age band of HRS (age 50–54), about 20 percent had died by 2010. About 10 percent had a nursing home stay, and the average number of stays was 0.18, indicating that some individuals had multiple stays. The average number of nights was twenty-three, including those with no nursing home exposure. These statistics increase with age. For all HRS cohort respondents the average number of stays was 0.26 and the average number of nights was about 33, indicating that the typical stay was about 130 nights. Among those who died before wave 10, eighteen years after wave 1, 26 percent had a nursing home stay and the average length of stay was eighty-three nights.

Table 2.5 shows the same statistics for the older AHEAD cohort. In the AHEAD cohort, mortality was essentially complete for those initially age 80–84. In that group 60 percent were in a nursing home at some time. The average number of nights was just under 310. With the exception of the youngest age group in the AHEAD cohort, the difference in nursing home exposure between everyone initially in an age band and those who died

Table 2.4   **HRS cohort: Mortality and cumulative nursing home frequencies, unconditional and conditional on dying between waves 2 and 10, weighted**

Age wave 1	N	Died waves 2–10	Any stay 2–10	Number stays	Number nights
50–54	3,889	0.20	0.10	0.18	22.6
55–59	4,178	0.25	0.14	0.30	34.9
60–64	1,371	0.33	0.18	0.36	58.0
All	9,438	0.24	0.13	0.26	33.3
		Conditional on dying in between waves 2 and 10			
50–54	828	1.00	0.26	0.52	78.8
55–59	1,115	1.00	0.29	0.67	73.7
60–64	484	1.00	0.30	0.68	108.1
All	2,427	1.00	0.28	0.62	82.5

Notes: Includes exit interviews. Respondent-level weight from baseline interview used throughout.

Table 2.5   **AHEAD cohort: Mortality and cumulative nursing home frequencies, unconditional and conditional on dying between waves 2 and 9**

Age wave 1	N	Died waves 2–9	Any stay 2–9	Number stays	Number nights
70–74	2,676	0.67	0.42	0.86	147.6
75–79	2,031	0.83	0.55	1.18	250.5
80–84	1,493	0.94	0.60	1.32	308.1
85–89	723	0.99	0.65	1.60	352.2
90–94	231	0.99	0.66	1.25	307.7
95 +	68	1.00	0.57	0.97	311.0
All	7,222	0.81	0.52	1.13	235.3
		Conditional on dying between waves 2 and 9			
70–74	1,802	1.00	0.49	1.02	166.8
75–79	1,678	1.00	0.58	1.25	256.6
80–84	1,400	1.00	0.62	1.35	311.4
85–89	715	1.00	0.65	1.61	350.7
90–94	229	1.00	0.66	1.25	309.6
95 +	68	1.00	0.57	0.97	311.0
All	5,892	1.00	0.57	1.24	255.1

Notes: Includes exit interviews. Respondent-level weight from baseline interview used throughout.

before 2010 is not substantial, indicating that right censoring is not very important; that is, among those initially age seventy-five or older we are close to observing rest-of-lifetime nursing home risk. For example, in the age group 75–79, 55 percent used a nursing home at some time before 2010. Thus, among those who survive to age 75–79, a lower bound on rest-of-life lifetime nursing home exposure is 55 percent. There is, of course left censoring, which would increase the lifetime risk of those who survive to that age.

Nonparametric Estimation of Lifetime Risk of any Nursing Home Stay

Our nonparametric estimation of nursing home exposure is based on figure 2.4. It combines nursing home exposure and transition probabilities from three cohorts. The main and central cohort is AHEAD wave 1 respondents whose initial ages were seventy to seventy-four. By 2010, at which time the cohort would have been eighty-seven to ninety-one years old, 67 percent of that cohort had died and 33 percent were still alive. Among those who died, 49 percent were in a nursing home sometime prior to death. Among the 33 percent who survived, 29 percent had nursing home exposure. To estimate the effect of right censoring among the 71 percent who survived and had no nursing home exposure, we use the AHEAD wave 1 respondents whose initial ages were eighty-five to eighty-nine. By 2010 all of that cohort had died, and 65 percent were in a nursing home prior to death but following the initial wave in 1993. These were "fresh" nursing home exposures because AHEAD wave 1 only sampled those in the community. Combining these probabilities, we estimate nursing home exposure of the initial AHEAD cohort age 70–74 to be 57.6 percent ($0.67 * 0.49 + 0.33 * (0.29 + 0.71 * 0.65)$).[4]

This figure needs to be adjusted in several ways. The initial AHEAD sample in 1993 excluded residents in nursing homes. Some initial AHEAD respondents age 70–74 had prior nursing home exposure. Some persons died before reaching age 70–74 and had nursing home exposure. To make these adjustments we use the HRS cohort. Combining HRS waves for respondents 50–54 years of age, we find that 20 percent died before reaching age seventy-two and that 26 percent of those who died were in a nursing home sometime prior to death. Among survivors, 1.3 percent were in a nursing home at age 70–74, and among those not in a nursing home, 5 percent had previously been in a nursing home. Combining these conditional probabilities with the AHEAD probabilities, we estimate that the lifetime exposure of HRS respondents initially age 50–54 in 1992 will be 53.4 percent when the last such respondent has died.

These calculations do not consider nursing home exposure prior to entering HRS. While we have no data on nursing home exposure prior to the initial wave of HRS, in the subsequent waves of HRS nursing home exposure is infrequent. For example, among those initially age 50–54 in HRS in 1992, 0.2 percent had nursing home exposure between waves 1 and 2, and an additional 0.6 percent had nursing home exposure between waves 2 and 3.

---

4. This calculation assumes that, conditional on being in the community at wave 1 and on reaching age 85–89 with no intervening nursing home exposure, the probability of nursing home exposure prior to death is the same as the probability of nursing home exposure of those in wave 1 age 85–89.

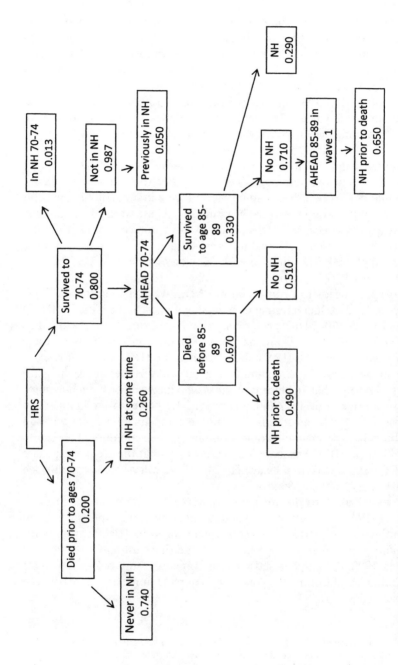

Fig. 2.4   Unconditional probabilities of nursing home exposure and transitions
Note: NH = nursing home.

2.4 Methodology of Parametric Estimation of Lifetime Exposure

We develop a simulation model that allows us to compute the lifetime distribution of nursing home stays and their length. Let $i = 1, \ldots, N$ denote respondents and $t = 1, \ldots, T_i$ denote the wave during which an interview takes place. Each wave takes place approximately every two years.[5]

We use two key pieces of information from the HRS in building the model. First, we use reports of any nursing home stays in the previous two years and reports of mortality to construct a combined status variable, d_{it}, which can take four values: (a) alive and living in the community, (b) alive and living in a nursing home, (c) died in the community, and (d) died in a nursing home. Because states (c) and (d) are absorbing, four transitions are possible from each of the two states where the respondent is alive (a and b). We define the probability of entering state $j = 1, \ldots, 4$ at $t + 1$ given a current state $k = 1, 2$ at t, a vector of sociodemographic characteristics x_i, and age a_{it} using a multinomial logit:

$$P(d_{it+1} = j \mid x_i, a_{it}, d_{i,t} = k) = \frac{\exp(x_i \gamma_{1,j,k} + \gamma_{a,j,k}(a_{it}))}{\sum_{j'} \exp(x_i \gamma_{1,j',k} + \gamma_{a,j,k}(a_{it}))}.$$

We do not impose parametric restrictions on the functions $\gamma_{a,j,k}$ and instead use categorical variables for age bands. Because data is scarce at older ages, we use five-year age groups from age 50 to 100. After obtaining estimates of the parameters by maximum likelihood, we interpolate linearly the age functions at single years of age intervals. We extrapolate for ages between 100 and 110 (maximum age in simulations).

Second, we use reports of the number of days spent in a nursing home between waves. Because the time of entry or exit is unknown and could vary on average depending on the state at t and the state at $t + 1$, we estimate separate models of the log of number of visits v_{it} between waves for (a) individuals transiting from living in the community to either living [or] died in a nursing home, and (b) for those transiting from living in a nursing home to the same two destinations. The models estimated take the form

$$\log v_{it} = x_i \beta_{j,k} + \beta_{a,j,k}(a_{it}) + \varepsilon_{it}$$
$$j = 2, 4, k = 1, 2$$

where ε_{it} is assumed normally distributed with mean 0 and variance $\sigma^2_{\varepsilon,j,k}$. Again, we assume the age functions are given by a set of categorical variables for different age bands (five-year age groups). We use interpolation for inter-

---

5. In future research, we plan to adjust the models presented to account for heterogeneity in exposure time (differences in time between interviews).

vening years. Given the log formulation of the conditional mean and the assumption of normality, the expected number of visits is given by

$$E[v_{it} \mid x_i, a_{it}, j, k] = \exp(x_i\beta_{j,k} + \beta_{a,j,k}(a_{it}) + \tfrac{1}{2}\sigma^2_{\varepsilon,j,k}).$$

The estimated equations for the transition probabilities and the process for the number of days in a nursing home can then be used to simulate histories of nursing home stays. The initial population for the simulation is those respondents 50–55 years of age in the War Babies and Early Baby Boomers cohorts. We draw with replacement 50,000 sets of sociodemographic characteristics x_i. We consider education, race, marital status at age fifty, number of children, whether the individual had daughters, and an indicator for whether the respondent was ever a smoker. We then simulate histories using the processes estimated earlier. Finally, we compute statistics of interest from the simulation using survey weights from the two waves used as the starting point.

2.5 Results for Parametric Model

2.5.1 Estimation

We first present estimation results of the transition models. We then present results for the number of days spent in a nursing home between waves. We obtain both sets of estimates using the HRS data as described in section 2.2. We use all cohorts in estimation, except the youngest (Mid–Baby Boomers) that was only inducted into the HRS in 2010. For the two cohorts who were older at baseline, AHEAD and CODA, we exclude the first two waves that each responded to so that our estimation sample does not suffer from underrepresentation of the nursing home population.

In table 2.6, we present multinomial logit estimates of transitions from the community to a nursing home. The reference category is living in the community (i.e., not in a nursing home). Since all age parameters go from negative to positive, this establishes that the fraction alive in the community decreases with age. Not surprisingly, transitions either to a nursing home or death increase in frequency with age. This is shown in figure 2.5, first panel, where we see that the average probability of staying in the community decreases from close to 100 percent for a fifty-year-old respondent to less than 50 percent for a ninety-five-year-old respondent. Before age sixty-five, most transitions out of the community are the result of death outside of nursing homes or residence in a nursing home. After age seventy-five, many more respondents die in a nursing home. The transition rate from the community to a nursing home increases steeply after age seventy.

Results from table 2.6 indicate that males face transition probabilities significantly different from those females face. Compared to females, males

Table 2.6   **Multinomial logit estimates: Transition from community**

Variables	Alive in NH	Died, not NH	Died in NH
Age (65 omitted)			
50	−1.872***	−1.052***	−1.967***
	(0.188)	(0.104)	(0.292)
55	−1.363***	−0.814***	−1.353***
	(0.113)	(0.074)	(0.168)
60	−0.733***	−0.370***	−0.603***
	(0.096)	(0.067)	(0.137)
70	0.663***	0.217***	0.729***
	(0.085)	(0.073)	(0.124)
75	1.141***	0.776***	1.258***
	(0.078)	(0.065)	(0.112)
80	1.779***	1.175***	1.917***
	(0.076)	(0.066)	(0.109)
85	2.338***	1.723***	2.776***
	(0.080)	(0.072)	(0.110)
90	2.693***	2.233***	3.582***
	(0.102)	(0.097)	(0.123)
95	2.710***	3.032***	4.135***
	(0.207)	(0.166)	(0.189)
Male	−0.414***	0.382***	0.205***
	(0.045)	(0.037)	(0.056)
Education (less than high school omitted)			
High school	−0.0748	−0.357***	−0.125*
	(0.050)	(0.044)	(0.064)
College	−0.156***	−0.513***	−0.399***
	(0.052)	(0.045)	(0.068)
Nonwhite	−0.0275	0.206***	−0.01
	(0.058)	(0.046)	(0.076)
Married at age 50	−0.317***	−0.144***	−0.352***
	(0.051)	(0.047)	(0.067)
Number of children (1–3 omitted)			
No children	−0.284	0.0159	0.199
	(0.231)	(0.186)	(0.225)
4+ children	−0.0585	0.0973**	−0.183***
	(0.044)	(0.038)	(0.059)
Has daughters	−0.00284	−0.0696	−0.0976
	(0.058)	(0.052)	(0.072)
Ever smoker	0.244***	0.612***	0.442***
	(0.042)	(0.041)	(0.058)
Constant	−3.640***	−3.702***	−4.584***
	(0.101)	(0.088)	(0.138)
Observations	108,186		
Log-likelihood	−31166		
Degrees freedom	54		
Chi-square	10,109		

Notes: Multinomial logit parameter estimates and standard errors. The base category is living in the community. NH refers to nursing homes.

***Significant at the 1 percent level.

**Significant at the 5 percent level.

*Significant at the 10 percent level.

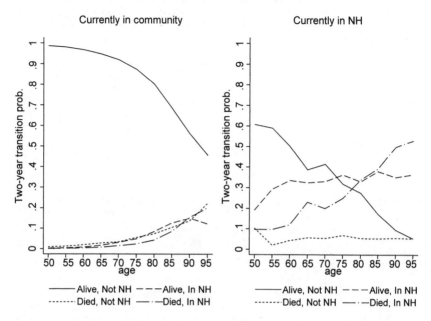

Fig. 2.5   Transition probabilities across states

who had been living in the community have a much lower chance of living in a nursing home two years (i.e., one survey wave) later. They also have a significantly higher risk of dying from one wave to the next, reflecting males' lower life expectancy—and, accordingly, higher death rates. This increased death probability is tilted toward death in the community: males are more likely to die in either setting, but almost twice as likely to die outside a nursing home.

Table 2.6 also shows that education, in particular college education, protects against both mortality and entering a nursing home. This reflects in part the SES-health gradient. Nonwhite respondents are more likely to die outside a nursing home but are about as likely as white respondents to enter a nursing home. Being married at age fifty also protects against entering a nursing home. Of course, the natural channel for this association is that one spouse may be able to provide help to the other who needs it. In addition, those married at age fifty are less likely to die, either in a nursing home or in the community. Interestingly, being childless does not appear to increase the probability of entering a nursing home (relative to having 1–3 children). Having four or more children appears to increase the probability that the respondent will die outside a nursing home, relative to dying in a nursing home. Having daughters appears to have no statistically detectable effect.

In table 2.7, we present multinomial logit estimates of transitions from

Table 2.7   **Multinomial logit estimates: Transition from nursing homes (NH)**

Variables	Alive, not NH	Died, not NH	Died in NH
Age (65 omitted)			
50	0.807	0.918	−0.409
	(0.635)	(0.917)	(0.883)
55	0.552*	−1.14	−0.813*
	(0.292)	(0.796)	(0.422)
60	0.283	−0.392	−0.699**
	(0.229)	(0.467)	(0.300)
70	−0.00192	−0.103	−0.154
	(0.196)	(0.365)	(0.223)
75	−0.386**	0.0381	−0.0505
	(0.183)	(0.322)	(0.198)
80	−0.468***	−0.0415	0.400**
	(0.177)	(0.317)	(0.186)
85	−1.057***	−0.175	0.427**
	(0.182)	(0.316)	(0.184)
90	−1.582***	−0.0102	0.766***
	(0.224)	(0.342)	(0.194)
95	−2.205***	−0.0373	0.809***
	(0.376)	(0.445)	(0.234)
Male	0.0932	0.640***	0.398***
	(0.100)	(0.162)	(0.093)
Education (less than high school omitted)			
High school	0.390***	−0.0948	−0.221**
	(0.108)	(0.183)	(0.095)
College	0.703***	0.233	−0.240**
	(0.114)	(0.184)	(0.103)
Nonwhite	−0.256*	0.203	0.00941
	(0.131)	(0.203)	(0.116)
Married at age 50	0.364***	0.239	0.0589
	(0.110)	(0.188)	(0.096)
Number of children (1–3 omitted)			
No children	−0.705	0.979	0.224
	(0.574)	(0.612)	(0.434)
4+ children	0.0996	0.00471	0.018
	(0.097)	(0.167)	(0.091)
Daughter	0.0948	0.123	−0.0509
	(0.128)	(0.211)	(0.107)
Ever smoker	−0.237**	0.0734	0.0923
	(0.095)	(0.162)	(0.086)
Constant	−0.406*	−2.370***	−0.407*
	(0.224)	(0.390)	(0.216)
Observations	3,798		
Log-likelihood	−4443		
Degrees freedom	54		
Chi-square	569.3		

Notes: Multinomial logit parameter estimates and standard errors. The base category is living in a nursing home.

***Significant at the 1 percent level.

**Significant at the 5 percent level.

a nursing home to one of the four states (living in the community, living in a nursing home, dying in the community, dying in a nursing home). The reference category is alive in a nursing home. From the estimates, we see that the exit probability from a nursing home to the community generally decreases with age. In figure 2.5, second panel, we see that the estimates imply that this probability goes from 60 percent at age fifty to less than 20 percent at age eighty-five. Hence, persistence increases with age, which likely reflects an increase in the severity of disabilities for those in a nursing home. Mortality rates in a nursing home are much higher than in the community. This can be seen in figure 2.5. For example, summing the two curves, the probability of dying either in the community or in a nursing home is 20 percent at age fifty, while it increases to about 60 percent by age ninety-five.

Table 2.7 indicates that gender differences are somewhat different for transitions originating in a nursing home. Specifically, and in contrast to the previous state of origin, males do not face a significantly different probability of exiting a nursing home alive. As well, their probability of dying between the two waves is much higher than females, with the difference being tilted again toward dying outside a nursing home. Gender differences are, however, markedly larger than they were for transitions originating in the community. This could perhaps be explained by a more severe disability for males when they finally enter a nursing home.

As for the other characteristics considered and likely to affect transitions out of nursing homes, college education appears to increase the likelihood of return to the community. Education also decreases the probability of dying in a nursing home, as was the case for those individuals who were initially living in the community (table 2.6). Being nonwhite reduces the probability of exiting a nursing home. Family background has no significant effect on exits from nursing homes, excepting those individuals who were married at age fifty, who are more likely to leave a nursing home for the community. Finally, being a smoker reduces the probability of returning to the community.

Estimates in tables 2.6 and 2.7 will play out in the simulations. On one hand, some characteristics such as education reduce the probability of entry into a nursing home and increase the exit probability from a nursing home. On the other hand, education also reduces the likelihood of dying, hence prolonging the exposure to nursing home risk. In the end, these opposing forces will yield ambiguous predictions of the effect of education on lifetime prevalence of nursing home stays.

We also look at the intensity of nursing home stays between waves. For this we turn to table 2.8, which reports estimation results for the number of days spent in nursing homes. Each column in the table reports estimates of the effect of variables on the log of the number of days spent in a nursing home for four different pairs of origin and destination states.

Table 2.8   **Regression estimates for number of days in nursing homes (NH)**

Variables	From community — Living in NH	From community — Died in NH	From nursing home — Living in NH	From nursing home — Died in NH
Age (65 omitted)				
50	−0.308	−0.299	0.946	−0.768
	(0.319)	(0.442)	(0.795)	(0.957)
55	−0.0242	−0.0822	0.333	−0.556
	(0.186)	(0.265)	(0.368)	(0.473)
60	−0.233	−0.192	0.0803	0.351
	(0.158)	(0.215)	(0.268)	(0.345)
70	0.025	−0.0379	0.465**	0.00768
	(0.138)	(0.191)	(0.225)	(0.238)
75	0.221*	0.0739	0.433**	0.174
	(0.126)	(0.174)	(0.205)	(0.205)
80	0.487***	0.474***	0.633***	0.00344
	(0.122)	(0.169)	(0.197)	(0.189)
85	0.694***	0.511***	0.828***	0.233
	(0.128)	(0.168)	(0.194)	(0.186)
90	1.046***	0.438**	0.857***	0.348*
	(0.160)	(0.182)	(0.213)	(0.190)
95	0.922***	0.413	1.234***	0.507**
	(0.313)	(0.256)	(0.261)	(0.221)
Male	−0.0905	−0.185**	−0.0724	−0.126
	(0.071)	(0.084)	(0.107)	(0.087)
Education (less than high school omitted)				
High school	−0.0266	−0.124	−0.147	−0.1
	(0.079)	(0.094)	(0.105)	(0.091)
College	−0.206**	−0.187*	−0.321***	−0.108
	(0.081)	(0.100)	(0.113)	(0.099)
Nonwhite	0.442***	0.0021	0.480***	0.0821
	(0.093)	(0.116)	(0.127)	(0.114)
Married at age 50	−0.0993	0.0881	0.00698	−0.176*
	(0.081)	(0.101)	(0.104)	(0.093)
Number of children (omitted 1–3)				
No children	−0.366	−0.104	0.388	−0.479
	(0.359)	(0.328)	(0.530)	(0.392)
4+ children	−0.222***	0.0693	0.0623	−0.119
	(0.070)	(0.090)	(0.099)	(0.088)
Daughter	−0.224**	−0.200*	−0.260**	−0.099
	(0.092)	(0.107)	(0.120)	(0.101)
Ever smoker	0.114*	−0.0481	−0.0938	−0.0432
	(0.068)	(0.087)	(0.095)	(0.083)
Constant	3.829***	3.488***	5.283***	5.207***
	(0.162)	(0.204)	(0.231)	(0.214)
Observations	2,579	1,488	1,272	1,226
Log-likelihood	−4882	−2710	−2349	−2074
Degrees of freedom	18	18	18	18
R-square	0.0662	0.0399	0.0608	0.034

Notes: Regression of the log of number of days in nursing homes between interviews. Each column refers to a different specification, estimated on the sample of respondents either living in the community or in a nursing home at t and who either survive in a nursing home at $t + 1$ or die in a nursing home by $t + 1$. Standard errors below point estimates.

***Significant at the 1 percent level.

**Significant at the 5 percent level.

*Significant at the 10 percent level.

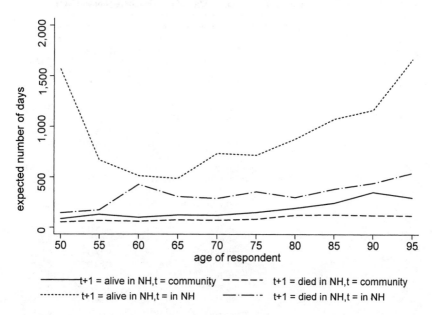

Fig. 2.6 Expected number of days in NH conditional on being in NH next wave

The first and second columns present results for transitions that originate from the community. In the first column, respondents are observed living in a nursing home at $t + 1$, while in the second they died in a nursing home by $t + 1$. We see for both these transitions an increase with age in the number of days spent in a nursing home. Figure 2.6 reports the average expected number of days spent in a nursing home by age. We can observe for both these transitions a small number of days (from roughly 100 days at age fifty to 350 days at age ninety-five) relative to other transitions that originate from nursing homes (see following). This partly reflects the fact that respondents experiencing the two transitions originating in the community will, on average, enter nursing homes in the middle of the time interval between waves. The average number of days is also smaller for those who died between waves. For these two transitions originating in the community, college education and having daughters appear to reduce the number of days spent in a nursing home, whereas being nonwhite and ever being a smoker both appear to increase it for those who are still living in a nursing home in the next wave.

The third and fourth columns of table 2.8 report regression results for transitions that originate from nursing homes. Not surprisingly, the number of days spent in a nursing home is much higher for those respondents, as shown in figure 2.6. Furthermore, the number of days increases with age (except for individuals staying in a nursing home at younger ages, for

Table 2.9   **Simulated lifetime exposure to nursing homes (NH) with and without exit interviews**

	With exit interviews	Without exit interviews
Prob(any stay)	0.577	0.368
E(no. of days)	214.7	136.6
E(no. of days| any stay)	371.9	370.4
Prob(dies in NH)	0.477	
Age first entry NH	76.8	75.9

Notes: Simulated outcomes from age 50, for 50,000 respondents drawn randomly from the pool of HRS respondents age 50–55 in the War Babies and Early Baby Boomers cohorts. Sample weights used.

whom the number is initially higher). In terms of characteristics, having a college degree and having daughters both decrease the number of days spent in a nursing home for individuals staying in a nursing home across waves. On the other hand, being nonwhite increases this number of days.

2.5.2 Simulation

We simulate the lifetime nursing home histories for an initial population with characteristics drawn from the pool of respondents 50–55 years of age in the War Babies and Early Baby Boomers cohorts. We draw (with replacement) 50,000 observations. We then simulate two-year transitions up to a maximum of 110 years of age.

In table 2.9, we present simulation results for five outcomes: the simulated probability of any stay, the average number of days in a nursing home (both conditional on having at least one stay and unconditional), the probability of dying in a nursing home, and, finally, the age at which individuals first enter a nursing home. We report these outcomes under two scenarios. The first includes the information from the exit interviews. Hence, we know whether—and when—someone died in a nursing home. For the second scenario we ignore the information from the exit interviews, so that nursing home stays prior to death are unobserved. Hence, we reclassify state $j = 4$ (Died this wave, in nursing home last two years) when computing outcomes to state $j = 3$ (Died this wave, no nursing home stay last two years). So all individuals who died will be attributed state $j = 3$.

Results are striking, especially when comparing the two scenarios (i.e., with and without exit interviews). When excluding exit interviews, the probability of ever experiencing a nursing home stay is 36.8 percent, which is consistent with prior literature (Kemper and Murtaugh 1991). When using exit interviews however, this probability increases to 57.7 percent. The average number of days spent in a nursing home increases from 136.6 to 214.7.

Table 2.10 Simulated lifetime exposure by sociodemographic characteristics

Subgroups of population	Prob(any stay)	E(no. of days)	Prob(dies in NH)	E(age first entry NH)	E(age of death)
Gender					
Female	0.649	284.9	0.536	76.8	79.3
Male	0.498	137.9	0.413	76.7	76.4
Race					
White	0.589	213.3	0.488	76.9	78.3
Nonwhite	0.512	222.5	0.419	75.9	76.1
Education					
Less than high school	0.486	188.7	0.411	74.3	74.3
High school	0.585	231.3	0.492	76.3	77.5
College	0.597	210.7	0.486	77.6	79.2
Number of children					
No children	0.502	139.1	0.402	76.5	75.6
1–3 children	0.598	222.5	0.496	76.9	78.2
4+ children	0.531	198.3	0.435	76.4	77.3
Ever smoker					
No	0.648	261.4	0.538	78.6	81.0
Yes	0.528	182.5	0.436	75.3	75.8
Married at age 50					
No	0.595	242.3	0.502	74.9	75.9
Yes	0.572	207.1	0.471	77.3	78.4
Has daughters					
No	0.594	231.6	0.501	76.5	77.6
Yes	0.574	211.3	0.473	76.8	77.9
Total	0.595	219.7	0.489	76.9	77.9

Notes: Simulated outcomes from age 50, for 50,000 respondents drawn randomly from the pool of HRS respondents age 50–55 in the War Babies and Early Baby Boomers cohorts. Sample weights used.

Conditional on having one stay, the average number of days spent over the lifetime of a fifty-year-old is 371.9 days, or just over a year. The probability of dying in a nursing home is 47.7 percent. Finally, the average age at first entry in a nursing home is 76.8 when using exit interviews, and 75.9 without. Overall, exit interviews are crucial in accurately establishing the lifetime prevalence and intensity of nursing home stays.

In table 2.10, we present table 2.9 results by sociodemographic groups. The lifetime prevalence of nursing home stays differs considerably by gender. Females face a 64.9 percent probability of having at least one stay, compared to 49.8 percent for males. This is due to both their longer life expectancy and to the fact that at every age, they face a higher probability of entering a nursing home (perhaps because their husband died before them). Females' average number of days spent in a nursing home is 284.9, compared to 137.9 for males. The probability that females will die in a nursing home is 53.6 percent, against 41.3 percent for males. Nonwhites have a lower probability of entering a nursing home, in part because of their lower life expectancy.

Differences in terms of education are ambiguous, as predicted earlier. Individuals with less than a high school diploma have a lower risk of ever entering a nursing home. Most of this difference is explained by their lower life expectancy (74.3 years, compared to 77.5 for those with a high school diploma and 79.2 for those with a college degree). At the same time, those with college degrees have a slightly lower lifetime exposure to nursing homes, driven in part by a delayed age of entry into nursing homes. Interestingly, individuals without children have a lower risk of ever entering a nursing home. Those who were a smoker at some point in their life are much less likely to ever enter a nursing home, but this effect is also driven by a lower life expectancy (75.8 compared to 81.0 for nonsmokers). We find little differences in lifetime prevalence by marital status or according to the presence of daughters.

Because some of the characteristics considered are correlated, the question arises as to whether differences remain over one characteristic when controlling for the others. Hence, we regress the simulated lifetime outcomes from age fifty on individuals' sociodemographic characteristics. This may be interpreted as a reduced-form equation of the transition and intensity equations mentioned earlier. Results are presented in table 2.11.

Results reveal that all else being equal, males have a 13.8 percent lower probability of ever entering a nursing home, and also spend 57.1 percent less time in a nursing home. Education effects are mostly driven by the distinction between having completed high school or not. Individuals with either high school or college degrees have a 7 to 8 percent higher chance of ever staying in a nursing home. Nonwhites, individuals without children or with many children, and those who were ever smokers are also less likely to enter a nursing home at any point in their life.

Table 2.11   Regression of lifetime measures on sociodemographic characteristics

Variables	P(any stay)	E(log days|any stay)
Male	−0.138***	−0.571***
	(0.004)	(0.022)
Education (less than high school omitted)		
High school	0.0717***	−0.034
	(0.006)	(0.032)
College	0.0830***	−0.0732**
	(0.006)	(0.031)
Nonwhite	−0.0591***	0.127***
	(0.005)	(0.027)
Married at age 50	−0.0259***	−0.0606**
	(0.006)	(0.027)
Number of children (1–3 omitted)		
No children	−0.0528***	−0.466***
	(0.020)	(0.105)
4+ children	−0.0507***	−0.0151
	(0.005)	(0.024)
Has daughters	0.0026	−0.0945***
	(0.006)	(0.029)
Ever smoker	−0.0860***	−0.156***
	(0.004)	(0.022)
Constant		5.262***
		(0.046)
Observations	50,000	28,547

Notes: Simulated outcomes from age 50 for 50,000 respondents drawn randomly from the pool of HRS respondents age 50–55 in the War Babies and Early Baby Boomers cohorts are regressed on other observed characteristics. The first model for the probability of any stay in a nursing home is estimated using a logit model, and average marginal effects on the probability of any stay are reported. In the second model, the log of the number of days spent in a nursing home, conditional on having at least one stay, is regressed on the same characteristics. Standard errors are reported in parentheses.
***Significant at the 1 percent level.
**Significant at the 5 percent level.
*Significant at the 10 percent level.

2.6 Discussion

Our estimates of lifetime risk are larger than those previously reported. Perhaps the most widely cited estimate is 37 percent in the population that survives to age sixty-five (Kemper and Murtaugh 1991). While our estimates are not directly comparable because of differences in initial age, mortality and nursing home exposure between ages fifty and sixty-five are much too small to account for the difference. The Kemper and Murtaugh estimate is based on the 1986 Mortality Followback Survey, which asked informants about the lifetime nursing home exposure of a sample of deceased in 1986. While this design likely obtains information about recent nursing home stays that is equivalent to the HRS exit interviews, it is probable that the informant either does not know about more distant stays or does not remember those stays. Indeed Kemper and Murtaugh state that such errors are likely to lead to underreporting "which would have caused us to underestimate lifetime nursing home use."

The study by Dick, Garber, and MaCurdy (1994) is similar to ours in method. Based on the National Long-Term Care Survey, they estimate transition probabilities between residence in the community, residence in a nursing home and death, and then via simulation estimate that lifetime risk is 35 percent conditional on survival to age sixty-five. Because of the complexities of the study design of the NLTCS, they combine three samples from the NLTCS, which leaves open the possibility that the populations represented do not mesh properly to form a complete population-representative sample. Indeed, addressing the reason for the lack of good estimates at the time of their paper, Dick, Garber, and MaCurdy state,

> Failure to address cumulative utilization in representative samples undoubtedly reflects the inadequacy of much existing data. No individual data sets have sufficiently complete longitudinal data to infer comprehensive measures of nursing home utilization for a nationally representative, random sample of elderly Americans. Ideally such a study would enroll a large number of elderly individuals, track them for several years, and obtain complete information on the number and timing of nursing home stays during the period of observation. (p. 366)

A major strength of this paper is the availability of the HRS, which satisfies the requirements of Dick, Garber, and MaCurdy. Further, the HRS used consistent, transparent recruitment methods over time, and the survey instrument is also consistent over time. The HRS exerted considerable effort in tracking subjects so the rate of complete unit loss over time is low: just 3.5 percent of our central cohort, the AHEAD cohort, which forms the basis for the bulk of the sample, has an unknown vital status (table 2.1), and 91 percent is either alive and in wave 10, or is dead with an exit interview.

Brown and Finkelstein (2004) estimate lifetime risk of nursing home exposure conditional on survival to age sixty-five to be 39 percent.[6] Their estimate is based on simulations of a model of Robinson of transitions between health states in the NLTCS 1982, 1984, 1989, and 1994 (Robinson 1999). Because the model predicts health status rather than nursing home status, additional data from the 1985 National Nursing Home Survey are used to link probabilistically health status to residence. As with Dick, Garber, and MaCurdy, the use of multiple data sets provides an opportunity of a mismatch between the populations represented by the different data sets.

---

6. Appendix table A1, Brown and Finkelstein (2004).

Table 2.12				Percentage residing in nursing homes at the time of interview, weighted				
	1996	1998	2000	2002	2004	2006	2008	2010
55–59	0.2	0.2	0.3	0.1	0.2	—	0.1	0.1
60–64	0.2	0.3	0.3	0.2	0.3	0.3	0.4	0.7
65–69	0.6	0.5	0.9	0.6	0.8	0.7	0.5	0.8
70–74	—	1.0	—	1.0	1.5	1.4	1.6	1.1
75–79	—	2.6	2.5	2.3	2.1	2.8	2.6	3.1
80–84	—	6.3	5.6	5.0	4.3	5.6	4.6	5.2
85+	—	18.5	18.9	18.8	18.2	16.0	14.3	15.0

Note: Does not include exit interviews.

It is unclear whether any of the three estimates use an equivalent of our exit interviews. However, it is striking that if we exclude the data from the exit interviews, we obtain an estimate of lifetime exposure conditional on survival to age fifty of 37 percent, which is similar to reported estimates in the literature. If we include the exit interview information, which accounts for stays at the end of life, our estimates are 53 and 59 percent for the non-parametric and simulations methods respectively.

Based on ten waves of data, our nonparametric method approaches a complete description of the nursing home experience of a cohort. As such that description does not rely on assumptions such as stationarity of the process of nursing home entry or exit. However, to extend the results to a statement about the nursing home experience of previous or future cohorts does require stationarity. Further, because we have not modeled any time trend or cohort effects in the transition probabilities, the para-metric methods require stationarity even as a description of our cohorts. Table 2.12 provides some evidence about stationarity. The table only includes observations from waves in which a particular cohort has been observed for three or more, because waves 1 and 2 do not adequately represent the nursing home population. Although there was a decline in the rate of nurs-ing home residency among those eighty-five or older between 2004 and 2008, the overall trend is a modest decrease of 3.5 percentage points over a fourteen-year period. In a number of the other age bands the rate increased. We conclude that there is little overall trend in the prevalence of nursing home residence in the HRS, so that stationarity of the process is a reasonable assumption.

2.7 Conclusion

In this chapter, we use both parametric and nonparametric approaches to calculate the lifetime risk of nursing home stays using rich data from the Health and Retirement Study. Both provide a similar estimate: a fifty-year-old has a 53–59 percent chance of ever staying in a nursing home, which is considerably higher than that reported in previous literature. Conditional on entering a nursing home, the average number of nights spent in a nursing home over the lifetime is just over a year (370 days). This average estimate hides considerable heterogeneity as the distribution is highly skewed.

Our results also highlight that there are two competing forces that affect lifetime risk: nursing home risk and mortality risk. Both of these depend in a nontrivial way on sociodemographic characteristics. For example, smokers have a higher risk of entering a nursing home conditional on being alive. But since they also face higher mortality risks, this reduces lifetime exposure to nursing home risk. We find that females, white, and nonsmokers face the highest risks of ever entering a nursing home.

References

Arling, G., S. Hagan, and H. Buhaug. 1992. "The Feasibility of a Public-Private Long-Term Care Financing Plan." *Medical Care* 30:699.

Brown, Jeffrey R., and Amy Finkelstein. 2004. "Supply or Demand: Why is the Market for Long-Term Care Insurance So Small?" NBER Working Paper no. 10782, Cambridge, MA.

———. 2008. "The Interaction of Public and Private Insurance: Medicaid and the Long-Term Care Insurance Market." *American Economic Review* 98 (3): 1083–102.

Cohen, M. A., E. J. Tell, and S. S. Wallack. 1986. "The Lifetime Risks and Costs of Nursing Home Use Among the Elderly." *Medical Care* 41 (6): 785–92.

Dick, A., A. M. Garber, and T. MaCurdy. 1994. "Forecasting Nursing Home Utilization of Elderly Americans." In *Studies in the Economics of Aging*, edited by David Wise, 365–94. Chicago: University of Chicago Press.

Juster, F. T., and R. Suzman. 1995. "An Overview of the Health and Retirement Study." *Journal of Human Resources* 30 (Suppl.): S7–S56.

Kelly, Anne, Jessamyn Conell-Price, Kenneth Covinsky, Irena Cenzer, Anna Chang, W. J. Boscardin, and Alexander Smith. 2010. "Length of Stay for Older Adults Residing in Nursing Homes at the End of Life." *Journal of the American Geriatrics Society* 58 (9): 1701–6.

Kemper, P., and C. M. Murtaugh. 1991. "Lifetime Use of Nursing Home Care." *New England Journal of Medicine* 324:595–600.

Liang, J., X. Liu, E. Tu, and N. Whitelaw. 1996. "Probabilities and Lifetime Durations of Short-Stay Hospital and Nursing Home Use in the United States, 1985." *Medical Care* 34 (10): 1018–36.

Robinson, Jim. 1999. "A Long-Term-Care Status Transition Model." In *The Old-Age Crisis—Actuarial Opportunities*: The 1996 Bowles Symposium, Society of Actuaries Monograph M-RS99-1.

Spillman, B. C., and J. Lubitz. 2002. "New Estimates of Lifetime Nursing Home Use: Have Patterns of Use Changed?" *Medical Care* 40 (10): 965–75.

Comment   David M. Cutler

For many purposes, we need to understand how likely people are to enter a nursing home. Many economists have wondered whether long-term care insurance is a good deal. Despite nursing homes being a major expense (a month in a nursing home costs about $6,000; Metlife Mature Market Institute 2009), only about 14 percent of the elderly possess a long-term care insurance policy (Brown and Finkelstein 2011). Is this because the residual risk is still large (Cutler 1996)? Because people are not financially or statistically literate (Lusardi and Mitchell 2007)? Because long-term care insurance is overpriced relative to relying on Medicaid (Brown and Finkelstein 2008)? Only by understanding the true probability of long-term care utilization can we answer these questions.

Similarly, many authors have considered whether people at or near retirement have savings adequate to finance their consumption during retirement years (Poterba, Venti, and Wise 2012). Normal consumption is relatively straightforward to estimate; it is typically assumed that the elderly will need about 80 percent of their consumption during working years when they are retired. But long-term care is a major additional expense. If the expected cost of long-term care is high, it implies that many people are undersaving. The key to determining this is again the lifetime risk of nursing home use.

Michael Hurd, Pierre-Carl Michaud, and Susann Rohwedder have done an enormous service by estimating the lifetime risk of nursing home care. They have taken data from the Health and Retirement Study and carefully estimated the probability that a person enters a nursing home. Along the way, they tackle several difficulties: the sampling frame for the HRS is people not in institutions; even though the HRS has been collecting data for nearly two decades, many of the original cohort have not lived long enough to measure total lifetime use; and so on. To address these problems, Hurd, Michaud, and Rohwedder estimate transition rates from one health state to another and then use these transition rates to simulate the probability that a random group of individuals will enter a nursing home before they die.

The final answer from Hurd and colleagues is that just about half of people age fifty and older (53 percent) will enter a nursing home before they die. That answer can then be plugged into equations for the value of long-term care insurance and for required saving to see how the elderly and near elderly are doing in their preparation for this event.

The most striking feature about the Hurd et al. result is that it is higher than comparable studies previously published. The most cited estimate of lifetime nursing home risk used to be Kemper and Murtaugh (1991). Using

David M. Cutler is the Otto Eckstein Professor of Applied Economics at Harvard University and a research associate of the National Bureau of Economic Research.

For acknowledgments, sources of research support, and disclosure of the author's material financial relationships, if any, please see http://www.nber.org/chapters/c12971.ack.

data from the National Mortality Followback Study, Kemper and Murtaugh estimated that 37 percent of people used a nursing home before they died. More recently, Brown and Finkelstein (2008) reported on lifetime nursing home risks as determined by a model commonly used by insurance actuaries in pricing long-term care insurance (Robinson 2002). That model suggests that lifetime nursing home risk for a sixty-five-year-old who is healthy enough to buy long-term care insurance is 27 percent for men and 44 percent for women—reasonably close to the estimate of Kemper and Murtaugh.

Hurd and colleagues claim that the difference between their estimates and those in the prior literature is that they include information provided by the next of kin in a postdeath survey, and there is significant use of nursing homes prior to death. A survey only of people who are alive would miss these stays. With regard to the Kemper and Murtaugh paper, however, this cannot be the sole explanation. Kemper and Murtaugh base their results entirely on a survey of next of kin. In principle, the National Mortality Followback Survey should pick up all people who used a nursing home, even in the period just before death. The Robinson model reported on by Brown and Finkelstein is a transition model just as Hurd et al. is. It is based on the early years of the National Long-Term Care Survey, in particular data from the 1982, 1984, and 1989 waves. I could not discern whether it used information from a next-of-kin survey on the use of nursing homes just prior to death, and would find clarification on this helpful.

If not a result of next-of-kin interviews, what else might explain the difference in nursing home rates between Hurd et al. and the prior studies? For starters, the data in the prior studies are relatively old. The National Mortality Followback Study was conducted in 1987 and was based on deaths in 1986. The Robinson model is based on transitions in the 1980s. Each of these is sufficiently old that newer data could give different results. The difficulty, however, is that the age-adjusted prevalence of nursing home residence is falling, so I would guess the trend would be for newer data to give lower values of nursing home care. In addition, the sample sizes for the older data are not huge—there are about 17,000 next of kin interviewed in the National Mortality Followback Survey and a comparable number in the National Long-Term Care Survey. The HRS is larger and perhaps more reliable. In the end, I am not sure how to explain the higher number here, and would like more clarification.

As Hurd et al. continue assembling their model, there are two elements I would like to see them add. First, they could differentiate between short- and long-term nursing home stays. There are two types of nursing home visits, and they are generally reimbursed differently. Short stays are used to recover from acute events: strokes and broken hips are the classic examples. They involve significant rehabilitation and have the endpoint of discharge to the community. Medicare generally pays for such stays, since the care provided is associated with recovery from an acute medical event. Long stays are associated with frail individuals or people with severe and worsening impairment. People with Alzheimer's disease, Parkinson's disease, and other degenerative physical and cognitive impairments are often in a nursing home for long periods of time. Medicare does not pay for these stays. Rather, payment comes from the individual, their family, or Medicaid if family funds are not sufficient. It is these stays that an individual may wish to insure against. The vast bulk of nursing home days are accounted for by long stay residents, but the share of stays will be tilted much more to the short stays.

In light of this mix, looking at whether people have any nursing home stay is not the best predictor of long-term care needs that an individual may wish to insure. I would like to see the analysis differentiate between Medicare-covered acute rehabilitation stays and long-term stays associated with frailty and decline.

The issue of distinguishing short and long stays is compounded by the fact that there are other alternatives for short stays beyond the nursing home. Inpatient rehabilitation facilities are alternatives to skilled nursing facilities, and one would not want to count a nursing home stay without also counting stays in a rehabilitation hospital. Otherwise, trends in the use of these two facilities would have major impacts on the estimated use of nursing care, which is not being affected nearly as much.

On the long-term stay side, the major alternative to using a nursing home is assisted living. The use of assisted living has increased immensely in recent years. For payment purposes and for evaluating the welfare of the elderly, we care about how stays in these two types of facilities are trending and how substitutable assisted living is for nursing homes. I believe it is possible to model assisted living facilities in the HRS, much as the authors have done for nursing homes, and I would encourage the authors to do so.

In sum, what seems like a small issue becomes big very rapidly. Hurd et al. start with a tightly focused question, and in no time the desired model grows. Hopefully, we will see the model evolve to incorporate these additional issues.

References

Brown, Jeffrey R., and Amy Finkelstein. 2008. "The Interaction of Public and Private Insurance: Medicaid and the Long-Term Care Insurance Market." *American Economic Review* 98 (3): 1083–102.
———. 2011. "Insuring Long-Term Care in the U.S." *Journal of Economic Perspectives* 25 (4): 119–42.
Cutler, David M. 1996. "Why Don't Markets Insure Long-Term Risk." Harvard University. Unpublished manuscript.
Kemper, Peter, and Christopher M. Murtaugh. 1991. "Lifetime Use of Nursing Home Care." *New England Journal of Medicine* 324:595–600.
Lusardi, Annamaria, and Olivia S. Mitchell. 2007. "Baby Boomer Retirement Security: The Role of Planning, Financial Literacy, and Housing Wealth." *Journal of Monetary Economics* 54 (1): 205–24.

MetLife Mature Market Institute. 2009. "The 2009 MetLife Market Survey of Nursing Home, Assisted Living, Adult Day Services, and Home Care Costs." October. http://www.metlife.com/assets/cao/mmi/publications/studies/mmi-market -survey-nursing-home-assisted-living.pdf.

Poterba, James R., Steven F. Venti, and David A. Wise. 2012. "Were They Prepared for Retirement? Financial Status at Advanced Ages in the HRS and AHEAD Cohorts." In *Investigations in the Economics of Aging*, edited by David Wise, 21–69. Chicago: University of Chicago Press.

Robinson, James. 2002. "A Long-Term Care Status Transition Model." University of Wisconsin, Madison. Unpublished manuscript.

A Comparison of Different Measures of Health and Their Relation to Labor Force Transitions at Older Ages

Arie Kapteyn and Erik Meijer

3.1 Introduction

Health, be it of an individual or of a population, can be characterized by a large number of indicators. For many purposes it is desirable to summarize the indicators by a limited number of indexes, possibly only one. Several health indexes have been proposed in the literature, varying in statistical methodology and the breadth of variables included in the index. Since health indexes may be constructed for different purposes, there is no need to settle on one preferred index. We are interested in the statistical properties of health indexes and how they are related to observed economic behavior. Health indexes can be classified by a number of different approaches. The simplest approach is to simply ask people to rate their own health on an

Arie Kapteyn is director of the Center for Economic and Social Research at the University of Southern California and a research associate of the National Bureau of Economic Research. Erik Meijer is a senior economist at the Center for Economic and Social Research at the University of Southern California and an adjunct economist at the RAND Corporation.

This chapter was prepared for the NBER conference on the economics of aging, held May 9–11, 2013, in Carefree, AZ. We thank Tatiana Andreyeva and Meena Fernandes, who were involved in the data construction for the MKA index that we draw upon. We thank Steven Venti for helpful comments. This chapter uses data from SHARE releases 2.0.1 (July 2007) and 2.5.0, as of May 24, 2011. The SHARE data collection has been primarily funded by the European Commission through the Fifth Framework Programme (project QLK6-CT-2001-00360 in the thematic program Quality of Life), through the Sixth Framework Programme (projects SHARE-I3, RII-CT-2006-062193; COMPARE, CIT5-CT-2005-028857; and SHARELIFE, CIT4-CT-2006-028812). and through the Seventh Framework Programme (SHARE-PREP, 211909; and SHARE-LEAP, 227822). Additional funding from the US National Institute on Aging (U01 AG09740-13S2, P01 AG005842, P01 AG08291, P30 AG12815, Y1-AG-4553-01, and OGHA 04-064, IAG BSR06-11, R21 AG025169) as well as from various national sources is gratefully acknowledged (see http://www.share-project.org for a full list of funding institutions). For acknowledgments, sources of research support, and disclosure of the authors' material financial relationships, if any, please see http://www.nber.org/chapters/c12972.ack.

ordinal scale. A more involved approach relates such self-reports to a number of explanatory variables, such as health conditions or difficulties with activities of daily living and uses a regression approach to determine the weights of each of the explanatory variables in the construction of a health index. A third approach considers health to be a latent construct for which a number of indicators exist. The indicators are then used to somehow estimate the underlying latent variable. In this chapter we aim at an empirical comparison of these approaches by taking prominent examples from the literature and comparing them among themselves as well as how well they explain economic behavior.

We focus on health measures that can be computed for individuals in widely available survey data. The data we use for the empirical part of this chapter are from the Survey of Health, Ageing and Retirement in Europe (SHARE), which is modeled after the Health and Retirement Study (HRS) in the United States. SHARE is a representative sample of individuals fifty and over and their spouses in a number of countries in continental Europe. We use data from waves 1 (2004–2005) and 2 (2006–2007), which include twelve and fourteen countries, respectively. We limit ourselves to the eleven countries that are present in both waves. The data contain extensive information about health, as well as many other topics of interest to economists and other social and behavioral scientists. The traditional health measure is self-reported general health (SRH), which has five categories: excellent, very good, good, fair, and poor.[1] SRH generally correlates strongly with objective measures of health in (rare) instances when both are available for the same individuals. It is a short and easy question, and as a result, widely available in many data sets. Because of properties and availability, it is generally considered a useful measure for many purposes. However, it is also a crude measure, and perhaps more importantly, it appears to be incomparable across countries without corrections: individuals with similar health as judged by more objective variables give widely different responses on average in different countries (Meijer, Kapteyn, and Andreyeva 2011; MKA hereafter). Hence, for comparing health across countries, it is not very suitable. Because of this, and the wealth of health data available in SHARE, MKA developed a health index for wave 1 of SHARE that uses much more information, is continuous, has a much higher reliability than SRH, and is comparable across countries. Jürges (2007), at the same time as MKA (but published earlier), also developed a health index for wave 1 of SHARE, with similar goals but a strikingly different methodology. Poterba, Venti, and Wise (2011, 2013) developed a health index for the HRS with yet another methodology, although comparability across countries does not appear to

---

1. This is the US version, which is also used in the HRS, PSID, and other survey data sets in the United States. SHARE wave 1 also includes a European version, with response categories of very good, good, fair, bad, very bad.

be a core goal of their effort. Our goal in this chapter is to study the theoretical and empirical differences between these indexes so that researchers who want to include a measure of health in their analyses can make a better informed choice as to which index is most appropriate for their analyses, and readers can interpret differences between results from different papers that use different indexes. Section 3.2 describes the construction of the indexes and highlights differences in methodology and variables used. Section 3.3 then studies empirical differences, and section 3.4 studies the differences in explanatory power in a simple model for labor force transitions at older ages. Section 3.5 explores issues of methodology and variable choice further by computing different variants of the indexes and studying their relations. Section 3.6 concludes.

3.2 Measuring Health: Variables and Approaches to Combining Them

This section describes the various health indexes that we aim to compare in the remainder of the chapter.

3.2.1 The Methodology Used by Meijer, Kapteyn, and Andreyeva

MKA estimate models of health that has a multiple indicators and multiple causes ([MIMIC] Jöreskog and Goldberger 1975) structure, analogous to the model of Börsch-Supan, McFadden, and Schnabel (1996): they assume that there is a single latent "true" health dimension, that a large number of observed health variables have this latent health dimension in common, and that true health is in turn related to a set of covariates. This leads to a system of equations

$$(1) \qquad\qquad y_{ni} = \tau_i + \lambda_i \eta_n + \varepsilon_{ni}$$

$$(2) \qquad\qquad \eta_n = x_n' \gamma + \zeta_{ni},$$

where y_{ni} is the i-th observed health measure for individual n, η_n is the true health of the individual, x_n is a vector of covariates, ε_{ni} and ζ_{ni} are error terms, and the other terms are parameters. Thus, equation (1) is a factor analysis model for the observed health measures, and equation (2) is a regression model for latent health.

This basic model structure is enriched along several lines. First, because most health measures used are binary or ordinal, the linear form of equation (1) is replaced by a binary or ordinal probit equation as appropriate, in which a linear equation like (1) is assumed to hold for an underlying continuous variable, and the relation between this underlying continuous variable and the categorical observed variable is a step function. Second, almost all parameters are allowed to be different across countries, reflecting differences in reporting behavior in the health measures across individuals from different countries (who often are faced with questions phrased in different languages), and institutional differences that might affect the relationship between health and the covariates. The exception is the equation for grip strength, which is an objective measure taken by the interviewer, which MKA assume to be free from differences in reporting behavior. This "anchoring" on grip strength ensures comparability across countries. A further refinement of this is that MKA use a grip strength residual measure instead of observed grip strength (see following) and analyze men and women separately, so that the index is not assumed to be comparable between men and women. Third, missing observations in the health measures are straightforwardly dealt with in this model structure (they are integrated out of the likelihood), so that these do not lead to dropping of observations. There were two (categorical) covariates with significant numbers of missings. For those, missingness was included as an additional category. This is not recommended for the purpose of unbiased estimation of regression models, but is more suitable for prediction purposes, which is what it is used for by MKA.

Some further technical assumptions (such as normal distributions and uncorrelatedness of the error terms) allow estimation by maximum simulated likelihood. With the model estimated, the MKA health index $\hat{\eta}_n$ is the conditional expectation of true health η_n given (all) the observed variables in the model.

3.2.2 The Methodology of Poterba, Venti, and Wise

We base the discussion here on the variant of their index discussed in Poterba, Venti, and Wise (2013; PVW hereafter). PVW start with a large set of variables that are assumed to be related to an underlying true health variable. This is similar to MKA, and to stress the similarity, we call the observed variables y_{ni} and true health η_n. PVW run a principal components analysis (PCA) and compute the first principal component $\hat{\eta}_n$, which is their health index. PCA can be defined and interpreted in various ways, but for our current purposes, the easiest interpretation is the following. Start with equation (1), and in addition to τ_i and λ_i, treat η_n as an additional parameter to be estimated. Estimate the model by minimizing the sum of squared errors. The resulting estimator of η_n is $\hat{\eta}_n$. No explicit assumptions about distribution or uncorrelatedness of the error terms are made. However, as noted by Wansbeek and Meijer (2000, 159), PCA is mathematically equivalent to a restricted form of factor analysis in which the error terms of the different observed variables not only are uncorrelated, but also have the same variance; in other words, equivalent to a form of factor analysis with much stronger assumptions than typically made in applications of factor analysis. On the other hand, as the number of observed variables increases, PCA and factor analysis solutions converge to each other. This finding underlies the estimation of "approximate factor models," which are often used in finance, by PCA. The number of measures used by PVW is large, but much smaller than the number typically used in applications in finance, and several orders of magnitude smaller than the number of observations, so there is likely to be some difference between PCA and factor analysis. With the interpretation as a restricted factor analysis model and the additional assumption of normally distributed variables, the principal component index is equal to the conditional expectation of true health given the observed variables used, up to a multiplicative constant. (The conditional expectation is "shrunken" toward zero and thus has lower variance.)

For PCA, binary observed variables can be treated as continuous variables. This is analogous to the treatment of dummy variables as covariates in regression analyses. However, binary variables are obviously not normally distributed, and thus the PCA index is not a conditional expectation, and likely not exactly equal to a scaled version of a conditional expectation that is consistent with the binary nature of the variables.

The description in PVW (especially their table 2-1) suggests that they coded all their measures as binary variables, although some of the original variables have more than two categories. Because PVW do not explicitly mention the treatment of missing data, we assume that observations with missing data are dropped. Because they only have one country, whether parameters are identical across countries is not a relevant issue. However, they use multiple waves of the HRS and data for both men and women. They include all of these in a single analysis, because it is found that coefficients are quite similar across waves and between men and women.

3.2.3 The Methodology of Jürges

Jürges (2007) uses a methodology that follows Cutler and Richardson (1997, 1999) and Lindeboom and van Doorslaer (2004). He also assumes that there is a single latent true health dimension, which we can again call η_n. He assumes that SRH is a categorical reflection of true health, and that a set of other observed variables x_n act as covariates. He estimates an ordinal probit model with SRH as dependent variable and x_n as explanatory variables. At an abstract level, this model structure is equivalent to the MKA model structure, in which the set of dependent variables y_{ni} consists of only one variable, SRH. However, as we will see, the set of variables that Jürges includes in x_n is very different from the covariates in MKA. The index of Jürges is defined as the predicted linear index from the ordinal probit model, that is, $\hat{\eta}_n = x'_n \hat{\gamma}$, which is the conditional expectation of true health given the covariates (but not conditional on the dependent variable SRH). Note that SRH is used in the estimation but not in the construction of the index: an individual who reports excellent health has the same value of the health index as another individual with the same values of the covariates but who reports being in poor health. MKA compare their index with an analogous index defined as just the predicted linear index from equation (2) and find that the linear index has much lower reliability. But in the case of MKA, this amounted to ignoring the information on twenty-five health measures, whereas in the case of Jürges, this only ignores the information from a single variable, and thus the inefficiency is much smaller.

Like MKA, Jürges allows for cross-country differences in reporting behavior in SRH by allowing the threshold parameters to be country specific, though not gender specific. The regression coefficients are assumed equal across countries. For low grip strength, Jürges adds a dummy for missingness to avoid having to drop a sizable fraction of the sample, and to reduce issues of selectivity (missingness of grip strength is strongly related to bad health). For the other covariates, there are no such dummies and we thus assume that records with missing data on these variables are dropped.

3.2.4 Variables Used in Constructing the Indexes

All three indexes use SRH, albeit in different ways. MKA and Jürges use it as an ordinal dependent variable and estimate a model with an ordinal probit equation. MKA include the information of SRH in the construction of their index, whereas Jürges ignores it in the construction. PVW include a binary indicator for whether SRH is fair or poor in their index. They also include an indicator for whether health was worse in the previous period, which MKA and Jürges do not have. Further, PVW include a dummy for whether health limits work, which MKA and Jürges do not have.

MKA and PVW include mobility, fine motor, and functional limitations (e.g., difficulty walking 100m), which are all binary, except that MKA use climbing stairs as an ordinal variable (0 = no difficulty, 1 = difficulty climbing several flights but not a single flight, 2 = difficulty climbing a single flight). MKA use difficulties with activities of daily living (ADLs, e.g., difficulty dressing) as separate measures, whereas PVW only include a binary indicator for at least one ADL. MKA also include difficulties with instrumental activities of daily living (IADLs, e.g., using a map), which PVW do not use. Jürges does not use any of these difficulties variables.

Both PVW and Jürges include doctor-diagnosed chronic conditions (e.g., ever had diabetes), but the set of conditions is larger for Jürges. PVW also include back pain, which is one of a number of "symptoms" variables. Another set of variables only included by PVW is health care utilization (doctor visit, hospital stay, nursing home stay, home care).

MKA and Jürges include grip strength. Grip strength in middle age has been established as a predictor of health problems and mortality at later ages. Both MKA and Jürges transform it before usage. MKA argue that grip strength is also a function of "size" (operationalized as height and weight) in a way that is unrelated to health. They correct for this by subtracting a predictive quadratic polynomial in height and weight and use the resulting grip stength residual as a dependent variable in their analyses. Jürges similarly corrects for height and sex and then defines low grip strength as being in the lowest tercile of the distribution of the residual. Jürges also includes an indicator for low walking speed (with individuals who were not subjected to the test assumed to have normal walking speed). MKA do not use walking speed and

PVW use neither walking speed nor grip strength. All three indexes use body mass index (BMI), which is derived from self-reported height and weight. PVW use BMI as a continuous variable, which makes it their only variable that is not binary. Based on National Institutes of Health (NIH) guidelines for classification, MKA use dummies (as covariates) for being underweight (BMI < 18.5), overweight (25–30), class I obese (30–35), and class II and III obese (> 35). Jürges uses dummies for BMI < 20, 25–30, and 30+.

Finally, MKA include a set of covariates not included by PVW and Jürges: age, whether living with a spouse or partner, household size, education, and household net worth.

In the empirical part of this chapter, we compare four indexes based on the ones described here. We have tried to closely approximate the indexes described in the literature, but there are some differences. Thus, although we will refer to the PVW or Jue index, they are not identical to the ones used by PVW or Jürges. However, we believe they are close enough to warrant this notation. The variables we have used in constructing the indexes are listed in table 3.1.

We use SRH as a linear index. That is, we treat the category scores 1–5 as being measured on an interval scale. Our MKA index for wave 1 is the same one as in the MKA article. For wave 2, we have used the estimates from the models estimated for wave 1 in MKA and computed the health index for each individual accordingly. For the PVW index, we used the list from table 2-1 in PVW and tried to mimic these as close as possible in SHARE. However, the wording and response categories occasionally differ from the ones in the HRS, and sometimes variables are not available. The most notable differences are the following:

- "Health problems limiting work" was not asked in SHARE wave 1. We have replaced it (for both waves) with health problems limiting "activities people usually do."
- "Health worse in previous period" is not available in wave 1, nor for the refreshment sample in wave 2. We excluded it.
- "Ever experience psychological problems" is operationalized as professional (doctor-psychologist) treatment for depression by a family doctor or psychiatrist, which was only asked if the respondent reported having suffered from depression in the last year (new interviews) or since the last interview (re-interviews).
- There was an error with the routing of the health care utilization section in wave 1 for Greece and Switzerland, which makes the home care variable missing for all respondents in these countries in wave 1. We considered two ways to deal with this: drop these countries from wave 1 or set home care to zero and add a "missing home care" dummy that is 1 for respondents in these countries in wave 1 and 0 otherwise. The two resulting indexes correlate almost perfectly for observations that have both. We use the second one in the following, so that we do not have to drop these two countries.

Table 3.1   **Variables included in the indexes**

	SRH	MKA	PVW	Jue
Self-reported health (US version)	linear	categories	fair/poor	(a)
Health limits activities			binary	
Mobility, fine motor, and functional limitations				
Walking 100 meters		x	x	
Sitting two hours		x	x	
Getting up from chair		x	x	
Climbing stairs		3 categories	binary	
Stooping, kneeling, crouching		x	x	
Reaching or extending arms above shoulder		x	x	
Pulling or pushing large objects		x	x	
Lifting or carrying weights over five kilos		x	x	
Picking up a small coin from a table		x	x	
Difficulties with activities of daily living (ADL)				
Dressing, including shoes and socks		x		
Walking across a room		x		
Bathing or showering		x		
Eating, cutting up food		x		
Getting in or out of bed		x		
Using the toilet, including getting up or down		x		
At least one ADL			x	
Difficulties with instrumental activities of daily living (IADL)				
Using a map in a strange place		x		
Preparing a hot meal		x		
Shopping for groceries		x		
Telephone calls		x		
Taking medications		x		
Doing work around the house or garden		x		
Managing money		x		
Doctor-diagnosed health conditions				
Heart problems			x	x
High blood pressure or hypertension			x	x
High blood cholesterol				x
Stroke			x	x
Diabetes or high blood sugar			x	x
Chronic lung disease			x	x
Asthma				x
Arthritis			x	x
Osteoporosis				x
Cancer			x	x
Stomach or duodenal ulcer, peptic ulcer				x
Parkinson's disease				x
Cataracts				x
Hip fracture or femoral fracture				x
Other conditions				x
Psychological problems			x	x
Bothered by (symptoms)				
Pain in back, knees, hips, or other joint			x	

(continued)

Table 3.1   (continued)

	SRH	MKA	PVW	Jue
Health care utilization				
Doctor visit			x	
Hospital stay			x	
Nursing home stay			x	
Home care			x	
Grip strength		(b)		(c)
Low walking speed (< 0.4 m/s)				x
Body mass index		categories	linear	categories
Demographics and socioeconomics				
Country		separate		(a)
Sex		separate		
Age		cubic polynomial		
Living with spouse or partner		x		
Household size		x		
Education in three classes		categories		
Net worth		(d)		

(a) Used in estimating the model but not in constructing the index.
(b) Residual after subtracting quadratic polynomial in height and weight and mean of the result (both gender specific).
(c) Low grip strength: lowest tercile after correcting for height and sex.
(d) Inverse hyperbolic sine of PPP-adjusted net worth.

Also, because PVW did not address cross-country comparability, we had to make a choice as how to implement it in a cross-country setting. The two ends of the spectrum are completely country specific, which by construction would imply that individuals for all countries are equally healthy on average, or joint, which assumes that there are no differences in reporting behavior. We chose the latter, which seems more in line with PVW's treatment of combining all waves and men and women. It would, however, be possible to create an intermediate index, by including some (but not all) interactions between country dummies and the variables that are now used.

The Jürges index was developed for SHARE and thus we are able to reproduce it quite closely. One presumably minor difference is that Jürges uses the maximum of two walking speed measures to measure low walking speed, whereas we use the SHARE-provided derived variable, which uses the average of the two. Also, wave 2 includes three health conditions that were not asked specifically in wave 1: other fractures, Alzheimer's disease or other memory problems, and benign tumor. We have combined these with the "other conditions" variable.

Table 3.1 summarizes the variables we have used in constructing the indexes in this chapter, and how we have used them. Observations with missings are generally dropped, with some exceptions, in particular dependent variables in MKA. This difference between MKA and the other indexes, and differences in which variables are used and how many missings they have, lead to differences in the number of respondents for which the indexes are available: for SRH we have 56,234 observations (across both waves and men and women), for MKA it is 54,388, for PVW 51,716, and Jue 52,324.

3.3 Empirical Properties of the Health Measures

The four health measures we consider vary in a number of different respects: they include different variables, are based on different statistical models, and vary in the extent they are assumed or constructed to be internationally comparable. To gain more insight in their comparative properties we present a number of descriptive tables and graphs. All tables and figures will be presented for males and females separately. As noted in the previous section, the number of observations varies by health measure due to the fact that they are based on different sets of underlying variables, which have different patterns of missings. To facilitate comparability we restrict the sample to observations that allow the construction of all four measures.

Table 3.2 presents sample characteristics of the measures. Since the measures have different scales, the means and standard deviations are not comparable. (Also note that the signs of the indexes are different: MKA is higher for better health, whereas the other indexes are higher for worse health.) It is of interest, however, to consider the kurtosis and skewness of the measures. To evaluate the numbers in the table, recall that the kurtosis of a normal distribution is three, while the skewness is zero. PVW and Jue show the highest kurtosis. Kurtosis is particularly high for males. For SRH and MKA, the kurtosis is close to that of a normal distribution. SRH and MKA also show the least skewness; they are both slightly skewed to the left. In contrast, PVW and Jue show considerable skewness to the right.

Figure 3.1 confirms these observations. To facilitate comparisons, the variables have been standardized so that they are measured on the same scale and better health is indicated by higher values. Clearly PVW shows a high peak at about one standard deviation above the mean, while at the same time exhibiting a long left tail. In other words, according to this index many individuals have similar (good) health, but there are also individuals with particularly bad health (those located in the left tail). When using the health measures to explain labor market status or labor market transitions, the PVW index may be able to distinguish between various degrees of bad health, while it may be less discriminating in the area of good health. MKA would appear to be better at discriminating between health states across the whole spectrum from very poor to excellent health, but may be less informative when it comes to distinguishing different levels of poor health. We return to this aspect in section 3.4.

Although the shape of the densities of the four health measures in figure

Table 3.2   **Distributional properties of the raw indexes**

	SRH	MKA	PVW	Jue
Males				
N	23,198	23,198	23,198	23,198
Mean	2.90	0.04	−0.39	0.84
SD	1.07	0.49	2.07	0.72
Skewness	−0.04	−0.60	1.71	1.29
Kurtosis	2.47	3.34	5.99	5.31
Females				
N	27,137	27,137	27,137	27,137
Mean	3.07	0.00	0.45	1.03
SD	1.06	0.39	2.57	0.82
Skewness	−0.16	−0.43	1.12	1.08
Kurtosis	2.54	2.96	3.57	4.42
Total				
N	50,335	50,335	50,335	50,335
Mean	2.99	0.02	0.06	0.94
SD	1.07	0.44	2.39	0.78
Skewness	−0.10	−0.51	1.37	1.19
Kurtosis	2.49	3.31	4.40	4.81

3.1 reveals considerable differences, it would be conceivable that they still rank the health of individuals in the same way and hence the measures may still exhibit high correlations (although obviously not equal to one). The correlations in table 3.3 vary between .54 and .86 (in absolute value). These numbers do not appear to be particularly high. For instance, the correlation between MKA and Jue for males of .61 would imply that in a regression of MKA on Jue less than 40 percent of the variance would be explained. Thus it appears that the various measures partly measure different things (as was also suggested by the discussion in section 3.2), which makes it worthwhile to investigate their relation with respondent characteristics and behavior.

Figure 3.2 shows the relation between the health measures and age. Once again the measures are standardized so that we can compare their scales. MKA shows the steepest decline with age, while the decline is least for SRH. PVW and Jue appear to be in between these two extremes. It is probably not surprising that SRH shows the smallest gradient with age. In expressing self-reports of health, respondents may very well compare themselves with others of the same age, which would lower the age gradient. In the extreme case that respondents would provide a completely relativistic evaluation (just comparing their health with others in their cohort), the age gradient might be zero. MKA is not only based on ADLs and IADLs, but also on grip strength, which is a physical measure with a pronounced negative age gradient.

A major point of interest is how health status compares across countries.

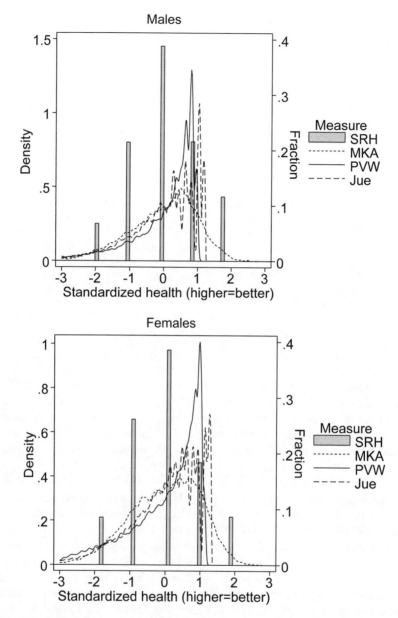

Fig. 3.1 Distributions of the standardized indexes

Table 3.3   **Correlations among the raw indexes**

	SRH	MKA	PVW	Jue
Males				
SRH	1.00			
MKA	−0.68	1.00		
PVW	0.64	−0.79	1.00	
Jue	0.54	−0.61	0.71	1.00
Females				
SRH	1.00			
MKA	−0.68	1.00		
PVW	0.66	−0.86	1.00	
Jue	0.57	−0.67	0.75	1.00

The four measures vary in the extent to which comparability issues are incorporated. SRH and PVW assume complete comparability, in the way we are using them. We could also have constructed the PVW by country, which would have avoided any assumptions about intercountry comparability. For SRH no obvious correction is available in the data, although we could have considered using the vignettes by health domain that have been collected in the SHARE data. This would have been a major task, as it requires not just the modeling of response scale corrections by health domain, but also a model that relates general health to health by domain. Somewhat similar modeling has been done by Kapteyn, Smith, and van Soest (2007) for several domains of work disability, while SHARE vignettes have been used in a number of different domains, but not for overall health; see for instance the special issue of *Social Indicators Research*, edited by Jürges and van Soest (2012), and Datta Gupta, Kristensen, and Pozzoli (2010). MKA assumes comparability by country of grip strength (or rather a transformation of grip strength that corrects for height and weight), which is used to rescale the within country measures. Jue assumes identical coefficients across countries, but with country-specific cutoff points for the conditional probits that explain SRH by country.

Figure 3.3 shows standardized means by country and sex. The first observation is that there is considerable correlation between mean female and mean male health across countries for every measure. If a country scores high in female health, it is likely to also score high in male health, and vice versa. The correlations between average male and female health are .95 for SRH, MKA, and Jue, and .90 for PVW. Regarding the correspondence between measures, we note that the signs are generally in agreement. If a country is below the mean according to one measure, it usually also is below the mean according to a different measure. There are a few exceptions to this rule. For instance for German males, SRH and PVW suggest that German health is below the mean, whereas MKA pegs it well above it. For both male and female Greeks, MKA suggests a mean health level below the sample

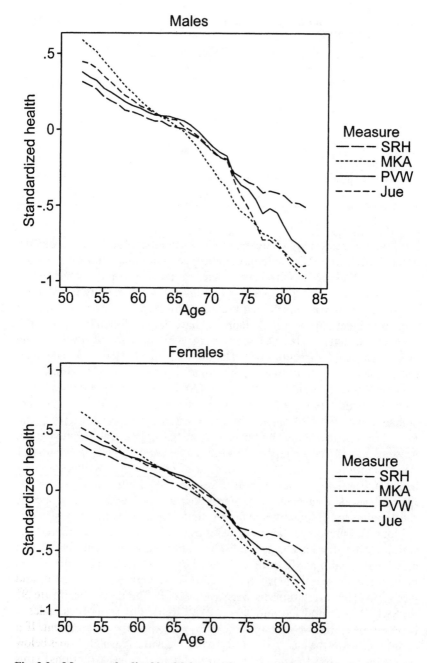

Fig. 3.2   Mean standardized health by age (five-year moving average centered at the given age)

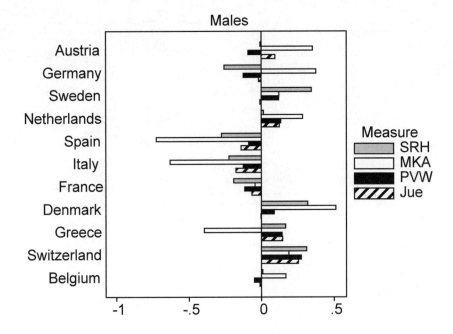

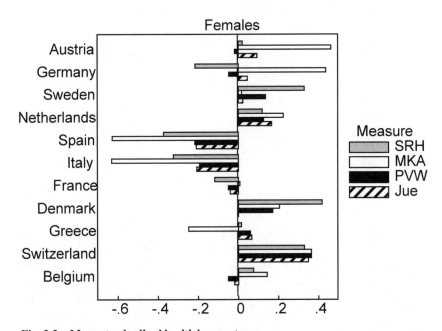

Fig. 3.3   Mean standardized health by country

Table 3.4   Correlations among different measures of country averages of health

	SRH	MKA	PVW	Jue
Males				
SRH	1.00			
MKA	0.45	1.00		
PVW	0.85	0.26	1.00	
Jue	0.63	0.49	0.78	1.00
Females				
SRH	1.00			
MKA	0.57	1.00		
PVW	0.89	0.61	1.00	
Jue	0.66	0.76	0.87	1.00

Table 3.5   Distribution of changes in standardized health indexes

	SRH	MKA	PVW	Jue
Males				
N	7,375	7,375	7,375	7,375
Mean	−0.15	−0.09	−0.11	−0.08
SD	0.89	0.64	0.75	0.77
Skewness	−0.13	−0.26	−0.61	−0.31
Kurtosis	4.03	5.04	8.81	8.13
Females				
N	8,703	8,703	8,703	8,703
Mean	−0.14	−0.07	−0.08	−0.09
SD	0.87	0.61	0.68	0.75
Skewness	−0.13	0.08	−0.28	−0.21
Kurtosis	3.78	5.45	6.03	5.12
Total				
N	16,078	16,078	16,078	16,078
Mean	−0.15	−0.08	−0.10	−0.08
SD	0.88	0.62	0.71	0.76
Skewness	−0.13	−0.09	−0.46	−0.26
Kurtosis	3.90	5.27	7.64	6.58

mean, while the other measures suggest Greek health to be about average or a little better than average. Table 3.4 shows the correlations between the country means of the four measures for males and females separately. The correlations of the country means appear of the same order of magnitude as the correlations between the individual measures presented in table 3.3.

Our interest is not only in the levels of health according to different measures and how they compare, but also in changes. Table 3.5 shows the distribution of health changes between 2004 and 2006. As these are changes

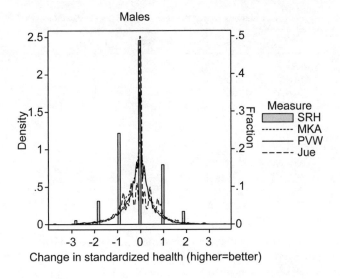

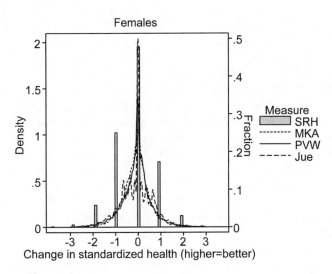

Fig. 3.4   Distributions of the changes in health

observed for the same respondents, it is not surprising that mean health changes are negative, since the respondents on average have aged about two years. Once again kurtosis is particularly high for PVW and to a slightly lesser extent for Jue. Skewness appears modest. Figure 3.4 shows standardized densities of the changes in health measures confirming the fact that the distributions of changes are indeed fairly symmetric. Table 3.6 shows that

Table 3.6   Correlations among the changes in the standardized indexes

	SRH	MKA	PVW	Jue
Males				
SRH	1.00			
MKA	0.55	1.00		
PVW	0.38	0.72	1.00	
Jue	0.22	0.28	0.43	1.00
Females				
SRH	1.00			
MKA	0.45	1.00		
PVW	0.35	0.78	1.00	
Jue	0.20	0.29	0.41	1.00

all changes are positively correlated, as one would expect. However, correlations are not particularly high.

Figure 3.5 shows how health changes are related to age. For females, all measures show an accelerating deterioration with age, with the possible exception of SRH. For males that pattern is somewhat less clear. In particular Jue and SRH show little sign of accelerating health deterioration for males. On the other hand, PVW indicates that health deteriorates at an accelerated pace with age.

Figure 3.6, once again provides a comparison across countries. As one would expect, nearly all measures show a decline, with some minor exceptions. The correlation between average male and female health changes is considerably lower than for levels. The correlation is .31 for SRH, .22 for MKA, .32 for PVW, and .61 for Jue. Table 3.7 shows the correlations between the country mean changes of the four measures for males and females separately. The correlations of the country mean changes appear of the same order of magnitude as the correlations between the individual measures presented in table 3.6, but they are definitely not the same. Remarkably, for females MKA and PVW correlate negatively with SRH. Generally, for females average SRH by country shows very small correlations with the other three measures.

The descriptive analyses so far have established that the various measures are positively correlated, but at the same time there are substantial differences in distributions, in their relations with age, and in how the measures rank countries by health. There is enough scope, therefore, to investigate how the measures relate to individual characteristics and behavior.

3.4 Labor Force Transitions

Within the age group of individuals fifty and older one would expect health to become an increasingly important determinant of transitions into retirement or into some kind of disability insurance scheme. To investigate

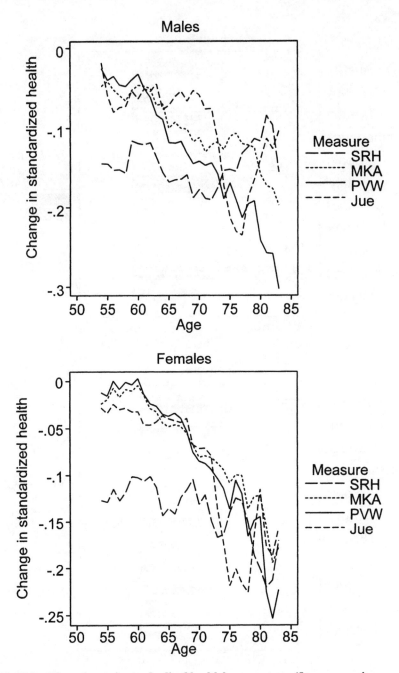

Fig. 3.5   Mean change in standardized health by current age (five-year moving average centered at the given age)

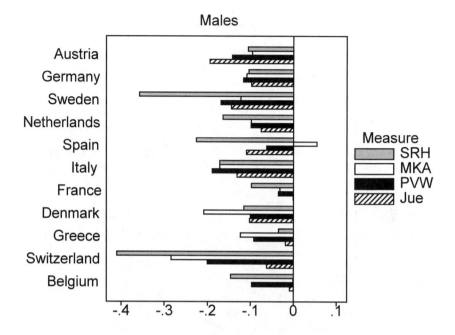

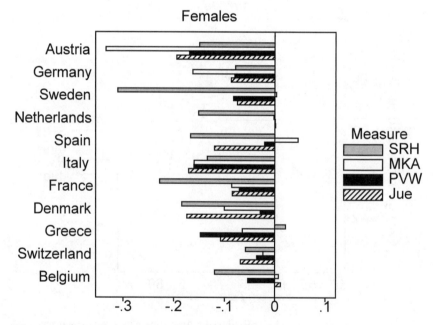

Fig. 3.6   Mean change in standardized health by country

Table 3.7   Correlation between different measures of country mean health changes

	SRH	MKA	PVW	Jue
Males				
SRH	1.00			
MKA	0.34	1.00		
PVW	0.61	0.72	1.00	
Jue	0.22	0.17	0.51	1.00
Females				
SRH	1.00			
MKA	−0.12	1.00		
PVW	−0.23	0.71	1.00	
Jue	0.03	0.67	0.57	1.00

the power of the various health measures in explaining such transitions we estimate linear probability models that explain labor market status in 2006, based on health status in 2004 and changes between 2004 and 2006. One might suspect that health status in 2006 could be endogenous with respect to labor market status in 2006. Empirical evidence, partly based on SHARE, suggests that retirement does not have adverse effects on health. Possibly retirement improves health. See, for instance, Coe and Zamarro (2011). To the extent that retirement improves health, we would underestimate the health change between 2004 and 2006 for those who have retired between waves. This would attenuate the estimated effect of a health change on the probability of a transition from work to retirement. The evidence is somewhat less clear with respect to the effect on receipt of disability insurance (DI), as one might worry about the possibility of self-reports being colored by justification bias (e.g., Bound 1991). The empirical evidence for the existence of justification bias appears to be limited, however, at least in Europe (Kapteyn, Smith, and van Soest 2011). In any case, the models to be presented are not meant to be full-fledged structural models of transitions into retirement or disability. Rather the analyses seek to establish the strength of the links between the various measures and observed transitions.

Table 3.8 presents transitions in labor market states between 2004 and 2006. Of those working in 2004, 13.6 percent are retired in 2006. Other less common pathways out of employment are to homemakers, unemployment, and disability. The probability of "unretiring" is very low. Less than 1 percent of those who were retired in 2004 report to be working in 2006. This contrasts with patterns in the United States where the probability of returning to work after retirement appears to be substantially higher (cf. Maestas 2010). Among the disabled in 2004, 7.3 percent report to be working in 2006. These are relatively small numbers though (thirty-six individuals).

To explain transitions we estimate a sequence of models with an increasing number of covariates. The first model only includes 2004 health (Lagged

Table 3.8   Labor force transitions

Wave 1 Labor force status	N	%	Wave 2 labor force status (row %)					
			Retired	Employed	Unemployed	Disabled	Homemaker	Other
Retired	7,685	47.5	91.5	1.0	0.2	1.6	4.9	0.9
Employed or self-employed	4,732	30.8	13.6	78.4	2.7	1.9	2.4	1.1
Unemployed	563	3.6	25.2	22.2	36.3	4.8	8.1	3.5
Permanently sick or disabled	449	2.8	32.8	7.3	1.4	51.8	5.1	1.6
Homemaker	2,501	15.2	18.7	3.0	1.1	2.5	71.9	2.8
Other	40	0.3	38.4	10.1	4.7	16.0	12.3	18.5
Total	15,970	100.0	52.3	26.1	2.4	3.4	14.4	1.4
N			8,554	3,970	373	526	2,349	198

health) and the difference in health between 2006 and 2004 (Health change) as explanatory variables. The health variables are all standardized to facilitate comparability between the estimated effects by health measure. The second model adds demographics (a third degree polynomial in age, education in three classes, living with a partner, change in the latter) and economic variables (working in the public sector, self-employed, eligible for public pension, eligible for private pension, reached early retirement age, reached normal retirement age, inverse hyperbolic sine of household net worth [PPP (purchasing power parity) adjusted], log household income [PPP adjusted], all as measured in 2004, plus reaching early and normal retirement age between 2004 and 2006). The third model adds country dummies. The models only consider binary choices: we estimate models for retiring versus working and becoming disabled versus working. That is, the sample for the first of these only consists of individuals who were working in 2004 and either working or retired in 2006, and the sample of the second only consists of individuals who were working in 2004 and either working or disabled in 2006.

For simplicity we do not present the estimation results for all the added covariates, but concentrate on the coefficients of lagged health and health change. Table 3.9 presents results for transitions between being employed in 2004 and being retired in 2006 for males. The dependent variable is equal to one if an individual is retired in 2006, so a negative sign implies an increase in the probability of being retired in 2006 if health falls. Both lagged health and health change have a highly significant effect on the probability of retirement. In this model without covariates, R^2 values are low. Adding demographics and economic variables raises the R^2s substantially and reduces the effect of the health variables. Self-reported health still shows significant effects (and to a lesser extent PVW and Jue). Conceivably, the significance of self-reported health is partly the result of justification bias. Adding country dummies further reduces the significance of the health variables, with only lagged self-reported health and health change as measured by Jue retaining significance.

Table 3.10 presents the same sequence of models for females. The conclusions are very similar to those for males. The simple model with just the health variables shows these variables to have highly significant effects. The significance reduces when demographics and economic variables are added and goes away once we also add country dummies, with the exception of lagged self-reported health and lagged health and health change as measured by Jue.

Table 3.11 contains estimation results for transitions into disability for males. The R^2s of the models without covariates are considerably higher than for the model explaining transitions into retirement. Furthermore, the health measures remain significant when we add additional covariates and the sizes of the regression coefficients of the health variables are hardly affected by the addition of covariates. The R^2s increase as a result of adding covariates, but the increase is modest, certainly in comparison with the

Table 3.9   Retiring versus staying employed or self-employed, males

	SRH	MKA	PVW	Jue
Health only				
Health change	−0.0277*	−0.0461***	−0.0500*	−0.0564***
	(0.0103)	(0.0139)	(0.0188)	(0.0157)
Lagged health	−0.0487***	−0.0781***	−0.0960***	−0.0748***
	(0.0100)	(0.0123)	(0.0176)	(0.0146)
R^2	0.011	0.022	0.020	0.017
Observations	2,464	2,464	2,464	2,464
+demographics, economic				
Health change	−0.0151	−0.00462	−0.0210	−0.0302**
	(0.00902)	(0.0118)	(0.0159)	(0.0131)
Lagged health	−0.0283***	−0.0112	−0.0432*	−0.0251**
	(0.00828)	(0.0114)	(0.0146)	(0.0114)
R^2	0.288	0.285	0.289	0.287
Observations	2,426	2,426	2,426	2,426
+country dummies				
Health change	−0.00977	−0.00996	−0.0191	−0.0273**
	(0.00888)	(0.0119)	(0.0153)	(0.0128)
Lagged health	−0.0158	−0.0169	−0.0291**	−0.0179
	(0.00860)	(0.0116)	(0.0140)	(0.0112)
R^2	0.308	0.308	0.309	0.309
Observations	2,426	2,426	2,426	2,426

Notes: Coefficients of demographic and economic variables and country dummies not shown. Standard errors in parentheses.
***Significant at the 1 percent level.
**Significant at the 5 percent level.
*Significant at the 10 percent level.

models explaining retirement. All this suggests that for the transition into disability, health is the main determinant with a rather modest role for demographics and socioeconomic variables.

Table 3.12 presents the results for females. Again, the health variables are highly significant and hardly affected by the addition of covariates. The R^2s are lower than for males.

When comparing across health measures, some tentative conclusions emerge. When it comes to explaining transitions into retirement, there is not much to choose between the various measures. MKA, PVW, and Jue all explain a relatively small percentage of the variance in the transition into retirement. The picture for disability is different. PVW explains a larger percentage of the variance of transitions into disability for both males and females, while the estimated coefficients are larger. It is of interest to speculate why this may be so. As noted in section 3.3, PVW has a long left tail and thus appears able to discriminate more finely between health levels at the poor end of the scale.

Another explanation might be that the health care utilization variables in

Table 3.10   Retiring versus staying employed or self-employed, females

	SRH	MKA	PVW	Jue
Health only				
Health change	−0.0274**	−0.0513*	−0.0733*	−0.0733***
	(0.0111)	(0.0172)	(0.0231)	(0.0189)
Lagged health	−0.0426***	−0.0602***	−0.0674***	−0.0750***
	(0.0117)	(0.0136)	(0.0189)	(0.0159)
R^2	0.010	0.014	0.013	0.020
Observations	1,881	1,881	1,881	1,881
+demographics, economic				
Health change	−0.0213**	−0.0173	−0.0442**	−0.0421**
	(0.0100)	(0.0160)	(0.0210)	(0.0178)
Lagged health	−0.0345***	−0.00693	−0.0365**	−0.0387*
	(0.00984)	(0.0122)	(0.0167)	(0.0150)
R^2	0.280	0.274	0.278	0.279
Observations	1,844	1,844	1,844	1,844
+country dummies				
Health change	−0.0171	−0.0144	−0.0401	−0.0385**
	(0.0102)	(0.0164)	(0.0210)	(0.0182)
Lagged health	−0.0287*	−0.0215	−0.0291	−0.0347**
	(0.0106)	(0.0138)	(0.0170)	(0.0154)
R^2	0.297	0.294	0.296	0.298
Observations	1,844	1,844	1,844	1,844

Notes: Coefficients of demographic and economic variables and country dummies not shown. Standard errors in parentheses.
***Significant at the 1 percent level.
**Significant at the 5 percent level.
*Significant at the 10 percent level.

the PVW index add explanatory power. This would be problematic from the standpoint of causal analysis. Presumably, one does not become disabled by going to the doctor, but one goes to the doctor because of a health problem that makes one disabled. Also, a doctor visit is often necessary to become classified as disabled for public disability insurance.

Noting that the doctor-diagnosed chronic health conditions and the health care utilization variables are the main components included in PVW but not in MKA, we investigate whether these are indeed the drivers of the additional explanatory power of the PVW index. We do this by estimating a fourth model, which adds wave 1 health conditions and changes in health conditions between 2004 and 2006 to the MKA-based model 3 (heart problems, high blood pressure, high cholesterol, stroke, diabetes, lung disease, asthma, arthritis, osteoporosis, cancer, ulcer, Parkinson's disease, cataracts, hip or femoral fracture, psychological problems, other), and a fifth model, which adds the health care utilization variables in 2004 and changes between 2004 and 2006 (doctor visit, hospital stay, nursing home stay, home care)

Table 3.11   Becoming disabled versus staying employed or self-employed, males

	SRH	MKA	PVW	Jue
Health only				
Health change	−0.0416***	−0.0511***	−0.0893***	−0.0529***
	(0.00767)	(0.0101)	(0.0159)	(0.0110)
Lagged health	−0.0448***	−0.0466***	−0.0756***	−0.0600***
	(0.00725)	(0.00845)	(0.0142)	(0.0119)
R^2	0.062	0.055	0.111	0.063
Observations	2,101	2,101	2,101	2,101
+demographics, economic				
Health change	−0.0395***	−0.0522***	−0.0862***	−0.0488***
	(0.00740)	(0.0103)	(0.0158)	(0.0107)
Lagged health	−0.0427***	−0.0521***	−0.0729***	−0.0584***
	(0.00710)	(0.00976)	(0.0143)	(0.0119)
R^2	0.083	0.080	0.128	0.084
Observations	2,079	2,079	2,079	2,079
+country dummies				
Health change	−0.0397***	−0.0601***	−0.0870***	−0.0492***
	(0.00736)	(0.0109)	(0.0156)	(0.0106)
Lagged health	−0.0433***	−0.0589***	−0.0731***	−0.0570***
	(0.00722)	(0.0103)	(0.0141)	(0.0118)
R^2	0.094	0.103	0.140	0.094
Observations	2,079	2,079	2,079	2,079

Notes: Coefficients of demographic and economic variables and country dummies not shown. Standard errors in parentheses.
***Significant at the 1 percent level.
**Significant at the 5 percent level.
*Significant at the 10 percent level.

to model 4. The results for all five models are given in appendix A, tables 3A.1 and 3A.2.

Most coefficients of the health conditions in the model for males becoming disabled are small and not significant, with two notable exceptions: stroke (both lagged and change; i.e., both having had one before 2004 and between 2004 and 2006, are significant and large) and psychological problems. These effects remain after inclusion of health care utilization variables. Several of the utilization variables have large and significant coefficients: lagged nursing home stay, lagged home care, and change in home care. For females, the results are slightly different: the utilization coefficients are generally not significant at the 5 percent level. However, for females, there are more health conditions that are significant, though not all with the expected sign: significant and positive (as expected) coefficients are change in stroke, lagged cancer, and change in cancer. Significant and negative are change in Parkinson's disease and lagged hip or femural fracture. Note, however, that these last two conditions are not included in PVW. The addition of the health conditions increases R^2 values

Table 3.12	Becoming disabled versus staying employed or self-employed, females			
	SRH	MKA	PVW	Jue
Health only				
Health change	−0.0322***	−0.0415***	−0.0783***	−0.0611***
	(0.00650)	(0.0106)	(0.0172)	(0.0128)
Lagged health	−0.0262***	−0.0306***	−0.0573***	−0.0428***
	(0.00690)	(0.00872)	(0.0153)	(0.0103)
R^2	0.035	0.029	0.071	0.056
Observations	1,647	1,647	1,647	1,647
+demographics, economic				
Health change	−0.0337***	−0.0461***	−0.0831***	−0.0638***
	(0.00686)	(0.0113)	(0.0178)	(0.0132)
Lagged health	−0.0279***	−0.0351***	−0.0604***	−0.0436***
	(0.00734)	(0.0103)	(0.0157)	(0.0105)
R^2	0.048	0.044	0.086	0.069
Observations	1,618	1,618	1,618	1,618
+country dummies				
Health change	−0.0354***	−0.0497***	−0.0836***	−0.0643***
	(0.00708)	(0.0119)	(0.0178)	(0.0133)
Lagged health	−0.0312***	−0.0420***	−0.0617***	−0.0451***
	(0.00828)	(0.0109)	(0.0159)	(0.0106)
R^2	0.058	0.056	0.093	0.075
Observations	1,618	1,618	1,618	1,618

Notes: Coefficients of demographic and economic variables and country dummies not shown. Standard errors in parentheses.
***Significant at the 1 percent level.
**Significant at the 5 percent level.
*Significant at the 10 percent level.

substantially. For males the R^2 increases from .115 to .205, while for females R^2 increases from .053 to .132. Adding health care utilization variables raises the R^2 further, to .281 for males and .145 for females. These values are substantially higher than the R^2 values for the other indexes in tables 3.11 and 3.12.

Summarizing, there is some evidence that the health care utilization components, and to a lesser extent some of the health conditions, give the PVW index some additional explanatory power over the MKA index in explaining transitions into disability.

3.5 Further Explorations of the Effects of Methodology and Choice of Variables

There are several dimensions along which the indexes differ. To understand the contribution of each of these dimensions to empirical differences between the indexes, we compare some variants of the indexes in which a subset of the dimensions is changed.

3.5.1 Model Structure

To investigate the effects of model structure, we have computed PCA-based indexes with the MKA variables and the Jue variables. For the MKA-PCA index, we considered two alternatives: one only using the indicators and one also including the covariates. These correlate 0.98 with each other, and thus the covariates play only a minor role in the construction of the index. The indicator-only index correlates 0.72 with the MKA index and the one that includes the covariates correlates 0.74 with the MKA index. At first sight, this seems rather low and seems to indicate an important role of methodology. Figure 3B.1 in appendix B gives more insight: the relation between the MKA index and its PCA counterpart is very strong and monotonic within each country, but highly nonlinear. It is shaped more like a logit curve. Hence, the methodological aspect that has the largest impact is the choice of using probit equations in (1) as opposed to linear equations. However, the strong monotonic relation implies that this only has the effect of nonlinearly transforming the index. PVW themselves nonlinearly transform their index to a percentile score, and in general given the arbitrariness of the health scale, one may need to consider different functional forms in any model that uses the health measures. Thus, this finding may be a reminder of this issue.

For the Jue-PCA index, we considered using only the covariates or including both self-reported health and the covariates. These two PCA indexes also correlate 0.98 with each other, and they correlate 0.93 with the probit-based Jue index. The PCA results with the Jue variables are strikingly different from the PCA results with the PVW and MKA variables: the eigenvalues of the correlation matrix of the PVW and MKA variable sets indicate that there is one dominant underlying dimension. For the PVW set, the first eigenvalue is 5.44, the second 1.46, and then it gradually decreases. For the MKA set, the first one is 9.15, then 2.50, 2.10, 1.39, and it gradually decreases. So in both cases the first one dominates, although there is some evidence that there may be a few minor underlying dimensions. The situation is very different for the Jue set: without including self-reported health, the first few eigenvalues are 2.00, 1.41, 1.37, and including self-reported health, they become 2.40, 1.41, 1.37, so the first dimension is not at all dominant. This is because the covariates used by Jürges are not highly correlated: most correlations are well below 0.10, with a few exceptions in the 0.2–0.3 range, whereas the PVW and MKA sets have many correlations in the 0.4–0.5 range. Thus, the Jue set is better suited for the type of model that he uses, in which they are covariates and the index is the one that predicts self-reported health best; whereas for the other sets, the index is what they have in common among themselves.

3.5.2 Country-Specific Reporting Behavior

MKA allow for country-specific reporting behavior in all variables except grip strength and country-specific relations between covariates and health whereas Jürges only allows for country-specific reporting behavior in self-reported health, and PVW as we have implemented it does not allow for any country-specific reporting behavior. We have computed an alternative version of the PVW index by estimating the PCA in each country separately. This results in an index that by construction has mean zero in each country, and thus is not suitable for comparing average health across countries. However, it correlates 0.99 with the earlier PVW index, and thus regression models using either should give virtually identical results, possibly with the exception of country dummies if they are included. This should not be taken as evidence that country differences are absent, but within-country health variation is much larger than between-country variation in average health. Similarly, we re-estimated the Jürges model without country-specific thresholds and constructed a corresponding index. This index correlates 0.9985 with the earlier Jue index. We have also constructed country-specific PCA indexes with the MKA and Jue variables, respectively. These correlate 0.98 with the corresponding indexes that do not allow country-specific reporting behavior. However, as figure 3B.1 in appendix B shows, the relation between the MKA index and its PCA counterpart is very strong (though nonlinear) within each country, but considerably blurred when combining the data from all countries, so this suggests that country-specific reporting behavior does matter much for the MKA index.

3.6 Discussion

As explained in section 3.2, the health measures used in this chapter are based on very different statistical models and make different assumptions about intercountry comparability. SRH and PVW (in the way we have constructed the index) assume complete comparability; Jue assumes comparability in the construction of the index, but allows for country-specific cutoff points in response scales; MKA makes the least assumptions about comparability, but uses a grip strength-related measure to scale the country and sex-specific indexes in order to attain comparability. In addition to different assumptions about comparability, the statistical models are different, which for our purposes implies different functional forms.

The most important difference, however, probably lies in the choice of variables that are included (or not) in the construction of the indexes, as summarized in table 3.1. By design, MKA includes difficulties with mobility, ADLs, and IADLs, plus self-reported health, and physical attributes like grip strength and body mass index. In the underlying MIMIC model, "causal" variables include sex, age, living with spouse or partner, household size, education, and net worth. PVW and Jue do not include these socioeconomic and demographic variables. On the other hand, Jue includes a long list of health conditions as well as grip strength and body mass index. PVW includes mobility limitations, body mass index, having at least one

ADL, a slightly more limited list of health conditions than Jue, and health care utilization variables. PVW is the only index including a pain variable. The importance of including certain variables can be seen by inspecting the model 5 regressions. For instance, in the model using MKA to explain transitions into disability of males, several of the health conditions are highly significant as are nursing home stays and home care. These variables are not included in MKA. Since PVW does include these variables, one would indeed expect PVW to have more explanatory power.

There are several potential exercises that potentially further enlighten these issues. As we have seen, MKA plus health conditions and health utilization gives a better fit than PVW, which in its turn gives a better fit than just MKA. However, the health conditions added in this exercise include some that were not included in PVW. We could additionally look at a regression in which only the ones in PVW are added to the MKA regression. Conversely, we could also run analogous regressions in which we add the additional health conditions and/or variables that are included in MKA but not in PVW to the regressions with the PVW index. Furthermore, MKA estimates a much larger set of parameters because most parameters are allowed to vary across countries, and thus MKA is much more flexible than PVW. We could investigate whether the PVW fit improves further by allowing a similar kind of flexibility in this index through adding interactions between country dummies and the variables currently in the PVW index, or at the extreme, constructing this index separately by country. Given the high correlation between the country-specific and country-independent PVW indexes, we do not expect this to affect the results materially, though.

Do our results imply that one should always include the maximum number of variables in a health index? Not necessarily. Health care utilization rates may vary by country for institutional reasons. So if the goal is to explain differences in health across countries, then one probably does not want to contaminate a health measure with institutional variables. But if one aims at explaining labor market transitions within a country, then including utilization variables may be a good idea.

A different dimension along which the measures differ is their complexity in estimation. Self-reported health is obviously the simplest of the four measures considered, but in a cross-country context its comparability is dubious, as has been argued, for instance, by Jürges (2007). The next simplest measure is PVW. Principal components analysis is available in many statistical packages and is quite standard. The health index proposed by Jürges is somewhat more complicated, as one has to parameterize the cut points in the probit analyses. MKA is the most involved, as it attempts to do full justice to the discrete nature of most of the variables and model these as the result of an underlying latent process. Although one might prefer a MIMIC-type approach as used in MKA on theoretical grounds, the empirical results in this chapter do not suggest that there is much by way of payoff in terms of improved explanatory power.

Appendix A

The Effects of Adding Health Conditions and Health Care Utilization Variables to the MKA Index

Table 3A.1   Becoming disabled versus staying employed or self-employed: MKA index for health, males

	Health only	+demogr, labor, financ	+country dummies	+health conditions	+utilization
Health change	-0.0511***	-0.0522***	-0.0601***	-0.0473***	-0.0371***
	(0.0101)	(0.0103)	(0.0109)	(0.00970)	(0.00876)
Lagged health	-0.0466***	-0.0521***	-0.0589***	-0.0402***	-0.0300***
	(0.00845)	(0.00976)	(0.0103)	(0.00886)	(0.00803)
w1 heart problems				0.0575**	0.0430
				(0.0273)	(0.0242)
Change heart problems				0.0715	0.0540
				(0.0379)	(0.0353)
w1 high blood pressure				-0.0157	-0.0175
				(0.0103)	(0.00996)
Change high blood pressure				-0.00464	-0.00771
				(0.0116)	(0.0118)
w1 high cholesterol				0.00922	0.0108
				(0.0123)	(0.0118)
Change high cholesterol				0.0108	0.0112
				(0.0106)	(0.0104)
w1 stroke				0.327*	0.299**
				(0.123)	(0.121)
Change stroke				0.301**	0.289**
				(0.139)	(0.137)
w1 diabetes				0.00653	0.00422
				(0.0249)	(0.0246)
Change diabetes				0.00935	0.00610
				(0.0251)	(0.0210)
w1 chronic lung disease				-0.00284	0.00346
				(0.0372)	(0.0346)
Change chronic lung disease				0.0172	0.0281
				(0.0504)	(0.0492)
w1 asthma				-0.0250	-0.0261
				(0.0188)	(0.0167)
Change asthma				-0.0603	-0.0634**
				(0.0316)	(0.0310)
w1 arthritis				-0.000798	-0.00535
				(0.0214)	(0.0189)
Change arthritis				-0.0123	-0.00821
				(0.0193)	(0.0176)
w1 osteoporosis				0.129	0.102
				(0.104)	(0.0870)
Change osteoporosis				0.00801	0.0199
				(0.0907)	(0.0811)

(continued)

Table 3A.1 (continued)

	Health only	+demogr, labor, financ	+country dummies	+health conditions	+utilization
w1 cancer				0.0736	0.0498
				(0.0443)	(0.0453)
Change cancer				0.0567	0.0312
				(0.0643)	(0.0616)
w1 ulcer				0.0168	0.00670
				(0.0322)	(0.0267)
Change ulcer				0.0253	0.0193
				(0.0410)	(0.0344)
w1 Parkinson's disease				−0.0256	−0.0126
				(0.0264)	(0.0261)
Change Parkinson's disease				0	0
				(.)	(.)
w1 cataracts				0.00870	−0.00662
				(0.0492)	(0.0464)
Change cataracts				−0.0558	−0.0546
				(0.0593)	(0.0580)
w1 hip or femoral fracture				0.161	0.140
				(0.166)	(0.169)
Change hip or femoral fracture				0.170	0.135
				(0.146)	(0.150)
w1 other conditions				0.0440**	0.0295
				(0.0205)	(0.0187)
Change other conditions				0.0190	0.00639
				(0.0157)	(0.0146)
w1 psychological problems				0.157*	0.157*
				(0.0581)	(0.0565)
Change psychological problems				0.143*	0.142*
				(0.0538)	(0.0522)
w1 doctor visit					−0.00551
					(0.00740)
Change doctor visit					−0.00851
					(0.00570)
w1 hospital stay					0.0643**
					(0.0271)
Change hospital stay					0.0354
					(0.0218)
w1 nursing home stay					0.899***
					(0.0726)
Change nursing home stay					−0.00219
					(0.0180)
w1 home care					0.335***
					(0.0904)
Change home care					0.283***
					(0.0753)
R^2	0.055	0.080	0.103	0.192	0.272
Observations	2101	2079	2079	2079	2079

Notes: Coefficients of demographic and economic variables and country dummies not shown. Standard errors in parentheses.

***Significant at the 1 percent level.

**Significant at the 5 percent level.

*Significant at the 10 percent level.

Table 3A.2: Becoming disabled versus staying employed or self-employed: MKA index for health, females

	Health only	+demogr, labor, financ	+country dummies	+health conditions	+utilization
Health change	−0.0415***	−0.0461***	−0.0497***	−0.0367*	−0.0355*
	(0.0106)	(0.0113)	(0.0119)	(0.0115)	(0.0113)
Lagged health	−0.0306***	−0.0351***	−0.0420***	−0.0293**	−0.0278**
	(0.00872)	(0.0103)	(0.0109)	(0.0119)	(0.0116)
w1 heart problems				0.0715	0.0663
				(0.0462)	(0.0445)
Change heart problems				0.0189	0.0132
				(0.0435)	(0.0441)
w1 high blood pressure				−0.00999	−0.00869
				(0.00982)	(0.0101)
Change high blood pressure				−0.00308	−0.00189
				(0.0135)	(0.0134)
w1 high cholesterol				−0.00777	−0.00518
				(0.0123)	(0.0122)
Change high cholesterol				−0.00459	−0.00415
				(0.0107)	(0.0107)
w1 stroke				0.224**	0.225**
				(0.112)	(0.113)
Change stroke				0.257**	0.256**
				(0.120)	(0.119)
w1 diabetes				0.00308	−0.000670
				(0.0164)	(0.0175)
Change diabetes				0.0614	0.0570
				(0.0518)	(0.0519)
w1 chronic lung disease				−0.0348	−0.0350
				(0.0279)	(0.0294)
Change chronic lung disease				0.0127	0.0108
				(0.0432)	(0.0433)
w1 asthma				0.0113	0.0117
				(0.0288)	(0.0292)
Change asthma				0.0397	0.0385
				(0.0348)	(0.0348)
w1 arthritis				0.0125	0.0138
				(0.0163)	(0.0166)
Change arthritis				0.00861	0.00890
				(0.0150)	(0.0149)
w1 osteoporosis				−0.0168	−0.0110
				(0.0229)	(0.0227)
Change osteoporosis				−0.00959	−0.00650
				(0.0250)	(0.0250)
w1 cancer				0.140**	0.125**
				(0.0577)	(0.0553)
Change cancer				0.177*	0.160*
				(0.0594)	(0.0577)
w1 ulcer				0.00521	0.00609
				(0.0332)	(0.0329)
Change ulcer				0.0292	0.0274
				(0.0284)	(0.0273)
w1 Parkinson's disease				0	0
				(.)	(.)

(continued)

Table 3A.2:   (continued)

	Health only	+demogr, labor, financ	+country dummies	+health conditions	+utilization
Change Parkinson's disease				−0.347* (0.128)	−0.332* (0.126)
w1 cataracts				−0.00342 (0.0202)	−0.00796 (0.0184)
Change cataracts				0.0531 (0.0493)	0.0489 (0.0447)
w1 hip or femoral fracture				−0.0850* (0.0295)	−0.109* (0.0384)
Change hip or femoral fracture				−0.0161 (0.0282)	−0.0206 (0.0323)
w1 other conditions				0.00666 (0.0159)	0.00491 (0.0157)
Change other conditions				0.0142 (0.0139)	0.0138 (0.0137)
w1 psychological problems				0.0360 (0.0199)	0.0331 (0.0200)
Change psychological problems				0.0272 (0.0237)	0.0225 (0.0237)
w1 doctor visit					−0.01000 (0.00991)
Change doctor visit					−0.00315 (0.00695)
w1 hospital stay					0.0161 (0.0328)
Change hospital stay					0.0131 (0.0247)
w1 nursing home stay					−0.152 (0.0878)
Change nursing home stay					−0.0628 (0.0418)
w1 home care					0.112 (0.0627)
Change home care					0.108 (0.0567)
Constant					
R^2	0.029	0.044	0.056	0.136	0.148
Observations	1647	1618	1618	1618	1618

Notes: Coefficients of demographic and economic variables and country dummies not shown. Standard errors in parentheses.

***Significant at the 1 percent level.

**Significant at the 5 percent level.

*Significant at the 10 percent level.

Appendix B

Relation of the MKA-PCA Index to the MKA-MIMIC Index by Country and Overall

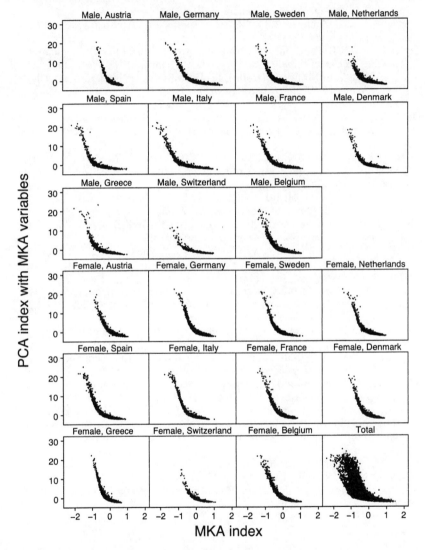

Fig. 3B.1   Relation between the MKA index and the PCA index based on MKA variables

References

Börsch-Supan, A., D. L. McFadden, and R. Schnabel. 1996. "Living Arrangements: Health and Wealth Effects." In *Advances in the Economics of Aging*, edited by D. A. Wise, 193–218. Chicago: University of Chicago Press.

Bound, J. 1991. "Self-Reported Versus Objective Measures of Health in Retirement Models." *Journal of Human Resources* 26:106–38.

Coe, N. B., and G. Zamarro. 2011. "Retirement Effects on Health in Europe." *Journal of Health Economics* 30:77–86.

Cutler, D., and E. Richardson. 1997. "Measuring the Health of the U.S. Population." *Brookings Papers on Economic Activity: Microeconomics* 1997:217–82.

———. 1999. "Your Money and Your Life: The Value of Health and What Affects It." In *Frontiers in Health Policy Research*, vol. 2, edited by A. Garber, 99–132. Cambridge, MA: MIT Press.

Datta Gupta, N., N. Kristensen, and D. Pozzoli. 2010. "External Validation of the Use of Vignettes in Cross-Country Health Studies." *Economic Modelling* 27 (4): 854–6.

Jöreskog, K. G., and A. S. Goldberger. 1975. "Estimation of a Model with Multiple Indicators and Multiple Causes of a Single Latent Variable." *Journal of the American Statistical Association* 70:631–9.

Jürges, H. 2007. "True Health vs Response Styles: Exploring Cross-Country Differences in Self-Reported Health." *Health Economics* 16:163–78.

Jürges, H., and A. van Soest, eds. 2012. "Comparing the Well-Being of Older Europeans." Special Issue of *Social Indicators Research* 105.

Kapteyn, A., J. P. Smith, and A. van Soest. 2007. "Vignettes and Self-Reports of Work Disability in the US and the Netherlands." *American Economic Review* 97(1): 461–73.

———. 2011. "Work Disability, Work, and Justification Bias in Europe and the U.S." In *Explorations in the Economics of Aging*, edited by D. A. Wise, 269–314. Chicago: University of Chicago Press.

Lindeboom, M., and E. van Doorslaer. 2004. "Cut-Point Shift and Index Shift in Self-Reported Health." *Journal of Health Economics* 23:1083–99.

Maestas, N. 2010. "Expectations and Realizations of Work after Retirement." *Journal of Human Resources* 45:718–48.

Meijer, E., A. Kapteyn, and T. Andreyeva. 2011. "Internationally Comparable Health Indices." *Health Economics* 20:600–19.

Poterba, J. M., S. F. Venti, and D. A. Wise. 2011. "Family Status Transitions, Latent Health, and the Post-Retirement Evolution of Assets." In *Explorations in the Economics of Aging*, edited by D. A. Wise, 23–69. Chicago: University of Chicago Press.

———. 2013. "Health, Education, and the Post-Retirement Evolution of Household Assets." NBER Working Paper no. 18695, Cambridge, MA.

Wansbeek, T., and E. Meijer. 2000. *Measurement Error and Latent Variables in Econometrics*. Amsterdam: North-Holland.

Comment   Steven F. Venti

The recent emergence of cross-national surveys based on a common research design has stimulated research on a number of important topics. Users of these data can take advantage of cross-national variation in public pension, health care, and disability programs to answer questions that were previously difficult to address using data from a single country. In many areas of comparative international research, health plays a key role. Because health is multidimensional it is often useful for researchers to summarize health in a single index that can be used to "explain" differences in nonhealth outcomes. A single index summarizing health is also valuable in its own right as a measure of what is happening to the health of the population. Kapteyn and Meijer (KM hereafter) have taken on the challenge of how to best summarize health in a single index using cross-national data. Their starting point is to compare the properties and performance of three indexes of health that have been proposed in the literature. Although they stop short of endorsing a particular index, their analysis provides a great deal of information about how to construct an improved index.

There are three issues that complicate the construction of a health index that can be used in cross-national comparisons. The first is the choice of a statistical model to summarize information on a variety of health measures (survey responses to questions about health difficulties and conditions) into a single index. The three statistical methodologies considered by the authors appear, at least superficially, to be quite different: a MIMIC model proposed by Meijer, Kapteyn, and Andreyeva (2011; MKA hereafter), an index based on self-reported health status (SRHS) adjusted for country effects proposed by Jürges (2007), and a principal components approach used by Poterba, Venti, and Wise (2013; PVW hereafter).

The second issue is the choice of which of many available health measures to include in the construction of an index. The original MKA and Jürges models use different subsets of the health measures available in SHARE for eleven European countries. The PVW model uses still another different subset of health measures available in the HRS for the United States. In both surveys there are a wide variety of health-related measures to choose from. Perhaps the most frequently used measure is self-reported health status (SRHS), a simple five-point scale describing the range of health from poor to excellent. As has been widely noted, country differences in SRHS reflect not just unobserved true health, but also systematic country reporting effects unrelated to true health. This shortcoming limits the usefulness of SRHS

Steven F. Venti is the DeWalt H. Ankeny '21 and Marie Ankeny Professor of Economic Policy and professor of economics at Dartmouth College and a research associate of the National Bureau of Economic Research.

For acknowledgments, sources of research support, and disclosure of the author's material financial relationships, if any, please see http://www.nber.org/chapters/c12973.ack.

Table 3C.1   Number of health measures used to construct each index

Health measure	MKA	PVW	Jürges
SRHS	1	2	no
ADL/IADL	15	1	no
Functional limitations	9	9	no
Health conditions	no	8	16
Utilization	no	4	no
Back pain	no	1	no
Grip strength	yes	no	yes
BMI	yes	yes	yes

in comparative analyses. As an alternative, a number of recent studies have developed indexes based on other, presumably more objective, health measures that are less susceptible to reporting bias. These include self-reported ADLs (e.g., difficulty bathing) and IADLs (e.g., difficulty shopping), self-reported functional limitations (e.g., difficulty climbing stairs), the prevalence of health conditions (e.g., has a doctor ever told you that you have diabetes?), or indicators of health utilization (e.g., number of doctor visits). These measures, though arguably more objective than SRHS, are still not immune to country-specific reporting bias. There are still other health measures such as mortality or grip strength for which systematic reporting errors are even less likely to be an issue. Table 3C.1 shows the health measures used to construct each of the three indexes KM analyze. There is some overlap, but the core subset of health measures used in each study is quite different.

The third issue that complicates the construction of a health index is how to account for country-specific reporting bias. As noted, cross-national variation in respondent-reported health measures may arise from two sources: differences in genuine health and systematic differences in the way residents of each country answer questions. Respondents asked to judge whether a task is "difficult" may apply different thresholds in different countries. Moreover, "difficult" may have different connotations when translated into different languages. The key is to distinguish genuine health effects from reporting bias. The most widely used way to do this is to assume that some health measures are "objective" and thus not affected by systematic reporting differences among countries. Given this assumption, one can interpret cross-national variation not explained by objective measures as reporting bias. The analysis by Jürges recognizes that SRHS is subjective, but implicitly assumes that the set of health measures used to predict SRHS are objective. Chief among these predictors are respondent reports of health conditions based on questions such as: "Has a doctor ever told you that you have high blood pressure?" If countries differ in access to health care or have different diagnostic thresholds for high blood pressure, then responses may systematically differ across countries or, to put it another way, persons in different countries with the same true blood pressure will provide different answers to the question. The MKA analysis assumes most health measures, other than grip strength, may not be objective. They use grip strength (adjusted for height and weight) as a benchmark to assess reporting bias in other health measures. The problem with this approach is that grip strength reflects only one dimension of genuine health. If mortality, walking speed, biomarkers, or some other (assumed) objective measure is used to identify reporting bias, then the results might be quite different. The third methodology (PVW) simply does not account for reporting bias.

I have no way of judging if one set of assumptions about the objectivity of particular measures of health is superior to another. However, one way to gauge the extent of the general problem is to use all three methodologies—each with a different adjustment for reporting bias—to produce health indexes and see if there are differences in these indexes. Similarity of the three indexes would suggest that reporting bias is not a major problem. KM reestimate the three indexes using the SHARE data, but preserving differences in the choice of variables made in the original studies. Summary measures indicate that the health indexes based on the three approaches are broadly similar. All display the expected downward sloping age profile and the distributions have similar shapes. However, the correlations between the indexes are between 0.54 and 0.86 and the figures show some variation in standardized health by country. That all three methods of accounting for reporting bias do not produce the same level of health in each country may indicate that reporting bias is an issue. However, the country differences may also be the consequence of using very different sets of health measures in the three models as well as differences in genuine health.

The KM implementation of the PVW model combines all countries in a single principal components model. This implementation assumes cross-country comparability. The assumption can be relaxed by estimating separate principal component models for each of the eleven SHARE countries to determine if the factor loadings are similar across countries. I obtain these estimates using a list of twenty-five health measures that is close, but not an exact match, to the list used by KM in their pooled version of the PVW model. If health measures have large reporting bias components, I would expect the factor loadings to vary among countries. In table3C.2 I show the correlations between the factor loadings on each health measure for each pair of countries. All entries in the table exceed 0.9 and most exceed 0.95 indicating that the relationship between each health measure and the overall index (the first principal component) is similar across countries. This suggests that country-specific response bias is probably not a major concern, at least for this subset of health measures.

KM evaluate the performance of the three models by including the lagged index and the change in the index as explanatory variables in simple linear models of the transition into retirement or disability. They find that none

Table 3C.2   Cross-country correlations for loadings on twenty-five health measures

	Austria	Germany	Sweden	Netherlands	Spain	Italy	France	Denmark	Greece	Switzerland	Belgium
Austria	1	0.984	0.967	0.945	0.956	0.961	0.963	0.942	0.938	0.949	0.948
Germany		1	0.973	0.945	0.969	0.975	0.964	0.948	0.966	0.975	0.956
Sweden			1	0.973	0.965	0.953	0.967	0.976	0.938	0.947	0.961
Netherlands				1	0.945	0.912	0.963	0.976	0.905	0.939	0.963
Spain					1	0.974	0.963	0.959	0.972	0.965	0.959
Italy						1	0.965	0.939	0.974	0.944	0.957
France							1	0.962	0.940	0.941	0.985
Denmark								1	0.923	0.940	0.968
Greece									1	0.960	0.939
Switzerland										1	0.945
Belgium											1

of the indexes have a statistically significant effect on retirement if demographic, economic, and country effects are included in the model. Although these estimates provide no information about the relative power of the three indexes, I did find it surprising that health is unrelated to retirement. I estimated a similar regression (not reported) employing the PVW index, using similar (but not exact) controls for the United States using HRS data for 2004 and 2006. The resulting estimates were statistically significant and larger in magnitude than those reported for European countries in tables 3.9 and 3.10 of KM. The source of the apparent difference between the European and United States' results is worthy of further analysis.

The authors next evaluate the performance of the three health indexes in a model of the transition to disability. All three indexes are statistically significant in all versions of the model (with and without covariates) and the R^2s are considerably higher than in the retirement models. Interestingly, the PVW index has greater explanatory power than the other indexes. Is this outcome the result of the statistical model or the choice of health measures used to construct the index? Noting that the PVW model includes measures of health conditions and health utilization, but the MKA model does not, the authors reestimate the disability equation supplementing the MKA index with health conditions and utilization variables. They find both sets of variables provide considerable explanatory power, although many of the individual estimates of health conditions are not statistically significant, especially for males.

These results suggest that disparities in performance between the three health indexes have more to do with the list of health measures used to construct the index rather than on the statistical model used. The utilization of health services and, to a lesser extent, the prevalence of health conditions help to explain the transition to disability. Presumably these measures contain information about genuine health that is not contained in other measures such as ADLs, IADLs, or functional limitations. So why not use them to construct an index regardless of which statistical model is used? The authors suggest that using these variables would be problematic for causal analysis. They argue: "Presumably, one does not become disabled by going to the doctor, but one goes to the doctor because of a health problem that makes one disabled." Their concern is justified, but going to the doctor may still be a useful, though imperfect, indicator of underlying health, particularly when used in a statistical model designed to extract the common factor (genuine health) from a large number of noisy health measures. A related concern raised by the authors is that utilization variables such as doctor visits or hospital stays confound institutional differences—in health care systems, in diagnostic standards, and so forth—with differences in genuine health. But genuine health and all of its other proxies, including ADLs, IADLs, diagnoses, grip strength, and even mortality, are to one degree or another, also "contaminated" by institutions. I thus find it difficult to draw the line between those health measures that are too closely related to institutions and those that are not. Their line of demarcation is that it may be problematic to use an index based in part on utilization variables to explain differences in health across countries, but using the index to explain retirement transitions is probably acceptable. I would argue for wider use of utilization variables because differences in institutions tell us something about genuine health differences.

In sum, my reading of the results is that country-specific response bias—known to be a serious problem if SRHS is used to measure health status—is probably less an issue for health measures such as ADLs, IADLs, and health conditions. Second, the choice of statistical model is relatively unimportant. Although there is more work to be done in this area, I suspect that the three models will perform similarly if they are based on the same set of health measures. The choice of a statistical model will then depend on other criteria. The PVW and Jürges models have the advantage of being easy to compute. However the MKA model explicitly yields estimates of reporting bias for each of the health measures (given the assumption that grip strength is reported without error). A third finding is that the estimated health index is sensitive to the choice of health measures used to construct the index. As far as what variables should be included, it is clear that there is no "one size fits all" solution. Despite some legitimate concerns raised by the authors, my reading of their results is that measures of health utilization and the prevalence of health conditions provide valuable information about genuine health and, for most purposes, should be included in the health index.

The recent availability of cross-national surveys such as the HRS, ELSA, and SHARE have allowed analysts to exploit new sources of variation in trying to address key issues in the areas of retirement, public pensions, disability, and well-being (among others). But the benefits of cross-national data are not without some difficult challenges, one of which is how to process the health content in these surveys. This chapter makes an important contribution to our understanding of how to construct a health index that concisely summarizes the data and is comparable across countries.

References

Jürges H. 2007. "True Health vs Response Styles: Exploring Cross-Country Differences in Self-Reported Health." *Health Economics* 16:163–78.

Meijer, E., A. Kapteyn, and T. Andreyeva. 2011. "Internationally Comparable Health Indices." *Health Economics* 20:600–19.

Poterba, J. M., S. F. Venti, and D. A. Wise. 2013. "Health, Education, and the Post-Retirement Evolution of Household Assets." NBER Working Paper no. 18695, Cambridge, MA.

II

Health and Financial Well-Being

4

The Nexus of Social Security Benefits, Health, and Wealth at Death

James M. Poterba, Steven F. Venti, and David A. Wise

The three-legged stool representing employer-provided pensions, private saving, and Social Security benefits is commonly used to describe support in retirement. However, a large fraction of retirees balance on only one leg, Social Security, and those balancing on this single leg are also in the poorest health. Poterba, Venti, and Wise (hereafter PVW) (2012) find that 40 percent of all persons approach their last year of life with less than $20,000 in annuity income and less than $10,000 in financial assets. Individuals in this group rely primarily on Social Security; for some, this income is supplemented by defined benefit pension benefits. Sixty-eight percent of those in this group also have no housing wealth, and they are also on average in much poorer health than persons with higher levels of income and liquid assets. This

James M. Poterba is the Mitsui Professor of Economics at the Massachusetts Institute of Technology and president and chief executive officer of the National Bureau of Economic Research. Steven F. Venti is the DeWalt Ankeny Professor of Economic Policy and professor of economics at Dartmouth College and a research associate of the National Bureau of Economic Research. David A. Wise is the John F. Stambaugh Professor of Political Economy at the Kennedy School of Government at Harvard University. He is the area director of Health and Retirement Programs and director of the Program on the Economics of Aging at the National Bureau of Economic Research.

This research was supported by the US Social Security Administration through grant #5 RRC08098100-04-00 to the National Bureau of Economic Research as part of the SSA Retirement Research Consortium. Funding was also provided through grant number P01 AG005842 from the National Institute on Aging. Poterba is a trustee of the College Retirement Equity Fund (CREF), a provider of retirement income services. We are very grateful to Jon Skinner for very helpful comments. The findings and conclusions expressed are solely those of the authors and do not represent the views of the SSA, any agency of the federal government, the TIAA-CREF, or the NBER. For acknowledgments, sources of research support, and disclosure of the authors' material financial relationships, if any, please see http://www.nber.org/chapters/c12964.ack.

raises the concern that adverse health events in old age may lead individuals to exhaust their assets.

We estimate how the drawdown of nonannuity wealth in the years preceding death is related to the receipt of Social Security benefits, defined pension benefits, and the level and change in health in the last years of life. In particular, we want to know whether Social Security income is protective of nonannuity assets. Are persons with more Social Security income able to cover health and other expenses with less need to drawdown savings? Our analysis is based on the drawdown of the nonannuity assets of persons in the Asset and Health Dynamics Among the Oldest Old (AHEAD) cohort of the Health and Retirement Study (HRS). We observe these persons from 1995 until their deaths. A large proportion of this cohort died between 1995 and the latest available survey wave in 2010.

The analysis of the postretirement evolution of nonannuity wealth also helps to fill a gap in what we know about income that older Americans draw from accumulated assets. Using the three-legged stool metaphor again, households may draw support in retirement from Social Security benefits, employer-provided pensions, income from accumulated assets, and by drawing down their asset holdings. Income from Social Security benefits and annuity income from the second leg—principally defined benefit (DB) pensions—are accurately measured in surveys such as the HRS. Some income flows from assets, such as interest and dividends, are well measured, but the accruing value of capital gains is likely to be measured with substantial error. Moreover, it is often difficult to measure the drawdown of assets that households use to supplement their other sources of support. This includes withdrawals from tax-deferred personal retirement accounts (PRAs) such as IRAs and 401(k)s, which are becoming increasingly important for recent retirees. Fisher (2007) and Anguelov, Iams, and Purcell (2012) provide summary information on these withdrawals. Households may draw on these asset reserves to bridge the gap whenever expenditures—particularly unanticipated expenditures—exceed annuity income.

In this chapter, we examine how the rate of asset spend-down is related to health and on the presence of other sources of income. By considering income from Social Security and DB pensions jointly with changes in asset stocks, we hope to develop a more complete picture of the financial resources available to the elderly. We are also interested in the association between health status and these other variables.

The analysis is based on wave-to-wave changes in the assets of AHEAD households. For persons with the same level of assets in a particular wave, we ask how the level of assets in the next wave depends on the initial level of health, the change in health between the waves, and the receipt of annuity income. We estimate how the level of assets in each wave is related to annuity income and health, given the level of assets in the prior wave. The links between health events and asset drawdown have been explored in a number of earlier studies. Smith(1999, 2004, 2005) and Coile and Milligan (2009) are notable contributions. In PVW (2010), we estimated the total cost of poor health by examining the association between poor health and the rate of change of wealth in retirement. In this chapter, we examine how annuitized income streams from Social Secuirty and DB pensions affect this association.

The chapter is divided into four sections. Section 4.1 describes the data that underlies the empirical analysis and explains briefly the health index that is a key component of the analysis. Section 4.2 presents descriptive data on the trajectory of assets during the retirement years. Section 4.3 reports our empirical results. Section 4.4 concludes and suggests several directions for further work.

4.1 The Data and Health Index

4.1.1 The AHEAD Survey

The analysis is based on data from the Asset and Health Dynamics Among the Oldest Old (AHEAD) survey of households that contained a person age seventy or older in 1993. These households were resurveyed again in 1995 and in every other year beginning in 1998 through 2010. In 1995 the AHEAD sample became one of several cohorts in the Health and Retirement Study (HRS). The AHEAD collects detailed information on household structure, sources of income, and assets. Because these households were at an advanced age when first surveyed in 1993, a large number of original respondents had died by 2010. This analysis focuses primarily on assets and income in the last survey wave prior to the wave in which a respondent is known to be deceased. We refer to this wave as the "last year observed" (LYO). Given the two-year spacing of waves (after 1998) in the AHEAD, the LYO will be within two years of the date of death. Persons who leave the sample, but are not known to have died, are excluded from the analysis.

The AHEAD respondents were first interviewed in 1993. However the data for 1993 are excluded from this analysis for two reasons. First, as Rohwedder, Haider, and Hurd (2006) explain, financial assets were underreported in 1993. Second, several of the key variables that we use to construct a health index were not included in the 1993 survey instrument. Our analysis therefore uses data for 1995, 1998, 2000, 2002, 2004, 2006, 2008, and 2010. All asset and income amounts are converted to 2010 dollars using the CPI-U (Consumer Price Index-Urban).

The unit of observation is the person. All income and asset amounts associated with the person are for the household. To structure the analysis we will first divide the AHEAD respondents into three groups defined by family status when first observed in 1993 and family status in the last year observed before death. These family "pathway" groups are: (a) persons in one-person households in 1993 that remain one-person households until last observed, (b) persons in two-person households in 1993 whose spouse is deceased in the last year observed before the person's death, and (c) persons in two-person households in 1993 whose spouse is alive when the person is last observed.[1] We often refer to the second group as "two-to-one" households (the number of persons in the household in 1995 and the number in the LYO) and to the third group as "two-to-two" households. Most analyses are performed separately for each of these family "pathway" groups.

4.1.2 The Health Index

We use an index of health based on the first principal component of responses to twenty-seven health-related questions contained in the AHEAD. These questions asked about functional limitations, the presence of health conditions, and other indicators of overall health. The list of questions used to construct the index and a discussion of the general properties of earlier versions of the index are reported in PVW (2010, forthcoming). The index used here is based on all respondents in all cohorts in the HRS between 1992 and 2010 with the exception of the 1993 AHEAD cohort. Initial analysis revealed that principal component loadings were stable over time and similar for men and women, so we have pooled waves and combined men and women. For each respondent a raw health score is obtained from the principal component loadings and the raw scores have been converted to percentiles (1 to 100). Thus a value of the health index of 25 implies that a person's health is at the 25th percentile of all HRS respondents in all years. The index has several important properties, which are summarized in more detail in PVW (forthcoming): (a) it is strongly related to the drawdown of assets as shown in our previous work, (b) it is stable over time—the weights given to each of the health variables vary very little as persons age, (c) it is strongly related to mortality, (d) it is strongly predictive of future health events such as stroke and the onset of diabetes, and (e) it is strongly related to economic outcomes *prior* to retirement as well as to postretirement outcomes. Figure 4.1 shows the 10th, 50th, and 90th percentiles of health by age. In reporting the results, we often refer to the effect of a 10 percentile point change in health. We can see in figure 4.1 that 10 percentile points covers a much greater portion of the total range in health for the oldest persons. For example, the difference between the health index value for the individual in the 10th percentile of all seventy-two-year-olds, and the value of that index for the individual in the 90th percentile at age seventy-two, is about 73 percentile points. The comparable difference is about 49 percentile points at age ninety.

4.2 Descriptive Findings

To motivate our descriptive analysis of wealth trajectories, health, and income flows, figure 4.2 illustrates the potential pathways through which poor health can affect wealth at older ages. The schematic suggests two potential

1. A fourth group, persons in one-person households in 1993 who later married, is excluded from the analysis because sample sizes are too small for meaningful analysis.

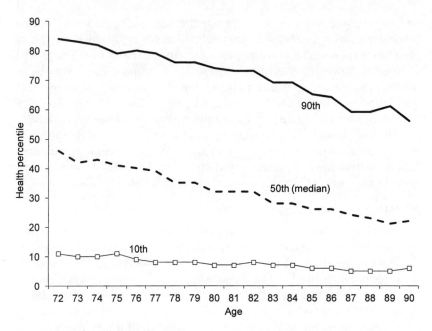

Fig. 4.1   The 10th, 50th, and 90th quantiles of the health index by age for all persons in AHEAD cohort, 1995–2010

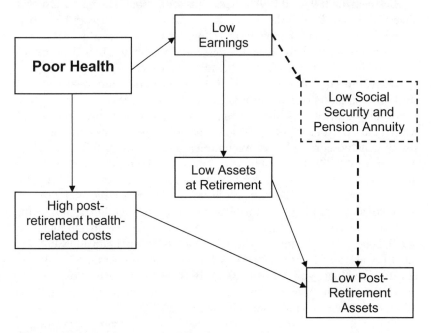

Fig. 4.2   Pathways from poor health to low postretirement assets

pathways between poor health and postretirement asset drawdown, keeping in mind the correlation between pre- and postretirement health status. First, poor health is associated with high postretirement medical costs, which may be financed by drawing on assets after retirement. Second, poor health contributes to low earnings prior to retirement. In turn low earnings reduce postretirement assets in two ways—(a) low preretirement earnings limit the accumulation of retirement assets, which in turn contributes to low asset levels at retirement; and (b) low preretirement earnings reduce the level of Social Security and private pension annuities paid after retirement. We are particularly interested in how the drawdown of nonannuity assets and the level of nonannuity assets at death are related to health status and to Social Security benefits.

4.2.1 Trends in Wealth from 1993 to the Last Year Observed

Several figures and tables help to motivate the analysis. Figure 4.3 shows the evolution of nonannuity wealth (primarily housing and other real estate, financial assets, and PRA balances) by last year observed (LYO) for each of the three family pathways. The last point plotted in each segment identifies the last year observed. Persons for whom the last year observed is 2006 or earlier died between the 2006 and 2008 waves; if the last year observed is 2010 (the "top" segment in each family pathway group) then the person is still alive in 2010, which is the last year data are available. Most waves in the AHEAD are spaced two years apart, with the exception of a three-year gap between the 1995 and 1998 waves. Thus for persons who have a last year observed before 2010, the last observation may be up to two years before the actual date of death (or three years if the last year observed is 1995). The estimation procedure discussed later essentially estimates how these trends for individuals are related to health and annuity income.

Two features of figure 4.3 stand out. First the nonannuity wealth of persons in the single-person pathway is much lower than the comparable wealth of persons in the two-to-one person pathway, who in turn have much lower wealth than persons in the two-to-two person pathway. Second, there is a strong negative correlation between nonannuity wealth in 1993 and subsequent mortality. Within each pathway, persons who began the period with higher wealth live longer. In each pathway group, the nonannuity wealth of persons who survive the longest is at least twice as large as the wealth of persons with the highest mortality. This is a startling illustration of the relationship between wealth and mortality noted by others, including Smith (1999, 2004, 2005), Adams et al. (2003), Wu (2003), Michaud and van Soest (2008), Case and Deaton (2005), Attanasio and Emmerson (2003), and Hurd, McFadden, and Merrill (2001). Both of these features of the data are also evident in profiles constructed for total wealth and for each of the other asset categories reported in PVW (2012).

Figure 4.4 shows median Social Security income by family pathway. The figure shows that for persons in one-person and two-to-two person house-

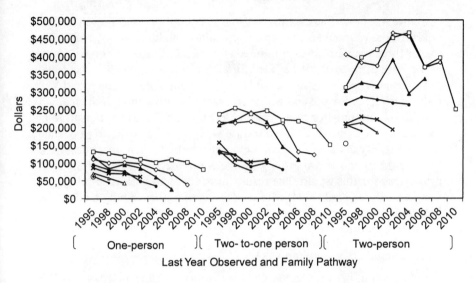

Fig. 4.3   Median nonannuity wealth by last year observed and family pathway

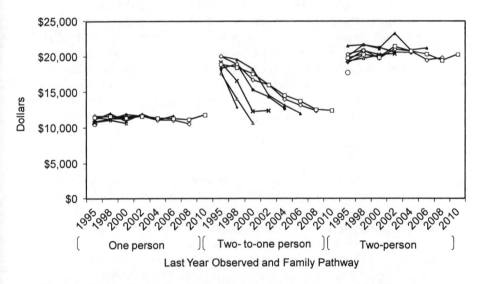

Fig. 4.4   Median Social Security income by last year observed and family pathway

holds there is little difference in Social Security income as persons age. But for the persons who transition from two- to one-person households, meaning that they outlived their spouses, there is a substantial decline in Social Security income with age. This presumably reflects the shift in many cases from two beneficiaries to one beneficiary.

Figure 4.5 shows the evolution of home equity. For one-person households the data show a very sharp decline in median home equity beginning two or three years before death. Indeed for each LYO, median home equity in the wave prior to death was zero for all but those whose LYO was 1993. For original two-person households with the spouse deceased at the LYO, a sharp decline near the end of life is also apparent, although the median at death is zero only for those whose LYO was 2002 or 2004. For original two-person households with the spouse alive at the LYO, there is a decline in home equity in the year or two before death, but it is more modest than that for the previous two groups. Home equity declines relatively little in prior years for this group. The results are consistent with the findings of Venti and Wise (2002, 2004) who emphasize that home equity tends to be husbanded until a precipitating shock such as entry to a nursing home or death of a spouse.

4.2.2 Nonannuity Assets and LYO

Figure 4.6 shows the median of home equity and financial assets (PRA assets and financial assets held outside of tax-deferred accounts) in 1995 by LYO and by pathway. The key feature of the figures is that persons with the greatest total nonannuity assets in1995 tend to live the longest, especially persons in one-to-one and in two-to-two households. The median for a third component—"other" nonannuity assets (mostly business assets, trusts, and vehicles)—is zero for each LYO for all pathways. The means of total nonannuity assets in 1995 (not shown) are not as strongly related to longevity and the mean of the "other" component is positive for all LYO and for each of the pathways.

4.2.3 The Distribution of the Change in Nonannuity
Wealth between 1995 and the LYO

Figure 4.3 shows the median decline in nonannuity assets by family pathway. The median does not capture, however, the substantial diversity in the decline that our analysis relies on. Table 4.1 shows the distribution of nonannuity asset change between 1995 and the LYO (the beginning and end points for each profile shown in figure 4.3), showing selected percentile changes—10, 30, 50, 70, and 90. For original singles, the median change is negative in all LYO. But for each LYO, the difference between the 30th and the 70th percentiles and especially between the 10th and the 90th percentiles is quite large. The difference between the 10th and 90th percentiles in particular may be affected substantially by the misreporting of asset balances discussed in detail in Venti (2011).

Figure 4.3 shows that the median decline in assets is largest for persons who were originally married but were predeceased by their spouse. The values for this group are shown in the second panel of table 4.1. The large decline for many persons in this pathway, as well as the wide range in the changes, is again especially evident in the 10th and 30th and the 70th and

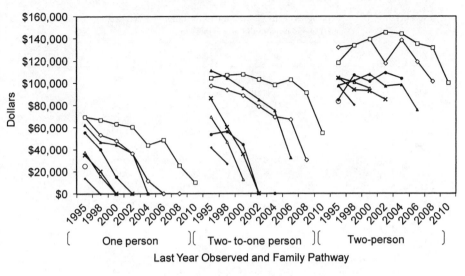

Fig. 4.5 **Median housing wealth by last year observed and family pathway**

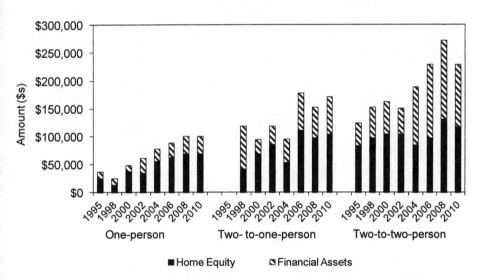

Fig. 4.6 **Median home equity and financial assets in 1995 by family pathway and last year observed**

90th percentiles. The bottom panel shows the median decline in assets for persons who were originally married and whose spouse was alive when they died. The median change is zero for the 2000 LYO and positive for the 2002 LYO. For other LYOs the medians are negative, but smaller than for the pathway shown in the middle panel.

Table 4.1   Percentiles of the distribution of the difference between nonannuity assets in LYO and nonannuity assets in 1995

LYO	10th	30th	50th	70th	90th
	Original singles				
1995	0	0	0	0	0
1998	−125,105	−21,102	−104	8,207	115,827
2000	−174,315	−40,782	−1,742	6,163	95,594
2002	−181,707	−41,702	−2,441	11,094	145,006
2004	−214,131	−57,687	−6,451	2,367	174,090
2006	−250,210	−83,403	−19,746	385	315,855
2008	−277,117	−69,503	−19,697	2,026	85,532
2010	−273,381	−83,403	−17,560	12,945	167,159
	Original two-person with spouse deceased in LYO				
1998	−794,458	−75,319	−2,696	5,672	125,891
2000	−579,605	−87,209	−19,768	0	74,761
2002	−302,770	−99,804	−13,472	30,155	149,042
2004	−517,101	−80,836	−9,361	12,806	168,856
2006	−416,367	−85,958	−73,714	−11	297,663
2008	−501,502	−54,432	−76,426	−7,411	232,418
2010	−520,941	−139,086	−43,558	−14,698	237,474
	Original two-person with spouse alive in LYO				
1995	0	0	0	0	0
1998	−254,517	−43,655	−2,174	35,349	246,125
2000	−328,204	−62,848	0	45,722	294,588
2002	−252,876	−72,025	970	43,734	288,280
2004	−355,825	−52,936	−2,780	85,256	279,605
2006	−726,559	−120,445	−24,396	89,251	341,245
2008	−394,767	−114,679	−10,969	79,876	503,577
2010	−344,674	−155,720	−37,365	19,516	351,595

Note: Persons whose LYO is 2010 were still alive when last observed.

The summary statistics in table 4.1 suggest that the median change in assets between 1995 and the LYO is rather modest, but there is enormous heterogeneity. For some the drawdown of nonannuity assets is very large; for other the increase in these assets is very large.

4.2.4 The Distribution of the Percent Change in Nonannuity Wealth between 1995 and the LYO

Table 4.2 shows the percentile distribution of the percentage change in nonannuity assets between 1995 and the LYO. While the median dollar declines in the singles group were small, the percentage declines are much larger, between 10 and 67 percent. That is, many persons in this group had very low nonannuity assets in 1995 and thus small dollar declines corresponded to large proportional declines. The median percent changes are smallest for persons in original two-person households whose spouse was

Table 4.2   **Percentiles of the distribution of the percentage change between nonannuity assets in LYO and nonannuity assets in 1995**

LYO	10th	30th	50th	70th	90th
	Original singles				
1995	0.0	0.0	0.0	0.0	0.0
1998	−100.0	−58.9	−10.2	15.5	237.4
2000	−100.0	−83.7	−33.9	17.8	203.7
2002	−100.0	−76.9	−27.3	21.1	192.2
2004	−100.0	−89.9	−41.3	9.2	178.3
2006	−100.0	−99.4	−67.3	−6.6	170.4
2008	−100.0	−92.7	−52.9	1.3	123.8
2010	−100.0	−72.9	−27.3	19.9	302.9
	Original two-person with spouse deceased in LYO				
1998	−80.7	−49.4	−32.4	12.1	200.6
2000	−100.0	−81.8	−41.2	−7.3	59.5
2002	−100.0	−78.4	−34.1	15.2	116.9
2004	−100.0	−82.7	−39.6	22.4	155.8
2006	−99.8	−81.2	−46.4	−6.0	130.8
2008	−100.0	−79.8	−45.6	−9.3	110.6
2010	−99.5	−70.2	−36.4	5.5	115.8
	Original two-person with spouse alive in LYO				
1995	0.0	0.0	0.0	0.0	0.0
1998	−82.2	−31.2	−4.6	21.5	110.7
2000	−81.4	−35.4	−0.9	38.6	181.1
2002	−81.2	−38.9	−0.7	25.7	116.3
2004	−80.1	−24.0	−2.6	41.9	172.9
2006	−91.0	−63.5	−12.9	45.9	138.5
2008	−73.8	−36.7	−6.8	39.8	151.0
2010	−80.9	−46.9	−19.2	9.7	103.7

Note: Persons whose LYO is 2010 were still alive when last observed.

still alive at their death. Thus, while we find modest median *dollar* drawdown in nonannuity assets for persons in single-person and in two-to-one households, we find that the median *percent* drawdown in these households is large. As with the dollar drawdown, there is enormous heterogeneity, with the drawdown as much as 100 percent for some and the addition to nonannuity assets well over 100 percent for others. For two-person households the median percent change is small. But again there is enormous heterogeneity.

Table 4.2 provides information that bears on the long-standing question of whether households draw down assets in retirement as the lifecycle hypothesis predicts. The results demonstrate that for each subgroup of the population, more than half of the households draw down assets by a substantial percentage, but that more than a quarter of the households seem to draw down assets by very little, or to accumulate assets, as they age.

Table 4.3   **Percentiles of the distribution of nonannuity assets in LYO (in 000s)**

LYO	10th	20th	30th	40th	50th	60th	70th	80th	90th
Original singles									
1995	0	2	14	38	63	95	143	232	411
1998	0	0	3	16	44	87	134	198	401
2000	0	0	3	18	43	75	125	190	341
2002	0	0	2	24	61	109	178	252	533
2004	0	0	1	12	35	72	174	283	606
2006	0	0	0	2	26	81	156	303	599
2008	0	0	4	17	38	76	152	253	387
2010	0	2	20	51	81	117	190	344	529
Original two-person with spouse deceased in LYO									
1998	0	6	40	72	120	217	305	426	559
2000	0	2	15	49	76	119	176	217	507
2002	0	2	23	61	106	138	232	379	800
2004	0	1	6	25	81	127	191	387	666
2006	0	3	29	60	108	183	289	389	800
2008	0	15	35	76	122	176	285	405	781
2010	1	20	51	96	150	220	305	473	860
Original two-person with spouse alive in LYO									
1995	14	42	77	113	153	221	313	503	851
1998	10	47	83	122	188	274	376	569	988
2000	19	48	94	133	184	257	367	526	1,089
2002	27	64	97	146	192	276	371	503	849
2004	35	100	130	187	262	320	456	615	860
2006	25	49	107	209	335	400	533	583	1,177
2008	35	101	191	258	382	447	613	901	1,059
2010	21	83	146	179	250	350	570	996	1,581
All pathways combined									
1995	0	14	39	70	104	145	225	343	623
1998	0	3	20	61	98	142	221	356	680
2000	0	2	23	51	94	135	199	328	648
2002	0	2	27	63	106	155	242	373	697
2004	0	1	12	51	104	175	260	404	706
2006	0	1	5	43	97	168	303	449	800
2008	0	4	28	61	118	188	308	432	821
2010	1	18	54	92	150	220	321	507	969

Note: Persons whose LYO is 2010 were still alive when last observed.

4.2.5 The Distribution of Nonannuity Assets in the LYO

Table 4.3 shows the distribution of the level of nonannuity assets in the LYO (in $000s). Among original singles over 40 percent have less than $40,000 in nonannuity assets in the last year observed before death—the 40th percentile ranges from $2,000 to $38,000 depending on the LYO (persons for whom the LYO is 2010 are excluded from this and subsequent calculations because these persons are still living when last observed). Among persons in

Table 4.4   Comparison of median nonannuity wealth in last year observed to median nonannuity wealth in 1995: Original one-person households

Health tercile in 1995	Age interval in 1995				
	70–74	75–79	80–84	85+	all
	Nonannuity wealth in 1995				
1	71,032	66,028	69,503	55,602	63,943
2	132,194	112,595	104,254	83,959	109,815
3	202,253	135,531	147,346	173,757	150,126
All	115,097	84,376	82,430	64,603	83,403
	Nonannuity wealth in last year observed				
1	25,532	19,247	29,210	14,548	20,265
2	115,172	48,494	59,405	57,536	63,042
3	170,600	99,854	86,593	102,844	115,757
All	65,861	37,481	43,644	26,493	39,516
	Percentage change from 1995 to LYO				
1	−64.1	−70.9	−58.0	−73.8	−68.3
2	−12.9	−56.9	−43.0	−31.5	−42.6
3	−15.7	−26.3	−41.2	−40.8	−22.9
All	−42.8	−55.6	−47.1	−59.0	−52.6

two-to-one households at least 30 percent have less than $40,000 in the LYO. But even in these pathways a large fraction of persons have substantial wealth in the LYO. Fewer persons in two-to-two households have little nonannuity wealth in the LYO and a large fraction has substantial wealth in the LYO. Over all pathways combined at least 30 percent have wealth less than $40,000 in the LYO. This amount ranges from $5,000 to $39,000 depending on the LYO. The table shows that while a large fraction of households have little or no wealth at retirement, a large fraction also have a great deal of wealth and indeed many households increased their wealth between 1995 and the LYO.

4.2.6 Health and the Change in Nonannuity
Assets between 1995 and the LYO

Table 4.4 shows the relationship between health and the decline in nonannuity assets between 1995 and the LYO for single persons. Survivors—those whose LYO is 2010—are excluded from the table. To facilitate health comparisons we have allocated persons to three health terciles based on the value of their health index in 1995. Over all age groups combined the decline was −68.3 percent for those in the lowest health tercile, −42.6 percent for those in the middle health tercile, and −22.9 for those in the third (best) health tercile. A similar trend holds for each of the age intervals.

Comparable information for persons in two-to-one and continuing two-person households are shown in tables 4.5 and 4.6, respectively. In each of

Table 4.5   Comparison of median nonannuity wealth in last year observed to median nonannuity wealth in 1995: Original two-person households with spouse deceased in LYO

	Age interval in 1995				
Health tercile in 1995	70–74	75–79	80–84	85+	all
Nonannuity wealth in 1995					
1	112,595	155,686	129,970	180,707	152,906
2	293,858	164,027	270,366	210,246	209,899
3	225,189	315,543	139,006	430,918	239,785
All	202,948	171,116	144,566	210,246	173,757
Nonannuity wealth in last year observed					
1	53,521	70,910	78,807	121,234	72,738
2	176,060	80,027	67,871	107,043	119,056
3	173,187	167,253	86,593	691,299	135,236
All	129,720	91,170	78,807	121,234	99,746
Percentage change from 1995 to LYO					
1	−52.5	−54.5	−39.4	−32.9	−52.4
2	−40.1	−51.2	−74.9	−49.1	−43.3
3	−23.1	−47.0	−37.7	60.4	−43.6
All	−36.1	−46.7	−45.5	−42.3	−42.6

Table 4.6   Comparison of median nonannuity wealth in last year observed to median nonannuity wealth in 1995: Original two-person households with spouse alive in LYO

	Age interval in 1995				
Health tercile in 1995	70–74	75–79	80–84	85+	all
Nonannuity wealth in 1995					
1	154,991	209,899	208,717	236,310	200,168
2	273,841	274,536	206,007	180,707	252,990
3	304,423	217,961	250,210	257,161	269,532
All	257,161	241,870	208,745	205,728	237,700
Nonannuity wealth in last year observed					
1	178,584	204,452	231,480	127,004	185,310
2	267,401	265,976	198,848	173,365	249,510
3	408,241	247,537	294,368	268,276	294,368
All	249,742	241,649	208,981	167,255	219,370
Percentage change from 1995 to LYO					
1	15.2	−2.6	10.9	−46.3	−7.4
2	−2.4	−3.1	−3.5	−4.1	−1.4
3	34.1	13.6	17.6	4.3	9.2
All	−2.9	−0.1	0.1	−18.7	−7.7

these pathways the health effects are also noticeable—for persons in the two-to-one pathway the decline is –52.4 percent for persons in the lowest health tercile versus –43.6 percent for persons in the highest; for persons in the two-to-one person pathway the decline is –7.4 percent for persons in the worst health tercile versus +9.2 percent for persons in the best. In percentage terms the difference is greatest for persons in the two-to-one person pathway.

4.3 Regression Models for Asset Evolution

The goal of our analysis is to determine the relationship between the post-retirement evolution of nonannuity assets and the health and the income flows of persons at advanced ages. We do this by estimating regression models in which assets in a given wave are explained by assets in the previous wave, as well as key health and income variables:

(1) $$A_w = k + \lambda * A_{w-1} + \alpha * H_{w-1} + \beta * \Delta H_{w.w-1} + a * SS_w$$
$$+ b * DB_w + c * Earn_w + m * M_w + \varepsilon_w.$$

In this equation, where the subscript w denotes wave, A_w denotes the level of assets, λ is the marginal effect of an additional dollar of assets in wave w-1, given the other covariates, on assets in wave w. H_{w-1} and $\Delta H_{w.w-1}$ denote the level of health in the previous wave and the change in health since the last wave respectively. Higher levels of H_{w-1} and $\Delta H_{w.w-1}$ are expected to reduce the need to rely on assets to finance health care needs and thus are likely to be associated with a positive change in assets. Higher levels of Social Security benefits SS_w and DB annuity income DB_w are also expected to be positively associated with asset change, given the level of assets in the previous wave, since persons with greater income should be able to cover the cost of health-related and other expenses with less need to draw down their accumulated assets. The M_w is an indicator of expected lifespan, which we discuss later. We also include year effects (not shown in the equation) that we interpret as controlling for differences in market returns across years. In PVW (forthcoming), we use a specification similar to equation (1) to investigate how education is related to the evolution of late-life asset holdings for households in the HRS.

One interesting feature of our data set and the specification in equation (1) is that real Social Security benefits are "fixed" at the date of first receipt for single-person households. Thus these benefits vary across households, but not over time for the same household, as shown by the flat profiles for continuously single and continuously married individuals in figure 4.4. The DB pension benefits are only partially indexed and thus real benefits will vary over time.

4.3.1 Baseline Estimates

Our baseline estimates of equation (1) are shown in table 4.7. We focus on persons in AHEAD in the three family pathway groups defined using

Table 4.7   Trimmed GLS estimates of the effect of health and annuity income on the evolution of nonannuity assets between 1995 and LYO, by family pathway

Variable	Continuously single		Original two-person household with spouse deceased in LYO		Original two-person household with spouse alive in LYO	
	Estimate	t-stat	Estimate	t-stat	Estimate	t-stat
Assets t-1	0.73	117.63	0.61	84.84	0.69	83.90
Age	−422	−1.00	391	0.55	−4,199	−3.54
Health(t-1)	638	6.67	1,216	6.82	1,445	5.97
Δ health	448	3.05	542	2.08	1,732	4.83
SS benefits	2.41	5.76	5.83	11.44	4.13	5.92
DB pension benefits	1.75	9.77	3.66	13.87	1.83	7.07
Year 2000	5,168	0.89	22,874	1.73	36,215	2.34
Year 2002	1,104	0.18	7,618	0.59	28,487	1.82
Year 2004	3,873	0.54	39,928	2.83	84,621	4.26
Year 2006	46,131	4.31	47,064	3.19	102,958	4.02
Year 2008	−8,084	−0.80	59,168	3.39	100,063	2.59
Year 2010	−13,070	−1.08	8,703	0.45	−19,581	−0.58
Constant	23,571	0.65	−103,600	−1.81	297,958	3.12
N	7,905		5,871		4,989	
Wald	16,172		9,291		8,460	

marital status in 1995 and marital status in the last year observed. We restrict the sample to persons who are known to be deceased and thus exclude all persons whose last year observed is 2010 (survivors). As noted earlier, there is substantial measurement error in assets. To minimize the effect of misreported asset values we trim the sample by running a first stage model and then excluding observations with residuals in the top or bottom 1 percent. Because lagged assets are likely to be measured with error, the coefficient on lagged assets (λ) may be biased toward zero and the coefficients on other variables, such as SS and DB, may be biased to the extent that these variables are correlated with the "true" value of lagged assets.

The best way to address this measurement error problem would be to find instrumental variables that are correlated with "true" lagged assets but can be excluded from the model for current assets. We are not convinced that the exclusion restrictions needed for such a strategy would be defensible. We therefore present the results from trimmed GLS estimation of equation (1), and then discuss several ways to evaluate the possibility that measurement error in lagged assets is leading to biased estimates on the SS and DB coefficients.

Several findings are noteworthy. First, the age effect is small and not significantly different from zero for the first two pathways. Thus, holding income and health constant, there is little evidence of purely age-related asset drawdown. However, the age effect is –$4,199 and statistically significant for persons in original two-person households whose spouse is alive at their death.

Second, the health variables and the annuity income variables are large and statistically significant. Figure 4.7 graphs the effect of a 10 percentile point increase in the level of health in the previous wave, a 10 percentile point change in health since the previous wave, a $5,000 increase in Social Security benefits, and a $5,000 increase in DB benefits on nonannuity assets. Each of the effects is large for each family pathway group, but is lower for single persons than for the other two family pathway groups, presumably because single persons have the lowest levels of nonannuity assets. The relationship between a 10 percentile point increment in lagged health and nonannuity wealth is over $6,000 for single persons, about $12,000 for persons originally in two-person households whose spouse predeceased them, and over $14,000 for persons originally in two-person households and whose spouse survives them. The relationship between a 10 percentile point increment in the change in health and nonannuity wealth ranges from over $4,000 for single persons to over $17,000 for persons originally in two-person households and whose spouse survives them. The relationship between nonannuity wealth and a $5,000 increment in Social Security benefits is about $12,000 for single persons, $29,000 for persons in original two-person households whose spouse was predeceased, and $21,000 for persons in original two-person households whose spouse survives them. The relationship between nonannuity wealth and a $5,000 increment in DB pension benefits ranges from about $9,000 in single-person households to over $18,000 for persons in original two-person households whose spouse predeceased them. This suggests that both Social Security income and DB income are "protective" of nonannuity wealth, while poor health is an important determinant of the drawdown of nonannuity wealth.

We have explored in some detail the concern that assets are measured with error. Our use of a trimmed sample (we trim the top and bottom 1 percent based on residuals of a preliminary regression) is an attempt to address this potential problem. Indeed, estimates based on untrimmed data show substantially lower coefficients on lagged assets and larger coefficients on SS and DB. Additional trimming however—as much as the top and bottom 3 percent of asset values and based on different methods of trimming—has very little effect on either the estimated coefficients on lagged assets or on the estimated coefficients of the SS or DB variables. In addition, estimates based on a similar specification used in Poterba, Venti, and Wise (forthcoming), which imputes a rate of return to lagged assets based on individual attributes, yields essentially the same results as those reported in table 4.7. The importance of this comparison is that the estimates on lagged assets in the earlier paper are in the 0.8 to 1.1 range. Whatever the extent of errors in variables, it is essentially the same in the data sets used in the two papers. The sample underlying table 4.7 is all AHEAD respondents who die by 2010, while that in Poterba, Venti, and Wise (forthcoming) is all persons over the age of sixty-five in all cohorts of the HRS.

We have also obtained median regression estimates comparable to the estimates shown in table 4.7. As expected, the estimates on health and annuity income are all smaller than the linear regression estimates—the largest is just over 2—but the median regression estimates on lagged assets are little different from the linear regression estimates. This finding suggests that while there may well be measurement error in lagged assets, this measurement error is not the primary reason for the large coefficients on SS and DB.

The size of the coefficients on both SS and DB suggest not only that the receipt of these annuitized income streams may help to avoid the drawdown of financial assets, but also that they may be correlated with other income streams or with an unobserved household propensity to save. Consider the coefficient on SS income for a married couple with both spouses still alive (coefficient 4.13) and with only one member of the couple still living (coefficient 5.83). Recall that the typical time period between two waves of the HRS is two years, so additional income of $1,000 per year would imply $2,000 of total payments between waves. If the individual saved all of the income from Social Security, the resulting coefficient would be somewhat larger than 2.0. The estimated coefficients more than twice this size raises the concern of omitted variables that are correlated with the SS variable. In the standard omitted variable setting, the estimated coefficient on SS in part reflects these omitted variable influences.

We suspect that the coefficient values on SS and DB in part reflect a correlation between these variables and unobserved individual attributes that affect the propensity to accumulate assets in retirement. As the descriptive tables 4.1, 4.2, and 4.3 show, many households increase assets substantially from wave to wave, even after retirement. These households tend to be those with substantial assets, and also to be those with high lifetime earnings and large SS benefits. If characteristics that permitted long, high-income labor market careers are correlated with individual attributes that persist over time, and that are related to late-life wealth accumulation behavior, then the cross-sectional variation in SS benefits that underlies our estimates will in part capture this variation in unobserved individual attributes, perhaps saving behavior that persists into old age but is not determined by Social Security benefits. This makes it difficult to interpret the coefficient estimate as purely a "protective effect" of Social Security income on assets. This issue merits further analysis.

4.3.2 Subjective Mortality

Life cycle theory suggests that all else being equal, those who expect to have long lives will spend down assets more slowly that those who expect

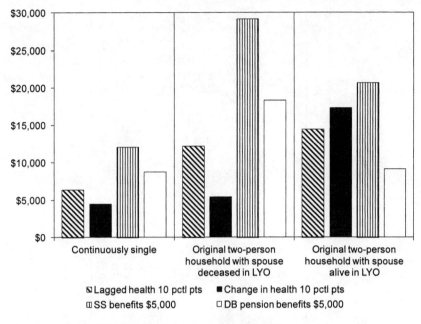

Fig. 4.7   Effect of health and income on assets, by family pathway

to live shorter lives. The next set of regressions adds a measure of the self-reported survival probability to the specification used in table 4.7. The subjective probability measure is the ratio of the probability that the respondent expects to live ten more years divided by the probability that the respondent will live ten more years based on the life table values for a person of the same age and gender. Unfortunately, the subjective probability of survival is only available for some respondents in most years and is not available for anyone in 1998. Thus the sample used in these regressions is smaller than that used in table 4.7. The reduction in the sample due to each of these reasons is described in table 4.8. Between 43 and 62 percent of the sample are missing the survivor probability variable and are thus excluded from the sample used to obtain the estimates in table 4.7.

The estimation results are shown in table 4.9. First, the estimated coefficients on the age, health, and income variables are in some cases very different from the estimates based on the full sample. This is perhaps not surprising given that 62 percent of the observations on singles, 43 percent for the second pathway, and 48 percent for the third pathway are excluded as the result of missing data. Because of the apparent nonrandomness of the missing observations, perhaps limited credence should be put in these results. Nonetheless, the estimated subjective probability coefficient is statistically insignificantly different from zero in each of the three pathways. It appears though that the restricted sample used in table 4.9 makes it difficult to draw

Table 4.8 Sample size (before trimming) when using subjective mortality

	1998	2000	2002	2004	2006	2008	2010	Total
			Singles					
Sample for table 7	2,161	1,764	1,381	1054	783	556	365	8,064
Delete if no 1998 mortality data	0	1,764	1,381	1054	783	556	365	5,903
Delete if no response to mortality question	0	1030	740	540	378	239	109	3,036
Percent decline	100%	−42%	−46%	−49%	−52%	−57%	−70%	−62%
		Two-person spouse deceased						
Sample for table 7	1,124	1,074	983	893	775	645	495	5,989
Delete if no 1998 mortality data	0	1,074	983	893	775	645	495	4,865
Delete if no response to mortality question	0	819	753	655	529	399	257	3,412
Percent decline	100%	−24%	−23%	−27%	−32%	−38%	−48%	−43%
		Two-person spouse alive						
Sample for table 7	1,417	1,093	829	639	480	373	259	5,090
Delete if no 1998 mortality data	0	1,093	829	639	480	373	259	3,673
Delete if no response to mortality question	0	825	599	474	331	257	156	2,642
Percent decline	100%	−25%	−28%	−26%	−31%	−31%	−40%	−48%

Table 4.9:   Trimmed GLS estimates of the effect of health and annuity income on the evolution of nonannuity assets between 1998 and LYO, by family pathway

Variable	Continuously single		Original two-person household with spouse deceased in LYO		Original two-person household with spouse alive in LYO	
	Estimate	t-stat	Estimate	t-stat	Estimate	t-stat
Assets t-1	0.68	60.82	0.62	61.23	0.75	65.48
Age	−1,840	−1.47	−391	−0.34	−4,555	−2.15
Health(t-1)	976	5.57	1,534	5.93	1,841	4.95
Δ health	1,103	3.98	469	1.24	3,117	5.69
SS benefits	1.48	1.94	5.89	8.18	4.38	4.22
Pension benefits	1.60	5.76	4.00	11.31	1.76	5.32
Prob(10 yrs) ratio	118	0.96	−39	−0.21	−367	−1.34
Year 2002	−4,898	−0.52	−38,574	−2.45	−20,848	−1.03
Year 2004	−3,144	−0.28	20,138	1.15	52,894	2.12
Year 2006	62,355	3.37	29,931	1.52	55,673	1.69
Year 2008	−13,973	−0.81	62,231	2.25	75,295	1.46
Year 2010	8,432	0.35	−48,014	−1.69	−102,789	−1.76
Constant	157,071	1.51	−28,066	−0.30	335,361	1.96
N	2,974		3,162		2,550	
Wald	4,336		4,931		5,103	

conclusions about the role of subjective life expectancy in contributing to asset drawdown. However, a similar specification was used in PVW (forthcoming) but estimation was based on all HRS cohorts. That analysis was not affected to the same extent by missing responses to the subject survival questions. The results also showed no statistically significant effect of the subjective probability of survival on assets.

4.4 Conclusions and Future Directions

Our analysis of asset drawdown at the end of life suggests that the median change in assets between 1995 and the last year observed (LYO) is rather modest, but that for more than half of households, assets when last observed are below those in the early retirement period. It is difficult to summarize the drawdown of assets in any simple way; however, there is enormous heterogeneity in the change. Because many individuals were observed in 1995 with relatively low levels of nonannuity assets, the median percent drawdown is sometimes quite large even though the dollar amount of drawdown is small. Persons who remained single and married persons predeceased by a spouse experienced median asset reductions of 30 to 50 percent between 1995 and the last year observed before their death. The reductions for persons whose spouse outlived them were much smaller.

We find that a large fraction of households have little or no wealth when they are last observed in the survey. Some might suggest that these households had "perfect foresight": they anticipated how long they would live and exhausted their wealth as they were approaching death. Several results are inconsistent with this view. First, most of those with little wealth at death also had little wealth in 1995. Thus the pattern is not one of wealth drawdown after retirement, but of arrival at retirement age without much wealth. Second, the drawdown of wealth is closely associated with poor health. In order to "time" the wealth profile to hit zero at death, persons would also have to anticipate health shocks. There is some evidence (Hurd and McGarry [2002]; Hurd, McFadden, and Merrill [2001]) that people are good judges of their own life expectancy, but the size and randomness of many health shocks would suggest that for many the depletion of assets was unanticipated and not planned for. Third, among those persons who had assets in 1995, many apparently exhausted their assets *before* death—our last measurement of assets is within two years of death, but many of these persons have yet to face large medical expenditures that occur disproportionately in the last six months of life. Finally, we find no significant relationship between the drawdown of assets and a variable that measures an individual's subjective life expectancy relative to population averages for persons of the same age and gender.

While we do not uncover significant links between subjective mortality and asset drawdown, we do find substantively important links with other variables. We estimate that a 10 percentile point increment in health in the previous wave is associated with over $6,000 more wealth for single persons in the current wave, over $12,000 more for persons originally in two-person households with a deceased spouse by the LYO, and over $14,000 more wealth for persons originally in two-person households with a surviving spouse at the LYO. The estimated effect of a 10 percentile point change in health between waves ranges from over $4,000 for single persons to over $17,000 for two-person households. A $5,000 increment in Social Security is associated with increments in wealth (over a two-year period) ranging from about $12,000 for single persons to over $29,000 for persons originally married with a deceased spouse in the LYO. The relationship between nonannuity wealth and a $5,000 increment (again over a two-year period) in DB pension benefits ranges from about $9,000 for single persons to over $18,000 for persons originally married with a deceased spouse in the LYO. Thus our estimates suggest that both Social Security income and DB income are "protective" of nonannuity wealth, while poor health is strongly associated with the drawdown of nonannuity wealth. Some of the estimated effects of annuity income on assets appear to be quite large, implying that one dollar of income is associated with more than one dollar of additional assets. We investigated measurement error in assets as a possible explanation for the magnitude of these estimates and we conclude that measurement error is not the key explanation for the large effects. A more likely explanation is that Social Security benefits are correlated with unobserved individual attributes that affect the propensity to accumulate assets in retirement. This explanation merits further investigation.

Our results raise a number of important questions about the preretirement planning of those who reach late life with essentially no nonannuity assets. These households are disproportionately dependent on Social Security as their primary source of income, and they are unlikely to be able to respond to financial shocks such as out-of-pocket medical costs by relying on their own resources. One question about this group is whether their level of consumption in retirement is lower than their preretirement standard of living. Some households may choose to accept low levels of consumption at advanced ages and thus save little for retirement while young. On the other hand, HRS data summarized in Venti and Wise (2001) show that two-thirds of respondents say they would save more if they "could do it again." And those who said they saved too little had assets at retirement that were a much lower proportion of lifetime earning than those who said their saving was "about right."

A second question is the extent to which low levels of retirement wealth accumulation reflect hardship prior to retirement. Particularly for households that have experienced chronic poor health, and associated low earnings, the observed level of assets at retirement may be the outcome of many years of financial struggle. For such households the level of Social Security benefits and other aspects of the social safety net, such as Medicare and Medicaid, are key determinants of retirement consumption.

Finally, the evidence that those with the lowest wealth in retirement are often those in the poorest health underscores the need to better understand the causal pathways linking health to wealth at older ages as well as during traditional working years. The prospect of continued increase in health care costs suggests that the financial burden of out-of-pocket medical spending may continue to grow; this could strengthen some of the channels linking health and wealth. Our findings highlight the need to search for opportunities to identify how both chronic health conditions, and acute health shocks, affect the trajectory of wealth.

References

Adams P., M. Hurd, D. McFadden, A. Merrill, and T. Ribeiro. 2003. "Healthy, Wealthy and Wise? Tests for Direct Causal Paths between Health and Socioeconomic Status." *Journal of Econometrics* 112 (1): 3–56.

Anguelov, Chris, Howard Iams, and Patrick Purcell. 2012. "Shifting Income Sources of the Aged." *Social Security Bulletin* 72 (3): 59–68.
Attanasio, Orazio, and Carl Emmerson. 2003. "Mortality, Health Status, and Wealth." *Journal of the European Economic Association* 1 (4): 821–50.
Case, Anne, and Angus Deaton. 2005. "Health and Wealth Among the Poor: India and South Africa Compared." *American Economic Review* (Papers and Proceedings) 95: 229–33.
Coile, Courtney, and Kevin Milligan. 2009. "How Portfolios Evolve After Retirement: The Effect of Health Shocks." *Review of Income and Wealth* 55:226–48.
Fisher, T. Lynn. 2007. "Estimates of Unreported Asset Income in the Survey of Consumer Finances and the Relative Importance of Social Security Benefits to the Elderly." *Social Security Bulletin* 67 (2): 47–53.
Hurd, Michael, Daniel McFadden, and Angela Merrill. 2001. "Predictors of Mortality among the Elderly." In *Themes in the Economics of Aging*, edited by D. Wise, 171–98. Chicago: University of Chicago Press.
Hurd, Michael, and Kathleen McGarry. 2002. "The Predictive Validity of Subjective Probabilities of Survival." *Economic Journal* 112 (482): 966–85.
Michaud, P. C., and A. van Soest. 2008. "Health and Wealth of Elderly Couples: Causality Tests using Dynamic Panel Data Models." *Journal of Health Economics* 27 (5): 1312–25.
Poterba, James, Steven F. Venti, and David A. Wise. 2010. "The Asset Cost of Poor Health." NBER Working Paper no. 16389, Cambridge, MA.
———. 2012. "Were They Prepared for Retirement? Financial Status at Advanced Ages in the HRS and AHEAD Cohorts." In *Investigations in the Economics of Aging*, edited by David A. Wise, 21–76. Chicago: University of Chicago Press.
———. Forthcoming. "Health, Education, and the Post-Retirement Evolution of Household Assets." *Journal of Human Capital*.
Rohwedder, Susann, Steven J. Haider, and Michael D. Hurd. 2006. "Increases in Wealth among the Elderly in the Early 1990s: How Much is Due to Survey Design?" *Review of Income and Wealth* 52 (4): 509–24.
Smith, James P. 1999. "Healthy Bodies and Thick Wallets: The Dual Relation between Health and Economic Status." *Journal of Economic Perspectives* 13 (2): 145–66.
———. 2004. "Unraveling the SES-Health Connection." *Population and Development Review Supplement: Aging, Health and Public Policy* 30:108–32.
———. 2005. "Consequences and Predictors of New Health Events." In *Analyses in the Economics of Aging*, edited by David A. Wise, 213–40. Chicago: University of Chicago Press.
Wu, Stephen. 2003. "The Effects of Health Status Events on the Economic Status of Married Couples." *Journal of Human Resources* 38 (1): 219–30.
Venti, Steven F. 2011. "Economic Measurement in the Health and Retirement Study." *Forum for Health Economics & Policy* 14 (3): 1–18.
Venti, Steven F., and David A. Wise. 2001. "Choice, Chance, and Wealth Dispersion at Retirement." In *Aging Issues in the United States and Japan*, edited by S. Ogura, T. Tachibanaki, and D. A. Wise, 25–64. Chicago: University of Chicago Press.
———. 2002. "Aging and Housing Equity." In *Innovations for Financing Retirement*, edited by O. Mitchell, Z. Bodie, P. Hammond, and S. Zeldes, 254–81. Philadelphia: University of Pennsylvania Press.
———. 2004. "Aging and Housing Equity: Another Look." In D. Wise, ed., *Perspectives in the Economics of Aging*, edited by D. A. Wise, 127–75. Chicago: University of Chicago Press.

Comment   Jonathan Skinner

For many years, Steve Venti and David Wise, later joined by James Poterba (hereafter PVW), have identified the key empirical facts essential to any understanding of retirement assets and wealth accumulation (e.g., Venti and Wise 1989; Poterba, Venti, and Wise 2011, 2012). Their findings often contradicted the implications of then-conventional life cycle models, and were instrumental in pushing researchers toward a newer wave of more realistic life cycle models. Gone was the idea that households spend their golden years dissaving optimally so as to end up with nothing at time T, the final year of life. Instead, the PVW research pointed to a world of surprising heterogeneity, where some households actually accumulate wealth through retirement, some arrive at retirement with virtually nothing, while others experience precipitous wealth declines, ending up with essentially no wealth prior to death (Poterba, Venti, and Wise 2012). Thus even those who might have been deemed to be saving adequately found themselves with virtually no financial wealth available during their last months of life.

In this chapter, they return to the question of how events preceding death affect wealth and consumption for older households in the Health and Retirement Study (HRS) study. They don't simply look at the wealth patterns of those who died, but instead consider wealth dynamics for everyone in the cohort (including those who didn't die by 2010, the last wave in the sample), stratified by three demographic groups: single households, two-person households where the spouse (or partner) is no longer present in the HRS wave prior to death, and two-person households where the spouse is present prior to death.

The authors make two primary observations. The first is that Social Security and defined benefit pensions can protect nonannuity wealth, in the sense that individuals with high levels of Social Security and defined benefit income are least likely to suffer downturns in their wealth, particularly as they approach death. And second, they note that poor health is central to dissaving and the consequent decline in nonannuity wealth, again for households close to death.

In this comment, I consider each point in turn. I am more equivocal about the interpretation of the first point, as measurement error in assets or (more likely) unobservable variations in consumption, could in theory generate the same empirical patterns they observe. I do agree entirely with the second point, that poor health is central to declines in wealth—and would further speculate that it is also a key reason for why people save in the first place.

Jonathan Skinner is the James O. Freedman Presidential Professor of Economics at Dartmouth College, the Professor of Family and Community Medicine at the Geisel School of Medicine and the Dartmouth Institute for Health Policy and Clinical Practice, and a research associate of the National Bureau of Economic Research.

For acknowledgments, sources of research support, and disclosure of the author's material financial relationships, if any, please see http://www.nber.org/chapters/c12965.ack.

Returning to the first point, the authors estimate a model that can be simplified and written as follows:

(1) $\Lambda_t = \alpha + \beta\Lambda_{t-1} + \gamma Y_t + \theta G_t + \lambda H_{t-1} + \omega\Delta H_t + \varepsilon_t$

where Λ_t, measured assets at time t, differ from true assets A_t because of the considerable measurement error in all wealth data, including the Health and Retirement Study (HRS) data used in their analysis (Venti 2011). In addition, the authors include an index of health status H_t (and the change in health status since the prior year, $H_{t\{nd\}1}$), along with measures of pension income Y_t and social security income G_t. (I ignore the other covariates in their regression model.) Their basic estimated model for the "two-to-one" group was as follows:

(2) $\Lambda_t = \alpha + 0.6\Lambda_{t-1} + 3.7Y_t + 5.8G_t + 1216H_{t-1} + 542\Delta H_t + \varepsilon_t.$

It is clear that higher levels of G and Y are strongly associated with higher levels of current measured assets, even after conditioning on lagged assets—that is, pension and Social Security income appears remarkably effective at preserving assets. Yet the coefficients are so large that they almost seem too effective; how can one dollar in annual Social Security income lead to six dollars more wealth in this year relative to last?[1]

One alternative interpretation relies on the well-known positive association between income, assets, and saving rates (e.g., Dynan, Skinner, and Zeldes 2004). Given that the coefficient on assets is relatively modest, just 0.6, other markers for wealth, such as pension income or Social Security income, could step up in the regression to account for the cross-sectional variation in assets explained by differences in life cycle income. In other words, the higher level of wealth and the higher pension and Social Security income may both reflect higher lifetime wealth, but one is not necessarily causal for the other.

Measurement error is one explanation for why the AR coefficient is so modest, but in unreported sensitivity analysis, PVW have found that median regressions—less sensitive to measurement error—are similar in magnitude to the regression reported earlier. Another possibility is that fluctuations in consumption are driving the remarkable heterogeneity in savings patterns. Because consumption is not included on the RHS of the regression, however, the coefficient on lagged wealth will be diminished, with the magnitude of the attenuation dependent on the extent of cross-sectional consumption variability.[2]

1. The HRS waves are over the space of two years, so the coefficient on Y and G, if not appropriately normalized for the two-year period, could well be 2.0.
2. A quick simulation with 10,000 observations, a log-normal distribution of consumption, interest rate of 0.03, lagged assets a variable fraction of consumption (from zero to four times consumption), and a constant income level suggested support for this case. When consumption was included along with income in a regression, the coefficient on lagged assets was 1.03, as one might expect from estimating a budget constraint. When consumption was excluded from the regression, the coefficient on lagged assets dropped to 0.7.

If consumption were measured as well on the right-hand side, then we would be confronted with the budget constraint:

$$(3) \qquad A_t = A_{t-1}(1 + r_t) + Y_t + G_t - C_t,$$

where C_t is consumption in year t. In this case, the coefficient on Y (and C) is restricted to be one. Of course, this requires measuring assets without error, but it is always best to put as much measurement error as possible on the left-hand side of the equation, as in the following equation (4):

$$(4) \qquad \Delta A_t = A_{t-1}r_t + Y_t + G_t - C_t.$$

This could prove to be a cleaner test of the hypothesis of whether Y or G is protective of assets, but we are still not out of the forest yet. First of all, this is a budget constraint, so the coefficients on Y and G are one (or two if measured over a two-year period); any divergence occurs solely because of measurement error. But consumption is rarely measured accurately in any survey, particularly near death, so even this regression is problematic. Second, measured wealth would still be included on the right-hand side of the regression, leading to a mechanical negative correlation between it and the dependent variable.[3]

As the authors note, health status is an important predictor of wealth accumulation or deaccumulation. It is unlikely that health status *per se* leads to less wealth through interest rate effects (except perhaps during the Great Recession), or lower pension and Social Security income—most of that dissaving will occur because of a jump up in consumption.[4] So one suggestion for future research would be to focus in more detail on the components of consumption that are most likely to be variable near death. In particular, one might rewrite the budget constraint as:

$$(7) \qquad A_t = A_{t-1}(1 + r_t) + Y_t + G_t - C_{ht} - C_{nht},$$

where C_{ht} is spending on out-of-pocket health-related consumption and C_{nht} is residual nonhealth consumption. There is good evidence on at least a limited set of health-related expenditures from the HRS, although even that may not entirely reflect the full gamut of consumption that responds strongly to poor health (Marshall, McGarry, and Skinner 2011). Presumably the PVW regression estimates reflecting how changes in health status affect wealth accumulation are working through this channel.

I think their focus on health status is exactly right. Previous work has suggested that mean levels of out-of-pocket expenditures in the last five years

---

3. Finally, there are a variety of ways to present the data on changes over time in wealth; the authors sensibly consider two cases—dollar changes and percentage changes in wealth. Each has its advantages, but a third middle ground is to consider ratios of asset changes to permanent income, defined to be some appropriately weighted combination of current and past income.

4. Drops in assets could be explained too by transfers to children, but this seems unlikely for people nearing death concerned about paying for visiting nurses or other services.

of life are remarkably large, ranging from about $30,000 for households whose decedents died of kidney disease or cancers, to more than $60,000 for decedents with dementia (such as Alzheimer's disease) (Kelley et al. 2013); given the modest size of financial wealth for most retirees, as shown in PVW and elsewhere, medical expenditures could in theory attenuate initial wealth holdings quite substantially.

Furthermore, the hypothesis tested in this chapter—whether Social Security and pension income is protective of wealth?—might be extended to a related question, which is whether wealth is then protective of being able to afford the expenses of a lengthy chronic disease, something that Kathleen McGarry and I have found in preliminary work. While a far more complicated problem, understanding how unexpectedly good pension and Social Security income affects not just asset accumulation, but also health and well-being more generally, could be of interest in assessing the value of tax incentives and other mechanisms to encourage retirement savings.

References

Dynan, Karen, Jonathan Skinner, and Steven Zeldes. 2004. "Do the Rich Save More?" *Journal of Political Economy* 112 (April): 397–444.
Kelley, Amy S., Katherine McGarry, Sean Fahle, Samuel M. Marshall, Quingling Du, and Jonathan Skinner. 2013. "Out-of-Pocket Spending in the Last Five Years of Life." *Journal of General Internal Medicine* 28 (2): 304–9.
Marshall, Samuel M., Kathleen McGarry, and Jonathan Skinner. 2011. "The Risk of Out-of-Pocket Health Care Expenditures at the End of Life." In *Explorations in the Economics of Aging*, edited by David A. Wise, 101–132. Chicago: University of Chicago Press.
Poterba, James, Steven F. Venti, and David A. Wise. 2011. "Family Status Transitions, Latent Health, and the Post-Retirement Evolution of Assets." In *Explorations in the Economics of Aging*, edited by David A. Wise, 23–74. Chicago: University of Chicago Press.
———. 2012. "Were They Prepared for Retirement? Financial Status at Advanced Ages in the HRS and AHEAD Cohorts." In *Investigations in the Economics of Aging*, edited by David A. Wise, 21–69. Chicago: University of Chicago Press.
Venti, Steven F. 2011. "Economic Measurement in the Health and Retirement Study." *Forum for Health Economics & Policy* 14 (3): 1–20.
Venti, Steven F., and David A. Wise. 1989. "Aging, Moving, and Housing Wealth." In *The Economics of Aging*, edited by David Wise, 9–54. Chicago: University of Chicago Press.

5

Understanding the SES Gradient in Health among the Elderly
The Role of Childhood Circumstances

Till Stowasser, Florian Heiss, Daniel McFadden, and
Joachim Winter

5.1 Introduction

It is the health economics version of the classic "chicken and egg" problem: We know that people with high socioeconomic status (SES) tend to be in better health and live longer than their economically disadvantaged counterparts but we are not sure which came first. Do economic resources determine health (hypothesis A)? Does health influence economic success (hypothesis B)? Or, are both health and wealth dependent on some third unaccounted factor (hypothesis C)? The body of literature dealing with this so-called socioeconomic gradient in health is impressive (for overviews see Smith [1999]; Cutler, Lleras-Muney, and Vogl [2011]; and Stowasser et al. [2012]).

The traditional view that causality flows from SES to health is especially common among—but not exclusive to—epidemiologists. Often-cited causal pathways are the affordability of health services, better health knowledge and lifestyles among the higher educated, environmental hazards associated with poorly paying occupations and low-income living conditions, or

Till Stowasser is assistant professor of economics at the University of Munich. Florian Heiss is chair of the Department of Statistics and Econometrics at the University of Düsseldorf. Daniel McFadden is a Professor of the Graduate School of the University of California, Berkeley, the Presidential Professor of Health Economics at the University of Southern California, a 2000 Nobel Laureate in Economics, and a research associate of the National Bureau of Economic Research. Joachim Winter holds the chair of the Department of Empirical Economic Research at the University of Munich.

We thank the Schaeffer Center for Health Policy and Economics at USC and the Center for Health and Wellbeing at Princeton University for their hospitality. Financial support was provided by the National Institute on Aging (NIA), grant no. P01 AG 005842. For acknowledgments, sources of research support, and disclosure of the authors' material financial relationships, if any, please see http://www.nber.org/chapters/c12976.ack.

the mere psychological burden that comes with a life of constant economic struggle. Economists were among the first to argue that causality may also work its way from health to economic outcomes, the most important channel being the development of human capital: physical frailty is likely to have adverse effects on educational attainment, occupational productivity, and, consequently, the accumulation of wealth. Finally, the statistical literature stresses the point that the persistent correlation between morbidity and SES may in fact be spurious and due to unobserved individual heterogeneity with a common influence on both health and wealth; see Heckman (1981b), inter alia. Prime candidates for such hidden third factors are genetic disposition and other family effects with an impact on preferences and health-relevant behaviors.

Discriminating among these rivaling hypotheses is important since policy recommendations will critically depend on the nature and the sources of the gradient. Methodologically, the estimation of credible causal effects in population data requires addressing the challenges of simultaneity (hypothesis A vs. hypothesis B) and unobserved common effects (hypotheses A/B vs. hypothesis C).[1] The conventional solution to both of these problems is to exploit natural experiments that provide instruments for either health or SES. While this strategy of isolating exogenous variation certainly works well on paper, it is not always persuasive in practice. The main caveat is that convincing instruments are generally in short supply. As discussed by Stowasser et al. (2012), even the availability of instruments that are clearly exogenous and that have an impact on the endogenous regressor they seek to replace may cause problems if the variation they reflect is not all that *relevant* for the dependent variable of interest. Moreover, since instrumental variable (IV) strategies usually rely on rather case-specific events, any uncovered effects may well be causal in nature but of questionable external validity; Deaton (2010) discusses these issues.

For these reasons, Adams et al. (2003) propose an alternative approach of uncovering causal links that makes use of the entire variation in health and economic variables. Using panel data, they test for Granger noncausality of SES for *innovations* in health, which deals with the econometric challenge of distinguishing hypotheses A and B.[2] Their purely statistical causality concept deviates from "true" causality in a structural sense, as their approach does not specifically address the issue of unobserved individual heterogeneity. As a consequence, the detection of Granger causality would not necessarily imply the validity of hypothesis A, since unobserved third factors may be at work instead. However, a finding that economic status is *not* Granger causal for health and that the relationship is invariant across a

---

1. For a detailed discussion, see Stowasser et al. (2012).
2. While Adams et al. (2003) studied both wealth-to-health and health-to-wealth causation, this study concentrates on the question of whether hypothesis A is correct.

wide range of SES and health histories would be informative, as this would rule out true causality as well.[3] Applying their framework to a representative sample of US Americans over the age of seventy, Adams et al. (2003) are unable to reject the hypothesis that economic status has no causal effect on mortality and most health innovations, once health history is controlled for. Despite the fact that this result may not be overly surprising in light of the subgroup's quasi-universal access to Medicare and considering that causal links may well have been active in the past,[4] their study stimulated some controversy in the literature.

On this account, Stowasser et al. (2012) revisit the approach introduced by Adams et al. (2003) and investigate whether the original findings are confirmed when their methodology is applied to a more encompassing set of data that covers health histories of different lengths and varying age compositions. In stark contrast to the original study, they find that it is much harder to reject the existence—or the activity—of causal links in more comprehensive samples. Importantly, this result is not exclusively driven by the inclusion of younger individuals, as the mere growth in sample size already leads to higher rejection rates of Granger noncausality, which indicates that the original results were partly driven by low test power. In light of their findings, Stowasser et al. (2012) discuss three avenues for improving the approach suggested by Adams et al. (2003). First, the underlying notion of health dynamics, with health being modeled as a first-order Markov process, falls short of reflecting the stock characteristics of latent health capital as envisioned by Grossman (1972). Second, the original approach does not account for individual heterogeneity, which makes it impossible to distinguish between true causal links and third-factor effects in case Granger causality is detected. Third, even if common effects were convincingly controlled for, the tests proposed by Adams et al. (2003) are only informative about the mere *presence* of causality but not of the mechanisms through which SES influences health. Although knowledge of this general link is important in its own right, the identification of specific pathways is equally critical from a policy perspective.

The present study aims at addressing these issues and gauges whether the main conclusion of Stowasser et al. (2012), that it is impossible to statistically reject SES-to-health causality even in a retired population age sixty-five and older, is robust to these methodological refinements. The research strategy rests on the increasing availability of retrospective life-history data within large panel studies that link economic and health data, such as the

3. The rationale for this reasoning is that Granger causality—or conditional dependence across time—is thought of as a necessary but insufficient condition for causality in a more structural sense.

4. Indeed, Adams et al. (2003) find a steep gradient in the initial cross-section, suggesting that a great deal of the relationship between health and wealth has already been determined during the (unexplained) first seven decades of a respondent's life courses.

US Health and Retirement Study (HRS) used for this analysis.[5] These data innovations are the response to the rapidly growing literature on childhood health that makes the point that a meaningful analysis of the gradient should incorporate a respondent's early-life information (for an overview, see Smith [2009]; Almond and Currie [2011]; and Currie [2011]). For instance, Case, Lubotsky, and Paxson (2002) suggest that part of the adult SES gradient in health originates in early childhood, as they find a strong relationship between parental economic status and childhood health that accumulates as children age. In another cohort study, Case, Fertig, and Paxson (2005) document that these early conditions have a lasting impact on adult health and—in line with hypothesis B—other outcomes such as education, labor supply, and income. As Currie (2009) notes, these findings are supported by many, albeit not all, of the myriad of studies that complement the literature by exploiting data from natural experiments.

Not only does this evidence suggest the use of available information on childhood circumstances to avoid bias from omitted variables when studying causal pathways in adulthood—the retrospective look at the beginning of life additionally has the potential to alleviate all three of the aforementioned problems in the Adams et al. (2003) framework. First, it provides an opportunity to incorporate longer health histories and, thus, a more realistic model of health dynamics. Second, to the extent that retrospective data also covers information on family backgrounds and parental SES, it will be possible to proxy control for some of the individual heterogeneity that is suspect of exerting a common influence on health and wealth. Third, controlling for both historic and contemporary variables may elucidate *when* the association between SES and health is established, which has important policy implications: if future outcomes are predetermined during childhood, resources spent on policies that aim at improving access to health care for adults and retirees may in fact be more wisely invested into educative and financial measures for young families.

In summary, the results of this study suggest that the findings of Stowasser et al. (2012) are largely insensitive to varying models of health histories. While SES is unlikely Granger causal for innovations in acute health insults, Granger noncausality can be statistically rejected for mental health conditions, mortality, and changes in overall health. Evidence for chronic diseases and functional health is a bit more inconclusive. However, since the detection of Granger causality for these health conditions is adversely related to sample size, it is possible that we merely observe the statistical artifact—as already reported by Stowasser et al. (2012)—that test power suffers considerably in small data sets. The fact that results are also quite robust to the

---

5. Comparable data collection efforts targeted at the population age fifty and older include the Survey of Health, Ageing and Retirement in Europe (SHARE), the English Longitudinal Study of Aging (ELSA), or the China Health and Retirement Longitudinal Study (CHARLS).

introduction of proxy controls for individual heterogeneity lends support to a causal interpretation of the observed gradient. In line with the literature on early-life circumstances, we find that childhood health has lasting predictive power for adult health. This, however, does not render contemporary factors unimportant. Finally, we uncover strong gender differences in the intertemporal transmission of SES and health: while the link between SES and functional, as well as mental health among men is established rather late in life, the gradient among women appears to originate from childhood circumstances.

The rest of this chapter is structured as follows. Section 5.2 presents the data used for analysis. This is followed by a brief description of the methodological framework—which closely resembles that of Adams et al. (2003) and Stowasser et al. (2012)—in section 5.3. The empirical analysis is presented in section 5.4. Section 5.5 concludes.

5.2 Data

In this chapter, we use data from the Health and Retirement Study (HRS), which is a representative panel of the US population age fifty and older. The design of the analysis sample and the constructions of the variables are natural extensions of Adams et al. (2003) and Stowasser et al. (2012).[6] Due to substantial deviations in survey design, observations from the first panel wave are dropped. As a result, the main working sample consists of 8 biennial waves covering interviews conducted between 1993 and 2008. In the spirit of the original study by Adams et al. (2003), we restrict our analysis to a mostly retired population of the age of sixty-five and older. On average, each wave contains roughly 11,400 individuals with usable records on health outcomes, SES variables, and demographic information.[7] Attritors and members of refreshment cohorts are kept in the sample for as long as they participate in the survey. This ensures that sample size is kept high enough for precise estimation and that up to 8 waves can be used simultaneously.

This study differs from Stowasser et al. (2012) in that it no longer estimates the incidence of twenty separate health conditions but combines some of them into disease clusters. As a result, health dimensionality is reduced to just six outcomes, which considerably facilitates concise interpretability of results. We consider these outcomes: the number of acute—and immediately life-threatening—conditions (cancer, heart disease, and strokes); the number of chronic diseases (lung disease, diabetes, hypertension, and arthritis); the number of functional health limitations (incontinence, severe falls, hip frac-

6. For further details on HRS, you may refer to Stowasser et al. (2012).
7. Just as in Stowasser et al. (2012), we exclude individuals that generally failed to disclose information on their health. Gaps from insular item nonresponse are filled via simulation-based imputation. For missing wealth and income measures, we use imputations readily available in the public release files provided by the RAND Corporation.

tures, ADL/IADL impairments, and an indicator for obesity); the number of mental illnesses (cognitive impairment, psychiatric disease, depression, and whether interviews were conducted with a proxy respondent); self-rated health status; and mortality. Summary statistics for these health indicators as well as for all SES variables used for analysis—namely wealth, income, education, dwelling condition, and neighborhood safety—are presented in appendix table 5A.1.

This contemporary data is complemented with information from retrospective questionnaires on respondents' health, living conditions, and family backgrounds when they were children, that has subsequently become available within HRS. While this method of retrieving information about panel members' lives before the survey's baseline year provides advantages—in the form of low cost, speed, and reduced sample attrition—over longitudinal cohort studies that follow respondents from cradle to grave, one may express doubt about the accuracy of responses. After all, interviewees are asked to recall circumstances that date back at least fifty years.[8] Yet, the growing literature on the reliability of retrospective surveys finds recall bias to be generally negligible (see Berney and Blane 1997; Garrouste and Paccagnella 2010). For instance, while Smith (2009) reports some unsystematic recall error in retrospective HRS data, he finds no evidence for "coloring"—the selective recall of health histories induced by adverse health events late in life—of responses.

Retrospective information on childhood health has been introduced to HRS in two stages. A general index of self-rated health (SRH) before age sixteen—which is constructed in the same way as HRS's five-point scale measure for contemporary SRH—is already available since panel wave 4, hence covering a rather large share of the entire HRS population. On the other hand, effective sample sizes are considerably smaller for the multitude of detailed child-health measures introduced in wave 9, since these are only available for respondents who were still sample members at this late stage. The latter list of variables includes twenty-one health conditions and whether respondents missed school for more than a month due to health problems. Once again, the individual health conditions are grouped to reduce complexity. We distinguish severe health problems (such as cancer or heart disease), less severe conditions (such as ear infections or allergies), mental health problems (such as depression or psychological problems), and classic child diseases (measles, chicken pox, and mumps).

The HRS early-life data also covers the economic living conditions during childhood as well as family background measures and certain child behaviors. Again, some measures are available as early as wave 4. These include a three-point index of self-assessed family SES, information on parental education, paternal unemployment, and whether the family ever solicited

8. The HRS questionnaire defines childhood as life before the age of sixteen.

Table 5.1   **HRS early life data, summary statistics**

Variables	N	Mean	Std. Dev.
Childhood health			
Poor/fair self-rated health	25,266	0.065	0.247
No. of severe conditions	11,624	0.243	0.526
No. of less severe conditions	11,625	0.345	0.665
No. of mental conditions	11,693	0.068	0.289
No. of childhood diseases	10,565	2.228	0.982
Missed school due to health problem	11,681	0.113	0.316
Family background			
Self-rated family SES above average	25,389	0.066	0.249
Self-rated family SES below average	25,389	0.317	0.465
Family needed financial help	24,994	0.125	0.331
Moved due to financial problems	25,246	0.180	0.384
Father's education (in years)	24,806	8.9	3.5
Mother's education (in years)	26,010	9.1	3.3
Father ever unemployed	25,045	0.290	0.454
Mother always worked	17,633	0.171	0.376
Mother sometimes worked	17,633	0.327	0.469
Any parent smoked	11,677	0.634	0.482
Both parents smoked	11,677	0.169	0.375
Smoked as child	15,219	0.185	0.389
Drugs or alcohol as child	11,722	0.005	0.071
Learning problems at school	15,218	0.027	0.162
Father's age (at death) (in years)	29,482	71.6	14.4
Mother's age (at death) (in years)	29,482	75.3	15.1
Adult height (in meters)	29,482	1.69	0.10

Note: N denotes the number of respondents for whom information on the respective variable is available.

financial help or had to move due to economic dire straits. Information on maternal labor-force participation and parental smoking were added in waves 8 and 9, respectively. In addition, starting with wave 9, HRS provides information on childhood smoking, drug and alcohol use, and whether the respondent experienced significant learning problems at school. Another pair of measures—already used by Adams et al. (2003) and Stowasser et al. (2012)—that also capture family effects, but which are not considered part of HRS's retrospective module, are the ages at death (or just the ages, in case they are still alive) of the respondents' parents. Similarly, respondents' adult height is often used as a proxy for health at birth and is correlated with the uterine environment the family provides (see Case and Paxson 2008; and Currie 2011).

Summary statistics for all early-life data used for analysis are provided in table 5.1. As indicated, the number of available observations differs considerably among variables. This needs to be taken into account when deciding which of these information to use for analysis in section 5.4, as statistical power will certainly suffer in case of severe sample-size loss.

5.3 Methodology

The econometric methods used in the present study are essentially those introduced by Adams et al. (2003), with some extensions introduced by Stowasser et al. (2012); we refer to the latter paper for a more detailed discussion. The analysis builds on a dynamic model of health incidence,

$$(1) \qquad f(HI_{it}^{j} \mid \mathbf{HI}_{it}^{k<j}, \mathbf{H}_{it-\tau}, \mathbf{S}_{it-1}, \mathbf{X}_{it-1}, I_{i}),$$

where i denotes the respondent and t indicates time. The dependent variable, HI_{it}^{j} measures a new incidence of a given health condition, where j stands for one of the six health clusters previously introduced. As in Adams et al. (2003), health innovations are thought to be influenced by the following explanatory variables: Instantaneous causal effects from concurrent health shocks on HI_{it}^{j}—such as the development of cancer that is followed by death within the same interwave spell—are captured by $\mathbf{HI}_{it}^{k<j}$, containing the incidence variables for all health indicators (1, . . . , k) that are causally arranged upstream of indicator j.[9] Furthermore, the model controls for health histories, $\mathbf{H}_{it-\tau}$, that capture state dependence and comorbidities, respectively. The vector $\mathbf{X}_{it-1}$ includes demographic controls. The vector of main interest, $\mathbf{S}_{it-1}$, contains lagged levels of wealth, income, educational attainment, and indicators for subpar living environments. If SES is truly causal for health changes in an elderly population, we should expect significant coefficients for at least some of these variables. Moreover, the null hypothesis that

$$(2) \quad f(HI_{it}^{j} \mid \mathbf{HI}_{it}^{k<j}, \mathbf{H}_{it-\tau}, \mathbf{S}_{it-1}, \mathbf{X}_{it-1}, I_{i}) = f(HI_{it}^{j} \mid \mathbf{HI}_{it}^{k<j}, \mathbf{H}_{it-\tau}, \mathbf{X}_{it-1}, I_{i}),$$

that is, that past SES is not Granger causal for health deteriorations, should be rejected, while invariance tests, as described in Adams et al. (2003), are expected to be confirmed.

Model 1 deviates from the original specification of Adams et al. (2003) in three dimensions. First, health histories are no longer assumed to be first-order Markov, as τ may take on values larger than one, to better accommodate the stock characteristics of latent health capital. This part of the analysis, in which we estimate model 1 with alternative specifications for $\mathbf{H}_{it\ \tau}$, is presented in section 5.4.1. Second, the model acknowledges

---

9. Similarly to Adams et al. (2003), the six health indicators are grouped in the order in which instantaneous causality is most likely to flow: acute conditions are listed first, as they can have an immediate impact on mortality. The remaining indicators are stacked as follows: acute conditions upstream of chronic conditions, upstream of functional conditions, upstream of mental conditions, and upstream of SRH.

Table 5.2   **Benchmark results, tests for Granger noncausality**

Health indicator	Test results (65+) W2–9 (N = 50,993)	
	F	M
Acute conditions		
Mortality	○	●●
Chronic conditions	●●●	●●●
Functional conditions	○○	●●●
Mental conditions	●●●	○○○
Self-rated health status	○○○	○○○

Notes: Results are for white females (F) and males (M). Abbreviations are as follows: Granger noncausality rejected at 5 percent level (●), rejected at 1 percent level (●●), or rejected at 0.1 percent level (●●●). Empty symbols indicate that the corresponding invariance test is rejected at the 5 percent level. Blank cells indicate that Granger noncausality cannot be rejected. N denotes the number of respondent-year observations.

the hypothetical presence of individual heterogeneity, I_i, that may induce spurious correlation between health and SES (see hypothesis C). The analysis in table 5.2 seeks to contain the confounding influence of such common effects by using proxy controls for family backgrounds and behavioral factors. Of main interest is whether the finding of Stowasser et al. (2012), that SES is Granger causal for innovations in health even in an elderly population, survives when more realistic health dynamics and a richer set of control variables are incorporated. A confirmation of their results would lend support to a causal interpretation of the observed association.

The final deviation from the original model proposed by Adams et al. (2003) concerns the reduction in health dimensionality by grouping certain medical conditions together. As a consequence, model 1 is fitted by ordered probit (except for mortality and the indicator for poor/fair SRH, which continue to be estimated with a probit model). To ensure the results are not driven by this modeling choice, and to provide a benchmark to which results from section 5.4 can be directly compared, we estimate model 1 with identical health histories and controls as in Adams et al. (2003). Evidently, results are largely insensitive to the aggregation of health measures and mirror the finding of Stowasser et al. (2012) that—with the exception of acute diseases—SES Granger causality cannot be rejected for medical events after the age of sixty-five. These results are at least significant at the 5 percent level, in many cases even at the 1 percent or 0.1 percent level, although model invariance across time is not always supported in a sample that spans over all 8 available panel waves.

5.4 Empirical Analysis

5.4.1 Health Dynamics

The notion of health being a latent capital stock that reflects the entire history of medically relevant events is not new. Ever since Grossman (1972) proposed his seminal health production framework, most health economists acknowledge the existence of "long memory effects" of the human body and mind. Heiss (2011) confirms that this feature characterizes the HRS population, too, as he detects a surprisingly high degree of state dependence in respondents' SRH. Studying the first seven panel waves, he finds that, even if the maximum number of six lags of SRH are included to predict SRH in the seventh wave, all historic variables have significant explanatory power on their own.

In light of this, modeling health dynamics as a first-order Markov chain is unlikely to provide an appropriate description of the evolution of health, as discussed by Stowasser et al. (2012, 494):

> Intuitively, this is because the Markov model assumes that all relevant information about the whole past is captured in the observed variables one period ago. This is unrealistic since knowledge of longer histories would better capture the stock characteristics of health capital [. . .]. Taking functional limitations as an example, a respondent who reported difficulties with walking one year ago and no limitations previously has a different outlook than a respondent who consistently reported difficulties with walking for the last ten years.

A straightforward way to improve the original Adams et al. (2003) model of health dynamics consists of increasing the length of health histories that model 1 controls for. While the performance of higher-order Markov models probably falls short of that of a fully fledged *hidden* Markov model, such as Heiss (2011), they will likely pick up many of the same effects. More importantly, however, there are practical limits to this strategy: the more lags of health conditions that are incorporated, the smaller the effective sample size that remains for analysis. On the one hand, it excludes all respondents that have been part of the sample for fewer waves than required by the desired history length. This may affect both sample attritors and members of refreshment cohorts, meant to keep the panel representative of the underlying population. On the other hand, the sample would even shrink if the panel was completely balanced, as each additional lag of control variables requires to drop one wave for the estimation of health innovations conditional on health histories.

As discussed by Stowasser et al. (2012), such large drops in sample size constitute a problem for the Adams et al. (2003) approach because it will be unable to reject Granger noncausality if test power becomes too small as the sample gets smaller. Given this apparent trade-off between richer health dynamics and the risk to obtain artifactual test results, the number of lags should only be increased with great care. On this account, the knowledge of health during childhood provides a promising alternative to control for even (much) longer histories without having to forego the potential scale limits in the data.

At the same time, the availability of information on child health alleviates the closely related problem of initial conditions—that is, life before respondents enter the panel (see Heckman 1981a). As Smith (2009, 388) notes,

> [k]nowing health or economic status beginning at [survey] baseline is not sufficient because the entire prior histories of health and economic trajectories may matter for current decision making. The absence of information on prebaseline health histories, including childhood health, means that researchers have to rely on a key untestable assumption: baseline health conditions sufficiently summarize individuals' health histories. If they do not, new health events unfolding during the panel may be the delayed (and perhaps predictable) consequence of some knowable part of an individual's health history. If so, health events within the panel cannot be used to measure effects of new exogenous, unanticipated events.

The extent to which retrospective data enables a look into the "black box" of early life, as compared to Adams et al. (2003) and Stowasser et al. (2012), is visualized in figure 5.1. Note that the effective health-history length is depicted to be by one wave (or two years) shorter than panel length theoretically permits.

Given these considerations, we gauge the sensitivity of model 1 to varying representations of health history by gradually increasing the lag length of adult health prevalence, by the inclusion of child health, and by combinations of the two. As argued earlier, these steps are associated with considerable reductions in effective sample size, which entails the risk of confounding any effect from longer health histories with the mere decline in test power. In order to separate these two effects, we also apply the original health-history specification of Adams et al. (2003) to these subsamples. These "dry runs" serve as the benchmarks to which results from models with more sophisticated health histories should be compared. The Granger noncausality test results for all of these specification are summarized in table 5.3.

The first alternative specification models health histories as a second-order Markov process (i.e., the number of health condition lags is increased to two), which reduces the size of the analyzable sample from 50,993 to 42,367 respondent-year observations. As is evident from comparing columns (C) and (D) with columns (A) and (B) of panel A in table 5.3, this has no significant impact on SES Granger causality tests. The same picture emerges when a third-order Markov model is used (see columns [G] and [H]). While with the latter specification, empirical p-values tend to be a bit higher than

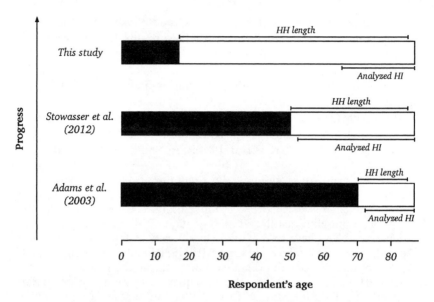

Fig. 5.1   Maximum health-history lengths, comparison between studies

Notes: White boxes indicate known health histories. Black boxes depict unknown health histories. "HH length" denotes the maximum length of health histories that can be exploited for analysis. "Analyzed HI" stands for the age range used to analyze health incidence.

with the lower-ordered Markov model (as indicated by fewer dots), this is clearly not driven by the inclusion of the additional lag but by the reduction in sample size. To see this, consider that p-values also increase for the benchmark case—compare columns (E) and (F) with columns (A) and (B)—whereas the actual switch to a higher-order Markov model—compare columns (G) and (H) to columns (E) and (F)—has no systematic impact at all. Results for even higher-order Markov models are not presented here, as these imply sample sizes too low to conduct meaningful analysis that stratifies by gender.

Panel B of table 5.3 contains results for specifications that use child health to incorporate longer health histories. Recall from section 5.2 that the number of respondents with data on childhood SRH greatly exceeds that of individuals for who we have detailed information on early-life health conditions. For this reason, we add these variables in two sequential steps. Results in columns (L) and (M) are for model 1 when controlling for first-order Markov health histories—the default in Adams et al. (2003)—and self-rated health during childhood. Once again, Granger noncausality tests are not systematically influenced by the incorporation of longer health histories and suggest that, with the exception of acute diseases, causal links from SES to health cannot be statistically rejected. In the second step, we additionally include the more specific data on childhood health conditions, which roughly cuts

Table 5.3:   **Results for varying health histories, tests for Granger noncausality**

A. Higher-order Markov models

Test results

Health indicator	Sample for 2nd-order Markov (N = 42,367)				Sample for 3rd-order Markov (N = 38,886)			
	Dry run		M2		Dry run		M3	
	F (A)	M (B)	F (C)	M (D)	F (E)	M (F)	F (G)	M (H)
Acute conditions								
Mortality	●●●	●●●	●●	●●●	●●	●●	●●	●●
Chronic conditions	●●●	●●	●●●	●●	●●●	●	●●	●
Functional conditions	○○	●●●	○○○	●●●	○○	●●●	○○○	●●●
Mental conditions	●●●	○○○	●●●	○○○	●●●	○○○	●●●	○○○
Self-rated health	○○○	○○○	○○○	○○○	○○○	○○○	●●●	○○○

B. Childhood health

Test results

Health indicator	Sample for SRH (N = 49,962)				Sample for conditions (N = 25,175)			
	Dry run		SRH		Dry run		HC	
	F (J)	M (K)	F (L)	M (M)	F (N)	M (O)	F (P)	M (Q)
Acute conditions								
Mortality	●●	●●●	●●●	●●●	n.a.	n.a.	n.a.	n.a.
Chronic conditions	●●●	●●●	●●●	●●●	●●	●●●	●●●	●●●
Functional conditions	○○	●●●	○○	●●●		●●		●
Mental conditions	●●●	○○○	●●●		●●●	○○○	●●●	●●●
Self-rated health	○○○	○○○	○○○	○○○	○○○	●●●	●●●	●●●

C. Third-order Markov model and childhood health

Test results

Health indicator	Sample for SRH (N = 34,136)				Sample for conditions (N = 19,527)			
	Dry run		M3 & SRH		Dry run		M3 & HC	
	F (R)	M (S)	F (T)	M (U)	F (V)	M (W)	F (X)	M (Y)
Acute conditions								
Mortality	●●	●●	●●	●●	n.a.	n.a.	n.a.	n.a.
Chronic conditions	●●●	●	●	●	●	●		●
Functional conditions	○○	●●●	○○○	●●●		●●●		●●

(*continued*)

Table 5.3: (continued)

	Test results							
	Sample for SRH (N = 34,136)				Sample for conditions (N = 19,527)			
	Dry run		M3 & SRH		Dry run		M3 & HC	
Health indicator	F (R)	M (S)	F (T)	M (U)	F (V)	M (W)	F (X)	M (Y)
Mental conditions	●●●	○○○	●●●	○○○	●●●	○○○	●●●	○○○
Self-rated health	○○○	○○○	●●●	○○○	●●●	●●●	●●●	●●●

Notes: Results are for white females (F) and males (M). Abbreviations are as follows: Granger noncausality rejected at 5 percent level (●), rejected at 1 percent level (●●), or rejected at 0.1 percent level (●●●). Empty symbols indicate that the corresponding invariance test is rejected at the 5 percent level. Blank cells indicate that Granger noncausality cannot be rejected. N denotes the number of respondent-year observations. SRH stands for self-rated health during childhood. HC denotes childhood health conditions. "Dry run" stands for dry runs that use the original specification by Adams et al. (2003). M2 and M3 abbreviate second-order and third-order Markov processes, respectively. That lack in variation impedes estimation of mortality models is indicated by "n.a."

the available sample size in half (49,962 to 25,175 respondent-year observations). The corresponding results in columns (P) and (Q) require some discussion. First of all, the effect of SES on mortality can no longer be studied because information on childhood health conditions is only available for respondents who were still alive in wave 9, which happens to be the most recent wave in the working sample. Furthermore, while it is true that Granger causality of SES is no longer supported for functional health conditions among women, this seems, once again, to be driven by the substantial reduction in sample size. Also note that, while the change in results for functional conditions among men (when comparing columns [O] and [Q]) seems substantial at first sight, a look at the actual *p*-values reveals that the change—from 0.0089 to 0.0104—is only marginal at best.

For results in panel C of table 5.3, we combine both ways of accommodating health histories, which should arguably provide the most comprehensive description of the long memory effects of latent health capital—although this comes at the cost of even greater sample-size loss. Test outcomes in columns (T) and (U) are from a model with third-order Markov health histories and childhood SRH. This specification is then amended with the data on childhood health conditions (see columns [X] and [Y]). Overall, test outcomes depicted here corroborate the findings from panels A and B. If anything, evidence for SES being Granger causal for the development of chronic conditions becomes a little weaker, as the null hypothesis of noncausality is only rejected at the 5 percent level for men and the 5 percent to 15 percent level for women (the corresponding *p*-value in column [X] equals 0.141). Similarly, results for functional conditions among females do again become barely insignificant ($p = 0.120$). While it is certainly possible to dismiss these observations as artifactual side effects of dwindling sample sizes, one should at least note that results are generally less stable for chronic and functional conditions than for mental health and SRH.

Finally, a look at the coefficients of the underlying prediction model 1— not reported here due to space limitations—confirms the earlier finding in the literature that even very long health histories have explanatory power for health innovations in an elderly population. For instance, Heiss's (2011) observation, that all lags of SRH have highly significant predictive power for current SRH, is confirmed even when controlling for SES and third-order Markov health-condition histories. The fact that the same holds true for SRH during childhood hints at an astounding degree of state dependence in latent health and confirms the long reach of childhood circumstances, established by the literature summarized in section 5.1. It is encouraging to observe that test results for Granger noncausality of SES are not significantly changed by accounting for these formerly omitted variables.

5.4.2 Common Effects

As argued earlier, the Granger causality framework proposed by Adams et al. (2003) cannot cleanly distinguish between hypotheses A and C—that is, between "true" causality and spurious correlation due to common effects. This identification problem arises because of unobserved individual heterogeneity—with respect to genetic endowment, family backgrounds, and early-life experiences—that influences both health and SES without there necessarily being a causal relationship between the two. Methodological solutions to this problem either require a set of valid instruments or the use of fixed-effects approaches. Since Adams et al. (2003), Stowasser et al. (2012), and the present chapter study whether the framework proposed by Adams et al. (2003) can serve as a viable *alternative* to IV estimation, it would not make much sense to go down the first mentioned route. Furthermore, while the HRS panel is certainly of sufficient length to estimate equations with individual fixed effects, it is not obvious that such models, which rely on the assumption that coefficients are constant over time, make sense when looking at health and wealth over a period spanning several decades.

For these reasons, this study follows a different strategy, which may well fall short of providing an outright solution to the problem, but should alleviate the confounding influence of unobserved third factors. Acknowledging the fact that the underlying problem is one of omitted variables—namely unobserved individual heterogeneity—we add control variables that should provide reasonable proxies for characteristics of the family and the home environment, as the latter are likely to play a central role in shaping individual preferences, behaviors, and genetic endowment. Naturally, the feasibility of this approach critically hinges on the data at hand. As extensively argued in the childhood-health literature, early-life data provides a number of variables that meet the aforementioned requirement (see—among several others—Case, Lubotsky, and Paxson [2002]; Berger, Paxson, and Waldfogel [2009]; Case, Fertig, and Paxson [2005]; Smith et al. [2010]; Mazzonna 2011; and Kesternich et al. [2012]). For instance, Case, Fertig, and Paxson (2005, 384):

> [. . .] include a large set of variables in [the control vector] C, and assume that this set of variables is rich enough to capture all individual heterogeneity. Indeed, our ability to control for a large set of childhood characteristics is an advantage over much of the previous literature that examines health and SES dynamics.

The fifteen family-background variables used to proxy control for individual effects are listed in table 5.1. As was the case for childhood health conditions, the number of available observations differs substantially among variables, which is why they are also added in two sequential steps. The first tier of controls includes the four proxies for family SES, parental education, paternal unemployment status, parental age (of death), and respondents' adult height. The second tier consists of the aforementioned data to which maternal labor-force status, parental and own smoking behavior as a child, drug use, and information on learning problems in school are added. Again, we estimate benchmark dry runs like those described in section 5.4.2 to distinguish the effects of adding the controls from those that are due to reductions in sample size. Results for Granger noncausality tests, conditional on model invariance, are summarized in table 5.4.

While p-values slightly increase across the board by the inclusion of both tier 1 and tier 2 variables, the changes in test results are not very substantial. Overall, the conclusion that Granger noncausality is statistically rejected for nonacute health events remains intact even after controlling for family backgrounds. The notable exception is functional health, for which results are a bit inconclusive. This underscores the earlier finding that the association between SES and this health dimension appears to be weaker than for other conditions.

In a final step, we estimate a version of model 1 that combines controls for family backgrounds with a more adequate model of health dynamics as developed in section 5.4.1. Note that, inasmuch as these longer histories capture the effect of latent health capital, they may also absorb some of the endogeneity imposed by genetic traits, with severe health problems in childhood being a signal for general frailty. To achieve the most conservative assessment for the presence of Granger causality, we model health histories as third-order Markov with controls for all available childhood health conditions and include the more encompassing second tier of early-life controls. Results are presented in table 5.5 and should be compared to columns (X) and (Y) of table 5.3 and columns (G) and (H) of table 5.4. Even in this most encompassing specification—that comes at the cost of an even smaller and

Table 5.4   **Results for varying family background controls, tests for Granger noncausality**

	Test results							
Health indicator	Sample for tier 1 ($N = 42{,}271$)				Sample for tier 2 ($N = 21{,}250$)			
	Dry run		Tier 1		Dry run		Tier 2	
	F (A)	M (B)	F (C)	M (D)	F (E)	M (F)	F (G)	M (H)
Acute conditions								
Mortality	●●	●●●	●●	●●	n.a.	n.a.	n.a.	n.a.
Chronic conditions	●●●	●●	●●●	●●	●●●	●●●	●●	●●
Functional conditions	○○	●●●	○	●●		●●		●
Mental conditions	●●●	○○○	●●●	●●●	●●●	○○○	●●●	○○○
Self-rated health	○○○	○○○	○○○	○○○	●●●	●●●	●●●	●●●

Notes: Results are for white females (F) and males (M). Abbreviations are as follows: Granger noncausality rejected at 5 percent level (●), rejected at 1 percent level (●●), or rejected at 0.1 percent level (●●●). Empty symbols indicate that the corresponding invariance test is rejected at the 5 percent level. Blank cells indicate that Granger noncausality cannot be rejected. N denotes the number of respondent-year observations. "Dry run" stands for dry runs that use the original specification by Adams et al. (2003). For definitions of tier 1 and tier 2, see text. That lack in variation impedes estimation of mortality models is indicated by "n.a."

less representative sample of just 16,335 respondent-year observations— SES Granger noncausality for mental health conditions and general health status is clearly rejected, which lends credibility to the interpretation that these associations do in fact reflect causal relationships. While results for chronic and functional health conditions are certainly less robust, it is not entirely clear how much of the increase in p-values is driven by the introduction of controls—which would in fact suggest the importance of third factors—and how much is due to dwindling test power that may occult the presence of true, albeit relatively weaker, causal links. A conclusive answer to this question will have to wait for the addition of refreshment cohorts, which will eventually increase the number of available observations for early-life conditions as well.

5.4.3 Pathways between SES and Health

So far, the focus of this study has been the ability of the approach introduced by Adams et al. (2003) to discriminate between true causality and the influence of third factors in case Granger causality is detected. While this general distinction is certainly of interest in its own right, it is equally important to go beyond broad causality tests and investigate more narrowly focused questions about the mechanisms that connect specific health outcomes to specific dimensions in SES. For this reason, we complete our analysis by discussing some key parameter estimates from the underlying

Table 5.5   Results for all controls, tests for Granger non-causality

| Health indicator | Test results ($N = 16{,}335$) | | | |
| | Dry run | | Tier 1 | |
	F (A)	M (B)	F (C)	M (D)
Acute conditions				
Mortality	n.a.	n.a.	n.a.	n.a.
Chronic conditions	●	●		
Functional conditions		●●		●
Mental conditions	●●●	○○○	●●	●●●
Self-rated health	●●●	●●●	●●●	●●●

Notes: Results are for white females (F) and males (M). Abbreviations are as follows: Granger noncausality rejected at 5 percent level (●), rejected at 1 percent level (●●), or rejected at 0.1 percent level (●●●). Empty symbols indicate that the corresponding invariance test is rejected at the 5 percent level. Blank cells indicate that Granger noncausality cannot be rejected. N denotes the number of respondent-year observations. "Dry run" stands for dry runs that use the original specification by Adams et al. (2003). For definition of tier 1, see text. That lack in variation impedes estimation of mortality models is indicated by "n.a."

prediction model, displayed in appendix tables 5A.2, 5A.3, 5A.4, and 5A.5, as they will shed light on the question of how and when links between SES and health are established.[10]

Acute Health Conditions

Results in table 5A.2 confirm our previous observation that adult SES is unlikely to be causal for the development of acute health conditions. In fact, in all of the specifications tested, there is not a single SES marker with a statistically significant impact on this health dimension. Reaffirmingly, estimates in columns (E) and (F) show that the same holds true for family SES during childhood, which is practically unrelated with the occurrence of acute health events in a population age sixty-five and older.

However, childhood health appears to have predictive power for adverse health shocks among retirees: results in columns (C) through (F) show that the number of diseases during childhood matters for women, whereas self-rated childhood health appears to be a sufficient statistic for male respondents. At the same time, the explanatory power of adult health histories is rather low, with first-order Markov processes representing an adequate

10. Note that, as expected, the number of classic child diseases has no explanatory power for any future health outcomes and are therefore excluded from regression tables 5A.2, 5A.3, 5A.4, and 5A.5.

modeling choice for both disease state dependence and comorbidities. While all higher-order lags—whose parameter estimates are not displayed due to space considerations—enter the model with intuitive signs, their effects are not statistically different from zero.

Chronic Health Conditions

As results in table 5A.3 show, evidence for chronic health conditions is less clear-cut. When childhood circumstances are ignored, wealth, income, and education are negatively related with the development of diseases such as diabetes or emphysema. This gradient gets considerably weaker—but does not fully disappear—when controlling for health and family background during early life (see columns [C] through [E]). Recall that these changes may partly be due to dwindling sample sizes that reduce test power, since point estimates for income among women, wealth among men, and college education among men remain rather constant whereas standard errors increase substantially. There is no evidence that the link between SES and chronic diseases is established during childhood, as none of the family background measures exerts any significant influence on adult health outcomes.

Yet, as was the case for acute illnesses, the development of chronic diseases appears to be partly predetermined by childhood health. Having experienced severe health spells before the age of sixteen significantly increases the likelihood of chronic morbidity. For men, the same is true for the number of less severe conditions. This evidence for strong intertemporal dependency is corroborated by estimates—which are again omitted to save space—of adult health histories that endorse a third-order Markov specification to model the evolution of chronic health conditions.

Functional Health Conditions

Mirroring the preceding analysis in sections 5.4.1 and 5.4.2, the strong link between *adult* SES and functional health detected in columns (A) and (B) of table 5A.4 is substantially weakened—and all but disappears for women—when early-life circumstances are added to the analysis. However, this should not automatically be taken as evidence against the general causality of SES for functional impairments. In fact, results in column (E) suggest that the SES gradient does survive even for women, but that it is already established during childhood: having grown up in a family with low SES and having been raised by guardians that smoked significantly impairs functional health for female retirees. Given the substantially higher labor market participation among men, it is not surprising that their link between SES and functional health seems to work through higher education, rendering family effects insignificant in column (F).

The long reach of early life is, once again, underlined by the fact that childhood health also affects functional well-being at higher ages. For women it is the number of mental health problems that matters, whereas men are sensitive to the number of less severe illnesses when growing up. With respect to adult health histories, third-order Markov processes fare much better than short-memory models. This is especially true for chronic comorbidities and indicators for subpar self-rated health, whose lagged values—not displayed here—all enter with significantly positive signs.

Mental Health Conditions

Finally, the nature of the SES gradient in mental health—under inspection in table 5A.5—closely resembles that of functional impairments. Again, the link appears to be established during childhood for women and later in life for men. Female retirees with mental health problems report that they suffered from learning difficulties, that they smoked as a child, and that their family had to change homes due to financial impasse.[11] In addition, mental health as a child is by far the strongest predictor for psychological and cognitive problems among elderly women. By contrast, childhood circumstances are far less consequential for men, whose mental well-being is primarily influenced by years of schooling and current financial wealth.

As was the case for chronic and for functional health conditions, the evolution of mental health is well described by third-order Markov models whose explanatory power clearly exceeds that of lower-order processes not reported here.

5. 5 Conclusion

This study addresses three critiques of the methodology for studying causality in the health-wealth nexus that was introduced by Adams et al. (2003). Building on Stowasser et al. (2012), we exploit the availability of retrospective data on early-life events, which allows for improved control of initial conditions and individual heterogeneity.

The first issue we address is the model of health dynamics. We implement higher-order Markov models and control for information on childhood health to accommodate the long memory effects of latent health capital. In line with the literature on early-life circumstances, we find that childhood health has lasting predictive power for adult health. This, however, does not render contemporary factors unimportant. Our analysis also suggests that— with the sole exception of acute health conditions—third-order Markov processes are a better description of health evolutions than shorter-memory models. At the same time, causality tests are largely insensitive to varying models of health histories.

Furthermore, we confirm the findings by Stowasser et al. (2012) that SES is unlikely to be causal for the development of acute health conditions but that Granger noncausality can—even in an elderly population age sixty-five

---

11. Note that the two latter indicators are only marginally significant at the 10 percent level.

and older—be statistically rejected for mental health conditions, mortality, and changes in overall health. Evidence for chronic diseases and functional health is somewhat inconclusive. This may simply reflect the problem that Granger causality tests require relatively large sample sizes to obtain adequate power, as discussed by Stowasser et al. (2012).

The second methodological issue is the inability to distinguish between true causal links and common effects in case Granger causality is detected. The present study alleviates this concern by conditioning on early-life events that may function as proxies for unobserved individual heterogeneity, with health problems in childhood being a signal for physical frailty, and parental SES and health-relevant behaviors capturing family effects. Results from this modification closely mirror those of accounting for longer health histories. The fact that results for mental health and overall health status are remarkably robust, lends support to a causal interpretation of the observed gradient for these health dimensions.

Ultimately, however, the assessment of this issue will depend on how narrowly one wishes to define "true" causality. In our opinion, it is fair to argue that SES may even have a causal effect—in a rather wide sense—on individual heterogeneity, rendering the distinction between hypotheses A and C almost arbitrary. In fact, there is increasing evidence that personal characteristics are not as immutable as was once believed. For instance, part of the literature on the education-health gradient argues that the years spent in education may not only change health-relevant knowledge, but also preferences, behaviors, and the way people think about their future (see Cutler and Lleras-Muney 2008). In a similar vein, Currie (2011) reports evidence that even the activation of genetic traits—once considered the holy grail of irrevocability—may depend on environmental factors as well.

Finally, we address a third critique of the Adams et al. (2003) approach, the lack of a microfoundation of the pathways between SES and health. We scrutinize the underlying prediction model, which reveals pronounced gender differences in the origin of the gradient. While the link between SES and chronic illness appears to be established rather late in life, the same cannot be said about functional and mental health conditions among female retirees. For them, low family SES and mental problems as a child are the most predictive markers for health deteriorations in late adulthood, hinting at an exceptionally high degree of intertemporal and perhaps even intergenerational transmission of health and SES. In contrast to this, the SES gradient in functional and mental health for men—whose past labor market participation is much higher than that of female HRS respondents—does not stem from childhood circumstances but is rather established during (secondary) education and adulthood.

Substantively, our findings add to the current debate about the role of early childhood circumstances for lifetime health. To the extent that future health outcomes are at least partly predetermined by childhood circumstances, public health policies should not neglect the importance of providing educative and financial support for young families. Our findings support the notion that social returns from such investments are likely to match those of measures that aim at altering the availability and use of health care in adulthood.

Appendix

Additional Tables

The following tables contain regression results from our underlying prediction model and summary statistics for the data set used in our analysis. Due to their large dimensions, they are each displayed on an individual page.

Table 5A.1   Contemporary health and SES variables used for analysis, summary statistics

Variable	Wave 2 (N = 8,726)		Wave 3 (N = 9,258)		Wave 4 (N = 11,916)		Wave 5 (N = 11,953)		Wave 6 (N = 12,273)		Wave 7 (N = 12,153)		Wave 8 (N = 12,502)		Wave 9 (N = 12,468)	
	Mean	StDev.	Mean	StDev.	Mean	StDev.	Mean	StDev.	Mean	StDev.	Mean	StDev.	Mean	StDev.	Mean	StDev.
No. of acute conditions	0.541	0.685	0.659	0.743	0.643	0.743	0.658	0.746	0.671	0.753	0.698	0.767	0.710	0.776	0.721	0.779
No. of chronic conditions	1.004	0.880	1.086	0.905	1.089	0.908	1.121	0.913	1.173	0.921	1.229	0.926	1.285	0.929	1.341	0.938
No. of functional conditions	1.316	1.120	1.535	1.264	1.562	1.278	1.654	1.299	1.171	1.303	1.768	1.311	1.851	1.316	1.905	1.308
No. of mental conditions	0.587	0.874	0.635	0.900	0.601	0.897	0.628	0.921	0.642	0.924	0.619	0.909	0.589	0.874	0.580	0.866
Poor/fair self-rated health	0.358	0.479	0.341	0.474	0.373	0.484	0.328	0.469	0.327	0.469	0.335	0.472	0.334	0.472	0.329	0.470
No. of acute conditions			0.244	0.491	0.277	0.522	0.219	0.471	0.236	0.486	0.219	0.471	0.218	0.467	0.221	0.475
Died since last wave			0.104	0.306	0.101	0.301	0.108	0.311	0.115	0.319	0.098	0.297	0.100	0.300	0.101	0.301
No. of chronic conditions			0.198	0.453	0.206	0.441	0.205	0.444	0.199	0.436	0.227	0.458	0.224	0.461	0.215	0.447
No. of functional conditions			0.843	1.072	0.874	1.077	0.798	1.018	0.830	1.038	0.836	1.042	0.931	1.068	0.908	1.040
No. of mental conditions			0.260	0.561	0.236	0.530	0.199	0.488	0.205	0.498	0.169	0.447	0.163	0.432	0.156	0.425
1st quartile wealth indicator	0.255	0.436	0.230	0.421	0.227	0.419	0.219	0.413	0.214	0.410	0.215	0.411	0.217	0.412	0.212	0.409
4th quartile wealth indicator	0.183	0.387	0.221	0.415	0.255	0.436	0.275	0.447	0.291	0.454	0.306	0.461	0.330	0.470	0.328	0.470
1st quartile income indicator	0.368	0.482	0.335	0.472	0.291	0.454	0.292	0.455	0.277	0.447	0.278	0.448	0.272	0.445	0.274	0.446
4th quartile income indicator	0.117	0.321	0.144	0.351	0.161	0.368	0.167	0.373	0.169	0.375	0.176	0.381	0.177	0.382	0.193	0.394
Poor/fair housing condition	0.133	0.340	0.128	0.334	0.114	0.318	0.106	0.308	0.097	0.296	0.116	0.320	0.108	0.310	0.104	0.305
Poor/fair neighborhood safety	0.145	0.325	0.132	0.338	0.101	0.302	0.089	0.284	0.075	0.263	0.086	0.281	0.096	0.294	0.094	0.291
High school (educ. > 10 y.)	0.613	0.487	0.629	0.483	0.672	0.469	0.692	0.462	0.716	0.451	0.735	0.441	0.754	0.431	0.766	0.423
College (educ. > 14 y.)	0.147	0.354	0.156	0.363	0.172	0.378	0.180	0.385	0.193	0.195	0.199	0.399	0.206	0.404	0.218	0.413

Note: Summary statistics are for the age-eligible sample (65+).

Table 5A.2   Prediction model for acute health conditions[a]

| | Ordered probit regression coefficients z-statistics in parentheses | | | | | |
| | Dry run | | Child health | | Family | |
Key explanatory variables	F (A)	M (B)	F (C)	M (D)	F (E)	M (F)
Current SES						
Wealth (1st qtl.)	0.023	0.031	0.000	0.005	0.012	0.008
	(1.02)	(1.19)	(0.08)	(1.03)	(0.24)	(1.40)
Wealth (4th qtl.)	−0.025	−0.044	0.012	−0.015	0.012	0.001
	(−1.15)	(−1.89)	(0.32)	(−0.37)	(0.29)	(0.11)
Income (1st qtl.)	−0.037	−0.044	−0.044	0.059	−0.026	0.018
	(−1.75)	(−1.86)	(−1.10)	(−1.31)	(−0.58)	(0.36)
Income (4th qtl.)	−0.005	−0.030	−0.012	−0.033	−0.009	−0.072
	(−0.19)	(−0.12)	(−0.27)	(−0.69)	(−0.17)	(−1.39)
High school	0.001	0.001	0.046	0.044	0.035	0.048
	(0.58)	(0.23)	(1.12)	(1.01)	(0.72)	(0.93)
College	−0.038	−0.001	−0.087	−0.030	−0.090	−0.010
	(−1.52)	(−0.38)	(−1.90)	(−0.68)	(−1.81)	(−0.21)
Child health history						
Poor/fair SRH			0.059	0.182***	−0.009	0.188**
			(0.94)	(2.67)	(−0.14)	(2.57)
Less severe cond.			0.034	0.054	0.050**	0.057
			(1.40)	(1.77)	(1.96)	(1.73)
Severe cond.			0.056	0.023	0.076**	0.030
			(1.87)	(0.65)	(2.28)	(0.80)
Mental cond.			0.135**	−0.129	0.180***	−0.012
			(2.45)	(−1.82)	(2.87)	(−1.52)
Family background						
Father's age	−0.001**	−0.002***	−0.000	−0.001	−0.001	−0.002
	(−2.23)	(−2.69)	(−0.11)	(−0.88)	(−0.56)	(−1.23)
Mother's age	−0.001***	−0.001**	−0.001	−0.001	−0.001	−0.001
	(−2.66)	(−2.03)	(−0.74)	(−1.33)	(−0.75)	(−0.44)

	M1	M1	M3	M3	M3	M3
Father's education					−0.007	0.009
					(−0.90)	(1.23)
Mother's education					0.011	−0.010
					(1.33)	(−1.25)
High family SES					0.005	0.105
					(0.07)	(1.24)
Low family SES					0.042	−0.027
					(1.07)	(−0.64)
Financial help					−0.033	−0.010
					(−0.56)	(−1.57)
Need to move					0.012	0.008
					(0.67)	(0.49)
Father unemployed					0.060	−0.027
					(1.52)	(−0.62)
Mother employed					0.020	0.007
					(1.56)	(0.48)
Parents smoked					0.012	−0.066**
					(0.76)	(−2.19)
Kid smoked					0.011	0.076
					(0.18)	(1.70)
Kid alcohol/drug					−0.000	0.152
					(−0.04)	(0.40)
Kid trouble learning					0.079	0.067
					(1.30)	(1.05)
Adult health history	M1	M1	M3	M3	M3	M3
N	31,805	23,268	11,573	7,954	9,630	6,705
Log likelihood	−16,668.7	−13,880.9	−4,637.9	−3,889.4	−3,845.1	−3,266.6

Notes: Results are for white females (F) and males (M). Abbreviations are as follows: *N* denotes the number of respondent-year observations. "Dry run" stands for dry runs that use the original specification by Adams et al. (2003). SRH stands for self-rated health during childhood. M1 and M3 abbreviate 1st-order and 3rd-order Markov processes, respectively.

ªDependent variable: number of acute health incidences.

***Significant at the 1 percent level.

**Significant at the 5 percent level.

*Significant at the 10 percent level.

Table 5A.3   Prediction model for chronic health conditions[a]

	Ordered probit regression coefficients z-statistics in parentheses					
	Dry run		Child health		Family	
Key explanatory variables	F (A)	M (B)	F (C)	M (D)	F (E)	M (F)
Current SES						
Wealth (1st qtl.)	0.005	0.112*	0.023	0.138***	0.02	0.144**
	(0.20)	(3.81)	(0.57)	(2.76)	(0.23)	(2.52)
Wealth (4th qtl.)	−0.028	0.005	−0.036	0.032	−0.048	0.051
	(−1.36)	(0.18)	(−1.10)	(0.79)	(−1.35)	(1.19)
Income (1st qtl.)	0.065***	−0.027	0.038	−0.015	0.086**	0.010
	(3.02)	(−1.04)	(1.06)	(−0.35)	(2.16)	(0.21)
Income (4th qtl.)	−0.012	−0.015	−0.006	−0.020	−0.007	−0.035
	(−0.49)	(−0.52)	(−0.14)	(−0.42)	(−0.17)	(−0.70)
High school	−0.083*	−0.008	0.017	−0.003	0.066	0.003
	(−3.81)	(−0.31)	(0.45)	(−0.78)	(1.51)	(0.93)
College	0.007	−0.092*	−0.087**	−0.100**	−0.063	−0.074
	(0.30)	(−3.58)	(−2.19)	(−2.31)	(−1.48)	(−1.58)
Child health history						
Poor/fair SRH			−0.002	0.088	0.012	−0.136
			(−0.03)	(−1.25)	(0.17)	(−1.79)
Less severe cond.			0.038	0.079***	0.035	0.067**
			(1.71)	(2.64)	(1.43)	(2.07)
Severe cond.			0.049	0.065	0.071**	0.092**
			(1.75)	(1.90)	(2.28)	(2.51)
Mental cond.			0.037	0.001	0.011	0.032
			(0.72)	(0.02)	(0.19)	(0.44)
Family background						
Father's age	−0.001**		−0.002**	0.001	−0.003**	−0.002
	(−2.35)		(−2.15)	(0.60)	(−2.53)	(−1.18)
Mother's age	0.001		0.000	0.001	0.001	0.000
	(0.08)		(0.44)	(0.69)	(0.73)	(0.30)

	M1	M1	M3	M3	M3	M3
Father's education					0.001	−0.005
					(0.20)	(−0.73)
Mother's education					−0.004	−0.004
					(−0.59)	(−0.47)
High family SES					0.001	0.037
					(0.02)	(0.43)
Low family SES					−0.011	0.026
					(−0.31)	(0.63)
Financial help					−0.087	0.007
					(−1.64)	(0.11)
Need to move					0.065	−0.023
					(1.55)	(−0.48)
Father unemployed					0.024	0.028
					(0.69)	(0.66)
Mother employed					−0.007	0.013
					(−0.61)	(0.92)
Parents smoked					0.000	0.035
					(0.02)	(1.20)
Kid smoked					−0.074	0.059
					(−1.35)	(1.34)
Kid alcohol/drug					−0.000	−0.028
					(−0.78)	(−0.07)
Kid trouble learning					−0.083	0.131
					(−0.58)	(1.13)
Adult health history	M1	M1	M3	M3	M3	M3
N	29,649	21,344	11,573	7,954	9,630	6,705
Log likelihood	−16,150.6	−10,997.9	−6,206.0	−4,031.0	−5,125.3	−3,389.1

Notes: Results are for white females (F) and males (M). Abbreviations are as follows: N denotes the number of respondent-year observations. "Dry run" stands for dry runs that use the original specification by Adams et al. (2003). SRH stands for self-rated health during childhood. M1 and M3 abbreviate 1st-order and 3rd-order Markov processes, respectively.

[a]Dependent variable: number of chronic health incidences.

***Significant at the 1 percent level.

**Significant at the 5 percent level.

*Significant at the 10 percent level.

Table 5A.4   **Prediction model for functional health conditions[a]**

| | Ordered probit regression coefficients z-statistics in parentheses | | | | | |
| | Dry run | | Child health | | Family | |
Key explanatory variables	F (A)	M (B)	F (C)	M (D)	F (E)	M (F)
Current SES						
Wealth (1st qtl.)	0.000	0.091*	0.024	0.081**	0.023	0.059
	(0.01)	(3.84)	(0.74)	(1.98)	(0.64)	(1.26)
Wealth (4th qtl.)	-0.012	-0.027	0.025	-0.010	0.010	-0.006
	(-0.74)	(-1.33)	(0.99)	(-0.31)	(0.37)	(-0.17)
Income (1st qtl.)	-0.009	0.020	-0.036	0.038	-0.016	0.043
	(-0.55)	(0.94)	(-1.29)	(1.27)	(-0.51)	(1.08)
Income (4th qtl.)	-0.010	0.017	-0.004	0.047	-0.006	0.030
	(-0.51)	(0.72)	(-0.13)	(1.24)	(-0.17)	(0.73)
High school	-0.044***	-0.017	-0.046	-0.009	-0.046	0.014
	(-2.61)	(-0.79)	(-1.58)	(-0.24)	(-1.34)	(0.34)
College	-0.062*	-0.060*	-0.041	-0.119*	-0.049	-0.129*
	(-3.33)	(-2.91)	(-1.35)	(-3.43)	(-1.46)	(-3.44)
Child health history						
Poor/fair SRH			-0.032	-0.011	-0.045	-0.027
			(-0.68)	(-0.19)	(-0.86)	(-0.44)
Less severe cond.			0.023	0.030	0.030	0.056**
			(1.30)	(1.22)	(1.54)	(2.09)
Severe cond.			0.054**	0.051	0.035	0.041
			(2.45)	(1.84)	(1.43)	(1.37)
Mental cond.			0.159*	0.039	0.156***	0.066
			(3.82)	(0.75)	(3.24)	(1.11)
Family background						
Father's age	0.000	0.000	-0.001	0.001	-0.001	0.001
	(0.89)	(0.63)	(-0.74)	(1.45)	(-1.17)	(1.45)
Mother's age	-0.000	0.001	0.001	-0.001	0.001	-0.000
	(-0.43)	(0.92)	(1.42)	(-0.68)	(1.05)	(-0.33)

	M1	M1	M3	M3	M3	M3
Father's education					0.000	−0.011
					(0.04)	(−1.87)
Mother's education					0.002	0.000
					(0.44)	(0.02)
High family SES					0.084	0.127
					(1.71)	(1.86)
Low family SES					0.122***	−0.017
					(4.45)	(−0.50)
Financial help					0.059	−0.001
					(1.46)	(−0.11)
Need to move					0.072**	0.032
					(2.20)	(0.80)
Father unemployed					−0.068**	0.026
					(−2.45)	(0.75)
Mother employed					−0.008	−0.001
					(−0.90)	(−0.08)
Parents smoked					0.055***	0.044
					(2.99)	(1.84)
Kid smoked					0.035	−0.013
					(0.80)	(−0.35)
Kid alcohol/drug					0.367	−0.049
					(0.76)	(−1.36)
Kid trouble learning					0.009	0.031
					(0.08)	(0.31)
Adult health history	M1	M1	M3	M3	M3	M3
N	29,649	21,344	11,573	7,954	9,630	6,705
Log likelihood	−66,786.2	−22,219.3	−13,213.0	−7,589.5	−10,870.5	−6,372.4

Notes: **Results are for white females (F) and males (M).** Abbreviations are as follows: N denotes the number of respondent-year observations. "Dry run" stands for dry runs that use the original specification by Adams et al. (2003). SRH stands for self-rated health during childhood. M1 and M3 abbreviate 1st-order and 3rd-order Markov processes, respectively.

[a]Dependent variable: number of functional health incidences.

***Significant at the 1 percent level.

**Significant at the 5 percent level.

*Significant at the 10 percent level.

Table 5A.5 Prediction model for mental health conditions[a]

	Ordered probit regression coefficients z-statistics in parentheses					
	Dry run		Child health		Family	
Key explanatory variables	F (A)	M (B)	F (C)	M (D)	F (E)	M (F)
Current SES						
Wealth (1st qtl.)	0.061**	0.156*	0.065	0.223*	0.088	0.279*
	(2.40)	(4.92)	(1.42)	(3.83)	(1.69)	(4.21)
Wealth (4th qtl.)	-0.016	-0.021	-0.024	-0.011	-0.020	-0.022
	(-0.65)	(-0.71)	(-0.60)	(-0.22)	(-0.46)	(-0.39)
Income (1st qtl.)	0.072***	0.087***	0.006	0.030	-0.051	0.028
	(3.17)	(3.00)	(0.13)	(0.56)	(-1.10)	(0.46)
Income (4th qtl.)	-0.088***	-0.065	-0.079	0.015	-0.105	0.030
	(-3.03)	(-1.88)	(-1.59)	(0.25)	(-1.94)	(0.45)
High school	-0.188*	-0.174*	-0.147*	-0.147*	-0.089	-0.146**
	(-8.19)	(-6.22)	(-3.58)	(-2.87)	(-1.82)	(-2.41)
College	-0.048	-0.081***	-0.104***	-0.118**	-0.089	-0.106
	(-1.72)	(-2.65)	(-2.09)	(-2.04)	(-1.64)	(-1.70)
Child health history						
Poor/fair SRH			0.023	-0.078	0.029	-0.097
			(0.34)	(-0.92)	(0.38)	(-1.03)
Less severe cond.			0.061**	0.013	0.064**	0.033
			(2.37)	(0.35)	(2.28)	(0.81)
Severe cond.			-0.003	0.068	0.002	0.074
			(-0.08)	(1.64)	(0.07)	(1.60)
Mental cond.			0.296*	0.210***	0.271*	0.156
			(5.43)	(2.88)	(4.27)	(1.82)
Family background						
Father's age	0.001	-0.000	0.001	0.000	0.001	-0.001
	(1.04)	(-0.31)	(1.19)	(0.02)	(0.74)	(-0.36)
Mother's age	0.000	0.001	0.001	0.000	0.001	-0.000
	(0.33)	(0.65)	(0.50)	(0.22)	(0.78)	(-0.23)

	M1	M3	M3	M1	M3	M3
Father's education					−0.008 (−1.10)	−0.010 (−1.01)
Mother's education					−0.009 (−1.03)	0.011 (1.05)
High family SES					−0.038 (−0.49)	−0.018 (−1.51)
Low family SES					0.013 (0.33)	−0.031 (−0.60)
Financial help					0.093 (1.54)	−0.043 (−0.57)
Need to move					−0.031 (−0.64)	0.055 (0.90)
Father unemployed					−0.057 (−1.36)	0.034 (0.62)
Mother employed					−0.006 (−0.45)	−0.004 (−0.25)
Parents smoked					−0.034 (−1.20)	0.023 (0.61)
Kid smoked					0.109 (1.73)	−0.023 (−0.40)
Kid alcohol/drug					0.246 (0.38)	−0.215 (−0.47)
Kid trouble learning					0.338** (2.41)	0.076 (0.52)
Adult health history						
N	29,649	21,344	11,573	7,954	9,630	6,705
Log likelihood	−12,117.7	−7,737.3	−4,177.3	−2,410.8	−3,410.6	−1,966.7

Notes: Results are for white females (F) and males (M). Abbreviations are as follows: N denotes the number of respondent-year observations. "Dry run" stands for dry runs that use the original specification by Adams et al. (2003). SRH stands for self-rated health during childhood. M1 and M3 abbreviate 1st-order and 3rd-order Markov processes, respectively.

[a]Dependent variable: number of mental health incidences.

***Significant at the 1 percent level.

**Significant at the 5 percent level.

*Significant at the 10 percent level.

References

Adams, P., M. D. Hurd, D. McFadden, A. Merrill, and T. Ribeiro. 2003. "Healthy, Wealthy, and Wise? Tests for Direct Causal Paths between Health and Socioeconomic Status." *Journal of Econometrics* 112:3–56.

Almond, D., and J. Currie. 2011. "Human Capital Development Before Age Five." In *Handbook of Labor Economics*, vol. 4b, *15*, edited by O. Ashenfelter and D. Card. Elsevier.

Berger, L. M., C. Paxson, and J. Waldfogel. 2009. "Income and Child Development." *Children and Youth Services Review* 31:978–89.

Berney, L., and D. Blane. 1997. "Collecting Retrospective Data: Accuracy of Recall after 50 years Judged Against Historical Records." *Social Science & Medicine* 45 (10): 1519–25.

Case, A., A. Fertig, and C. Paxson. 2005. "The Lasting Impact of Childhood Health and Circumstance." *Journal of Health Economics* 24:365–89.

Case, A., D. Lubotsky, and C. Paxson. 2002. "Economic Status and Health in Childhood: The Origins of the Gradient." *American Economic Review* 92 (5): 1308–34.

Case, A., and C. Paxson. 2008. "Height, Health, and Cognitive Function at Older Ages." *American Economic Review: Papers & Proceedings* 98 (2): 463–7.

Currie, J. 2009. "Healthy, Wealthy, and Wise: Socioeconomic Status, Poor Health in Childhood, and Human Capital Development." *Journal of Economic Literature* 47 (1): 87–122.

———. 2011. "Inequality at Birth: Some Causes and Consequences." *American Economic Review: Papers & Proceedings* 101 (3): 1–22.

Cutler, D. M., and A. Lleras-Muney. 2008. "Education and Health: Evaluating Theories and Evidence." In *Making Americans Healthier: Social and Economic Policy as Health Policy*, edited by J. House, R. Schoeni, G. Kaplan, and H. Pollack, 29–60. New York: Russell Sage Foundation.

Cutler, D. M., A. Lleras-Muney, and T. Vogl. 2011. "Socioeconomic Status and Health: Dimensions and Mechanisms." In *The Oxford Handbook of Health Economics*, edited by S. Glied and P. C. Smith, 124–163. New York: Oxford University Press.

Deaton, A. 2010. "Instruments, Randomization, and Learning about Development." *Journal of Economic Literature* 48:424–55.

Garrouste, C., and O. Paccagnella. 2010. "Data Quality: Three Examples of Consistency Across SHARE and SHARELIFE Data." In *Retrospective Data Collection in the Survey of Health, Ageing amd Retirement in Europe*, edited by M. Schröder, 62–72. Munich: Mannheim Research Institute for the Economics of Aging (MEA).

Grossman, M. 1972. "On the Concept of Health Capital and the Demand for Health." *Journal of Political Economy* 80 (2): 223–55.

Heckman, J. J. 1981a. "The Incidental Parameters Problem and the Problem of Initial Conditions in Estimating a Discrete Time-Discrete Data Stochastic Process." In *Structural Analysis of Discrete Data and Econometric Applications*, edited by C. F. Manski and D. McFadden, 179–196. Cambridge, MA: MIT Press.

———. 1981b. "Statistical Models for Discrete Panel Data." In *Structural Analysis of Discrete Data and Econometric Applications*, edited by C. F. Manski and D. McFadden, 114–178. Cambridge, MA: MIT Press.

Heiss, F. 2011. "Dynamics of Self-Rated Health and Selective Mortality." *Empirical Economics* 40 (1): 119–40.

Kesternich, I., B. Siflinger, J. P. Smith, and J. Winter. Forthcoming. "The Effects of World War II on Economic and Health Outcomes across Europe." *Review of Economics and Statistics*.

Mazzonna, F. 2011. "The Long-Lasting Effects of Family Background: A European Cross-Country Comparison." Working Paper 245-2011, Munich Center for the Economics of Aging.

Smith, J. P. 1999. "Healthy Bodies and Thick Wallets: The Dual Relationship between Health and Economic Status." *Journal of Economic Perspectives* 13 (2): 145–66.

———. 2009. "Reconstructing Childhood Health Histories." *Demography* 46 (2): 387–403.

Smith, J. P., Y. Shen, J. Strauss, Y. Zhe, and Y. Zhao. 2010. "The Effects of Childhood Health on Adult Health and SES in China." Working Paper 809, RAND Corporation.

Stowasser, T., F. Heiss, D. McFadden, and J. Winter. 2012. "'Healthy, Wealthy and Wise?' Revisited: An Analysis of the Causal Pathways from Socio-Economic Status to Health." In *Investigations in the Economics of Aging*, edited by D. A. Wise, 267–317. Chicago: University of Chicago Press.

Comment   Robert J. Willis

This is the tenth anniversary of the publication of Adams et al. (2003) that introduced the idea of using Granger causality to test hypotheses about causal factors that underlie correlations between health and socioeconomic status. This paper generated a great deal of controversy about the interpretation of the Granger approach—and the meaning of causality more generally—and the implications of their empirical results in the context of conflicting literatures in epidemiology and economics about causal factors underlying the SES gradient in health. Using longitudinal data from the AHEAD cohort of the HRS containing persons age seventy and over at baseline, they found that health shocks Granger-cause changes in wealth but they rejected the hypothesis that SES Granger-causes health.

The Adams et al. (2003) finding of a causal effect of health on SES, a line of causation largely ignored by epidemiologists, was uncontroversial. However, their finding of Granger noncausation of SES on health flew in the face of an epidemiology literature in which virtually all correlations between SES and health were assumed to reflect this line of causation. Although Granger causation provides little insight into the particular mechanisms that may connect innovations in socioeconomic variables to changes in health, rejection of Granger causation may seem to undermine much of the epidemiological literature in one fell swoop because, if the noncausality results

Robert J. Willis is professor of economics and research professor in the Department of Economics and the Institute for Social Research at the University of Michigan and a research associate of the National Bureau of Economic Research.

For acknowledgments, sources of research support, and disclosure of the author's material financial relationships, if any, please see http://www.nber.org/chapters/c12977.ack.

are taken at face value, all possible causal mechanisms by which SES affects health are shown to be statistically insignificant.

Of course, such a sweeping conclusion is too strong because the Adams et al. (2003) results were for a particular sample of given size of quite elderly people who are largely retired and covered by Medicare. Granger causation might be found in a larger sample of persons with a longer period of observation, especially in age groups in which economic and social factors might play a larger role in determining access to care or motivation for the maintenance of health. With these possibilities in mind, Stowasser et al. (2012) replicated the methodology of Adams et al. (2003), adding data from the younger HRS cohorts when they reach age sixty-five to the then longer histories of the AHEAD cohort. With the additional statistical power provided by this enlarged sample, Stowasser et al. (2012) found that they could not generally reject Granger causation from SES to health. Thus, they could not rule out any of the three possible hypotheses concerning the correlation between SES and health: SES causes health, health causes SES, or that both health and SES are caused by some third set of unmeasured factors.

In the current chapter, Stowasser et al. continue to use the Granger methodology, with a focus on seeing what they can say about the line of causation from SES to health, while doing what they can to control for unmeasured heterogeneity that might lead to spurious correlations between SES and health, by allowing for higher than first-order Markov dependence of current health on past health to capture the capital-like character of health and by including measures of childhood health and family background. Although more elaborate controls and longer lags result in losses in sample size, overall they conclude that there is credible evidence of causal impacts of SES on health, with the exception of acute conditions.

Given the original emphasis in Adams et al. (2003) on the strong implications of findings of Granger noncausality, I found it surprising that the current chapter provides little discussion of the implications of what they find to be quite strong evidence of noncausality for heart attacks, stroke, and cancer, which comprise the aggregate category they label as acute life-threatening conditions. These conditions are, of course, among the major killers in advanced societies that are well past the epidemiological transition in which death from infectious disease is replaced by death from chronic illness. A finding of Granger noncausality for SES on these conditions implies that no pathway involving economic resources would have any effect on the incidence of heart attack, stroke, or cancer among the population of people over age sixty-five.

To me, this seems to be a potentially major finding worthy of further discussion. What are the specific hypotheses put forward by economists, epidemiologists, or others that are ruled out by the finding of Granger noncausality of SES for heart attack, stroke, or cancer among older people? I am not an expert in this area, so I do not know whether this finding would (or should) change the views of experts in epidemiology or health economics. For example, do many of the experts believe that the extra access to care afforded by the purchase of medigap insurance provides no extra protection beyond what basic Medicare provides in the case of acute disease? Actually, I suspect that most experts would say that money buys little protection against the occurrence of these diseases, but may help prevent or delay death from them once they occur by providing access to more or better quality medical care. The failure of the authors to reject noncausality for mortality would support this argument.

Stowasser et al. find significant effects of higher-order Markov dependency and, often, of childhood health and family background variables, which implies that one's current health status depends on a "long memory" of past health shocks. This important finding suggests that any causal account of the determinants of the SES-health gradient is likely to be very complex, with room for feedback loops involving causation running in both directions in a high dimensional state space. The authors present the Granger causality approach as an alternative to structural models that require some kind of exogenous instrument to identify causal effects. Valid instruments are difficult to find and, even when available, may not identify causal effects of general interest. However, the Granger approach, at best, seems to offer clues for more focused research on particular issues. For example, what should one make of their finding that mental health problems are linked to childhood conditions for females, but not for males? Assuming this differential to be a true empirical regularity, it still requires some theoretical ideas or hunches about differences in the underlying mechanisms that determine mental health to indicate which among many possible lines of focused research might provide a causal explanation of this finding.

In sum, the line of research that began a decade ago with Adams et al. (2003) has shown that it is imperative to view the determinants of health within a dynamic framework encompassing the entire life cycle. Their data-hungry research program has been aided enormously—and increasingly—by availability of longitudinal data from the HRS, which grows in length with each wave and, in recent waves, has attempted to capture early life SES and health conditions. The early hope that the Granger methodology could reject whole classes of potential true causal models has not been fulfilled. Rather, as more and better data have been brought to bear, most fully in this chapter, their findings suggest that an understanding of the SES-health gradient must include causal arrows running in both directions, along with a host of third factors that drive both SES and health in a dynamic process with many feedback loops and a long memory. Needless to say, this won't be quick work.

III

Determinants of Health

6

Early Retirement, Mental Health, and Social Networks

Axel Börsch-Supan and Morten Schuth

6.1 Introduction

This chapter explores the interrelationships between early retirement, mental health—including cognition and subjective well-being—and the size and composition of social networks among older individuals in the Survey of Health, Ageing and Retirement in Europe (SHARE). We argue that early retirement has negative side effects on the size and intensity of the retirees' social networks. These side effects appear to explain part of the accelerated cognitive aging that occurs after early retirement.

Early retirement is popular in Europe. It is seen as a much appreciated social achievement that increases personal well-being, particularly among

Axel Börsch-Supan is director of the Munich Center for the Economics of Aging (MEA) of the Max Planck Institute for Social Law and Social Policy, professor of economics at the Technical University of Munich, and a research associate of the National Bureau of Economic Research. Morten Schuth is a PhD student at the MEA.

We are grateful to Elaine Kelly and the participants of the 2013 NBER conference on the economics of aging in Carefree, Arizona, and to Howie Litwin for helpful comments. Klaus Härtl provided excellent research assistance. The SHARE data collection has been primarily funded by the European Commission through the Fifth Framework Programme (project QLK6-CT-2001-00360 in the thematic program Quality of Life), through the Sixth Framework Programme (projects SHARE-I3, RII-CT-2006-062193; COMPARE, CIT5-CT-2005-028857; and SHARELIFE, CIT4-CT-2006-028812), and through the Seventh Framework Programme (SHARE-PREP, 211909; SHARE-LEAP, 227822; and SHARE-M4, 261982). Additional funding came from the US National Institute on Aging (U01 AG09740-13S2, P01 AG005842, P01 AG08291, P30 AG12815, Y1-AG-4553-01 and OGHA 04-064, IAG BSR06-11, R21 AG025169) as well as from various national funding agencies, especially the German Ministry for Science and Education (BMBF) for the international coordination. The findings and conclusions expressed are solely those of the authors and do not represent the views of any agency of the German or US government, the NBER, or any other sponsor. For acknowledgments, sources of research support, and disclosure of the authors' material financial relationships, if any, please see http://www.nber.org/chapters/c12982.ack.

employees who suffer from work-related health problems. First introduced in the 1970s and 1980s, generous early retirement provisions in most European countries were instituted with few actuarial adjustments, if any (Gruber and Wise 1999). But times have changed since then. In response to the growth of the older segment of the population and to the precarious financial state of the public pension system, the costs of early retirement have come under increased scrutiny. This has led to a string of pension reforms in Europe since the 1990s, reducing pay-as-you-go pension benefits and introducing multipillar pension systems with supplemental occupational and individual pensions, in addition to the traditional unfunded retirement insurance (Börsch-Supan 2012).

Despite the enormous increase in life expectancy all over Europe, policymakers are still largely unwilling to challenge the widely popular early and normal retirement ages. Politically speaking, reducing the generosity of early retirement is often seen as "touching the third rail," with a fatal shock delivered at the next election. A case in point is France, where a timid increase in the retirement age, from sixty to sixty-two years, was partially reverted after the most recent presidential elections.

While many studies have addressed the macro connotations of early retirement, particularly its large costs, another body of literature has looked at the individual implications of early retirement. An immediate benefit from early retirement is the receipt of income support without the necessity to continue working, enabling individuals to enjoy more leisure. Moreover, early retirement relieves workers who feel constrained in their place of work, whether due to stressful job conditions or to work-impeding health problems. For such individuals, early retirement should manifest itself in an improvement of well-being and, potentially, also health. On the other hand, early retirement might also be harmful, because individuals who stop working may lose a purpose in life. This might, in turn, decrease subjective well-being and mental health. Early retirement may after all not be the bliss that many individuals hope for.

Börsch-Supan and Jürges (2006), using the German Socio-Economic Panel data, found that individuals were less happy in the year of early retirement than in the years before and after retirement. Moreover, individuals generally attained their preretirement satisfaction levels relatively soon after retirement. Hence, the early retirement effect on well-being appears to be negative and short lived rather than positive and long lasting, similar to what occurs in the set point model of happiness by Clark et al. (2003). Charles (2002) studied the effect of retirement on depression, and Lindeboom, Portrait, and van den Berg (2002) studied the effect of retirement and other factors (a significant decrease in income, death of the spouse, disability, and a move to a nursing home) on the mental health of individuals, using data from the Longitudinal Aging Study Amsterdam (LASA).

A seminal paper by Adam et al. (2007) based on SHARE found that cognition—measured mainly by memory abilities such as delayed word recall—

declined during retirement. This controversial finding has sparked an entire literature. While there are a few papers with the opposite result (Coe and Lindeboom 2008; Coe et al. 2012) based on US data exploiting variation in occupational pension plans, studies based on European data confirm the early findings (Bonsang, Adam, and Perelman 2010; Kuhn, Wuellrich, and Zweimüller 2010; Rohwedder and Willis 2010; and Mazzonna and Peracchi 2012) and show that the negative effect on cognition increases with the time in retirement. For a given age, these studies suggest that early retirees suffer more from cognitive and health decline than later retirees.

Research on these often emotional and highly contested issues is complicated by the fact that the measures of well-being, cognition, and health that are commonly available in general purpose surveys may suffer from justification bias (Bound 1991). That is, early retirees may report worse health in order to justify their early exit from the workforce. Moreover, early retirement is not an exogenous outcome, but is likely to be related to ill health and lower cognitive abilities. For example, persons in bad health are likely to retire earlier but also to report worse life satisfaction. Finally, those that hope or believe that life satisfaction will increase after retirement are more likely to retire at any age. We thus face the usual task of disentangling cause and effect.

The separation of selection effects and reverse causality from the genuine impacts of early retirement on well-being and health requires advanced econometric techniques that tend to make results controversial. The econometric problem is to find a counterfactual value for well-being and health had a person not taken early retirement. The usual instruments for identifying such a counterfactual are policy changes in early retirement rules, such as changes in the pensionable age or changes in the actuarial adjustments. The Survey of Health, Ageing and Retirement in Europe (SHARE), used for this chapter and described in section 6.2, is useful in this respect, as it provides institutional and credibly exogenous variation across countries to provide the necessary counterfactual. Moreover, since SHARE is a panel, the data also include conditioning variables describing health and well-being in earlier stages of life. Part of the difference between the US studies based on occupational pension plans and the European studies based on social security laws may reflect the better identification possible in the SHARE data.

This chapter goes one step further and investigates potentially causal mechanisms for the effects of early retirement on mental health, especially cognition. Its central hypothesis is derived from the anchoring function of employment: work, even if unpleasant and arduous, provides social contacts. Even disliked colleagues and a bad boss, we argue, are better than social isolation because they provide cognitive challenges that keep the mind active and healthy.

We briefly describe our data in section 6.2. The current analysis takes advantage of a major innovation in SHARE wave 4, the social network data based on a name generator that identifies those persons with whom the respondents "discuss things that are important to them," that is, "good or bad things that happen to you, problems you are having, or important concerns you may have."[1] In the first step, we find significant correlations among early retirement, mental health and social networks, which give first evidence for our line of reasoning (section 6.3). This explanation is confirmed and strengthened in the second step when we control for other possible determinants (section 6.4). Unobserved common factors and potential reverse causality, however, call for an instrumental variable approach. This is done in section 6.5, which is the core of the paper. Using instruments describing the retirement regulations, similar to the approaches taken by Rohwedder and Willis (2010); Bonsang, Adam, and Perelman (2010); and Mazzonna and Peracchi (2012), plus regional variables describing social capital as instruments for the size and intensity of individual social networks confirms our findings. Section 6.6 concludes.

6.2 The SHARE Data

The Survey of Health, Ageing and Retirement in Europe (SHARE, see Börsch-Supan and Jürges [2005] and Börsch-Supan et al. [2005, 2008, 2011, 2013]) is a unique multidisciplinary and cross-national panel database of ex ante harmonized micro data on health, socioeconomic status, and social and family networks covering most of the European Union and Israel. To date, SHARE has collected three panel waves (2004, 2006, 2010) of current living circumstances and one wave of retrospective life histories (2008, SHARELIFE). Six additional waves are planned until 2024. SHARE gives a broad picture of life after age fifty, measuring physical and mental health, both objectively and subjectively; economic and noneconomic activities, income and wealth by sources; intergenerational transfers of time and money within and outside of the family; as well as life satisfaction and well-being. SHARE is modeled after, and harmonized with, the US Health and Retirement Study (HRS) and the English Longitudinal Study of Ageing (ELSA). In turn, together with these two surveys, SHARE has become a role model for further aging surveys worldwide. SHARE's scientific power is based on three key features: its panel design that grasps the dynamic character of the aging process, its multidisciplinary approach that delivers the full picture of the individual and societal aging, and its cross-nationally ex ante harmonized design that permits international comparisons of health, economic, and social outcomes within Europe and between Europe and the United States.

In four waves of SHARE, more than 150,000 interviews have been conducted with about 86,000 respondents age fifty and over and their poten-

1. Quotes from the SHARE wave 4 questionnaire (see Malter and Börsch-Supan 2013).

tially younger partners in nineteen countries (Austria, Belgium, Switzerland, Czech Republic, Germany, Denmark, Estonia, Spain, France, Greece, Hungary, Ireland, Israel, Italy, Netherlands, Poland, Portugal, Sweden, and Slovenia).

The SHARE target population consists of all persons born in 1954 or earlier in wave 1 (2004–2005), 1956 or earlier in wave 2 (2005–2006), and 1960 or earlier in wave 4 (2010–2011), who have their regular domicile in the respective SHARE country. A person is excluded if she or he is incarcerated, hospitalized, or out of the country during the entire survey period, unable to speak the countries' language(s) or has moved to an unknown address. In addition, current partners living in the household are interviewed regardless of their age. All SHARE respondents that were interviewed in any previous wave are part of the longitudinal sample. They are traced and reinterviewed if they moved within the country.

Covering the key areas of life, namely health, socioeconomics and social networks, SHARE includes a great variety of information: health variables, physical measures and biomarkers, psychological variables, economic variables, and social support variables as well as social network information. While the regular waves of SHARE, such as waves 1, 2, and 4, deal with the respondents' current living conditions, wave 3 (SHARELIFE) was conducted as a retrospective survey in order to collect information about the respondents' life histories.

The interviewers used computer-assisted personal interviewing (CAPI) to collect most of the data in all waves. In addition, self-administered (drop-off) questionnaires were handed out in waves 1, 2, and 4 after completion of the CAPI. If respondents deceased, end-of-life interviews were conducted face-to-face (CAPI) or by telephone (CATI) with a proxy, collecting the information regarding the respondent's last year of life. Proxy interviews were also used when respondents were not able to do an interview; for example, due to health reasons.

Even though SHARE is a panel survey with a stable core questionnaire over time, innovative research questions, physical measurements, or modules have been incorporated in each wave. For example, in wave 2, two physical measurements—peak flow and chair stand—were added (see next section for details). In wave 4 a completely new module—the social networks module based on a name-generator approach—has been implemented to learn more about the social connectedness of respondents. It is one of the key variables in this chapter.

In SHARELIFE, retrospective data with respect to childhood living circumstances, partners, children, accommodation, employment, socioeconomic and health conditions were collected with the help of a "Life History Calendar" similar to the one applied in ELSA. In this chapter, the life histories are essential to reconstruct the life courses of the respondents. One may suspect that this retrospective information provided by respondents is incomplete or inaccurate. SHARE has therefore cooperated with the German Pension Fund (DRV) and linked the German survey data with administrative data held by the DRV. These administrative data are much more complete and accurate since they are process generated. We have used these administrative data for this chapter to check the validity of the self-reported employment histories in Germany and found a very close match (Korbmacher 2013).

From the first wave on, SHARE combined self-reports on health with physical performance measurements. In this chapter, we use grip strength as the most objective measure of physical health available in SHARE.

The core variables in this chapter are based on wave 4 of SHARE. Explanatory and auxiliary variables, however, are taken from all waves. We restrict our analyses on all individuals who are retired, for whom the retirement year could be ascertained (some 21,000 individuals), and who retired at or after the applicable statutory retirement age.

6.3 The Triangle of Early Retirement, Mental Health, and Social Networks

Figures 6.1 and 6.2 visualize the main story behind this chapter. Figure 6.1 shows the decline of cognition by age, separately for early and normal retirees. Cognition is measured by memory ability: the single values in immediate and delayed recall of a ten-word list and the sum of these two scores. The main point is that cognition is at all ages lower for early retirees, corresponding to about 1.5 years of aging on average.

Figure 6.2 shows the number of friends and former colleagues in the social network. While the relation is noisier than that of figure 6.1, it exhibits the same pattern: the number of friends and former colleagues in the social network also declines with age, and it is lower at all ages for early retirees.

Not only are cognition and social network size associated with early retirement, they are also correlated with each other, and these triangular relations hold for a broad set of measurement concepts for each of the three domains (see figure 6.3).

Figure 6.3 also serves to explain the key variables involved in this chapter. Individuals are categorized as retired when they self-report as retired. We then measure the time elapsed since retirement (time distance since retirement). We distinguish two retirement pathways: normal retirement (NR) at or after the statutory retirement age, and early retirement (ER) for all other labor force exits in the window of early retirement; that is, between the applicable statutory early retirement age and the normal statutory retirement age in each country. The two key variables for retirement are the interactions of a pathway dummy with the time elapsed since retirement: "NRdist" and "ERdist." These variables are of particular interest since they best describe the "dose" of retirement exposure that may have triggered a "response" in terms of social networks and mental health, using the parlance of epidemiology.

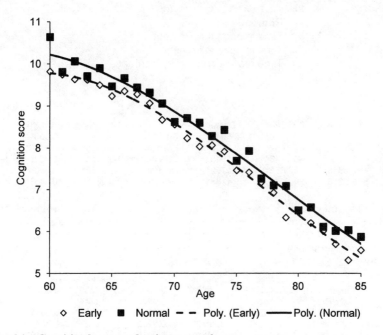

◇ Early   ■ Normal   − − Poly. (Early)   ——— Poly. (Normal)

Fig. 6.1   **Cognition by age and retirement pathway**
Source: Own calculations from SHARE waves 1–2, release 2.5.0; wave 3, release 1; wave 4, release 1.1.1; full data set.

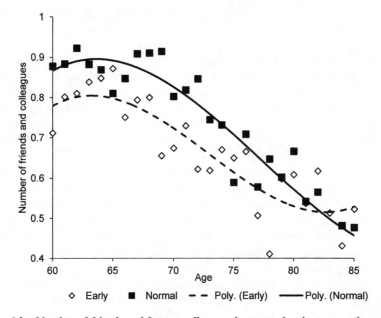

◇ Early   ■ Normal   − − Poly. (Early)   ——— Poly. (Normal)

Fig. 6.2   **Number of friends and former colleagues by age and retirement pathway**
Source: Own calculations from SHARE waves 1–2, release 2.5.0; wave 3, release 1; wave 4, release 1.1.1; full data set.

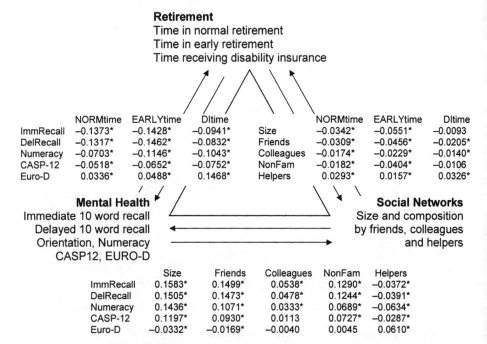

Fig. 6.3   Correlations in the triangle of early retirement, mental health, and social networks

Source: Own calculations from SHARE waves 1–2, release 2.5.0; wave 3, release 1; wave 4, release 1.1.1; full data set.

Mental health is measured by five variables: the number of words recalled from a list of ten—both immediately (ImmRecall) and delayed (after about thirty minutes) (DelRecall)—and a composite indicator of numeracy. In our later analyses, we will add the scores of immediate and delayed recall and simply call it "Cognition." We add a twelve-item composite scale (CASP-12) designed to measure the quality of life in old age, adapted by SHARE from the original nineteen-item scale (Hyde et al. 2003), and a depression scale (EURO-D) targeted at severe depression symptoms (Prince et al. 1999).

We characterize social networks, the third domain in this chapter, by their size (number of individuals mentioned as close confidants) and their composition, focusing on nonfamily members, including friends and colleagues. More precisely, the variable "sn_size" counts all members of the social network and "friends&c" counts the number of friends and former colleagues/coworkers in the network.

Figure 6.3 reports the correlations among these variables, based on the working sample that includes all individuals who have retired by wave 4. Asterisks mark statistically significant relationships between the variables (at 1 percent).

Time since retirement is significantly related to all mental health variables: it affects cognition and well-being negatively and increases the measure of depressive symptoms. Moreover, the time elapsed after an early retirement has stronger associations with worsening mental health than the time elapsed since normal retirement, although individuals retiring early are almost always younger than those retiring at the pensionable age.

Time elapsed since retirement is also correlated with smaller social networks, both overall and concerning colleagues, friends, and other nonfamily members. Again, this time effect is stronger for early retirees than normal retirees. Correlations with the number of formal helpers have, as expected, exactly the opposite pattern.

Finally, the association between social networks and mental health is highly significant. Larger social networks are strongly associated with better cognitive abilities, higher subjective well-being, and less depression.

The main questions of this chapter are now whether these relations uphold when the influence of other variables (section 6.4) and potential reverse causality are accounted for (section 6.5).

6.4 Controlling for Other Determinants

The correlations depicted may have many reasons. An underlying common cause could be physical health. Individuals with worse physical health tend to retire earlier. They may have mobility problems and therefore less ability to maintain their social network. Suffering from bad physical health is likely to reduce well-being and increase depression, and to reduce mental health and cognition either directly (biologically) or indirectly (psychologically).

Demographic variables such as age, gender, and marital status also affect all three variables. Retirement rules are age and gender specific in all SHARE countries; age, gender, and marital status are significant factors influencing morbidity, and they are associated with the size and closeness of social networks. Also education is likely to modify all the observed associations.

The following regression analyses control for these background variables. Health is characterized by functional abilities (basic activities of daily living, denoted by ADL, independent activities of daily living, denoted by IADL, and the global activity limitation indicator developed by van Oyen et al. 2006, denoted by GALI), the presence of one or more chronic illnesses (longill), and the objective measure of grip strength (maxgrip) measured in kilograms. We do not correct for subjective health as this is highly correlated with well-being once objective health is controlled for.

Age enters the regression as a quadratic polynomial, education is measured in years, and "couple" indicates that the respondent lives in a partnership, whether married or not.

Table 6.1 reproduces the findings quoted in the introduction to this chapter. Dependent variables are the cognition measures described in section 6.3,

Table 6.1   The influence of retirement on cognition

	ImmRecall (1)	ImmRecall (2)	DelRecall (3)	DelRecall (4)	Cognition (5)	Cognition (6)
ERdist	−0.013***	−0.004	−0.029***	−0.010***	−0.042***	−0.013**
	(0.003)	(0.003)	(0.003)	(0.003)	(0.006)	(0.005)
NRdist	−0.013***	−0.003	−0.031***	−0.009**	−0.044***	−0.012**
	(0.003)	(0.003)	(0.004)	(0.004)	(0.007)	(0.006)
Female	0.829***	0.694***	0.920***	0.782***	1.748***	1.475***
	(0.033)	(0.034)	(0.040)	(0.040)	(0.066)	(0.067)
Age	0.037	0.007	0.061**	0.018	0.096*	0.024
	(0.025)	(0.025)	(0.029)	(0.029)	(0.049)	(0.049)
Age_sq	−0.001***	−0.000**	−0.001***	−0.000**	−0.001***	−0.001***
	(0.000)	(0.000)	(0.000)	(0.000)	(0.000)	(0.000)
Couple	0.098***	0.119***	0.037	0.054*	0.134***	0.172***
	(0.025)	(0.025)	(0.031)	(0.031)	(0.051)	(0.050)
Edu_years	0.092***	0.094***	0.096***	0.105***	0.188***	0.200***
	(0.003)	(0.003)	(0.003)	(0.003)	(0.005)	(0.006)
Maxgrip	0.025***	0.020***	0.027***	0.022***	0.051***	0.042***
	(0.002)	(0.002)	(0.002)	(0.002)	(0.003)	(0.003)
Longill	−0.092***	−0.055**	−0.143***	−0.062**	−0.236***	−0.118**
	(0.025)	(0.026)	(0.031)	(0.031)	(0.051)	(0.051)
ADL	−0.027	−0.013	−0.028	−0.016	−0.054	−0.028
	(0.021)	(0.021)	(0.023)	(0.022)	(0.039)	(0.039)
IADL	−0.204***	−0.204***	−0.198***	−0.188***	−0.404***	−0.394***
	(0.018)	(0.018)	(0.018)	(0.018)	(0.032)	(0.032)
GALI	−0.072***	−0.072***	−0.135***	−0.095***	−0.208***	−0.168***
	(0.026)	(0.026)	(0.032)	(0.032)	(0.052)	(0.052)
COUNTRY FE		YES		YES		YES
Constant	3.032***	4.241***	0.481	2.109*	3.542*	6.393***
	(0.921)	(0.930)	(1.083)	(1.079)	(1.808)	(1.808)
N	19,893	19,893	19,887	19,887	19,897	19,897
Adj. R-sq	0.231	0.252	0.191	0.229	0.244	0.277

Note: Robust standard errors in parentheses.
***Significant at the 1 percent level.
**Significant at the 5 percent level.
*Significant at the 10 percent level.

and the main explanatory variables are two variables indicating time spent in early and normal retirement (ERdist and NRdist). Columns (1), (3), and (5) show that retirement affects cognition even when other potential determinants are held constant. We are aware that such a regression may possibly reflect reverse causality. We will address this in section 6.5.

Table 6.2 shows that part of the explanation for this relation may be social networks. Adding the social network variables to the regression in table 6.1 increases the fit of the regression and reduces the coefficients of the early retirement variables. The social network variables have significant effects

Table 6.2   **The influence of retirement and social networks on cognition**

	ImmRecall (1)	ImmRecall (2)	DelRecall (3)	DelRecall (4)	Cognition (5)	Cognition (6)
ERdist	−0.011***	−0.003	−0.026***	−0.010***	−0.037***	−0.013**
	(0.003)	(0.003)	(0.003)	(0.003)	(0.005)	(0.005)
NRdist	−0.010***	−0.002	−0.028***	−0.009**	−0.038***	−0.011*
	(0.003)	(0.003)	(0.004)	(0.004)	(0.006)	(0.006)
Sn_size	0.058***	0.054***	0.075***	0.062***	0.133***	0.116***
	(0.008)	(0.008)	(0.010)	(0.010)	(0.016)	(0.016)
Friends&c	0.076***	0.058***	0.092***	0.051***	0.167***	0.109***
	(0.009)	(0.009)	(0.012)	(0.012)	(0.019)	(0.019)
Female	0.785***	0.657***	0.864***	0.743***	1.648***	1.399***
	(0.033)	(0.034)	(0.040)	(0.040)	(0.066)	(0.067)
Age	0.029	0.003	0.052*	0.015	0.080	0.018
	(0.025)	(0.025)	(0.029)	(0.029)	(0.049)	(0.049)
Age_q	−0.000***	−0.000**	−0.001***	−0.000**	−0.001***	−0.001**
	(0.000)	(0.000)	(0.000)	(0.000)	(0.000)	(0.000)
Couple	0.122***	0.134***	0.065**	0.064**	0.186***	0.197***
	(0.026)	(0.026)	(0.032)	(0.031)	(0.052)	(0.051)
Edu_years	0.088***	0.090***	0.090***	0.101***	0.179***	0.190***
	(0.003)	(0.003)	(0.003)	(0.003)	(0.005)	(0.006)
Maxgrip	0.025***	0.020***	0.026***	0.022***	0.051***	0.042***
	(0.002)	(0.002)	(0.002)	(0.002)	(0.003)	(0.003)
Longill	−0.101***	−0.069***	−0.155***	−0.077**	−0.256***	−0.147***
	(0.025)	(0.026)	(0.031)	(0.031)	(0.051)	(0.051)
ADL	−0.029	−0.014	−0.030	−0.016	−0.058	−0.029
	(0.021)	(0.021)	(0.023)	(0.022)	(0.039)	(0.039)
IADL	−0.198***	−0.201***	−0.191***	−0.185***	−0.392***	−0.389***
	(0.018)	(0.018)	(0.018)	(0.018)	(0.032)	(0.032)
GALI	−0.061**	−0.068***	−0.122***	−0.091***	−0.184***	−0.161***
	(0.026)	(0.026)	(0.032)	(0.032)	(0.052)	(0.052)
COUNTRY FE		YES		YES		YES
Constant	3.148***	4.250***	0.614	2.107**	3.794**	6.402***
	(0.916)	(0.926)	(1.074)	(1.073)	(1.793)	(1.798)
N	19,893	19,893	19,887	19,887	19,897	19,897
Adj. R-sq	0.239	0.257	0.200	0.233	0.254	0.282

Note: Robust standard errors in parentheses.
***Significant at the 1 percent level.
**Significant at the 5 percent level.
*Significant at the 10 percent level.

on cognition: network size in general and the number of friends and former colleagues in particular significantly increased cognition.

Indeed, as table 6.3 shows, early retirement has a direct effect on the total size of the social network, and also on the number of friends and former colleagues in the social network.

We tested the robustness of these results against unobserved coun-

Table 6.3   The influence of retirement on social networks

	Sn_size (1)	Sn_size (2)	Friends&c (3)	Friends&c (4)
ERdist	−0.014***	−0.002	−0.018***	−0.002
	(0.003)	(0.003)	(0.003)	(0.002)
NRdist	−0.016***	−0.004	−0.022***	−0.004
	(0.003)	(0.003)	(0.003)	(0.003)
Female	0.445***	0.453***	0.245***	0.223***
	(0.032)	(0.033)	(0.026)	(0.027)
Age	0.046*	0.023	0.068***	0.039**
	(0.024)	(0.024)	(0.019)	(0.019)
Age_sq	−0.000*	−0.000	−0.000***	−0.000***
	(0.000)	(0.000)	(0.000)	(0.000)
Couple	0.168***	0.180***	−0.440***	−0.426***
	(0.026)	(0.025)	(0.023)	(0.022)
Edu_years	0.024***	0.036***	0.037***	0.046***
	(0.003)	(0.003)	(0.002)	(0.003)
Maxgrip	0.002	0.004**	−0.001	−0.001
	(0.001)	(0.002)	(0.001)	(0.001)
Longill	0.129***	0.169***	0.019	0.085***
	(0.026)	(0.026)	(0.021)	(0.022)
ADL	0.003	0.001	0.022*	0.017
	(0.018)	(0.019)	(0.014)	(0.013)
IADL	−0.011	−0.004	−0.076***	−0.059***
	(0.015)	(0.015)	(0.010)	(0.010)
GALI	−0.067***	−0.018	−0.079***	−0.042*
	(0.026)	(0.026)	(0.022)	(0.022)
COUNTRY FE		YES		YES
Constant	0.107	0.306	−1.813***	−0.663
	(0.878)	(0.877)	(0.703)	(0.698)
N	20,003	20,003	20,003	20,003
Adj. R-sq	0.026	0.053	0.063	0.102

Note: Robust standard errors in parentheses.
***Significant at the 1 percent level.
**Significant at the 5 percent level.
*Significant at the 10 percent level.

try effects since there are large differences in all three domains across the SHARE countries. The northern countries are healthier, while the social networks in the southern countries are larger. Retirement rules are also very different across countries. These differences may reflect cultural and historical differences common to the three domains (retirement, cognition, and social networks) and might thus cause the observed correlations without a genuine relationship among the three domains. We therefore reestimated the aforementioned regressions with country fixed effects (columns [2], [4], and [6] in tables 6.1, 6.2, and 6.3). Results change only very little, indicating

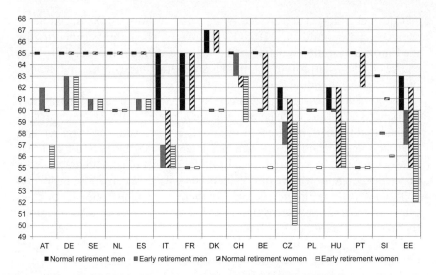

Fig. 6.4   Variation in early and normal retirement ages across time, cohorts, and gender

Source: Own calculations from national authority data, the Social Security Association, and the MISSOC database, 1992–2012.

that the correlations between the three domains are not due to unobserved country specificities.

6.5 Accounting for Reverse Causality and Common Unobservable Factors

The regressions in section 6.4 may suffer from endogeneity bias. As pointed out in the introduction, the correlation between early retirement and weak cognition may be due to two mechanisms that run in opposite directions: in addition to the causal effect of retirement on cognition and, more general, mental health, weak cognitive abilities may precipitate early retirement because employers tend to hold on to the most productive workers, selecting out less productive ones.

In order to isolate the first of the two mechanisms, we use instruments that capture retirement regulations. Such instrumental variables will change cognition if the first mechanism is active, but are not affected by individual cognition. This identification strategy is similar to the approaches taken by Bonsang, Adam, and Perelman (2010), Rohwedder and Willis (2010), and Mazzonna and Peracchi (2012), but we exploit more individual variation (see figure 6.4). More precisely, we instrument the time after early retirement by the difference of the individual's age and the statutory eligibility age for early retirement (LERdist), and the time after normal retirement by the difference of the individual's age and the statutory eligibility age for normal retirement (LNRdist), both based on the information about the statutory eligibility age provided by national authorities, the Social Security Association, and the MISSOC database.[2] The latter is generated by the European Commission (various years) and various other auxiliary data sources.[3] These statutory eligibility ages vary by time, cohort, and gender, providing the individual variation mentioned earlier.

There is a good reason to also be careful with the exogeneity of the number of friends and former colleagues in the social network. While it appears far-fetched that the size and intensity of social networks cause early retirement, cognition and social network size and intensity may be caused by similar unobserved variables. Unobserved health and psychological characteristics may reduce cognition and cause an increasing distance to friends and former colleagues as these individuals age. We therefore exploit regional variables drawn from external sources that describe social capital to instrument for the size and intensity of individual social networks. Specifically, we use the regionally aggregated means of the variable called "trust in other people" (agg_trust) from the European Social Survey (ESS) wave 2 (2004), which is available for all involved SHARE countries. The regions (on the so-called NUTS-1 level) represent states or departments within each country. A second instrumental variable is the logarithm of population density in 2010 by NUTS-1 regions (lpden) from Eurostat. Note that it is unlikely that these variables affect individual cognition directly while they affect cognition indirectly through their effect on social networks.

Tables 6.4, 6.5, and 6.6 report the first stage regressions and show the predictive power of the instruments for the potentially endogenous variables. The rightmost columns include country dummies and interactions of the country dummies with age. The cognition measure is the sum of the scores from the immediate and the delayed word recall. All F-tests are highly significant. The policy variables (LRNdist and LERdist) are highly significant for the time since retirement, while the social capital variables (agg_trust and lpden) are highly significant for the number of friends and former colleagues in the social networks.

Our main results from the second stage are displayed in tables 6.7, 6.8, and 6.9. Table 6.7 confirms our findings from figure 6.2 and table 6.2 in this instrumental variable regression. The number of friends and colleagues in the social network declines with the time since retirement, holding age and age squared constant. This effect is larger for the early retirees as compared to the normal retirees. Note that both effects are highly significant in the full specification.

Table 6.8 shows the effects for the time since retirement on cognition, corresponding to figure 6.1 and table 6.1, but taking account of potential endogeneity. It has the same pattern: cognition declines with time spent in retirement, and this effect is larger for early retirees than normal retirees. Both effects are highly significant in the full specification.

2. We are grateful to Fabrizio Mazzonna who provided the statutory eligibility ages for Italy.
3. Data available on request.

Table 6.4   **First stage: Time elapsed since early retirement**

	ERdist (1)	ERdist (2)	ERdist (3)	ERdist (4)
LERdist	0.740***	0.608***	0.581***	0.367***
	(0.037)	(0.044)	(0.045)	(0.045)
LNRdist	−0.506***	−0.424***	−0.391***	0.004
	(0.038)	(0.046)	(0.048)	(0.047)
Agg_trust	0.418	0.432	0.454*	0.375
	(0.270)	(0.271)	(0.276)	(0.267)
Lpden	−0.250***	−0.220**	−0.214**	−0.182**
	(0.089)	(0.089)	(0.090)	(0.088)
Female		−0.012	−0.144	−0.615***
		(0.113)	(0.165)	(0.164)
Age		0.902***	1.001***	1.349***
		(0.158)	(0.168)	(0.167)
Age_sq		−0.006***	−0.006***	−0.010***
		(0.001)	(0.001)	(0.001)
Couple		0.607***	0.618***	0.567***
		(0.117)	(0.119)	(0.118)
Edu_years		−0.052***	−0.052***	−0.051***
		(0.012)	(0.013)	(0.013)
Maxgrip			−0.013*	−0.013*
			(0.007)	(0.007)
Longill			−0.045	0.009
			(0.119)	(0.117)
ADL			0.094	0.021
			(0.110)	(0.109)
IADL			−0.017	0.038
			(0.093)	(0.091)
GALI			−0.083	−0.086
			(0.119)	(0.117)
N	19,944	19,944	18,531	18,531
F	300.787	255.826	199.315	231.266
Fp	0.000	0.000	0.000	0.000

Notes: Column (4) also includes country dummies and age interactions with country dummies. Robust standard errors in parentheses.

F-test of excluded instruments:

$F(4,19924) = 310.77$ $F(4,19919) = 51.73$ $F(4,18501) = 46.21$ $F(4,18488) = 41.49$

Prob > F = 0.0000   Prob > F = 0.0000   Prob > F = 0.0000   Prob > F = 0.0000

Angrist-Pischke multivariate F-test of excluded instruments:

$F(2,19924) = 303.82$ $F(2,19919) = 18.05$ $F(2,18501) = 20.17$ $F(2,18488) = 21.21$

Prob > F = 0.0000   Prob > F = 0.0000   Prob > F = 0.0000   Prob > F = 0.0000

***Significant at the 1 percent level.

**Significant at the 5 percent level.

*Significant at the 10 percent level.

Table 6.5   First stage: Time elapsed since normal retirement

	NRdist (1)	NRdist (2)	NRdist (3)	NRdist (4)
LERdist	−0.769***	−0.928***	−0.876***	−0.684***
	(0.082)	(0.125)	(0.127)	(0.142)
LNRdist	1.421***	0.964***	0.938***	0.504***
	(0.080)	(0.064)	(0.065)	(0.068)
Agg_trust	−0.328	−0.207	−0.127	−0.040
	(0.258)	(0.245)	(0.250)	(0.241)
Lpden	0.099	0.049	0.056	0.026
	(0.102)	(0.096)	(0.099)	(0.096)
Female		0.990***	1.003***	1.626***
		(0.319)	(0.352)	(0.369)
Age		−0.207	−0.253	−0.684***
		(0.223)	(0.233)	(0.221)
Age_sq		0.006***	0.006***	0.009***
		(0.001)	(0.001)	(0.001)
Couple		−0.553***	−0.555***	−0.502***
		(0.111)	(0.112)	(0.110)
Edu_years		−0.001	0.002	−0.004
		(0.011)	(0.011)	(0.011)
Maxgrip			0.008	0.009
			(0.006)	(0.006)
Longill			0.103	0.037
			(0.105)	(0.102)
ADL			−0.080	0.012
			(0.106)	(0.103)
IADL			0.149*	0.073
			(0.089)	(0.085)
GALI			0.080	0.102
			(0.105)	(0.102)
N	19,944	19,944	18,531	18,531
F	762.791	743.866	588.702	596.536
Fp	0.000	0.000	0.000	0.000

Notes: Column (4) also includes country dummies and age interactions with country dummies. Robust standard errors in parentheses.

F-test of excluded instruments:

$F(4,19924) = 2192.68$ $F(4,19919) = 79.10$ $F(4,18501) = 70.35$ $F(4,18488) = 20.08$

Prob > F = 0.0000   Prob > F = 0.0000   Prob > F = 0.0000   Prob > F = 0.0000

Angrist-Pischke multivariate F-test of excluded instruments:

$F(2,19924) = 586.17$ $F(2,19919) = 10.35$ $F(2,18501) = 11.89$ $F(2,18488) = 26.85$

Prob > F = 0.0000   Prob > F = 0.0000   Prob > F = 0.0000   Prob > F = 0.0000

*** Significant at the 1 percent level.

**Significant at the 5 percent level.

*Significant at the 10 percent level.

Table 6.6   **First stage: Size of social network (friends and ex-colleagues)**

	Friends&c (1)	Friends&c (2)	Friends&c (3)	Friends&c (4)
Agg_trust	0.167***	0.166***	0.144***	0.138***
	(0.052)	(0.051)	(0.054)	(0.054)
Lpden	0.082***	0.056***	0.061***	0.062***
	(0.019)	(0.018)	(0.019)	(0.019)
LERdist	−0.001	0.016**	0.015*	0.011
	(0.008)	(0.008)	(0.008)	(0.009)
LNRdist	−0.013*	−0.032***	−0.032***	−0.035***
	(0.008)	(0.009)	(0.009)	(0.010)
Female		0.248***	0.244***	0.260***
		(0.024)	(0.032)	(0.032)
Age		0.051***	0.040*	0.033
		(0.019)	(0.021)	(0.021)
Age_sq		−0.000***	−0.000**	−0.000
		(0.000)	(0.000)	(0.000)
Couple		−0.406***	−0.422***	−0.420***
		(0.022)	(0.023)	(0.023)
Edu_years		0.046***	0.047***	0.047***
		(0.003)	(0.003)	(0.003)
Maxgrip			−0.001	−0.001
			(0.001)	(0.001)
Longill			0.085***	0.084***
			(0.022)	(0.022)
ADL			0.013	0.012
			(0.014)	(0.014)
IADL			−0.056***	−0.060***
			(0.011)	(0.011)
GALI			−0.037*	−0.037*
			(0.022)	(0.022)
N	19,944	19,944	18,531	18,531
F	60.674	89.676	71.463	50.639
Fp	0.000	0.000	0.000	0.000

Notes: Column (4) also includes country dummies and age interactions with country dummies. Robust standard errors in parentheses.

F-test of excluded instruments:

$F(4,19924) = 54.06$	$F(4,19919) = 10.44$	$F(4,18501) = 9.19$	$F(4,18488) = 10.00$
Prob > F = 0.0000	Prob > F = 0.0000	Prob > F = 0.0000	Prob > F = 0.0000

Angrist-Pischke multivariate F-test of excluded instruments:

$F(2,19924) = 19.35$	$F(2,19919) = 12.58$	$F(2,18501) = 11.32$	$F(2,18488) = 11.11$
Prob > F = 0.0000	Prob > F = 0.0000	Prob > F = 0.0000	Prob > F = 0.0000

***Significant at the 1 percent level.

**Significant at the 5 percent level.

*Significant at the 10 percent level.

Table 6.7   Second-stage IV estimation: The effect of (early) retirement on the number of friends and ex-colleagues in the social network

	Friends&c (1)	Friends&c (2)	Friends&c (3)	Friends&c (4)
ERdist	−0.021***	−0.069	−0.065	−0.097***
	(0.007)	(0.046)	(0.045)	(0.037)
NRdist	−0.015***	−0.060**	−0.059**	−0.068***
	(0.003)	(0.025)	(0.024)	(0.021)
Female		0.302***	0.292***	0.308***
		(0.049)	(0.049)	(0.044)
Age		0.104**	0.092*	0.118**
		(0.051)	(0.056)	(0.059)
Age_sq		−0.000**	−0.000	−0.000
		(0.000)	(0.000)	(0.000)
Couple		−0.392***	−0.413***	−0.398***
		(0.025)	(0.027)	(0.028)
Edu_years		0.044***	0.044***	0.042***
		(0.004)	(0.004)	(0.003)
Maxgrip			−0.001	−0.002
			(0.001)	(0.001)
Longill			0.089***	0.087***
			(0.022)	(0.023)
ADL			0.013	0.015
			(0.014)	(0.015)
IADL			−0.051***	−0.055***
			(0.011)	(0.012)
GALI			−0.035	−0.035
			(0.022)	(0.023)
Constant	0.841***	−4.342*	−3.838	−5.208**
	(0.031)	(2.521)	(2.621)	(2.470)
N	20,770	20,770	19,007	19,007
F	69.429	95.598	74.487	47.815
Fp	0.000	0.000	0.000	0.000

Notes: Column (4) also includes country dummies and age interactions with country dummies. Robust standard errors in parentheses.
***Significant at the 1 percent level.
**Significant at the 5 percent level.
*Significant at the 10 percent level.

Table 6.9 adds the number of friends and former colleagues in the social network to the IV-regression in table 6.8. It is significant in all specifications and reduces the coefficients of the retirement duration variables by about a third, relative to the full specification. We conclude that part of the nexus between retirement and cognition works through the shrinkage of social networks, here measured by the declining number of nonfamily members, namely friends and former colleagues.

Tables 6.10, 6.11, 6.12, and 6.13 explore the robustness of this result.

Table 6.8   Second-stage IV estimation: The effect of (early) retirement on cognition

	Cognition (1)	Cognition (2)	Cognition (3)	Cognition (4)
ERdist	−0.255***	−0.218*	−0.214*	−0.259***
	(0.023)	(0.119)	(0.119)	(0.084)
NRdist	−0.166***	−0.173***	−0.180***	−0.172***
	(0.009)	(0.065)	(0.062)	(0.052)
Female		1.020***	1.710***	1.710***
		(0.122)	(0.123)	(0.108)
Age		0.279**	0.196	0.264*
		(0.132)	(0.145)	(0.135)
Age_sq		−0.002***	−0.001	−0.001*
		(0.001)	(0.001)	(0.001)
Couple		0.218***	0.175***	0.205***
		(0.063)	(0.065)	(0.063)
Edu_years		0.212***	0.197***	0.193***
		(0.009)	(0.009)	(0.008)
Maxgrip			0.042***	0.041***
			(0.003)	(0.003)
Longill			−0.114**	−0.119**
			(0.054)	(0.056)
ADL			−0.016	−0.016
			(0.042)	(0.043)
IADL			−0.365***	−0.370***
			(0.035)	(0.036)
GALI			−0.159***	−0.157***
			(0.055)	(0.056)
Constant	9.846***	−4.001	−3.613	−5.856
	(0.093)	(6.451)	(6.820)	(5.605)
N	20,348	20,348	18,906	18,906
F	252.401	318.501	265.404	169.087
Fp	0.000	0.000	0.000	0.000

Notes: Column (4) also includes country dummies and age interactions with country dummies. Robust standard errors in parentheses.
***Significant at the 1 percent level.
**Significant at the 5 percent level.
*Significant at the 10 percent level.

Tables 6.10 and 6.11 employ alternative social network variables. In table 6.10, we replace the size by the intensity of the contacts to friends and former colleagues. We obtain very similar results, although the significance levels are lower. The same holds if we use the distance as an indicator for the quality of the social network (table 6.11).

Tables 6.12 and 6.13 finally employ interactions between the size and the quality of the social network. We obtain results very similar to tables 6.9 through 6.11, confirming the robustness of our findings.

Table 6.9   **Second-stage IV estimation: The effect of (early) retirement and social networks on cognition**

	Cognition (1)	Cognition (2)	Cognition (3)	Cognition (4)
ERdist	−0.218***	−0.149	−0.180*	−0.185**
	(0.027)	(0.099)	(0.104)	(0.088)
NRdist	−0.138***	−0.106	−0.136**	−0.120*
	(0.012)	(0.065)	(0.064)	(0.063)
Friends&c	1.919***	1.177**	1.067**	1.037**
	(0.473)	(0.507)	(0.512)	(0.516)
Female		0.664***	1.420***	1.411***
		(0.194)	(0.192)	(0.193)
Age		0.167	0.130	0.162
		(0.118)	(0.132)	(0.130)
Age_sq		−0.001**	−0.001	−0.001
		(0.001)	(0.001)	(0.001)
Couple		0.692***	0.627***	0.624***
		(0.208)	(0.219)	(0.213)
Edu_years		0.161***	0.147***	0.148***
		(0.023)	(0.024)	(0.023)
Maxgrip			0.043***	0.043***
			(0.004)	(0.004)
Longill			−0.212***	−0.210***
			(0.073)	(0.073)
ADL			−0.028	−0.029
			(0.044)	(0.043)
IADL			−0.310***	−0.313***
			(0.044)	(0.045)
GALI			−0.117*	−0.116*
			(0.062)	(0.062)
Constant	8.233***	0.572	−1.205	−1.589
	(0.412)	(5.587)	(6.077)	(5.480)
N	19,944	19,944	18,531	18,531
F	185.946	272.813	228.672	155.855
Fp	0.000	0.000	0.000	0.000

Notes: Column (4) also includes country dummies and age interactions with country dummies. Robust standard errors in parentheses.
***Significant on the 1 percent level.
**Significant on the 5 percent level.
*Significant on the 10 percent level.

6.6 Conclusion

Is early retirement bliss? Evidence from earlier studies has placed this assumption in doubt. Early retirement may actually be a mixed blessing because cognition declines. Moreover, the effect of early retirement on subjective well-being seems to be negative and short lived rather than long lasting and positive.

Table 6.10   **Second-stage IV estimation: The effect of (early) retirement and contact intensity with friends and ex-colleagues in the social network on cognition**

	Cognition (1)	Cognition (2)	Cognition (3)	Cognition (4)
ERdist	−0.215***	−0.134	−0.167	−0.180*
	(0.030)	(0.103)	(0.107)	(0.092)
NRdist	−0.139***	−0.100	−0.131**	−0.120*
	(0.013)	(0.067)	(0.066)	(0.065)
Sn_contact	0.633***	0.371**	0.334**	0.328*
	(0.165)	(0.166)	(0.170)	(0.172)
Female		0.665***	1.424***	1.421***
		(0.198)	(0.197)	(0.196)
Age		0.142	0.108	0.139
		(0.125)	(0.137)	(0.139)
Age_sq		−0.001**	−0.001	−0.001
		(0.001)	(0.001)	(0.001)
Couple		0.753***	0.681***	0.685***
		(0.242)	(0.258)	(0.255)
Edu_years		0.166***	0.153***	0.152***
		(0.022)	(0.023)	(0.022)
Maxgrip			0.043***	0.043***
			(0.004)	(0.004)
Longill			−0.206***	−0.206***
			(0.074)	(0.074)
ADL			−0.023	−0.023
			(0.043)	(0.043)
IADL			−0.312***	−0.315***
			(0.044)	(0.045)
GALI			−0.124**	−0.124**
			(0.061)	(0.062)
Constant	8.281***	1.591	−0.296	−0.776
	(0.424)	(5.862)	(6.260)	(5.839)
N	19,944	19,944	18,531	18,531
F	170.492	265.172	223.018	151.052
j	0.048	0.460	2.394	2.383
jp	0.827	0.498	0.122	0.123

Notes: Column (4) also includes country dummies and age interactions with country dummies. Robust standard errors in parentheses.
***Significant at the 1 percent level.
**Significant at the 5 percent level.
*Significant at the 10 percent level.

This chapter has explored one mechanism that may explain why early retirement contains negative effects: the erosion of social networks after retirement. Social isolation, in turn, diminishes the day-to-day challenges that keep people mentally fit and well because, ultimately, human beings are social entities. We find evidence that retirement in general, and early retirement in particular, reduces the size of the social network, and in particular

Table 6.11   Second-stage IV estimation: The effect of (early) retirement and the distance to friends and ex-colleagues in the social network on cognition

	Cognition (1)	Cognition (2)	Cognition (3)	Cognition (4)
ERdist	−0.219***	−0.150	−0.178*	−0.177*
	(0.028)	(0.099)	(0.104)	(0.090)
NRdist	−0.135***	−0.107	−0.132**	−0.121*
	(0.012)	(0.065)	(0.065)	(0.063)
Sn_distance	0.604***	0.400**	0.389**	0.380**
	(0.154)	(0.175)	(0.181)	(0.182)
Female		0.697***	1.453***	1.446***
		(0.185)	(0.179)	(0.177)
Age		0.174	0.127	0.146
		(0.118)	(0.132)	(0.135)
Age_sq		−0.001***	−0.001	−0.001
		(0.001)	(0.001)	(0.001)
Couple		0.647***	0.618***	0.612***
		(0.192)	(0.210)	(0.201)
Edu_years		0.151***	0.133***	0.134***
		(0.028)	(0.030)	(0.029)
Maxgrip			0.045***	0.044***
			(0.004)	(0.004)
Longill			−0.196***	−0.195***
			(0.069)	(0.069)
ADL			−0.022	−0.022
			(0.044)	(0.044)
IADL			−0.320***	−0.320***
			(0.041)	(0.042)
GALI			−0.131**	−0.130**
			(0.061)	(0.061)
Constant	8.486***	0.490	−0.982	−0.782
	(0.363)	(5.630)	(6.098)	(5.713)
N	19,944	19,944	18,531	18,531
F	188.529	261.769	216.740	149.263
j	0.025	0.056	1.434	1.519
jp		0.875		0.813

Notes: Column (4) also includes country dummies and age interactions with country dummies. Robust standard errors in parentheses.
***Significant at the 1 percent level.
**Significant at the 5 percent level.
*Significant at the 10 percent level.

the number of friends and other nonfamily contacts in the interpersonal milieu (and not only the number of immediate colleagues).

Our findings are robust and take account of the potential endogeneity of cognition and common unobservables in cognition and social network size and quality. The instruments seem to work well. An even better identification strat-

Table 6.12   **Second-stage IV estimation: The effect of (early) retirement and the number of friends and ex-colleagues in the social network *interacted with the contact intensity* on cognition**

	Cognition (1)	Cognition (2)	Cognition (3)	Cognition (4)
ERdist	−0.216***	−0.150	−0.182	−0.199**
	(0.033)	(0.108)	(0.111)	(0.094)
NRdist	−0.142***	−0.117*	−0.146**	−0.139**
	(0.013)	(0.067)	(0.066)	(0.064)
Friends_x_contact	0.157***	0.090**	0.078*	0.077*
	(0.045)	(0.043)	(0.044)	(0.044)
Female		0.752***	1.509***	1.510***
		(0.176)	(0.176)	(0.171)
Age		0.172	0.135	0.164
		(0.127)	(0.139)	(0.143)
Age_q		−0.001**	−0.001	−0.001
		(0.001)	(0.001)	(0.001)
Couple		0.638***	0.565**	0.572***
		(0.205)	(0.222)	(0.218)
Edu_years		0.167***	0.154***	0.153***
		(0.023)	(0.024)	(0.024)
Maxgrip			0.043***	0.043***
			(0.004)	(0.004)
Longill			−0.177***	−0.177***
			(0.068)	(0.069)
ADL			−0.016	−0.016
			(0.043)	(0.043)
IADL			−0.327***	−0.329***
			(0.041)	(0.043)
GALI			−0.132**	−0.131**
			(0.061)	(0.062)
Constant	8.638***	0.468	−1.283	−1.660
	(0.363)	(6.062)	(6.467)	(6.062)
N	19,944	19,944	18,531	18,531
F	161.092	250.813	213.993	145.033
j	0.226	0.578	2.656	2.642
jp	0.634	0.447	0.103	0.104

Notes: Column (4) also includes country dummies and age interactions with country dummies. Robust standard errors in parentheses.
***Significant at the 1 percent level.
**Significant at the 5 percent level.
*Significant at the 10 percent level.

egy would be to exploit variation in social networks over time. While SHARE contains some indicators of social isolation in earlier waves, the sample sizes of these prototypical earlier waves were much smaller and this strategy failed due to too few observations. Since SHARE will include the social network measures again in wave 6, such analyses will be part of our future work. A

Table 6.13   **Second-stage IV estimation: The effect of (early) retirement and the number of friends and ex-colleagues in the social network** *interacted with the distance to these friends and ex-colleagues in the social network* **on cognition**

	Cognition (1)	Cognition (2)	Cognition (3)	Cognition (4)
ERdist	−0.219***	−0.183*	−0.208*	−0.216**
	(0.031)	(0.105)	(0.110)	(0.089)
NRdist	−0.141***	−0.136**	−0.161**	−0.150**
	(0.012)	(0.065)	(0.064)	(0.061)
Friends_x_distance	0.146***	0.091**	0.086*	0.083*
	(0.040)	(0.042)	(0.044)	(0.044)
Female		0.809***	1.558***	1.554***
		(0.158)	(0.156)	(0.150)
Age		0.215*	0.168	0.191
		(0.122)	(0.138)	(0.138)
Age_q		−0.001***	−0.001	−0.001
		(0.001)	(0.001)	(0.001)
Couple		0.561***	0.524***	0.524***
		(0.165)	(0.185)	(0.177)
Edu_years		0.156***	0.139***	0.139***
		(0.027)	(0.030)	(0.029)
Maxgrip			0.044***	0.044***
			(0.004)	(0.004)
Longill			−0.164**	−0.164**
			(0.065)	(0.066)
ADL			−0.014	−0.014
			(0.044)	(0.044)
IADL			−0.332***	−0.332***
			(0.040)	(0.041)
GALI			−0.148**	−0.146**
			(0.061)	(0.061)
Constant	8.797***	−1.427	−2.805	−2.706
	(0.307)	(5.907)	(6.449)	(5.831)
N	19,944	19,944	18,531	18,531
F	175.000	244.751	204.089	140.116
j	0.088	0.172	1.806	1.897
jp	0.767	0.678	0.179	0.168

Notes: Column (4) also includes country dummies and age interactions with country dummies. Robust standard errors in parentheses.
***Significant at the 1 percent level.
**Significant at the 5 percent level.
*Significant at the 10 percent level.

second direction of our future work will exploit the job characteristics available in SHARE to account for differences in the physical demands, the stress levels, and the effort-reward balance in the last working place.

References

Adam, Stéphane, Eric Bonsang, Sophie Germain, and Sergio Perelman. 2007. "Retirement and Cognitive Reserve: A Stochastic Frontier Approach Applied to Survey Data." CREPP Working Paper no. 2007/04, HEC-ULg.

Bonsang, Eric, Stéphane Adam, and Sergio Perelman. 2010. "Does Retirement Affect Cognitive Functioning?" *ROA Research Memorandum* 2010/1, Maastricht University.

Börsch-Supan, Axel. 2012. "Entitlement Reforms in Europe: Policy Mixes in the Current Pension Reform Process." In *Fiscal Policy after the Financial Crisis*, edited by Alberto Alesina and Fracesco Giavazzi, 405–442. Chicago: University of Chicago Press.

Börsch-Supan, Axel, M. Brandt, K. Hank, and M. Schröder, eds. 2011. *The Individual and the Welfare State. Life Histories in Europe*. Heidelberg: Springer.

Börsch-Supan, Axel, M. Brandt, H. Litwin, and G. Weber, eds. 2013. *Active Ageing and Solidarity between Generations in Europe. First Results from SHARE after the Economic Crisis*. Berlin: DeGruyter.

Börsch-Supan, Axel, A. Brugiavini, H. Jürges, A. Kapteyn, J. Mackenbach, J. Siegrist, and G. Weber, eds. 2008. *Health, Ageing and Retirement in Europe (2004–2007). Starting the Longitudinal Dimension*. Mannheim: Mannheim Research Institute for the Economics of Aging.

Börsch-Supan, Axel, A. Brugiavini, H. Jürges, J. Mackenbach, J. Siegrist, and G. Weber, eds. 2005. *Health, Ageing and Retirement in Europe—First Results from the Survey of Health, Ageing and Retirement in Europe*. Mannheim: Mannheim Research Institute for the Economics of Aging (MEA).

Börsch-Supan, Axel, and H. Jürges, eds. 2005. *The Survey of Health, Ageing and Retirement in Europe—Methodology*. Mannheim: Mannheim Research Institute for the Economics of Aging (MEA).

Börsch-Supan, Axel, and Hendrik Jürges. 2006. "Early Retirement, Social Security and Well-Being in Germany." In *Developments in the Economics of Aging*, edited by David Wise, 173–99. Chicago: University of Chicago Press.

Bound, John. 1991. "Self-Reported Versus Objective Measures of Health in Retirement Models." *Journal of Human Resources* 26:106–38.

Charles, Kerwin Kofi. 2002. "Is Retirement Depressing? Labor Force Inactivity and Psychological Well-Being in Later Life." NBER Working Paper no. 9033, Cambridge, MA.

Clark, Andrew, Ed Diener, Yannis Georgellis, and Richard Lucas. 2003. "Lags and Leads in Life Satisfaction. A Test of the Baseline Hypothesis." German Institute for Economic Research. DIW Discussion Paper no. 371.

Coe, Norma, and Maarten Lindeboom. 2008. "Does Retirement Kill You? Evidence From Early Retirement Windows." CentER Discussion Paper Series 2008-93.

Coe, Norma, Hans-Martin von Gaudecker, Maarten Lindeboom, and Jürgen Maurer. 2012. "The Effect of Retirement on Cognitive Functioning." *Health Economics* 21 (8): 913–27.

European Commission. Various years. MISSOC data base. http://ec.europa.eu/employment_social/social_protection/missoc_tables_en.htm.

Gruber, Jonathan, and David Wise, eds. 1999. *Social Security and Retirement Around the World*. Chicago: University of Chicago Press.

Hyde, Martin, Richard Wiggins, Paul Higgs, and David Blane. 2003. "A Measure of Quality of Life in Early Old Age: The Theory, Development and Properties of a Needs Satisfaction Model (CASP-19)." *Aging Mental Health* 7:186–94.

Korbmacher, Julie. 2013. "The Validity of Life-History Data Vis-à-vis Administrative Records." In *"Eine neue Perspektive der empirischen Alternsforschung in Deutschland: Verknüpfung von medizinisch-biologischer und sozio-ökonomischer Forschung und Verknüpfung von sozio-ökonomischen Umfragen, Prozessdaten und Biomarkern"*, edited by Axel Börsch-Supan. Final report to the Volkswagen Foundation, Munich, Germany.

Kuhn, Andreas, Jean-Philippe Wuellrich, and Josef Zweimüller. 2010. "Fatal Attraction? Access to Early Retirement and Mortality." IEW Working Papers 499, Institute for Empirical Research in Economics, University of Zurich.

Lindeboom, Maarten, France Portrait, and Gerard van den Berg. 2002. "An Econometric Analysis of the Mental-Health Effects of Major Events in the Life of Elderly Individuals." *Health Economics* 11:505–20.

Malter, F., and A. Börsch-Supan, eds. 2013. *SHARE Wave 4: Innovations & Methodology*. Munich: Munich Center for the Economics of Aging (MEA), Max-Planck-Institute for Social Law and Social Policy.

Mazzonna, Fabrizio, and Franco Peracchi. 2012. "Aging, Cognitive Abilities and Retirement." *European Economic Review* 56 (4): 691–710.

Prince, Martin, Friedel Reischies, Aartjan Beekman, Rebecca Fuhrer, Cara Jonker, Sirkka-Liisa Kivela, Brian Lawlor, et al. 1999. "Development of the EURO-D Scale-A European Union Initiative to Compare Symptoms of Depression in 14 European Centres." *British Journal of Psychiatry* 174:330–8.

Rohwedder, Susann, and Robert Willis. 2010. "Mental Retirement." *Journal of Economic Perspectives* 24 (1): 119–38.

van Oyen, Herman, Johan van der Heyden, Rom Perenboom, and Carol Jagger. 2006. "Monitoring Population Disability: Evaluation of a New Global Activity Limitation Indicator (GALI)." *Sozial-und Präventivmedizin* 51 (3): 153–61.

Comment   Elaine Kelly

A recent literature has shown that retirement has a negative impact on cognition (Adam et al. 2007; Bonsang, Adam, and Perelman 2012; Rohwedder and Willis 2010). Börsch-Supan and Schuth's chapter uses data on European retirees from SHARE to extend this work along two margins. First, by considering the impacts on cognition of different types of retirement. Second, by assessing whether the effect of retirement on cognition operates in part through changing social networks. Understanding the mechanisms

Elaine Kelly is a senior research economist at the Institute for Fiscal Studies.

For acknowledgments, sources of research support, and disclosure of the author's material financial relationships, if any, please see http://www.nber.org/chapters/c12983.ack.

behind the relationship between retirement and cognition is particularly important if research is to be used to derive policy implications. At present, it is unclear whether workers should be discouraged from retiring early to protect their cognition, or whether cognition could be safeguarded through changing behaviors or systems of support for retirees.

The chapter is motivated by two observations. First, that cognition declines with age, but is lower for early retirees than normal retirees. Second, that the number of friends and colleagues in a person's social network declines with age, but is lower and declines more steeply for early retirees. Börsch-Supan and Schuth assess whether these patterns are related, and in particular whether the relationship between early retirement and social networks explains part of the association between early retirement and cognition.

The challenge for identification is that both early retirement and the size of social networks are not exogenous. Perhaps most importantly, the timing of retirement may be determined by both current and expected future health and cognition. Lower cognition among early retirees might therefore reflect who retires early, rather than the effect of early retirement on cognition. Similarly, unobserved health and psychological characteristics might affect cognition, early retirement, and the extent of social networks. The authors address these potential sources of endogeneity by instrumenting both early retirement and social networks.

I start by providing comments on the background to early retirement and the identification strategy, before moving on to suggestions about how to extend the analysis in future work.

Early and normal retirement ages in Europe are complex and differ by country, age, gender, work history, and disability status. The chapter starts to exploit this rich source of variation and therefore builds on variation in legal retirement ages used by Rohwedder and Willis (2010). There are, however, two pieces of additional information that would be useful when interpreting the results. The first is the relative prevalence of normal, early, and disabled retirement. Given the focus on social networks, the extent to which people retire at the same time as their peers is potentially very important. The impact of retiring early on your social network when the early retirement rate is 5 percent is plausibly very different from when the rate is 40 percent. The second is evidence for why people retire early. For some older people, early retirement is the result of an active decision to give up work; for others, early retirement is the result of redundancy or unemployment. The composition of early retirees is likely to vary by cohort, depending on the strength of the job market around the time of retirement.

The omission of this information does not affect identification, but inclusion could make the chapter richer, the results easier to interpret, and provide potential extensions to baseline specifications.

The strategy for identifying the impact of early retirement on cognition borrows from Bonsang, Adam, and Perelman (2012) and Rohwedder and Willis (2010), who define the cognition of individual i as the following:

$$(1) \qquad c_i = r_i\beta_1 + x_i\beta_2 + \varepsilon_i,$$

where r_i is an indicator for whether the individual is retired, and x_i are exogenous characteristics. To address the endogeneity of retirement decisions, r_i is instrumented using statutory early and normal retirement ages (Bonsang, Adam, and Perelman 2012; Rohwedder and Willis 2010), or aggregate employment rates by age and sex (Bonsang, Adam, and Perelman 2012).

The baseline specification used by Börsch-Supan and Schuth is different. Rather than considering the effect of retirement relative to remaining in work, the chapter seeks to identify the impacts on cognition of different types of retirement among retirees. Early retirement is thus an object of interest, as opposed to statutory early retirement laws providing an instrument for retirement. Börsch-Supan define two retirement types (normal and early) and specify the cognition of retiree i along the following lines:[1]

$$(2) \qquad c_i = \alpha_1 RetE_i + \alpha_2 YrsRet_i + \alpha_3(RetE_i YrsRet_i) + x_i\gamma_1 + \varepsilon_i,$$

where $RetE_i$ is a dummy for early retirement, and $YrsRet_i$ represents years since retirement. The coefficients of interest are therefore α_2, the effect of years since retirement on cognition for normal retirees, and α_3 the differential effect of years since retirement for early retirees.

Comparing specifications equations (1) and (2) illustrates that Börsch-Supan and Schuth are estimating something different and more complex than Bonsang, Adam, and Perelman (2012) and Rohwedder and Willis (2010). The chapter would therefore benefit from a more thorough discussion about how the estimation strategy relates to existing work, and whether any further identifying assumptions are required.

I next turn to the treatment of social networks, and their relationship to early retirement and cognition.

Social networks are regarded as important sources of information, support, and mental stimulation for older people (Pinquart and Sörensen 2000; Stoddart 2000). However, as in most contexts, social networks are almost certainly not exogenous, with the same unobserved factors that impact social network size also likely to affect cognition. The authors' solution is to instrument social networks with population density and regional variation in average "trust in people" from the European Social Survey. For these instruments to be valid they must: (a) be correlated with individual social networks; and (b) influence cognition only through their effects on social networks. The first condition is certainly fulfilled, as demonstrated in table 6.7, but the second is unlikely to hold. Take the example of Italy, which has

---

1. No specification is provided in the chapter, so this specification represents an interpretation of the approach.

five NUTS-1 regions: Northwestern, Northeastern, Central, Southern, and Insular. The Southern and the Northeastern regions differ from each other in population density and average levels of "trust in people" in ways that correlate with individual social networks. However, both instruments are almost certainly correlated with other aspects of health and behavior, such as diet, exercise, and occupational mix, through mechanisms other than social networks. The authors use the Angrist-Pischke F-test for excluded instruments, but this is only informative when at least one of the instruments is valid.

Finding an instrument that fulfills both conditions (a) and (b) is difficult. One possibility is to exploit variations in the number and sex of family members, such as siblings or children. The number of siblings or children may not be entirely exogenous, but at least predate retirement. Conditional on having children, the sex of the oldest child should be random. If, as seems likely, daughters are more involved in caregiving than sons, and the relationship is sufficiently strong, this could prove a suitable alternative instrument.

My final set of comments relates to potential ways to extend the current analysis, and assumes that the previous concerns over identification can be addressed.

In the chapter, all the specifications are linear and do not allow for heterogeneity in the relationships between cognition, social networks, and early retirement across individuals. This is a sensible baseline approach and mirrors earlier work on the impacts of retirement on cognition, which estimate average or local average treatment effects. However, it seems very likely that the impact of early retirement and both social networks and cognition could depend upon factors such as sex, occupational background, education, and marriage or partnership status. Understanding the nature of this heterogeneity is important for at least two reasons. First, where effects are heterogeneous, the instrument will identify a local average treatment effect rather than an average treatment effect, with the estimated coefficient depending on who is affected by the instruments (retirement regulations for early retirement, and population density or regional variation in trust for social networks). This means the estimated effects using alternative instruments might be quite different, potentially limiting external validity.

Second, variation in how social networks relate to early retirement and cognition might reveal more about how the social network effect operates. Where the impacts of retirement upon cognition are concentrated among individuals with certain characteristics, it may be easier to formulate theories about the mechanisms behind the estimated effects. This speaks to a broader point about how to interpret the results in the chapter and what conclusions to draw. The authors find that declining social networks do explain a proportion of the negative impact of early retirement on cognition, but the question that remains is why. How does early retirement affect different elements of the social network, and what part of the decline in social networks explains a portion of the early retirement effect? The descriptive evidence in tables

6.2 and 6.3 does not provide any strong priors. Does the social network effect operate through the reduction in colleagues? If not, what aspects of an individual's social life change on retirement? Does the relationship between social networks and early retirement depend on whether partners, peers, and other potential members of a social network continue to work? Answering these questions is particularly important, if results are to be used to derive policy implications about how to support or advise people around retirement. Given the rich data available in SHARE, the authors should be able to explore some of these issues in future work.

In summary, this chapter provides an interesting and important first step in understanding the relationship between retirement and cognition.

References

Adam, S., E. Bonsang, S. Germain, and S. Perelman. 2007. "Retirement and Cognitive Reserve: A Stochastic Frontier Approach Applied to Survey Data." CREPP Working Paper no. 2007/04, HEC-ULg.

Bonsang, E., S. Adam, and S. Perelman. 2012. "Does Retirement Affect Cognitive Functioning?" *Journal of Health Economics* 31:490–501.

Pinquart, M., and S. Sörensen. 2000. "Influences of Socioeconomic Status, Social Network,and Competence on Subjective Well-Being in Later Life: A Meta-Analysis." *Psychology and Aging* 15:187–224.

Rohwedder, S., and R. Willis. 2010. "Mental Retirement." *Journal of Economic Perspectives* 24:119–38.

Stoddart, H. 2000. "Social Networks are Important in Preventing Dependency in Old Age." *British Medical Journal* 320 (7244): 1277.

7

Spousal Health Effects
The Role of Selection

James Banks, Elaine Kelly, and James P. Smith

Partner selection is a potentially important and underresearched aspect of levels and inequality of health in all countries. If the healthy marry the healthy and the unhealthy the unhealthy and the health of partners matters as seems likely, then partner selection will exacerbate health inequalities in a population. Health histories of partners may matter for at least three reasons (Monden 2007; Oreffice and Quintana-Domeque 2010; Silventoinen et al. 2003). First, individuals may select their partners in part based on observable and unobservable aspects of their potential partner's prior health. Second, partner selection may depend on factors such as education and health behaviors (smoking, drinking, and exercise), which are correlated with current and future health. Third, couples typically share a common lifestyle and the same household environment. Health outcomes may therefore become more correlated over time as partners are exposed to similar environmental risks, whether through choice or unexpected shocks.

Partner selection may matter as well for international differences in health outcomes. In some countries, partner selection is at the discretion of parents and may be heavily influenced by customs and only take place within

James Banks is professor of economics at the University of Manchester and deputy research director of the Institute for Fiscal Studies (IFS). Elaine Kelly is a research economist at the IFS. James P. Smith holds the Distinguished Chair in Labor Markets and Demographic Studies at the RAND Corporation.

This chapter was supported by grants from the National Institute on Aging and by the Economic and Social Research Council via cofunding through the Centre for Microeconomic Analysis of Public Policy at the IFS. It was presented at the NBER conference on the economics of aging in Carefree, Arizona, in May 2013. The expert programing assistance of Iva Maclennan is gratefully acknowledged. We appreciate the excellent comments of our discussant, Amitabh Chandra, and other participants at the conference. For acknowledgments, sources of research support, and disclosure of the authors' material financial relationships, if any, please see http://www.nber.org/chapters/c12968.ack.

narrowly defined and highly stratified groups. Even in industrialized countries with similar levels of average incomes, heterogeneity and geographic mobility may vary a good deal, producing quite different degrees of partner selection. The case we analyze in this chapter—England and the United States—is a good example since the United States is a more heterogeneous country (if only due to their immigration history and size), and there is much more geographical mobility in the United States than in England (Banks et al. 2012).

There are two aspects of the existing scientific infrastructure that have limited research on this question. Until recently, our major surveys have been focused on individuals, or when there was information on couples there would be only a single household reporter for both individuals in the partner/spousal unit. That is a major limitation, especially when we need to know prepartnership data about both people (Smith 2009). The partner/spouse data in our analysis were reported by each partner about themselves. Secondly, comparable cross-national data did not exist. These two limitations do not restrict our research here since our two data sets for England and the United States (the English Longitudinal Survey for England [ELSA] and the Health and Retirement Study for the United States [HRS]) made international data comparability an essential part of their design. Both surveys also included in their later waves detailed childhood health and background histories that allow us to investigate prepartnership information on health and other relevant traits.

This chapter is divided into four sections. The next section highlights the main attributes of the English and American data we use in this research. Section 7.2 summarizes our results on the nature of the association between spouses and partners in terms of their prepartnership health and socioeconomic status (SES) backgrounds as well as their contemporary health status and health behaviors at the time of the two surveys. The third section examines models of marital dissolution as affected by prior-to-relationship childhood health and the pre- and postmarital patterns of partnership smoking behavior. The final section highlights our main conclusions.

7.1 Data

This research primarily uses data from two surveys—the English Longitudinal Survey of Aging (ELSA) and the American Health and Retirement Survey (HRS). Both collect longitudinal data on health, economic status, work, and well-being from a representative sample of the English and American populations age fifty and older. The ELSA and HRS are strong in the measurement of socioeconomic variables and health (self-reported subjective general health status, prevalence and incidence of physical and mental disease during the post-age-fifty adult years) and salient health behaviors (smoking, alcohol consumption, and physical activity). An important advantage of both data sets for our research in this chapter is that each spouse/partner reports separately about their own health status and health behaviors as well as many aspects of their prepartnership lives, including their family SES and their childhood health.

One limitation of ELSA and HRS is that data collection only begins at age fifty (and even later for older cohorts at the time of the initial baseline interview). Fortunately, this limitation was recognized, and both HRS and ELSA included very similar retrospectively reported childhood health histories.[1] In addition to a subjective question rating their childhood health before age sixteen on the standard five-point scale from excellent to poor, respondents in both surveys were asked about the occurrence of a set of common childhood illnesses. If the condition did exist, they were asked the age of first onset. The age fifty restriction is also recognized later in the chapter when we use two data sets that represent the entire adult age distribution in the two countries—Understanding Society in England and the Panel Survey of Income Dynamics in the United States.

The list of childhood illnesses that were asked was very similar in the two surveys but not identical—some diseases were asked in one survey but not the other.[2] Even within these sets of childhood conditions, there are differences in wording or inclusion that must be taken into account. The following childhood diseases have basically the same wording in both surveys—asthma, diabetes, heart trouble, chronic ear problems, severe headaches or migraines, and epilepsy or seizures. For the common childhood infectious diseases, HRS respondents were asked about mumps, measles, and chicken pox separately while ELSA respondents were asked a single question about all infectious disease with the question wording mentioning these three diseases, but also including polio and tuberculosis (TB).[3]

1. ELSA fielded their childhood health history between its wave 3 and wave 4 core interviews between February and August 2007. The HRS childhood health history was initially placed into an Internet survey in 2007 for those respondents who had Internet access and who agreed to be interviewed in that mode. The remainder of HRS respondents received the same childhood health history as part of the 2008 core interview. For details about the nature of these histories see Smith (2009) and Banks, Oldfield, and Smith (2012).

2. For example, the following childhood conditions and diseases were asked in ELSA but not in HRS—broken bones and fractures; appendicitis; leukemia or lymphoma; cancer or malignant tumor. The following conditions were asked in HRS but not in ELSA—difficulty seeing even with glasses or prescription lenses; a speech impairment; stomach problems; high blood pressure; a blow to the head; head injury or trauma severe enough to cause loss of consciousness or memory loss for a period of time.

3. The biggest difference between the two surveys involves allergies and respiratory problems. In HRS respondents were asked about respiratory disorders, which included bronchitis, wheezing, hay fever, shortness of breath, and sinus infections and were separately asked about any allergic conditions. ELSA respondents were asked about allergies including hay fever and then separately about respiratory problems. Thus, hay fever shows up in a different category in the two surveys. The other difference of possible significance concerns the category of emotional and psychological problems, which included two questions about depression and other emotional problems in HRS and one question about emotional, nervous, or psychiatric problems in ELSA. In addition to any impact of these wording differences, the form in which the questions

Both HRS and ELSA have measures of the family background of respondents although the measures are more similar in concept than in execution between the surveys. In the HRS, we know the occupation of the father when the respondent was sixteen years old, the education of both mother and father, whether each parent is alive, and if not, the age of death, and the economic status of the family during the respondent's childhood years.[4]

In ELSA, we have information on the occupation of the father when the respondent was fourteen years old, the education of both parents, whether each parent is alive, and if not the age of death, and some more limited information on the economic status of the respondent's family in childhood. Finally, in both surveys when there was only a single lifetime relationship, we know the pre- and postrelationship patterns of the smoking behavior of both partners.

7.2 Selection Effects of Partners

7.2.1 Relationships between Spousal Attributes

Table 7.1 documents estimated relationships between early and later life attributes of spouses in terms of health outcomes, health behaviors, and SES background in both England (using ELSA) and the United States (using HRS). Health outcomes are provided separately for the childhood years and for contemporary health outcomes at the time of the HRS and ELSA surveys. In this research, we are using the 2006 (for the health information) and 2008 (to retrieve the childhood health information) waves of HRS and the 2006 ELSA wave when the life history module was administered.

Much of the literature on intercouple correlations in health has focused on height and weight, where studies consistently find strong positive associations (Tambs et al. 1992; Tambs et al. 1991; Oreffice and Quintana-Domeque 2010; Silventoinen et al. 2003). A smaller literature focuses on health conditions and finds positive correlations for the majority of conditions considered (Di Castelnuovo et al. 2009; Wilson 2002; Monden 2007).

Table 7.1 lists age-adjusted associations between spouses/partners in anthropometric measurements, their health conditions and self-reported health in both adulthood and childhood, the standard list of health behaviors (exercise,

---

were asked also differed between the two surveys. HRS respondents were asked separate questions about each condition while ELSA respondents were shown a "show card," which contained a list of conditions and then asked to identify any that they may have had before age sixteen. The show card format could lead to lower reported prevalence if respondents that had multiple conditions only identify a subset from show cards, while they would have answered in the affirmative to each of the questions individually had they been asked.

4. The HRS respondents were asked the following question, "Now think about your family when you were growing up, from birth to age sixteen. Would you say your family during that time was pretty well off financially, about average, or poor?" The categories of response were pretty well off financially, about average, or poor.

Table 7.1   **Estimated relationship of woman's attribute with partner attribute**

	ELSA	HRS		ELSA	HRS
Adult health			Adult behaviors		
Diabetes	.023	.041***	Exercise mod	.316***	.146***
HBP	.020	.047***	Ever smoke	.229***	.198***
Cancer	−.019	.013	Now smoke	.329***	.265***
Lung	.049**	.085***	Quit smoking	.194***	.120***
			Drinks lots	.442***	.305***
Major	.076***	.069***	Overweight	.144***	.205*
Minor	.084***	.089***	Obese	.121***	.151***
Stroke	−.005***	−.024***	BMI	.257***	.285***
Heart conditions	.045**	.029*			
Arthritis	.103***	.114***			
Ex VG	.323***	.197***			
Fair/Poor	.248***	.195***			
Pain	.196***	.103***			
Childhood health			Background		
Height	.240***	.213***			
Major	.141***	.005	Ed partners years	.549***	.482***
			Ed Parents years	NA	.603***
Minor	.035*	.080***	SES as a kid	NA	.080***
Poor	.063**	.013	Father profess	.294***	.132***
Excel	.115***	.051***	Mom died	.020	.034**
Ear	−.016	−.009	Dad died	.018	.030**
Respiratory	.056**	.031*	Mom disease	.078**	NA
Allergies	.032	.010	Father disease	.080***	NA
Month ill	.009	NA	Parents unemployed *	.017	NA
			Black	NA	.923***
Month not in school	−.026	.022	Hispanic	NA	.823***
Emotion problem kid	.128*	.020	Ed Mothers	NA	.457***
Depression	NA	.028	Ed Fathers	NA	.400***
Diabetes	NA	−.002**			
Disability	NA	−.001			
Learning Disability	NA	.057***			
Contagious disease	.126***	.057***			

Notes: Woman's attribute is the outcome—the model contains her male partner's attribute (coefficients in table) and a quadratic in both partners' ages. The sample consists of all current relationships.
***Significant at the 1 percent level.
**Significant at the 5 percent level.
*Significant at the 10 percent level.

drinking, smoking, and body mass index [BMI]–type outcomes), as well as their SES background during childhood and parental attributes both now and in childhood. The estimated coefficients in table 7.1 are all derived from a series of regressions of the female attribute on that of her male partner's attribute in the same domain in a model that also includes age quadratics in both partners' ages. We also estimated a parallel set of models where the male partner trait was the outcome variable and the female partner trait was the regressor (still including the two age quadratics). The coefficient estimates were as expected given the male and female differences in the range of the specific outcomes. None of the substantive conclusions of this chapter is affected by which spouse is used as the right-hand-side explanatory trait.

Our adult health indicators consist at this point of adult self-reports of specific diseases and general health status on the standard five-point scale from excellent to poor. In keeping with existing work on the spousal correlations in health conditions (Monden 2007; Di Castelnuovo et al. 2009), both partners' age-adjusted specific disease prevalences are positively associated across spouses. These associations appear generally to be somewhat higher in the United States compared to England. In our view, we would characterize these associations as positive but not particularly large.

We tend to find the reverse country level relationship when we examine reports of childhood disease, in that in this case, the spousal association in childhood disease appears to be definitely higher in England. This seems particularly true for emotional issues as a child and contagious diseases such as mumps, chicken pox, and measles, which are far more positively associated in England compared to the United States. While we can only measure this in the US data, learning disabilities as children exhibit one of the stronger associations across partners. Even the more objective height measure, often used as an indicator of childhood nutrition, is somewhat more positively associated across partners in England.

There are much higher partner relationships between health measures that rely on subjective reports on health than on reports of disease, and these correlations now tend to be distinctly higher in England than in the United States. For example, the association across spouse/partners in reporting age-adjusted adult health as excellent or very good is 0.32 in England compared to 0.20 in the United States. Similarly, being in excellent or poor health as a child has an association that is twice as large in England compared to the United States. If fair or poor childhood health is used instead, the association is three times larger in England. Since the existence of adult disease appears on average to be slightly more positively correlated in the United States compared to England, the higher association in subjective reports of health suggests that health reporting thresholds of spouse/partners are more similar in the more culturally homogenous England than in the more heterogeneous America.

When we examine adult health behaviors (exercise, smoking, drinking, and indicators of obesity), the results are strikingly uniform in that these health behaviors are strongly positively associated across partners and much more so in England compared to the United States. Couples in England are much more likely to both smoke, drink, and engage in vigorous exercise, if not together at least as a parallel common part of their lives. The only exception to that cross-national comparison is that the BMI-type measures such as obesity and being overweight are slightly more closely related in the United States. That may indicate that types and quantities of food are more commonly consumed among partners in the United States. This greater similarity in health behaviors in England is interesting in that health outcomes across partners/spouses appear somewhat more positively correlated in the United States.

One particularly interesting relationship in the adult behaviors subsegment of table 7.1 concerns quitting smoking. When one of the partners quits smoking, the odds are more than 50 percent larger in England compared to the United States that the other partner will also quit smoking. Part of the much higher similarity among partners in currently smoking compared to ever smoking most likely reflects the fact that "ever" includes a long period of time that the partners were not together and their behaviors could not influence each other. We will model these patterns of smoking behavior in the next section.

Turning to the family background variables on which the most research has been done (Mare 1991; Pencavel 1998), the association in education of partners is slightly higher in England compared to the United States (0.55 compared to 0.48). In the United States in HRS we also know the education of the parents of both partners. The education of the parents is even more positively associated than that of the partners (about 0.6). In fact, the education of both partners' mothers and both partners' fathers are also highly positively associated (0.46 and 0.40 respectively), indicating that much more so than in health social background is highly socially stratified.

Not surprisingly, other aspects of partners' SES backgrounds also appear to be positively associated. One difficulty in making these cross-national comparisons in the domain of family background is that there are only a few background variables that are strictly comparably defined in HRS and ELSA. One such variable that is reasonably comparably defined is whether the father of the respondent had an occupational code labeled professional. In ELSA, a respondent's father is defined as professional if the respondent defines his main job as "manager or senior official in someone else's business," "running their own business," or "profession or technical." This association across partners is twice as high in England compared to the United States.

Table 7.1 presents measures of association of partners only adjusting for their ages. There may be other characteristics that matter in influencing the strength of this association. For example, spousal attributes (at least for first marriages) may be more positively associated the older one is when one gets married. This may partially reflect a more mature judgment in choosing a partner, an ability to obtain more information on the potential partner, or a greater realization of the consequences of early life influences on adult life outcomes. Similarly, these early life associations may vary with whether this is a first marriage or not since a previous marriage failure may lead to choosing a different set of traits in a partner. To investigate these conjectures, we reran these models that underlie table 7.1, controlling for age at marriage of both partners and whether this is a first marriage. Age of partner was not statistically significant, so we concentrated on the changing association of these spousal attributes with the number of lifetime relationships.

Table 7.2 displays changes in partner relationships by the number of relationships for the United States while table 7.3 does the same for England. Because sample sizes in HRS are higher than in ELSA, we present a three-way partnership classification in HRS (1, 2, 3+) and a two-way partnership classification in ELSA (1, 2+). These models are estimated separately by these relationship categories, and once again also include an age quadratic for both partners.

The most distinct pattern we find, and it is present in both countries, is that associations in SES background clearly fall in multiple marriages. In the United States, even the association of education of partners is half as large in three-plus relationships compared to single relationships that endure. The same is true, if to a lesser degree, in the size of this association in education of parents and in education of mothers and fathers of partners. If not as sharp, a similar pattern is found in England. While there is a slight decline in the association between partners in race and much more so in Latino ethnicity with multiple partnerships in the United States, the association remains highly positive in all marriage groups in the US sample in these age cohorts. Most of the recent increase in intermarriage across race and ethnicity postdated the age groups in the age fifty-plus HRS sample.

In terms of adult health behaviors, we find a quite uneven pattern with more similarity in some behaviors (smoking) but less of an association in others (drinking a lot). In the United States and England, childhood health is generally more positively associated in first relationships while the opposite is true for adult health.

7.3 Marriage Models

The theoretical impact of health on the probability of marriage or cohabitation is ambiguous. Healthier individuals will attract a higher "price" on the marriage market, but marriage provides a form of insurance that is of greater benefit to the less healthy. Lillard and Panis (1996) used the Panel Survey of Income Dynamics (PSID) to show that among men better health (on a composite measure) is associated with greater hazard of marriage and

Table 7.2   Estimated relationship of woman's attribute with partner attribute by number of partnerships—HRS

	1st	2nd	3+		1st	2nd	3+
Adult health				**Adult behaviors**			
Diabetes	.054***	.005	.007	Exercise mod	.150***	.128***	.190***
HBP	.066***	−.004	.028	Ever smoke	.208***	.143***	.092*
Cancer	.015	.026	−.049	Now smoke	.243***	.217***	.415***
Lung	.044**	.101***	.275***	Quit smoking	.126***	.077***	.151***
Major	.070***	.052*	.084	Overweight	.012	.065**	.048
Minor	.080***	.100***	.114**	Obese	.151***	.154***	.152***
Stroke	−.022*	−.043***	.001	BMI	.284***	.270***	.313***
Heart condition	.017	.056***	.055	Drinks a lot	.304***	.317***	.286***
Arthritis	.104***	.158***	.083*				
Ex VG	.218***	.165***	.114**				
Poor	.202***	.178***	.166***				
Pain	.085***	.137***	.134**				
Childhood health				**Background**			
Height	.229***	.161***	.185***	Ed spouse years	.541***	.351***	.262***
Major kid	−.000	.001	.025	Ed parents years	.628***	.547***	.547***
Minor kid	.085***	.085***	.024	SES as a kid	.082***	.062***	.110
Poor kid	.005	.026	.043	Father profess	.131***	.100**	.210***
Excel kid	.054***	.044	.044	Mom died	.050***	.032	.060
Emotion problem as kid	.010	.027	.028	Black	.935***	.928***	.902***
Depress kid	.008	.022	.136	Hispanic	.872***	.676***	.549***
Drugs and booze	−.005*	−.007*	−.019**	Ed mothers	.486***	.340***	.373***
Respiratory	.021	.045	.057	Ed fathers	.436***	.297***	.233***
Disability kid	−.021**	.057	.009				
Learn disability kid	.075**	.035	.036				
Kid contagious	.066***	.037	.009				

Notes: Woman's attribute is the outcome—the model contains her partner's attribute (coefficients in table) and a quadratic in both partners' ages. The sample consists of all current relationships.

***Significant at the 1 percent level.

**Significant at the 5 percent level.

*Significant at the 10 percent level.

Table 7.3   Estimated relationship of woman's attribute with partner attribute by number of partnerships—ELSA

	1st	2+		1st	2+
Adult health			Adult behaviors		
Diabetes	.016	.047	Exercise mod	.312***	.326***
HBP	.026	−.016	Ever smoke	.213***	.236***
Cancer	−.019	−.022	Now smoke	.307***	.347***
Lung	.054**	.085***	Quit smoking	.193***	.191***
Asthma	.027	.087*	Drinks lots	.442***	.387***
Major	.067***	.106**	Overweight	.160***	.074
Minor	.082***	.087**	Obese	.116***	.137**
Stroke	−.006	−.006	BMI	.282***	.159**
Heart condition	.040*	.058			
Arthritis	.101***	.120***			
Ex VG	.320***	.197***			
Poor	.224***	.342***			
Pain	.221***	.114***			
Childhood health			Background		
Height	.256***	.177***	Parents argue	.082***	.023
Major kid	.151**	.110	Ed spouse years	.578***	.460***
Minor kid	.024	.069			
Poor kid	.072***	.034	Father profess	.310***	.232***
Excel kid	.117***	.105**	Mom died	.023	.032
Ear kid	−.007	−.038	Dad died	.021	−.002
Respiratory kid	.082**	.007	Mom disease	.068**	.069
Allergies kid	.007	.091	Father disease	.086***	.032
Asthma kid	−.003	.025			
Emotion problem as kid	.134*	.117			
Kid contagious	.098***	.204***			

Notes: Woman's attribute is the outcome—the model contains her partner's attribute (coefficients in table) and a quadratic in both partners' ages. The sample consists of all current relationships.
***Significant at the 1 percent level.
** Significant at the 5 percent level.
*Significant at the 10 percent level.

a lower hazard of divorce. However, once they condition on socioeconomic characteristics, healthier men are less likely to marry, supporting the insurance hypothesis. The results therefore point toward strong positive selection into marriage on the basis of factors correlated with health (such as income and education), which dominate the negative selection generated by the insurance motivation. Fu and Goldman (1994) also find evidence of selection with risky behavior such as smoking and drug taking, and physical characteristics such as obesity and short stature delaying entry into marriage.

Data limitations mean that there is far less work on the impact of childhood health on marriage. That is principally because there are few panels that go from childhood to the later life years collecting prospective health

Table 7.4   **Models of marriage outcomes for women**

VARIABLES	Ever cohabit (1)	Multiple marriages (2)	Ever divorced (3)	Age first cohabit (4)
	A. Marriage female—England			
Female major kid	−0.015	0.078**	0.092**	−0.584**
Female minor kid	0.007	0.031**	0.036**	−0.339**
F Dad died < 70	0.008	−0.010	−0.001	−0.122
F Mom died < 70	0.002	−0.001	0.023	−0.147
Female father prof	0.010	0.026	0.003	0.073
Female ed normed	−0.007***	−0.014***	−0.011***	0.556***
Observations	4,305	3,860	4,146	4,143
R-squared	0.015	0.041	0.060	0.086
	B. Marriage female—United States			
Female major kid	0.003	0.060***	0.080***	−0.122*
Female minor kid	0.001	0.032***	0.025**	−0.069
F Dad died < 70	0.000	0.008	−0.004	−0.169
F Mom died < 70	0.011**	0.010	0.017	0.013
Female father prof	−0.006	−0.002	0.000	0.325
Female ed	−0.000	−0.000	0.003*	0.216**
Observations	9,391	9,391	9,391	9,001
R-squared	0.001	0.012	0.014	0.076

Notes: Models also include age quadratics of both partners. Robust standard errors in parentheses.

***Significant at the 1 percent level.

**Significant at the 5 percent level.

*Significant at the 10 percent level.

outcomes and fewer still that collect information on both partners. These constraints are relaxed with the data we use in this study.

Tables 7.4 (for women) and 7.5 (for men) summarize results from our models estimating effects of childhood health and background variables on a set of marriage-related outcomes in the two countries. The English models are in the A panels of these tables and the American models are in the B panel. The marriage outcomes we investigate include whether a respondent ever cohabited (including marriage), experienced multiple marriages/cohabitatons, were ever divorced, and the age of first cohabiting or marriage. Separate models are estimated for women and men in both England and the United States.

In addition to an age quadratic and constant term (not displayed in the tables), these models include controls for having a major illness and a minor illness as a child, whether one's mother or father died before age seventy, whether one's father was in a professional job when one was a child, and education of respondent. In England the education variable is labeled "Ed normed," which is equal to the number of years of education minus the

Table 7.5   Models of marriage outcomes for men

VARIABLES	Ever cohabit (1)	Multiple marriages (2)	Ever divorced (3)	Age first cohabit (4)
	A. Marriage male—England			
Male major kid	−0.021	0.016	0.037	0.616
Male minor kid	0.001	0.018	0.018	−0.155
M Dad died < 70	−0.005	0.035**	0.046***	−0.191
M Mom died < 70	0.011	0.002	0.004	−0.347*
Male father prof	0.002	0.012	0.007	0.233
Male ed normed	−0.000	−0.009***	−0.013***	0.273***
Observations	3,344	3,055	3,187	3,185
R-squared	0.001	0.021	0.042	0.038
	B. Marriage male—United States			
Male major kid	−0.036**	0.015	0.046*	0.457
Male minor kid	−0.008	0.001	−0.003	−0.013
M Dad died < 70	−0.004	0.014	0.010	0.000
M Mom died < 70	−0.010	−0.013	−0.015	0.051
Male father prof	0.009	0.000	0.006	0.506**
Male ed	0.001	−0.001	0.001	0.069**
Observations	6,585	6,585	6,585	6,266
R-squared	0.031	0.001	0.053	0.057

Notes: Models include an age quadratic and constant term. Robust standard errors in parentheses.
***Significant at the 1 percent level.
**Significant at the 5 percent level.
*Significant at the 10 percent level.

compulsory school-leaving age. Hence, normed is equal to 0 if the cohort member left school at the compulsory school-leaving age, −1 if they left the year before, and 1 if they left the year after. This is to take into account the change in the compulsory schooling age implemented in 1947. The estimated effects of the other variables in these models are not sensitive to the inclusion of own years of schooling as a control variable.

Among English and American men and women, illness during childhood has little effect on whether one ever cohabited, in large part since most people in age group fifty and over have had at least one relationship.[5] The only exception to this generalization is that having experienced a major illness during childhood reduced the probability of cohabiting/marriage among American men.

In contrast, we find statistically significant effects of both major and minor illnesses during childhood on whether one has had multiple partner-

5. The fraction who had been in a relationship are: .962 (American men), .991 (American women), .968 (English men), and .971 (English women).

ships or has even been divorced for both English and American women (see table 7.4). We also find that these childhood illnesses reduced the age of first relationship for women in both countries. Table 7.5 shows that these effects of childhood illness on our measures of relationship stability are much weaker for men, particularly in England. The only exception is that major childhood illness increases the probability of divorce among American men.

Why would childhood illness effects on relationship stability be there for women but not for men? The fact that this gender difference exists in both countries suggests that the explanation is not specific to unique aspects of the culture of each country, but lies instead in gender roles. One gender role that may well come into play is that within relationships, especially in these age groups; women are the caregivers and are a force in improving the health of their spouses. Poor health in childhood for women, which eventually will be transmitted to poorer health in adulthood, may make the relationship less stable since not only might women find it more difficult to help their partners but their male partners may not be willing to provide the help needed with the adult health problems of the woman.[6]

7.3.1 Smoking Models

In this section, we analyze patterns of smoking behavior pre- and post-marriage to assess the influence of partners on smoking behavior. Table 7.6 summarizes basic patterns of pre- and postmarriage smoking behavior as revealed in the HRS for the United States and in ELSA for England, and shows that on almost all dimension the countries are very similar.

The birth cohorts in HRS and ELSA, and especially the men, were clearly heavy smokers in the past who also exhibited significant quitting behavior, a part of which, at least in the United States, no doubt was induced by the Surgeon General's report. In both countries, about two-thirds of men and two-fifths of women were ever smokers. Current smoking behavior is much lower than ever smoking, with about 10 percent of men and women still smoking in both samples.

Most smoking behavior is initiated before marriage. Among men who ever smoked, 87 percent in the United States and 96 percent in England started before marriage. For women ever smokers, there is a more sizable difference with 68 percent starting before marriage in the United States, compared to 88 percent in England. This is the most sizable cross-country difference in table 7.6, and is also reflected in the proportion of women who start smoking before marriage (27 percent in the United States compared to 38 percent in

6. Differences in the effects of individual characteristics on marriage by gender are not limited to childhood health. Oreffice and Quintana-Domeque (2010) find strong interspousal correlations in height and weight, but additional penalties from poor health characteristics vary by gender. Shorter men are more likely to marry shorter, heavier women with a lower level of education. The husbands of heavier women tend to be shorter, poorer, and less educated. The marriage market does not additionally penalize short women or heavier men.

Table 7.6   Patterns of smoking behaviors pre- and postmarriage in the United States and
                   England

	United States		England	
	Men (%)	Women (%)	Men (%)	Women (%)
Ever	62.4	39.0	62.7	43.4
Now	10.8	8.3	10.9	10.1
Both partners never smoked	27.9	27.9	26.1	26.1
Fraction of smokers who quit	82.7	78.7	82.7	76.8
Start before marriage	55.4	27.3	59.9	38.1
Fraction of smokers who started < marriage	87.1	67.9	95.5	87.9
Smoked after marriage	58.6	36.9	52.4	37.4
Smokers before marriage who married smokers	33.9	68.5	44.5	69.9
Nonsmokers before marriage who married smokers	21.0	51.6	28.7	53.8

Source: Calculations by authors from the HRS and ELSA.

England). In England, among those who started smoking before marriage, the average time before (first) marriage was 5.0 years for women and 8.6 years for men. A significant fraction of those who smoked before marriage continued that behavior after the start of their marriage.

The final two rows show the smoking behavior of this sample before marriage so that it reflects smoking selection associated with marriage. In the United States, among male smokers before marriage, 34 percent of them married a smoker while among male nonsmokers before marriage, 21 percent married a smoker. The corresponding numbers for American women are as follows—among female smokers at marriage 69 percent married a smoker, while for female nonsmokers 52 percent married a smoker. Thus, while there is a distinct positive association at marriage between smoking behaviors of partners, it remains the case that many nonsmokers also marry smokers. This is especially true for American women, which may not be surprising since so many men smoked during that time period in the HRS birth cohorts.

The corresponding numbers for England in table 7.6 show similar assortative mating in premarital smoking behavior for English women, with 70 percent of English female smokers at the time of their marriage also married smokers compared to only 54 percent for female nonsmokers marrying smokers. Assortative mating for English men is of a similar magnitude, with 45 percent of male smokers marrying smokers compared to only 29 percent for male nonsmokers.

Table 7.7 presents results of models estimating the relationship between postmarriage and current smoking behavior to smoking before marriage of both partners in the United States. In addition to our standard age quadratics, our American models also include controls for education (three

Table 7.7   Models of smoking behavior in United States

	Married men currently smoke	Married women currently smoke	Married men smoke > marriage	Married women smoke > marriage
Male smoked < marriage	0.116***	0.025***	0.770***	0.070***
Female smoked < marriage	0.020	0.089***	0.044	0.785***
Male and female smoked < marriage	0.009	0.043	-0.036	-0.048*
Ed 0–11	0.050***	0.064***	0.020	0.062***
Ed 16+	-0.065***	-0.039***	-0.058***	-0.069***
African American	0.063***	0.000	0.072***	0.009
Hispanic	-0.024	-0.031	-0.006	-0.055**
Constant	-0.077	-0.154**	0.221***	-0.191*

Source: Data from the HRS.

Note: Models also include an age quadratic.

***Significant at the 1 percent level.

**Significant at the 5 percent level.

*Significant at the 10 percent level.

dummy variables for years of education—0–11 years, 12–15 years, and 16 or more years with the middle group serving as the reference group), African American race, and Hispanic ethnicity. Our corresponding English models are presented in table 7.8 with the only difference being the absence of the two American ethnicity variables and the use of the education normed variable instead of the American education dummies.

Consider the American models first. Among men, African Americans smoke more, both at the time of the administration of our HRS sample and postmarriage, while there are no statistically significant between-group differences for African American women. These differences are much smaller for Hispanics, with the only statistically significant difference existing for Latinas who smoked somewhat less after marriage. Education differences in smoking are well established in the United States (Goldman and Smith 2011) and these patterns are replicated in table 7.7. Smoking is highest among the least educated and lowest among the most educated for both genders. We find a similar negative effect of education in the English models in table 7.8.

Our main interest in the models in table 7.7 concerns estimated effects of own and spousal premarriage smoking. In terms of ever smoking after marriage, not surprisingly, smoking before marriage is a very strong predictor for both men and women. When we examine current smoking, the estimated effects of premarriage smoking are considerably smaller, illustrating once again the significant degree to which these generations quit smoking.

Perhaps the most interesting result in table 7.7 is the asymmetric gender effects of premarriage partner smoking in the United States. Controlling for male partner premarriage smoking, female partner premarriage smoking has no statistically significant effect on postmarriage male smoking. In sharp contrast, the estimated effects of male partner premarriage smoking remain statistically significant and nontrivial, even after we control for female premarriage smoking. To put it simply, at least in the domain of smoking, men influence women while women do not influence men, on average, to the same degree. By marrying a male smoker, women's health could be influenced in two ways—first, the widely cited negative effects of exposure to second-hand smoke, and in addition, the enhanced probability of becoming a smoker.

The parallel results for England are presented in table 7.8. The own sex premarriage estimates on current smoking are evidence of significant quitting behavior in England as well. The other lagged premarriage coefficients are similar to what they were in the United States. In England, if both partners smoked it was apparently more difficult for both women and men to cease their smoking after marriage. As for the United States, the estimated effects of male premarital smoking on female smoking are larger than the estimates for the effects of female smoking on male smoking. However, the magnitudes are smaller, and only the association between male premarital smoking and female smoking after marriage is statistically different from zero.

Table 7.8   Models of smoking behavior in England

	Married men currently smoke	Married women currently smoke	Married men smoke > marriage	Married women smoke > marriage
Male smoked < marriage	0.138***	0.014	0.751***	0.055***
Female smoked < marriage	−0.009	0.189***	0.036	0.662***
Male and female smoked < marriage	0.061*	0.015	0.052	0.136***
Ed normed	−0.008**	−0.014***	−0.009***	−0.013***
Constant	0.096	0.691**	−0.221	0.102
Observations	1,616	1,613	1,586	1,606

Source: Data from the ELSA.

Note: Models also include an age quadratic.

***Significant at the 1 percent level.

**Significant at the 5 percent level.

*Significant at the 10 percent level.

Table 7.9   Models of quitting behavior

	United States		England	
	Married men quit smoking	Married women quit smoking	Married men quit smoking	Married women quit smoking
Partner smokes now	−0.277***	−0.337***	−0.336***	−0.310***
Partner quit	−0.004	−0.032	0.041*	0.095***
Ed normed	NA	NA	0.008	0.025***
Ed 0–11	−0.054**	−0.100***	NA	NA
Ed 16+	0.084***	0.031	NA	NA
Constant	0.953***	1.169***	0.689	−0.668

Note: Sample consists of ever smokers.
***Significant at the 1 percent level.
**Significant at the 5 percent level.
*Significant at the 10 percent level.

Table 7.9 contains our models for quitting smoking behavior for residents of both countries. We restrict the sample in these models for each gender to those that ever smoked and add categorical variables for your partner's smoking behavior (never smoked, still smokes, quit smoking) with never smoked the reference group in the models. In both countries relative to partners who never smoked, individuals are less likely to quit if their partners are currently smoking, with the magnitudes of these effects quite similar in both countries. We find a stronger influence of partner behavior in England compared to the United States in that having a partner who quits smoking is positively associated with you also quitting smoking in England for both men and women. We find no such relationship in our American models.

7.3.2 Smoking Models for Younger Cohorts

Attitudes toward smoking have changed dramatically since the ELSA and HRS cohorts started smoking and formed partnerships. In this section, we use alternative sources of data to consider whether our results hold for younger cohorts and the extent to which partnership sorting by smoking behavior has changed. Data for England comes from Understanding Society, a United Kingdom–wide longitudinal survey covering 40,000 households. We use data on smoking behavior from the second wave, conducted in 2010. Information on marriage and cohabitation is available. The American data come from the 2007 wave of the Panel Survey of Income Dynamics (PSID), the premiere all age group income panel in the United States.

Table 7.10 shows patterns of smoking behavior pre- and postmarriage, for cohorts aged 50+ and 30–49 in both countries. The A panel of table 7.10 has data for England, while the B panel contains the American results. Comparing the first two columns of table 7.10 panel A and 7.10 panel B to the ESLA and HRS figures in table 7.6 for essentially the same age group

Table 7.10   Patterns of smoking behaviors pre- and postmarriage in the United States and England

	Men 50+ (%)	Women 50+ (%)	Men 30–49 (%)	Women 30–49 (%)
A. England				
Ever	68.5	53.8	61.3	52.4
Now	17.1	16.0	29.0	22.6
Both partners never smoked	18.9	18.9	25.6	25.6
Fraction who quit	76.6	68.3	52.8	57.0
Start before marriage	58.9	42.5	52.7	44.5
Fraction of smokers who started < marriage (ever)	85.9	79.0	91.5	84.5
Smoked after marriage	56.7	47.3	52.2	43.6
Smokers before				
Marriage who married smokers	47.1	65.3	53.8	67.9
Nonsmokers before marriage who married smokers	35.8	54.1	32.6	46.7
B. United States				
Ever	53.1	33.4	33.6	26.4
Now	13.3	7.3	15.4	11.1
Both partners never smoked	36.7	36.7	55.5	54.1
Fraction who quit	74.9	78.1	54.2	58.0
Start before marriage	43.6	23.8	29.2	21.9
Fraction of smokers who started < marriage (ever)	82.1	71.3	86.9	83.0
Smoked after marriage	42.5	27.8	26.0	20.6
Smokers before				
Marriage who married smokers	33.7	60.5	39.3	52.8
Nonsmokers before marriage who married smokers	17.7	38.7	14.4	23.4

Sources: For panel A, Understanding Society, wave 2. Respondents in England who have partners, have nonmissing partnership and smoking information, and whose partners have nonmissing partnership and smoking information. For panel B, sample is from the PSID.

(ages 50+) shows that levels of previous and current smoking among the 50+ are somewhat higher in Understanding Society than in ELSA. In contrast, they are generally somewhat lower in PSID than in HRS, but the general patterns remain remarkably the same. The American result is not surprising in that the PSID sample of 50+ is younger than the HRS sample.

The comparison between the two age-defined birth cohorts in Understanding Society and PSID gives the combined effect of differences by age and cohort. As expected, the proportion who ever smoked is lower for those ages 30–49 than for those 50+, with a difference of 6.3 percentage points for men and 0.8 percentage points for women in England, and even larger in the PSID where it is a difference of 19.5 percentage points for men and 7.0 percentage points for women, most likely reflecting the large secular decline in male smoking in the United States. The proportions that smoke now are higher for the younger cohort, in part because the probability of quitting rises with age.

The final two rows show the relationship between smoking and partner selection. Even though the shares that smoked before marriage are very similar across the two cohorts, the difference in proportion of smokers and nonsmokers who married a smoker is much higher for those age 30–49 than for those 50+, indicating greater premarital smoking selection in partners in the younger cohorts. While this is true in both countries, it is especially the case in England.

Table 7.11 decomposes the last two rows in table 7.10 into those with compulsory education or less and more than compulsory education in England, and for those with less than a high school degree and with a college degree or more in the United States. For both birth cohort groups, the proportions of smokers who married smokers and nonsmokers who married smokers are lower for those with more than compulsory education. This in part reflects lower overall smoking rates among the more educated. Within cohort differences by education level show no large changes.

For both education groups in England, smoking selection is greater for the younger cohort, with higher proportions of smokers marrying smokers and lower proportions of nonsmokers marrying smokers. The largest cross-cohort differences are in the (increased) proportions of male smokers that marry smokers and the (reduced) proportions of female nonsmokers that marry nonsmokers. The change in the former does not differ by education level; the change in the latter is much larger for more educated women. The remaining two groups, female smokers and male nonsmokers, are most likely to marry someone with the same smoking behavior, and this increases only slightly over time. One explanation is that female smoking has always been undesirable to men who do not smoke. Over time and cohorts, this has strengthened slightly. The bigger change is in women's attitudes to men who smoke.

Table 7.12 provides models of smoking behavior in Understanding Society and the PSID that correspond to the models in tables 7.7 and 7.8. The own

Table 7.11   **Partner selection and smoking behavior, by age and education**

Understanding Society in England

	Compulsory only		More than compulsory	
	Men (%)	Women (%)	Men (%)	Women (%)
Age 50+				
Smokers at marriage who married smokers	50.0	65.7	43.9	63.5
Nonsmokers before marriage who married smokers	41.5	56.4	33.8	53.0
Age 30–49				
Smokers at marriage who married smokers	56.5	68.1	51.5	66.8
Nonsmokers before marriage who married smokers	37.6	52.5	30.6	44.2

Panel Survey of Income Dynamics in USA

	Less than 12		16 or more	
	Men (%)	Women (%)	Men (%)	Women (%)
Age 50+				
Smokers at marriage who married smokers	50.0	69.2	39.5	59.6
Nonsmokers before marriage who married smokers	25.0	47.5	26.4	31.1
Age 30–49				
Smokers at marriage who married smokers	38.5	90.0	23.3	50.0
Nonsmokers before marriage who married smokers	19.2	38.7	12.6	19.5

effects in ELSA and 50+ Understanding Society cohorts are roughly similar, although own premarriage smoking has a larger effect on current smoking in Understanding Society, particularly for women. The partner effects are more consistently significant in the female smoking models.

As would be expected, the association between smoking and own premarriage smoking are stronger for the younger Understanding Society cohort, as the quit rate increases over time. However, the associations with partner's smoking behavior are also stronger and similar across men and women in the younger age group. For current smoking, this may be explained by increasing quit rates as cohorts age. However, the result for smoking after marriage suggests an increased responsiveness to partner behavior. This still largely remains not the case in the United States for the younger cohort in that they largely remain uninfluenced by a partner's smoking. The main exception is that when both partners smoked before marriage, married women are much more likely to be current smokers.

Table 7.13 provides models of quitting behavior that mirror those for the HRS and ELSA in table 7.9. As in table 7.9, there is a strong negative association between quitting smoking and having a partner that currently

Table 7.12   **Models of smoking behavior by age**

	50+				30–49			
	Married men currently smoke	Married women currently smoke	Married men smoke > marriage	Married women smoke > marriage	Married men currently smoke	Married women currently smoke	Married men smoke > marriage	Married women smoke > marriage
	Understanding Society for England							
Male smoked < marriage	0.150***	0.055**	0.731***	0.074***	0.366***	0.071***	0.851***	0.104***
Female smoked < marriage	0.048	0.205***	0.031	0.798***	0.055*	0.279***	0.125***	0.743***
Male and female smoked < marriage	0.050	0.040	–0.014	–0.088***	0.070*	0.084***	–0.100***	–0.007
Ed normed	–0.013***	–0.009***	–0.008***	–0.008***	–0.012***	–0.015***	–0.002	–0.008***
Constant	0.597	–0.187	–0.324	–0.434	0.257	0.251	0.272	–0.460
Observations	1,376	1,375	1,132	1,279	1,689	1,688	1,491	1,541
	United States—PSID							
Male smoked < marriage	0.228***	0.039**	0.769***	0.065***	0.395***	0.025	0.710***	0.030
Female smoked < marriage	0.031	0.180***	0.028	0.633***	0.013	0.304***	–0.017	0.618***
Male and female smoked < marriage	–0.055	–0.077	0.031	0.116*	0.022	0.102*	0.137**	0.176***
Ed 0–12	0.273***	–0.005	0.005	0.102**	0.227***	0.092**	0.119**	0.037
Ed 16 plus	–0.039	–0.047**	–0.125***	–0.040*	–0.030	–0.044***	–0.053**	–0.047**
Constant	0.031	0.032***	0.092***	0.078***	0.028***	0.026***	0.043***	0.046***

***Significant at the 1 percent level.
**Significant at the 5 percent level.
*Significant at the 10 percent level.

Table 7.13   **Models of quitting behavior**

	Age 50+		Age 30–49	
	Married men quit smoking	Married women quit smoking	Married men quit smoking	Married women quit smoking
England—Understanding Society				
Partner smokes now	−0.416***	−0.317***	−0.442***	−0.386***
Partner quit	−0.032	−0.010	0.029	0.092***
Ed normed	0.010**	0.015***	0.015***	0.011***
Constant	1.555*	−0.224	0.634	0.411
United States—PSID<set panel head>				
Partner smokes now	−0.305***	−0.331***	−0.313***	−0.333***
Partner quit	0.083**	0.041	0.093	0.060
Ed 0–11	−0.332***	0.043	−0.237***	−0.288***
Ed 16 plus	0.032	0.063	0.027	0.083
Constant	0.768***	0.801***	0.604***	0.665***

***Significant at the 1 percent level.
**Significant at the 5 percent level.
*Significant at the 10 percent level.

smokes. The association is stronger for the Understanding Society over 50 cohort than in ELSA. By contrast, the association between quitting and a partner quitting is only statistically significant for the age 30–49 sample in Understanding Society and the 50+ sample in the PSID.

7.4 Conclusion

In this chapter, we investigated the issue of partner selection in the health of individuals who are at least fifty years old in England and the United States. Such an investigation is now possible since data sets such as ELSA and HRS interview both partners in the relationship and also ask questions about central prepartnership variables that include family background and childhood health.

We find a strong and positive association in family background variables including education of partners and their parents. Adult health behaviors such as smoking, drinking, and exercise are more positively associated in England compared to the United States. Childhood health indicators are also positively associated across partners. In general, these correlations are more positive for first than for subsequent partnerships. Especially for women, poor childhood health is associated with future marital disruptions in both countries.

Because of the better availability of the necessary data, we investigated more closely the pre- and postpartnership smoking behavior of couples. There exists strong positive assortative mating in smoking in that smokers are much more likely to partner with smokers and nonsmokers with non-smokers. This relationship is far stronger in England compared to the United States. In the United States, we find evidence of asymmetric partner influence in smoking in that men's premarriage smoking behavior influences his female partner's postmarriage smoking behavior, but there does not appear to be a parallel influence of women's premarriage smoking on their male partner's postmarital smoking. These relationships are much more parallel across genders in England.

In the age cohorts in our samples, there was historically strong quitting behavior in smoking. Once again, we find stronger evidence of spousal influence in England as being partnered with a smoker who quit smoking makes it more likely for the partner to quit as well. This relationship does not exist in the United States.

References

Banks, James, Richard Blundell, Zoe Oldfield, and James P. Smith. 2012. "Housing Mobility and Downsizing at Older Ages in Britain and the USA." *Economica* 79 (313): 1–26.

Banks, James, Zoe Oldfield, and James P. Smith. 2012. "Childhood Health and Differences in Late Life Outcomes between England and America." In *Investigations in the Economics of Aging*, edited by David Wise, 321–43. Chicago: University of Chicago Press.

Di Castelnuovo A., G. Quacquaruccio, M. Benedetta Donati, G. de Gaetano, and L. Iacoviello. 2009. "Spousal Concordance for Major Coronary Risk Factors: A Systematic Review and Meta-Analysis." *American Journal of Epidemiology* 169 (1): 1–8.

Fu, H., and N. Goldman. 1994 "Are Healthier People More Likely to Marry? An Event History Analysis Based on the NLSY." Working Paper 94-5, Office of Population Research, Princeton University, Princeton, NJ.

Goldman, Dana, and James P. Smith. 2011. "The Increasing Value of Education to Health." *Social Science and Medicine* 72 (10): 1728–37.

Lillard, Lee, and Constantijn Panis. 1996. "Marital Status and Mortality: The Role of Health." *Demography* 33 (3): 313–27.

Mare, R. D. 1991. "Five Decades of Educational Assortative Mating." *American Sociological Review* 52:15–32.

Monden, C. 2007. "Partners in health? Exploring Resemblance in Health between Partners in Married and Cohabiting Couples." *Sociology of Health & Illness* 29:391–411.

Oreffice, S., and C. Quintana-Domeque. 2010. "Anthropometry and Socioeconomics Among Couples: Evidence in the United States." *Economics & Human Biology* 8 (3): 373–84.

Pencavel, John. 1998. "Assortative Mating by Schooling and the Work Behavior of Wives and Husbands." *American Economic Review* 88:326–9.

———. 2009. "Re-constructing Childhood Health Histories." *Demography* 46 (2): 387–403.

Silventoinen, K., J. Kaprio, E. Lahelma, R. J. Viken, and R. J. Rose. 2003. "Assortative Mating by Body Height and BMI: Finnish Twins and Their Spouses." *American Journal of Human Biology* 15:620–7.

Tambs, K., T. Moum, L. Eaves, M. Neale, K. Midthjell, P. G. Lund-Larsen, S. Naess, and J. Holmen. 1991. "Genetic and Environmental Contributions to the Variance of the Body Mass Index in a Norwegian Sample of First and Second-Degree Relatives." *American Journal of Human Biology* 3:257–67.

Tambs, K., T. Moum, L. J. Eaves, M. C. Neale, K. Midthjell, P. G. Lund-Larsen, S. Naess. 1992. "Genetic and Environmental Contributions to the Variance of Body Height in a Sample of First and Second Degree Relatives." *American Journal of Physical Anthropology* 88:285–94.

Wilson, S. E. 2002. "The Health Capital of Families: An Investigation of the Inter-Spousal Correlation in Health Status." *Social Science and Medicine* 55 (7): 1157–72.

Comment   Amitabh Chandra

In this remarkable chapter, we learn that the health of spouses is positively correlated. To illustrate with a few examples from the analysis, consider a simple regression of a wife's health outcome on her husband's (adjusting for the ages of both partners): in the United States, if the husband has arthritis the wife is 10 percentage points more likely to have this condition; if the husband is in fair or poor health, then his wife is about 20 percentage points more likely to be similarly disposed. These associations are similar, but slightly larger, in the United Kingdom and are noted for adult health, adult behaviors (such as smoking), childhood health (as measured by height), and background (such as education). It is also interesting to note that these associations are larger for the first relationship than subsequent ones. So much for the idea that first love is a little foolish.

There are several implications of these findings that are worth exploring. The first, and most salient, is the linkage to Nicholas Christakis's work on "Mortality after the Hospitalization of a Spouse," which was published in the *New England Journal of Medicine* and summarized in many news outlets (Christakis and Allison 2006). In this work, Christakis's team makes three points: First, that having a sick spouse is about one fourth as bad for a partner's health as having a spouse actually die. Second, some spousal diseases, such as hip fracture or psychiatric conditions, were nearly as bad for partners as if the spouse actually died. Third, the period of greatest risk is over the short run, within thirty days of a spouse's hospitalization or death, when the

Amitabh Chandra is professor of public policy and director of health policy research at the Kennedy School of Government at Harvard University and a research associate of the National Bureau of Economic Research.

For acknowledgments, sources of research support, and disclosure of the author's material financial relationships, if any, please see http://www.nber.org/chapters/c12969.ack.

risk of death upon a spouse's hospitalization is almost as great as that when a spouse dies. When this chapter came out the principal concern with these findings was that the husbands and wives suffered correlated health shocks (and that it was the common shock, as opposed to the health of one partner, that resulted in their correlated outcomes). But what we learn from the new chapter by Banks, Kelly, and Smith is that another source of bias may also be at work: if the marriage markets result in assortative mating (where healthy men marry healthy women and unhealthy men are more likely to be matched to unhealthy women), then it may be unsurprising to find that one spouse's hospitalization predicts another spouse's hospitalization. I do not believe that the entirety of Christakis's results would be defined by this explanation, and it is highly unlikely that the increased risk of hospitalization within thirty days of a spouse's hospitalization would be, but the point here is that assortative mating in health means that the Christakis studies are biased in the direction of finding what they did. Exploring the empirical content of this hypothesis would be a fruitful area for future research, especially because the odds ratios for elevated hospitalization in the Christakis studies are small (less than 1.5) and we know that it does not take a lot of selection to undo these effects.

The chapter also opens up a number of interesting questions for future research. Do "spousal health effects" (what I call assortative mating on health) persist even after controlling for race and income? First, this is an important distinction to what is presented in the chapter, because to the degree that most marriages in the United States are still within race and within income group, it is possible that the facts presented here are picking up assortative mating on the basis of race and income. Second, the analysis motivates us to ask whether assortative mating on the basis on health increased over time? I would suspect that it has, if nothing else, because of the increasing concentration of income, wealth, and opportunity. Robert Mare, the distinguished sociologist at UCLA, has noted that the fraction of marriages that are educationally homogamous (i.e., marriages where both spouses have the same educational levels) have increased from 44 percent of all marriages in 1960 to over 55 percent in the 2000s. Building on my first comment, these trends may imply higher assortative mating on the basis on health (either causally or because both trends have a common causal factor).

Understanding why assortative mating occurs is beyond the scope of this chapter, but certainly within the scope of economics. In the world of biology, scientists have studied assortative mating in arthropods in great detail (arthropods are invertebrate animals having an exoskeleton, a segmented body, and jointed appendages; they include insects, arachnids, and crustaceans). The leading theories are: (a) mate choice—where larger (healthier?) arthropods are better able to exercise choice; (b) mate availability—where larger agents are differentially available for mating; and (c) mating constraints—where size differences (here, health differences) cause physical or energetic difficulties. The role of the last constraint is likely to be falling in human populations as a result of superior medical care (sick children are more likely to be healthy adults today than in the past). But the case for the mate choice hypothesis is likely increasing.

An increasing amount of assortative mating has large implications for inequality and the political economy of transfer programs. Healthier and richer parents are more likely to produce healthier children who will receive many educational advantages. Connecting the theory to the evidence, for human marriage markets as opposed to arthropods markets, would make a terrific research program.

References

Christakis, Nicholas A., and Paul D. Allison. 2006. "Mortality after the Hospitalization of a Spouse." *New England Journal of Medicine* 354:719–30.

8

Grandpa and the Snapper
The Well-Being of the Elderly
Who Live with Children

Angus Deaton and Arthur A. Stone

8.1 Introduction

This chapter lies at the intersection of two literatures, one on whether children bring well-being to those who live with them, and one on the living arrangements of the elderly. Whether or not children make their parents' lives better is an old question that remains unsettled; see Hansen (2012) and Stanca (2012) for recent surveys of the literature, both of these argue that most studies find a negative effect of children on their parents' well-being. Our own work, Deaton and Stone (2014), argues that, in line with what might be expected from rational choice under uncertainty with life evaluation as a target, parents' life evaluation is no different from that of nonparents on average, at least once we allow for differential selection into parenthood. However, we also find that parents of children have different

Angus Deaton is the Dwight D. Eisenhower Professor of Economics and International Affairs at the Woodrow Wilson School of Public and International Affairs and at the Economics Department at Princeton University and a research associate of the National Bureau of Economic Research. Arthur A. Stone is the Distinguished Professor of Psychiatry and of Psychology, vice-chair of the Department of Psychiatry and Behavioral Science, and director of the Applied Behavioral Medicine Research Institute at Stony Brook University.

We are grateful to Gallup for granting us access to the Gallup-Healthways Well-Being Index data and the Gallup World Poll. Both authors are consulting senior scientists with Gallup. We gratefully acknowledge financial support from Gallup and from the National Institute on Aging through the National Bureau of Economic Research, grants 5R01AG040629–02 and P01 AG05842–14. We are grateful to Anne Case and to David Laibson for comments on previous versions. For acknowledgments, sources of research support, and disclosure of the authors' material financial relationships, if any, please see http://www.nber.org/chapters/c12962.ack.

Snapper is an Irish term for a child, abbreviated from *whippersnapper*. It is a term that a grandpa would use to indicate his irritation with an unruly child.

emotional lives, with more happiness and more enjoyment, as well as more stress and more worry.

The literature on the living arrangements of the elderly in the United States argues that the elderly value their ability to live independently. In consequence, those who are living with children under age eighteen, who are unlikely to be their own, are likely to be selected on factors such as low income or poor health (see Börsch-Supan, Kotlikoff, and Morris 1988). Low income and poor health have well-attested negative effects on both evaluative and emotional well-being. It is also possible that living with young people brings fewer positive and more negative emotions for the elderly than for the parents themselves; the ability to tolerate the more difficult parts of childhood may diminish with age. Such effects would add to the effects of negative selection, and we might expect especially poor outcomes for the elderly living with children.

Outside of the United States and other rich countries, it is common for the elderly to live in multigenerational families. Where this is the case, there is less reason to believe that there is negative selection into living with children among the elderly. In such places, we should observe something closer to the direct effects of living with children. It has often been argued that, prior to the demographic transition, "the elderly are an integrated, useful, and respected part of their families," Deaton and Paxson (1992, 165) who are summarizing an earlier extensive literature. If so, living with a younger generation of children may bring positive emotional and evaluative experience in pretransition countries.

We use two large data sets collected by Gallup; one for the United States, the Gallup-Healthways Well-Being Index, and one for 161 countries around the world, the Gallup World Poll, with sample sizes of 1.8 million and 1.1 million individuals, respectively. These data sets are rich in well-being questions, and include measures of life evaluation as well as a range of emotional well-being measures or hedonics. They also have the advantage of using identical questions in all locations. These advantages are offset by incomplete information on living arrangements. In particular, we have information on one respondent from each household, and know only whether or not there is a child at home, not the relationship of the respondent to that child.

Our primary focus is on the well-being of the elderly, though we shall typically compare outcomes for the elderly with those for the younger generation who are actually the parents of the children.

8.2 Well-Being, the Elderly, and Children in the United States

Figure 8.1 is a starting point for our investigation, and uses the Gallup-Healthways Well-Being Index data from the United States, which has collected 1,000 daily observations from adults (age eighteen or older) from the beginning of 2008 through to the end of 2012. The two lines show average

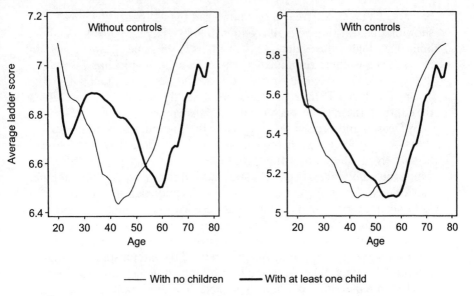

Fig. 8.1   Mean life evaluation by age, with and without children, and with-out covariates

life evaluation by age for those who do and do not report the presence of a child living with them; a child is defined as anyone younger than eighteen, no matter what their relation to the respondent. The life evaluation measure here is the Cantril Ladder, running from 0 (the worst possible life for you) to 10 (the best possible life for you), and these numbers are averaged for all people by single years of age. The left-hand graph has no controls, while the right-hand graph controls for income categories, education categories, and sex; missing values—of which there are a substantial number for income— are handled by treating missing as a category. Both plots show five-year triangularly weighted moving averages of the age coefficients in a regression of the ladder on the presence of at least one child interacted with indicators for single years of age, together with covariates when they are included.

The graphs show that both those with and without children have the famil-iar U-shaped profile of life evaluation by age (Blanchflower and Oswald 2008; Stone et al. 2010). Interestingly, in the left-hand graph where there are no controls, the onset of the U is postponed for those with children, opening up a gap between those with and without children during ages thirty to fifty; the midlife dip in well-being is two decades later among people with children. We have used the 2008 American Community Survey to investigate how many of the people living with children are the parents of those children. Figure 8.3 plots this fraction by age, and shows that at each age from thirty-four to forty-six, more than 90 percent of adults who have a child at home are the parents of that child. We can therefore read the left panel of figure 8.1 as showing that, for those age thirty-four to forty-six, *parents* with a child at home have higher life evaluation than adults in the same age range who do not. Among younger respondents, where the child is most likely a sibling, life evaluation is lower in the presence of a child, something that is also true among the elderly. In the right-hand part of the figure, where we have added the controls, the gaps between the two lines are much smaller.

In Deaton and Stone (2014) we show that, for the parental group age thirty-four to forty-six, the higher well-being of those with children can be entirely attributed to a fuller set of covariates than those used in the figure, including race, Hispanic status, marital status, religiosity, smoking, and a range of health conditions. Those with children in the thirty-four to forty-six age range are different from those without children in ways that promote higher life evaluation on their own account. This is consistent with the idea that the positive effect of children on life evaluation comes entirely from the life evaluation–enhancing effects of the circumstances—higher income, education, religiosity, and health—that differentially cause people to select into parenthood. It is also possible that some or all of these conditions may be a result of being a parent, so the ability to explain the evidence by covariates does not conclusively imply that children do not enhance life evaluation. "Good" characteristics cause selection into parenthood, but are in part induced by parenthood—parents giving up smoking, or exercising more frequently—and this part of the increase in well-being should properly be attributed to the presence of the children.

One aim of this chapter is to make a similar accounting for the elderly. We start by examining uncontrolled differences in outcomes by age, and then document the differences in background characteristics between the elderly who do and do not live with children. We then present regressions of outcomes on the presence of a child with a range of controls for background characteristics.

Figure 8.2 shows the (uncontrolled) *difference* in the ladder and in hedonic outcomes between those with and without children; here we use five-year (except for first and last) age groups as an alternative to the smoothing in figure 8.1. The top-left panel for the ladder shows the differences between the two lines in the top panel of figure 8.1. The various hedonic experiences in the other panels come from questions in which respondents are asked whether or not they experienced X "during a lot of the day yesterday." We average over the dichotomous response to obtain the fractions in each age group who experience X, and then plot the differences in prevalence between those with and without children at home. Figure 8.2 shows the results of this calculation for X equal to happiness, enjoyment, stress, worry, and anger. Note that the scales in figure 8.2 are different for different outcomes.

The panels show that the average hedonic well-being of older Americans living with children is considerably worse than the average hedonic well-

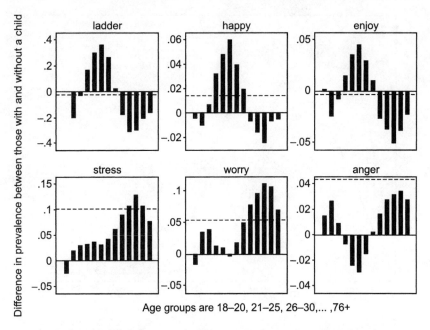

Age groups are 18–20, 21–25, 26–30,... ,76+

Fig. 8.2   Mean ladder and average prevalence of affect by five-year age groups

being of older Americans who do not. The second panel on top, for example, shows that those age forty-one to forty-six with children were 6 percent *more* likely to experience happiness yesterday, while those age sixty-six to seventy were 2 percent *less* likely to do so. These are large effects, at least in terms of other variables that affect happiness; for example, an increase in log income of 0.3 increases the probability of reporting happiness by 1 percent. The patterns for enjoyment and smiling (not shown) have a similar life cycle shape to that for happiness, as does sadness (with the sign reversed) and this too is not shown. The negative emotions of stress, worry, and anger are shown in the other three panels. Stress is worse among those with children, and especially so among the elderly. Worry is not much worse for adults in their thirties and early forties, and anger is substantially less prevalent for adults in the same age range. But worry and anger are much elevated among the elderly who live with children. Among adults age thirty-four to forty-six who live with children, the presence of children is associated with more positive and more negative affect; emotional life is more extreme with children. But for the elderly, there is no upside: all of the positive emotional experiences are *less* prevalent when they live with children, and negative emotional experiences are *more* prevalent.

The horizontal lines in these figures show the *average* difference between those with and without children irrespective of age. These numbers—particularly for anger, but see also stress—provide spectacular examples of

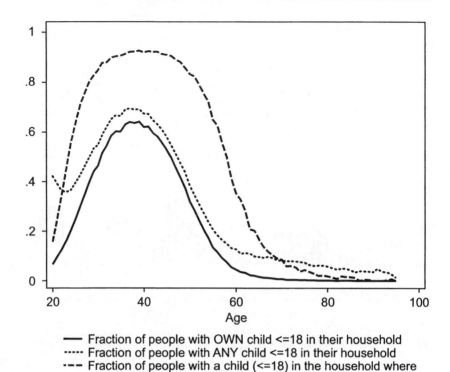

— Fraction of people with OWN child <=18 in their household
···· Fraction of people with ANY child <=18 in their household
·—— Fraction of people with a child (<=18) in the household where
    the child is their own = ratio of two lower curves

Fig. 8.3   Fractions of people with a child at home and who are child's parents
Source: American Community Survey (2008).

Simpson's paradox, that the average over everyone can lie outside the interval defined by the age-specific averages. Such findings illustrate the importance of appropriate conditioning and undermine the often convenient intuition that omitting a covariate will lead to estimates that are averages of the estimates for each value of the covariate. We suspect that some of the confusion in the literature on the well-being effects of children comes from insufficient attention to controls.

An immediate question is whether the negative outcomes for the elderly can be explained by the circumstances that select the elderly into living with children. We turn first to the question of how the elderly living with children differ from those living without children. Figure 8.3, which is calculated from the 2008 American Community Survey, shows the fractions of people at each age who live with children, and what fraction of those people are the parents (including stepparents and parents through adoption) of the children with whom they live. The graph shows the fractions of people with a child in their household by age, the fraction with their own child in the

Table 8.1   **Characteristics of those age 65–94 with and without children living at home**

	No children	Children	Difference	t-value
Married	0.55	0.51	−0.04	12.0
Female	0.57	0.58	0.01	2.4
Hispanic	0.04	0.10	0.06	37.4
Black	0.07	0.20	0.13	52.4
White	0.92	0.76	−0.16	59.1
Asian	0.00	0.01	0.01	9.0
Age	74.2	71.4	−2.84	60.8
No high school	0.19	0.27	0.08	27.1
HS diploma	0.41	0.39	−0.02	5.8
College	0.27	0.24	−0.02	7.7
Postgraduate	0.12	0.09	−0.03	14.1
Log income	7.96	7.93	−0.02	3.6
Religious	0.75	0.80	0.04	13.7
Health limitation	0.34	0.39	0.05	14.3
Disabled	0.33	0.38	0.04	51.7
Health status	2.79	2.95	0.16	18.6
Smoker	0.10	0.14	0.04	20.7

Notes: "Religious" is 1 if the respondent said that religion is very important in his or her life, "log income" is the natural log of household monthly income, "disabled" is 1 if the respondent reported that he or she had a health problem that prevented him or her from doing the things that people his or her age can normally do, "health limited" is 1 if the respondent reported that there was at least one day in the last month when poor health prevented him or her from doing his or her usual activities. "Health status" is the mean of self-reported health status scored as 1 for excellent, 2 very good, 3 good, 4 fair, and 5 poor; so higher numbers mean worse health.

household, and the ratio of the two. Note first that the fraction of people living with someone below eighteen years of age is only 12.6 percent at age sixty, and only a third of those are the child of the respondent. By age sixty-five, the numbers are 9.6 percent and 16.5 percent respectively, and they decline with age thereafter. In the Gallup data—unlike the American Community Survey—we do not know the relationship of the respondent to the child, but the most obvious possibility is that the elderly are living with their own adult children, so that the people under eighteen are their grandchildren. The literature on living arrangements in the United States argues that the elderly are reluctant to live with their children, so that the presence of someone under age eighteen may indicate poor health, low income, or an inability to live alone; indeed, low income and functional limitations are predictive of not living independently. Other possibilities include grandparents looking after their grandchildren in the absence of the child's parents—their own children—an outcome that would not suggest poor health.

Table 8.1 looks at the population age sixty-five and older in the GHWI data and shows the characteristics of those with and without children.

There are more than half a million observations in this age group, though some data are missing and some comparisons involve smaller numbers. The elderly who live with children are more likely to be black or Hispanic, and much less likely to be white. They are less well educated, more religious, less likely to be married, a little poorer, and much more likely to report poor health, disability, or health conditions that limit daily activities. Poor health outcomes have strong negative associations with life evaluation and with all hedonics, and are associated with lower happiness, enjoyment, and smiling, and more stress, worry and anger. Income comes with better life evaluation and better hedonics, but is not very different between the two groups. Religiosity comes with higher life evaluation, more of the positive emotions, and with less anger. Education comes with higher life evaluation, but has little effect on hedonics. Women have higher life evaluation, and more of both positive and negative emotions; similar differences characterize blacks and Hispanics relative to whites. Taken together, the poorer health of the elderly who live with someone younger than eighteen can predict some of their poorer outcomes, but their other characteristics have mixed effects on subjective well-being.

If table 8.1 is repeated for those in the parental age group, from thirty-four to forty-six, we find that the circumstances of those who live with children are uniformly well-being enhancing compared with the circumstances of those who do not live with children. They are healthier, better off, better educated, more religious, more likely to be black or Hispanic, and less likely to smoke. This is in contrast to the negative health selection into living with children among the elderly, and the mixed positive and negative selection on other factors. These differences between young and old will go at least some way to explaining what we see in figures 8.1 and 8.2.

Table 8.2 presents regression coefficients on an indicator for the presence of at least one child in regressions for the ladder and for a range of hedonic experiences as well as physical pain; as before, the age group is sixty-five to ninety-five. The first column reports the coefficient when the regression contains, not only the presence of children, but also a range of socioeconomic characteristics (income, education, single years of age, sex, race, marital status, religiosity, state of residence, and smoking status) together with controls for disability, the presence of a health limitation, and the five categories of self-reported health status. The middle column reports the same results, but without the health controls, while the column on the right reports the results for the average difference in outcomes between those who do and do not have a child at home.

All of the estimates in the table show worse outcomes for elderly people who live with children, and all but the coefficient for happiness in the first column are statistically significant. Adding more controls reduces the size of the effects, which grow absolutely smaller as we move along rows from right to left. As might be expected, it is the addition of the health controls

Table 8.2   Coefficients on presence of children with alternative sets of controls

	Full controls		No health controls		No controls	
	β	t	β	t	β	t
Ladder	−0.105	(6.9)	−0.215	(14.5)	−0.278	(18.5)
Happiness	−0.003	(1.4)	−0.011	(5.1)	−0.021	(9.5)
Smiling	−0.010	(3.4)	−0.015	(5.5)	−0.018	(6.8)
Enjoyment	−0.020	(8.3)	−0.028	(12.3)	−0.040	(17.4)
Sadness	0.022	(7.8)	0.033	(12.9)	0.044	(16.9)
Anger	0.037	(18.3)	0.042	(22.7)	0.050	(27.0)
Worry	0.053	(17.3)	0.072	(25.1)	0.090	(31.3)
Stress	0.061	(20.1)	0.078	(27.6)	0.096	(33.7)
Physical pain	0.018	(5.8)	0.043	(13.8)	0.055	(17.6)

Notes: Each β is the coefficient on an indicator for the presence of children in a regression with the outcome as dependent variable. The columns differ in which other covariates are included in the regression. The "full controls" are marital status, household size, single years of age, religiosity, smoking, race, Hispanic status, education, income categories, sex, state of residence, disability, presence of a health limitation, and categories of self-reported health. "No health controls" refers to the full controls except for health, and "No controls" is simply the average difference between those with and without children.

that reduces the size of the negative effects of children on well-being; for life evaluation, the coefficient is reduced from −0.28 without controls to −0.22 with demographic and income controls to only −0.11 with full health controls. People age sixty-five and older who live with children have worse evaluative and emotional outcomes, even when we control for health. Of course, we cannot rule out that there are health conditions beyond those that we can take into account, and it is not the effect of the living arrangements— whether snappers or daughters-in-law. On the other side, we have included self-reported health status in the regression and this arguably overcontrols for health because both it and the outcome variables are self-reported and almost certainly contain common dispositional factors that are spurious in this context.

These results for the elderly are quite different from those for the parents of the children (more precisely, adults age thirty-four to forty-six) in Deaton and Stone (2014). There, life evaluation is higher for those with children, but the difference can be entirely accounted for by their more favorable background characteristics. Adults age thirty-four to forty-six also suffer more worry and stress, but also more happiness and enjoyment, and less anger, and those differences survive the controls. These results are consistent with the fact that the presence of children does indeed produce those emotional outcomes, and the lack of a difference in (conditional) life evaluation is what would be predicted by rational choice if parents aim to maximize life evaluation and anticipate the emotional (and other) effects of having children. Hence, apart from the selection covariates, there should be no difference *on average* between those with and without children.

For the elderly, by contrast, our evidence suggests that living with children under eighteen is associated with worse outcomes on all measures, in part because of the selection into living with a child—primarily health selection—and in part because living with a child and/or his or her parents is unpleasant in itself. None of this is to argue that some of the elderly do not take pleasure in their grandchildren or in the children of those with whom they live. But, on average, we can find no evidence of it. Controlling for their background characteristics does nothing to contradict the generally bleak picture of evaluative and emotional well-being of the elderly who live with children.

We have replicated table 8.2 for Hispanic and black elderly only, for whom living with children is more common, perhaps because living with their own children is seen as less undesirable. The results (not shown) replicate the generally negative consequences for worry, anger, stress, happiness, and enjoyment, but the negative effect on life evaluation is smaller and statistically insignificant, with or without controls. Note that we still have more than 20,000 observations for elderly blacks and Hispanics, so the insignificance is not simply the effect of having too few observations.

The United States has a relatively high fertility rate compared with other rich countries, although not compared with much of the rest of the world. Within the United States, there are marked differences in fertility rates across states, from 1.63 children per woman in Rhode Island and 1.66 in Massachusetts to 2.35 in Alaska and 2.44 in Utah. While the Mormon presence in Utah makes it exceptional, fertility rates are generally higher in the west and lower in the east. It would not be surprising if these fertility variations were linked to the emotional impacts of living with children. In particular, in high fertility settings, the elderly may find a greater role in childcare, elders may enjoy living with children more, and the selection into living with children may be less averse.

To test this possibility, we have computed, for those age sixty-five to ninety-five, the difference in evaluative and emotional outcomes between those who are or are not living with someone under age eighteen, and correlated those with total fertility rates state by state. In addition to the ladder, we looked at a measure of positive affect, defined as the sum of happiness, smiling, and enjoyment, less sadness, divided by four. A parallel construct of negative affect is defined as the average of stress, worry, and anger. We compute the unconditional differences, because for this comparison we want to include the selection effects as well as the possible direct effects of living with children.

The three cross-state correlations are small and insignificant, 0.05 for the ladder, 0.16 for negative affect, and –0.08 for positive affect. As we shall see, the findings are quite different when we look across countries.

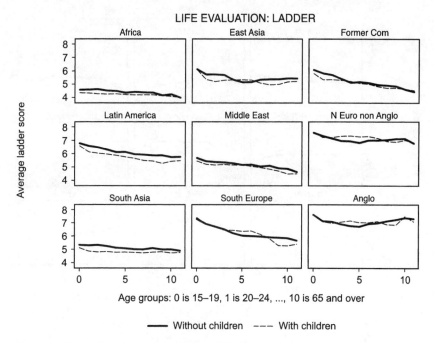

LIFE EVALUATION: LADDER

Age groups: 0 is 15–19, 1 is 20–24, ..., 10 is 65 and over

——— Without children   ––– With children

Fig. 8.4   **Life evaluation and age for world regions**

8.3 Well-Being, the Elderly, and Children around the World

One of the surprising findings from the Gallup World Poll, which has collected data from a total of 161 countries from 2006 to 2012, is that the age pattern of life evaluation does *not* show the standard U-shape in all countries or regions of the world. This is in spite of a literature that claims an almost biological necessity of the shape around the world (Blanchflower and Oswald 2008), holding not only in people, but also in nonhuman primates (Weiss et al. 2012), though see Frijters and Beatton (2012) for a dissenting view, and Ulloa, Møller, and Sousa-Poza (2013) for a review with many contrary findings. Figure 8.4 shows the age patterns of the ladder in the World Poll, split by people who do and do not live with children; it is the counterpart of the left panel of figure 8.1 for the United States, but splits the world into nine geographical regions. In most cases, we have chosen obvious geographical groupings, but we have also distinguished regions where previous work has suggested interesting regional patterns. This accounts for the former communist countries, including the former Soviet Union and its erstwhile satellites in Eastern Europe, for the group of rich English-speaking countries (the United States, Canada, the United Kingdom, Ireland, Australia, and New Zealand) as well as for the division of Europe into North (excluding the Anglo countries) and South. Note also that in the World

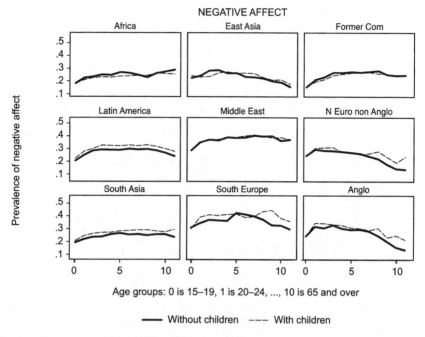

Age groups: 0 is 15–19, 1 is 20–24, ..., 10 is 65 and over

——— Without children   – – – With children

Fig. 8.5   Negative affect and age for world regions

Poll, as opposed to the Gallup-Healthways Well-Being Index poll for the United States, children are defined as those less than fifteen years of age, not eighteen.

The bottom right-hand panel of figure 8.4, for the rich English-speaking countries, looks like figure 8.1 for the United States. The familiar U-shaped pattern is evident here, though it is obscured somewhat by using identical scales for the different regions of the world, most of which have much lower ladder scores than do the rich Anglo countries. The U-shape is also visible in northern Europe and to some extent in East Asia, but it is absent elsewhere. This is particularly obvious in the ex-communist countries, where life evaluation declines steadily with age. This is almost certainly a feature of the transition from communism, where the elderly have lost the world they used to know, and in some cases their pensions and health care, while the young have seen a new world of opportunity open up. But the pattern of life evaluation declining with age is not specific to these countries. It occurs also in Latin America, the Middle East, and southern Europe. In the other two regions—which are also the poorest regions—South Asia and Africa, there is little or no age pattern in the average ladder score.

Looking next at figure 8.5 (we shall come back to the comparison of those with and without children) we see the age patterns of negative affect for the same regions. Negative affect is the same summary measure defined earlier

Table 8.3   Percentages of elderly living with a child by global regions

Region	55–59	60–64	65–69	70 plus
North Europe non-Anglo	6.8	3.1	2.0	1.8
Rich Anglo	9.6	5.2	3.5	2.0
Southern Europe	11.1	6.6	6.2	4.3
Ex-communist	23.8	21.3	17.6	16.3
East Asia	31.2	32.2	26.4	20.1
Latin America and Caribbean	43.2	38.1	34.6	27.6
Middle East	49.0	43.3	40.8	43.2
South Asia	53.4	53.5	54.2	50.9
Africa	75.8	71.9	72.1	69.9

Notes: "Rich Anglo" comprises the English-speaking rich countries: the United States, Canada, Ireland, Britain, Australia, and New Zealand. "North Europe" is the non-Anglo part of northern Europe: France, Germany, Netherlands, Belgium, Sweden, Denmark, Austria, Finland, Iceland, Luxembourg, Norway, and Switzerland. "Southern Europe" is Spain, Italy, Greece, Israel, Malta, Cyprus, Portugal, and Northern Cyprus. "Ex-communist" comprises the formerly communist countries of Eastern Europe, Russia, and Central Asia.

for the United States. The plots show the averages of the fractions of the population who experienced each of the emotions. Stone et al. (2010) show that these negative emotions decline with age in the United States, which is consistent with theories in which people learn to better handle their emotions with age and experience (Carstensen, Fung, and Charles 2003). This pattern is evident in the bottom right panel for the aggregate of the rich Anglo countries. The same pattern is also clear in northern Europe, and to a lesser extent in East Asia (which includes Japan.) But in the rest of the world, there is no evidence that people learn to better handle their negative emotions as they get older. Instead, people just get angrier, more stressed, and more worried as they age. Perhaps anger management, like a well-developed and generous Social Security system, is something that comes only in the richest countries of the world.

We have also drawn a parallel figure for positive affect, the average of happiness, smiling, enjoyment, and negative sadness. The figure is quite similar to that for the ladder in its age patterns, and shows little difference in positive affect between those with and without a child at home so it adds little to the discussion.

Figures 8.4 and 8.5 also show differences between those with and without a child at home. Before looking at these, we look at the prevalence of having a child in the home around the world. It is unusual for an elderly person in the United States to live with a child younger than age eighteen (or fifteen). It is even more unusual in northern Europe, and unusual too in southern Europe, but not at all in the rest of the world. Table 8.3 shows the fractions of the elderly living with children younger than age fifteen. For the rich English-speaking countries (including the United States), for northern Europe and for southern Europe, the fractions of people age seventy and older who live with someone younger than fifteen is 2 percent, 1.8 percent, and 4.3 percent, respectively. In the Middle East, South Asia, and Africa the corresponding figures are 43.2, 50.9, and 69.9 percent, with intermediate numbers for the Eastern European and other formerly communist countries, for East Asia, and for Latin American and the Caribbean. In the high fertility regions of the world, it is common for the elderly to live with children, and in South Asia and Africa, most of the elderly live with at least one child younger than fifteen. When living with children is normal, it is unlikely to be seen as undesirable, though it is still possible that poor health will make it more likely that the elderly do so.

Returning to figure 8.4, the Anglo panel shows again what we found in section 8.1, that people with children have higher life evaluation than people without when they are in the parenting years, but that the elderly living with children have lower life evaluation. This pattern holds in both northern and southern Europe, and in an attenuated form in East Asia and the Middle East. In Africa, South Asia, and Latin America, people with children have lower life evaluation throughout life. Figure 8.5 shows that negative affect is higher among the elderly with children in Europe and the Anglo countries. In Latin America and South Asia, negative affect is associated with children throughout life. Once again, there is little to see in the corresponding graphs for positive affect. These results, with the sharp differences between the rich and poor regions of the world, which are also the high fertility and low fertility regions of the world, suggest a line of investigation in which the emotional consequences of children depend on how scarce or plentiful they are. We shall return to this later.

Table 8.4 tabulates the differences in outcomes for each region and for the world as a whole. For each outcome, the first pair of columns show the uncontrolled difference (and *t*-value) for people age sixty-five and older between those who do or do not live with a child; these are computed from regressions of each outcome on an indicator for the presence of children and dummy variables for each country, either in the world as a whole, or in a region. The second pair of columns shows the difference when we control for sex, single years of age, education, income, religiosity, and indicators for satisfactory self-reported health status and disability. These estimates should not be treated overly seriously, given the difficulties of measuring income, education, and health status (and even age) in some countries.

The estimates in table 8.4 confirm what we have already seen in figures 8.4 and 8.5, that life evaluation is lower for those with children among the elderly in the richest countries, and that children in the homes of the elderly are associated with more negative affect in most regions, but more so in the richest countries. The controls do little to explain the negative association between the ladder and life evaluation; indeed, for regions other than the Anglo region, the association with children is *smaller* or *more negative* in the

Table 8.4   Children, life evaluation, and emotions around the world

	Ladder				Positive affect				Negative affect			
	No controls		Controls		No controls		Controls		No controls		Controls	
	b	t	b	t	b	t	b	t	b	t	b	t
World	−0.01	0.5	−0.06	3.5	0.01	4.5	0.01	3.0	0.02	6.3	0.02	7.3
Africa	0.02	0.4	−0.01	0.1	0.01	1.1	0.01	0.1	−0.03	2.7	−0.02	2.6
E. Asia	−0.16	2.7	−0.21	3.8	0.00	0.5	0.00	0.0	0.04	5.3	0.04	5.5
Ex-comm	0.19	5.1	0.02	0.7	0.05	5.8	0.03	3.7	−0.00	0.2	0.01	1.2
LAC	−0.09	1.9	−0.13	2.8	0.01	1.3	0.01	0.8	0.02	4.2	0.02	4.0
M East	−0.09	1.6	−0.14	2.4	−0.01	0.8	−0.01	0.8	0.03	2.9	0.04	3.3
N Europe	−0.02	0.2	−0.05	0.6	0.00	0.0	−0.01	0.5	0.07	5.1	0.07	4.8
S Asia	0.00	0.1	−0.10	2.1	0.02	2.5	0.01	1.3	0.02	2.2	0.03	3.3
S Europe	−0.21	1.8	−0.29	2.5	−0.01	0.6	−0.02	0.9	0.06	3.3	0.06	3.7
Anglo	−0.12	1.0	−0.09	0.8	−0.03	1.6	−0.03	1.8	0.08	4.5	0.08	4.8

Notes: "Positive affect" is the sum of happiness, enjoyment, and smiling less sadness, all divided by 4. "Negative effect" is the average of worry, stress, and anger. The estimates come from regressions that either, in the uncontrolled case, contain country fixed effects, or in the controlled case, country fixed effects plus controls for income, sex, education, single years of age, marital status, religiosity, disability, and self-reported health status.

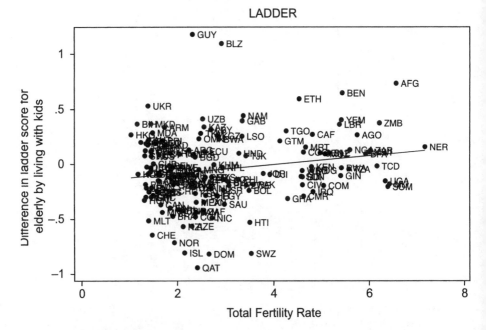

Fig. 8.6   Differences in ladder scores between those who do and do not have a child at home in relation to total fertility rates

presence of the controls. For most of the world, there is thus little evidence of negative selection into living with a child. That there is typically more negative and positive affect among the elderly living with children is essentially unaffected by the presence of the controls. Outside of the English-speaking world, the emotional and evaluative patterns of the elderly living with children look very similar to the patterns among parents living with children.

A final way of looking at these estimates is shown in figures 8.6 and 8.7, which looks at total fertility rates around the world. For each country we have computed the difference in average ladder and negative affect scores for all adults age fifty-five and older (the ten-year extension is to increase the sample sizes for some countries that have only been sampled once). The two figures then plot these differences against the total fertility rate for each country. For figure 8.6, which shows differences in ladder scores between those with and without children, there is a positive correlation with total fertility, whereas in figure 8.7, which shows differences in negative affect between those with and without children, there is a somewhat stronger negative correlation. (There is considerable sampling variability for the outcome measures in several countries, which weakens both scatters, though both are statistically significant.) In places where fertility is high the elderly generally have relatively higher life evaluation when they live in a household contain-

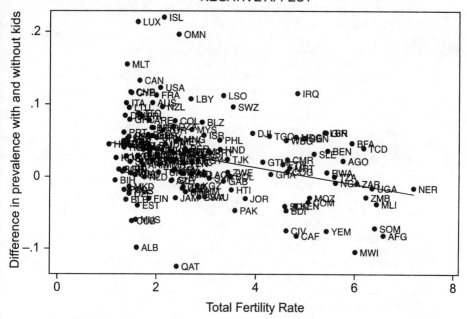

Fig. 8.7   Differences in negative affect between those who do and do not have a child at home in relation to total fertility rates

ing a person under fifteen, and where fertility is low they generally have lower life evaluation. Where high fertility is seen as desirable, older people do not feel that their life is compromised by living in a family with a young child. In such countries they are also less likely to be angered, stressed, or worried by the presence of children. Our results are consistent with the view that the negative evaluative and emotional consequences for the elderly of living with children are most likely a consequence of the fertility transition.

References

Blanchflower, David G., and Andrew J. Oswald. 2008. "Is Well-Being U-Shaped Over the Life-Cycle?" *Social Science and Medicine* 66:1733–49.

Börsch-Supan, Axel, Laurence J. Kotlikoff, and John N. Morris. 1988. "The Dynamics of the Living Arrangements of the Elderly." NBER Working Paper no. 2787, Cambridge, MA.

Carstensen, L. L., H. H. Fung, and S. T. Charles. 2003. "Socioemotional Selectivity Theory and the Regulation of Emotion in the Second Half of Life." *Motivation and Emotion* 27 (2): 103–23.

Deaton, Angus, and Christina Paxson. 1992. "Patterns of Aging in Thailand and Côte d'Ivoire." In *Topics in the Economics of Aging*, edited by David A. Wise, 163–206. Chicago: University of Chicago Press.

Deaton, Angus, and Arthur A. Stone. 2014. "Evaluative and Hedonic Wellbeing Among Those with and without Children at Home." *Proceedings of the National Academy of Sciences* 111 (4): 1328–33.

Frijters, Paul, and Tony Beatton. 2012. "The Mystery of the U-Shaped Relationship between Happiness and Age." *Journal of Economic Behavior and Organization* 82:525–42.

Hansen, Thomas. 2012. "Parenthood and Happiness: A Review of Folk Theories Versus Empirical Evidence." *Social Indicators Research* 108:29–64.

Stanca, Luca. 2012. "Suffer the Little Children: Measuring the Effects of Parenthood on Well-Being Worldwide." *Journal of Economic Behavior and Organization* 81:742–50.

Stone, Arthur A., Joseph E. Schwartz, Joan E. Broderick, and Angus Deaton. 2010. "A Snapshot of the Age Distribution of Psychological Well-Being in the United States." *Proceedings of the National Academy of Sciences* 107 (22): 9985–90.

Ulloa, Beatrice Fabiola López, Valerie Møller, and Alfonso Sousa-Poza. 2013. "How Does Subjective Well-Being Evolve with Age? A Literature Review." IZA Discussion Paper No. 7328. http://ssrn.com/abstract=2250327.

Weiss, Alexander, James E. King, Miho Inoue-Murayama, Tetsuro Matsuzawa, and Andrew Oswald. 2012. "Evidence for Midlife Crisis in Great Apes Consistent with the U-Shape in Human Well-Being." *Proceedings of the National Academy of Sciences*. www.pnas.org/cgi/doi/10.1073/pnas.1212592109.

Comment   David Laibson

This is another chapter in a line of influential and important subjective well-being research by Angus Deaton and Arthur Stone. The current chapter features the following findings. In the United States: (a) older adults living with kids have lower life satisfaction than older adults not living with kids; (b) older adults living with kids have fewer positive emotions and more negative emotions than older adults not living with kids; and (c) these associations are considerably weakened by the addition of controls, but the signs of the associations do not change and the magnitudes remain large. Throughout my discussion, I willl reserve the word kids to mean "kids under the age of eighteen." I will refer to "the negative association" as the robust negative association between living with kids and (various measures) of subjective well-being (among older adults). I will also assume that the older adults living with kids are typically living with their middle-aged children and grandchildren. It is the grandchildren that are the "kids" in most of these cases.

David Laibson is the Robert I. Goldman Professor of Economics at Harvard University and a research associate of the National Bureau of Economic Research.

For acknowledgments, sources of research support, and disclosure of the author's material financial relationships, if any, please see http://www.nber.org/chapters/c12963.ack.

The results are a bit different outside of the United States. The first two results are unchanged and the third result is more paradoxical: the negative associations are unchanged or even *strengthened* by the addition of controls. Finally, the authors show that the results reverse in high fertility countries, where older adults living with kids show *higher* levels of life satisfaction, *higher* frequencies of positive emotion, and *lower* frequencies of negative emotion.

As the authors point out, these relationships need not be causal. Indeed, I believe that selection probably lies behind most of the results in this chapter, a position that is probably aligned with that of the authors. Four kinds of selection—both adverse and advantageous—are present in this setting:

1. Adverse selection on the characteristics of older adults: "Grandpa is disabled so he's going to move in with us so we can take better care of him."

2. Adverse selection on the characteristics of middle-aged adults: "We need to move in with Grandpa, since we can no longer afford to live independently."

3. Advantageous selection on the characteristics of older adults: "Grandpa is rich and has invited us to move in with him."

4. Advantageous selection on the characteristics of middle-aged adults: "We have decided to ask Grandpa to move in with us since we are doing so well."

Adverse selection will induce a negative association between subjective well-being and living with kids. Moreover, the existence of adverse selection would imply that adding the relevant controls weakens the magnitude of this negative effect. On the other hand, advantageous selection will induce a positive association between subjective well-being and living with kids. The existence of advantageous selection would imply that adding the relevant controls weakens the strength of this positive effect. In most societies, both adverse and advantageous will be present, generating scope for a wide range of reduced form associations.

To illustrate the potential richness of these various mechanisms, consider the following hypothetical example. First assume that most selection is adverse (e.g., older adults with low cognitive function are more likely to move in with their kids). However, some selection is advantageous (e.g., older adults with high levels of pension income are more likely to support their middle-aged kids by allowing them to move in). Assume as well that advantageous channels have less measurement error than the adverse channels. Then it follows that there will be a negative association between subjective well-being and living with kids (among older adults), and that adding controls *increases* the magnitude of the negative association (since the advantageous channels are disproportionately partialed out).

On a related point, survey responses from older adults are likely to have higher measurement error than survey responses from middle-aged adults for two reasons. First, a substantial fraction of older adults have cognitive deficits. For example, about half of people age 80–89 have dementia or CIND (cognitive impairment not dementia). Second, older cohorts have relatively lower levels of literacy than middle-aged adults (particularly in developing countries), reducing their ability to comprehend survey questions (even when they are asked verbally). So it is natural that adding controls absorbs more variance for middle-aged adults than it does for older adults. Consequently, adding controls is more likely to control for selection effects of middle-aged adults than it is to control for selection effects of older adults.

To further explore the selection issues raised in this chapter, consider a simple model of cross-country differences. Assume that countries differ (exogenously) on two dimensions: the "taste" for independence and intergenerational income growth. The taste for independence varies from cultures that value personal space and personal autonomy (like the United States) to cultures that take a more communal view of family duties and intergenerational caregiving (like traditional societies). Note that these communal societies may still value independence/autonomy, just not as much. For example, in the United States, living with your kids/grandkids is a sign of distress—why else would an independence-valuing household give up independence? In communal societies, living with your kids/grandkids is not a sign of distress and might even be a sign of high social capital (e.g., intergenerational ties, filial bonds, etc.).

We formalize these ideas in the following way. For an older adult, living independently yields utility:

$$u(y) + \alpha.$$

For an older adult, living communally yields utility:

$$u\left(\frac{y + y_{+1}}{\sqrt{2}}\right),$$

where y is own income for the older adult and y_{+1} is the income of the middle-aged child of the older adult. The utility function also reflects returns to scale from living together. The strength of the taste for independence is capture by the parameter α. We further assume ln utility. Let $\theta = y/y_{+1}$, so θ is the inverse of the (gross) rate of intergenerational income growth. Finally, assume that the grandparents make the decision about whether they will or will not move in with their adult children. Then the indifference value of α is

$$\alpha = \ln\left(\frac{\theta + 1}{\theta}\right) - \frac{\ln 2}{2}.$$

This yields the equilibrium diagram in figure 8C.1. Older adults will live independently when the taste for independence, α, is sufficiently high and when the inverse of the rate of intergenerational income growth, θ, is

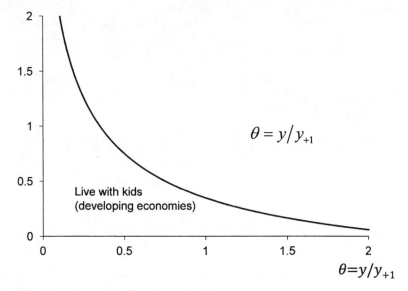

α = taste for independence

$\theta = y/y_{+1}$

Live with kids
(developing economies)

$\theta = y/y_{+1}$

Fig. 8C.1   Selection in choice of household structure

Notes: Older adults above the curve choose to live independently. Older adults below the curve choose to live with their children. In developed countries, living with your children (as an older adult) is atypical, so those households tend to have unobserved adverse characteristics. In developing countries, living with your children (as an older adult) is typical, so those households tend not to have unobserved adverse characteristics.

sufficiently high. These features tend to be associated with developed countries, which also tend to be countries with low rates of fertility.

Finally, there is a natural extension of the model that further links this model to the findings in the chapter. In developed countries, living with your children (as an older adult) is not typical, and older adults with this arrangement tend to have *adverse* characteristics. In developing countries, living with your children is the norm, so those households will not tend to have adverse characteristics and might tend to have advantageous characteristics. Hence, one would expect that in developed countries (low fertility countries) older adults who live with their adult children would tend to have low levels of subjective well-being, whereas in developing countries (high fertility countries), older adults who live with their adult children would tend to have high levels of subjective well-being. This is what Deaton and Stone find in their data, since living with kids (children under eighteen) is a proxy for living with your adult children.

9

Expectations, Aging, and Cognitive Decline

Gábor Kézdi and Robert J. Willis

This study explores the relationships between expectations, aging, and cognitive decline, a topic that has previously received little research. The empirical literature on the individual heterogeneity of expectations is relatively new, and little has been published in this area, especially with respect to the general population. (See Hurd [2009] for a review of the empirical literature.) However, heterogeneity in expectations is likely to play an important role in accounting for heterogeneity in decisions made in the presence of uncertainty. If aging has direct effects on the ways in which people form expectations, then those effects may affect the quality of important decisions made in old age.

In this chapter we use data from the Health and Retirement Study (HRS) to document general patterns in expectations in various domains with respect to aging and investigate the potential role of cognitive decline in those patterns. We focus on two aspects of expectations: optimism and uncertainty. The HRS measures expectations by asking about the probability of various events (see Manski [2004], for the case for probabilistic measurement of expectations using surveys). We define optimism as the assignment of higher

Gábor Kézdi is associate professor of economics at Central European University and a research fellow of the Institute of Economics at the Hungarian Academy of Sciences. Robert J. Willis is professor of economics and research professor in the Department of Economics and the Institute for Social Research at the University of Michigan and a research associate of the National Bureau of Economic Research.

We are grateful to the Behavioral and Social Research Program of the National Institute on Aging (NIA) for supporting through grant U01-AG09740 the collection of the HRS data used in this chapter and for research support through NIA grant P01AG026571. We are also grateful to Péter Hudomiet for excellent research assistance. For acknowledgments, sources of research support, and disclosure of the authors' material financial relationships, if any, please see http://www.nber.org/chapters/c12980.ack.

probabilities to events with positive consequences. We define uncertainty as a person's inability or unwillingness to state a probability belief or evidence of ambiguity or vagueness in the beliefs that they do report. Our measure of uncertainty is the propensity to answer "don't know" or "50 percent." (Hudomiet and Willis [2013] use a similar concept of uncertainty but measure uncertainty in a different way.) Both optimism and uncertainty should be important for decision making: optimism can have direct effects by shifting the level of expectations, while uncertainty can affect decisions through interactions with risk aversion or through more subtle preferences such as ambiguity aversion or loss aversion.

Our major aim in this chapter is to provide descriptive evidence using longitudinal data from the HRS without imposing much theoretical structure or seeking causal results. We do, however, pay close attention to methodological issues involving measurement error, calendar time effects, cohort differences and mortality selection to avoid findings that are statistical artifacts rather than patterns associated with aging. Our treatment of cohort effects and mortality selection builds on the approach of Agarwal et al. (2009), who argue that roughly after age fifty, aging leads to an increase in "mistakes" in decision making that may be due to cognitive decline. Our treatment of calendar time effects makes use of variation in wave-to-wave changes in age induced by variation of the timing of interviews within a survey wave. We document substantial measurement error in cognitive decline and discuss its consequences for our joint analysis of cognitive decline and expectations. We minimize the consequences of measurement error by determining the individual rates of change in the variables across all the survey waves rather than analyzing wave-to-wave changes. We perform several robustness checks to substantiate the resulting associations.

Although both optimism and uncertainty can be specific to the events in question, we show empirically that aging may have general effects on both optimism and uncertainty. In most cases, aging appears to decrease optimism and increase uncertainty. Optimism with respect to stock market expectations, expectations that income will keep up with inflation, and expectations of sunshine the next day all decline strongly with age. The increase in uncertainty is less robust and depends on the measure of uncertainty. Survival expectations are an exception, with a significant increase in optimism and potentially a decrease in uncertainty observed with age. Increasing optimism about survival was documented earlier by Hurd, Rohwedder, and Winter, (2005) for the European countries in SHARE and by Hudomiet and Willis (2013) using data from the HRS with a different measurement strategy.

Aging could have these general effects for several reasons. One possibility is that cognitive decline associated with aging affects an individual's view of the world and their ability to process information about the world, causing a person to overstate the likelihood of negative events and to hold less precise probabilistic beliefs. Our results provide some support for this possibility, as we find that cognitive decline plays a modest but statistically significant and robust role in explaining the decline of optimism with the exception of survival expectations. Somewhat surprisingly, we do not find an association between cognitive decline and increasing uncertainty.

Another possibility is that the increase in the awareness of mortality that accompanies aging leads to decreased attention to events that are far in the future, thus reducing incentives to acquire knowledge about those events.[1] As an individual's economic focus shifts from work to retirement and from the accumulation of wealth to managing that wealth during retirement, the relevance of particular types of economic events may change. In the same way, from a psychological point of view, Carstensen (2006) theorizes that aging makes people focus less on long-term goals and more on near-term emotional sources of satisfaction. These economic and psychological dimensions of an individual's changing perspective of time suggest that aging may lead to reduced attention to macroeconomic events. Our results on the differential effects of age and cognitive decline on survival expectations may be interpreted as support for this theory. However, the tendency for aging and cognitive decline to reduce optimism in most of the domains we investigate seems contrary to Carstensen's theory.

We begin our analysis by deriving simple measures of optimism and uncertainty about particular topics from HRS questions about subjective probability beliefs regarding stock market returns one year in the future, the chance of a future economic depression, whether tomorrow will be a sunny day, whether one's income will keep up with inflation, job loss, and survival to a specific age.[2] Next, we show how these measures change with age, employing methods to isolate "pure" age effects by eliminating cohort and time effects. We then turn our attention to measures of cognition from the HRS and describe the process of cognitive decline with age. We provide evidence of substantial survey noise in the cognitive measures and discuss the implications of this noise for our analysis. Finally, we examine how changes in optimism and uncertainty in each domain are related to cognitive decline using techniques that minimize the potential of spurious relationships.

9.1 Data

This study uses data from seven waves of the Health and Retirement Study (HRS), spanning from 1998 to 2010. The HRS began in 1992 with a cohort of individuals age fifty-one to sixty-one and their spouses. In 1998,

---

1. See Kézdi and Willis (2012) for a model showing how expectations about stock market returns are affected by incentives to learn about the history of returns and other aspects of financial investment. They also show that greater stock ownership is associated with more optimistic expectations.
2. The sunny day question of the HRS has been used as a measure of optimism by Bassett and Lumsdaine (1999).

Table 9.1   The expectation questions of the HRS used in this analysis

Question label	Exact wording of the question
Stock market	By next year at this time, what is the percent chance that mutual fund shares invested in blue chip stocks like those in the Dow Jones Industrial Average will be worth more than they are today?
Economic depression	What do you think are the chances that the US economy will experience a major depression sometime during the next ten years or so?
Sunny day	What do you think are the chances that it will be sunny tomorrow?
Income growth	What do you think are the chances that your income will keep up with inflation for the next five years?
Job loss	What are the chances that you will lose your job during the next year?
Survival to age A	What is the percent chance that you will live to be A or more? (with A being a function of the age of the respondent)

the sample was refreshed to make it representative of all age groups above fifty years of age. The spouses of all respondents were also interviewed, regardless of their age. The sample has been refreshed with a new six-year cohort of fifty-one to fifty-six-year-olds and their spouses every six years (in 2004 and 2010), and 2010 is the currently the last wave with available data. We use data on all individuals who were interviewed in at least two survey waves and were between fifty-one and ninety years old at the time of each interview. Proxy interviews were discarded because they lack observations on expectations. Altogether, we analyzed 107,024 observations of 20,938 individuals.

The HRS has asked respondents to assess the probability of various outcomes since its beginning in 1992. This analysis focuses on the six questions listed in table 9.1.

Respondents were invited to answer these expectation questions in percentage terms. The question sequence was introduced by explaining the task and providing an example of the chance of rain on the day following the interview. The sunny day question was used as a warm-up question in some survey waves. Not every question was asked in every wave of the HRS: of the six questions we analyze here, only the survival question was asked every time. We display the number of individuals in our sample who were asked each question in each survey wave in table 9.2. Not every expectation question was asked of each respondent, but five of the six questions we analyze were asked of all participants in at least some of the survey waves (the exception is the job loss question, which was restricted to respondents who were employed). Aside from general availability, the main motivation behind selecting these six questions is the fact that it is relatively straightforward to assign positive or negative meaning to these questions, which is important for our analysis of optimism.

We analyze two aspects of expectations: optimism and uncertainty. We define optimism as assigning higher probabilities to events that have positive consequences. It is relatively straightforward to operationalize this definition for the probability answers examined here: the measure of optimism is the probability answer itself. We redefined answers to the economic depression and job loss questions by subtracting them from 100 percent so that the resulting percentages also correspond to the positivity of the answer. To handle potential spurious trends in the underlying "true" probabilities, we made two additional adjustments. First, we discarded the sunny day answers of respondents who moved between interviews. This allows us to ensure that age-related changes in residence (e.g., to retirement communities in southern states) do not affect measured changes in responses to the sunshine question. Seasonal changes are accounted for by dummy variables expressing the month of the interview as described later. Second, we replaced the answer to the survival question with the difference between the respondent's answer and the corresponding probability reported by life expectancy tables.[3]

Conceptually, we define uncertainty as a person's inability to form a probabilistic belief or his admission that his beliefs are imprecise. For each expectation question, we measure uncertainty in terms of the propensity to answer "don't know" or "50 percent." "Don't know" clearly signals an inability to form probabilistic expectations. The "50 percent" answers are interpreted in a similar way based on the assumption that most respondents mean "unsure" when they say "50 percent." This assumption is supported by evidence. Beginning in 2006, the HRS asked a follow-up question to people who answered "50 percent" to the stock market question and the survival expectation question. For example, among respondents who answered "50" to the stock market question, a follow-up question asked whether they thought it was equally likely that the market would go up or go down or whether they were "just unsure." Seventy percent of these respondents for both the stock market and survival questions answered that they were unsure. The results are qualitatively the same but quantitatively stronger when we exclude the 50 percent answers and measure uncertainty only by the propensity to answer "don't know."

In addition to establishing the effects of aging, our analysis aims to uncover whether those effects are related to the decline of cognitive functioning. Cog-

---

3. These implied survival probabilities were compiled from the appropriate life table for each gender, year of age, and survey year. The variable is part of the RAND distribution, which expresses the HRS as the ratio of the answer to the survival probability question divided by the probability implied by the life expectancy tables. We transformed that variable to measure the difference instead of the ratio. The RAND documentation is available at http://www.rand .org/content/dam/rand/www/external/labor/aging/dataprod/randhrsL.pdf, pages 1019–1025.

nitive functioning is measured by a composite twenty-seven-point variable that combines results from four short cognitive tests that were administered in each wave of the HRS that we use. These four tests were two word recall tests, a counting backward test, and the "serial sevens" test. The first test asked respondents to recall ten words immediately after hearing them from the interviewer, within one minute, while the second test asked respondents to complete the same task some time later after answering other survey questions. These two tests were scored according to the number of correctly recalled words. The third test asked respondents to count backward from 20, with a score of 1 assigned for a correct answer. The fourth test asked respondents to subtract 7 from 100, subtract 7 from the result, and so forth for 6 subtractions. The score for this test is the number of correct subtractions. We quantify cognitive functioning with the combined score that has previously been used in the literature investigating cognitive functioning using HRS data.[4]

In some of our analyses, we examine the association with normal cognitive aging as distinct from associations with the onset of dementia. Dementia is a loss of cognitive functioning beyond normal aging. Dementia may cause people to be unable to answer complex survey questions such as the expectation questions. Most severely demented respondents participate in the HRS via proxy interviews, and these respondents are not asked to perform the cognitive tests and answer the expectation questions. Therefore, it is not possible to directly analyze the association between dementia and expectations in these data. At the same time, signs of the onset of dementia can be detected in our sample using the prediction model developed by Hurd et al. (2013). Using a clinical diagnosis of dementia in the ADAMS study of a subset of HRS respondents (Plassman et al. 2007), Hurd et al. (2013) assigned predicted probabilities of dementia status one year after the interview for every respondent in the HRS. These predictions use variables observed in the HRS and combine those variables into probabilities using an ordered probit model with three outcomes (dementia, severe impairment without dementia, and normal aging). For nonproxy interviews, this prediction uses the cognitive score, the change in the cognitive score from the previous interview, demographic characteristics, and measures of assistance with activities of daily living (ADL). The correlation between the decline in the cognitive score and the predicted probability of dementia would make joint analysis of cognitive ability and dementia problematic. The predicted probability of dementia is practically zero below age seventy, which further limits the ability to conduct joint analysis. Instead, we use the predicted probability of dementia in our robustness checks to determine whether asso-

4. A fifth measure is often added to the score to control for dementia (Crimmins et al. 2011), but we use a different, more reliable measure of dementia and do not include that score in our cognitive measure. The HRS cognitive measures are described in more detail in Fisher et al. (2012).

Table 9.2   **Number of observations for the expectation questions and cognitive measures by survey wave**

Question label	HRS survey wave						
	1998	2000	2002	2004	2006	2008	2010
Stock market	0	0	13,412	16,647	15,874	15,045	13,491
Economic depression	3,400	108	149	16,647	15,874	15,045	0
Sunny day	0	14,792	15,451	16,867	0	0	0
Income growth	14,591	14,792	15,451	16,867	16,266	0	0
Job loss	4,847	4,506	3,943	4,925	4,393	0	3,192
Survival to age A	7,169	13,894	14,807	15,899	15,241	15,040	13,432
Cognitive score	14,591	14,792	15,463	16,912	16,280	15,358	13,628
Probability of dementia	0	4,299	5,005	5,320	5,572	5,802	5,662

Source: HRS waves from 1998 through 2010. Sample includes respondents ranging in age from fifty-one to ninety years old, without the new respondents in 2010 and without the proxy interviews. The number of observations refers to the number of individuals in the sample who were asked the relevant question (including individuals who refused to answer or who responded that they did not know).

ciations with cognitive decline correspond to normal aging or early signs of dementia.

The income growth question was discontinued in 2008. The economic depression question was discontinued in 2010, and prior to 2004, it was asked of new respondents only (new spouses and the new cohort in 1998). The stock market question was first asked in 2002. The job loss question was asked in all waves except for 2008, but only of the subset of respondents who were employed at the time of the interview. Survival expectations were asked of the entire sample in all waves except in 1998, when it was only asked of a subsample.

9.2 Expectations and Aging

The effect of aging on expectations is difficult to measure for many reasons. Cross-sectional age profiles blend the effect of aging with differences across birth cohort and selective mortality. Cohort differences may lead to cross-sectional age differences in expectations if older birth cohorts have different expectations than younger birth cohorts, even when their answers are compared at the same age. Selective mortality may lead to cross-sectional age differences in expectations if mortality is correlated with expectations (perhaps due to common factors).

Examining changes in expectations for the same individuals eliminates confounding cohort effects. Age profiles can be constructed from the individual changes by creating aggregate slopes and combining those slopes (this method was used by Agarwal et al. [2009]). The slopes of the average measures are defined as

(1)
$$s(x)_a = \frac{1}{N_{\Omega(a)}} \sum_{i \in \Omega(a)} \frac{x_{i,w+1} - x_{i,w}}{age_{i,w+1} - age_{i,w}},$$

where x is the relevant variable, $s(x)_a$ is the slope starting with integer age a, i refers to individuals, w refers to the survey wave, age in the denominator is measured in fine detail (in 1/12th years, calculated from the month of birth of the individual to the month of the interview), and $\Omega(a)$ refers to the set of individuals belonging to an age group defined by integer age a. Once the slopes are estimated, they can be added from a prespecified starting value to create age profiles identified from wave-to-wave changes.

However, wave-to-wave changes blend the effects of aging with the effects of calendar time. Calendar time may affect most of the expectations measured here, including those regarding income growth, economic depression, the stock market, or the probability of a sunny day.

Fortunately, the features of the data collection help us to control for calendar time effects. The data collection of any survey is spread out over time. In a typical HRS wave, over 80 percent of the interviews are completed within six months, and the remaining interviews take another five to eight months to collect. This leads to interindividual variation in the time that passes between interviews. Measured to monthly precision, the median amount of time between two interviews is exactly two years, the 1st decile is 1 and 9/12 years, the 9th decile is 2 and 6/12 years, and the tails are long. As a result, the wave-to-wave difference in any measure may be related to different age differences between waves for different individuals.

We control for calendar time effects by replacing each expectation variable with its deviation from the mean measured in the year-month of the interview. That is, we replace variable x in equation (1) by the following variable:

(2)
$$\tilde{x}_{iw} = x_{iw} - \frac{1}{n_m} \sum_{j \in \Omega(m)} x_{jw},$$

where m refers to the year-month of the interview and $\Omega(m)$ refers to the set of all observations in our sample in year-month m. Identifying the age slopes from the year-month adjusted variables uses the assumption that calendar time has an equal effect for all respondents.[5] Under that assumption, the age

---

5. The age slopes of the year-month adjusted variables are identified from differences-in-differences-in-differences. Consider two respondents of exactly the same age interviewed in the same month in the base wave. One respondent is interviewed in exactly two years in the following wave, by which time her age increased by two years. The other respondent is interviewed six months later, so that his age increased by 2.5 years. The difference in the changes of their answers may reflect differences in aging or differences in the calendar time of the second wave. If we assume that the differences resulting from the difference in calendar time are the same for all respondents, we can estimate that difference using pairs of respondents with the same calendar time difference between their second interviews and the same time elapsed from their base interview to their second interview. If there is a difference in this second comparison, we record that difference and subtract it from the difference measured in the first comparison.

profiles constructed using age slopes of the year-month adjusted variables $s(\tilde{x})_a$ show the effects of age without cohort effects and without calendar time effects.

9.2.1 Age Profiles of Optimism

We first show the age profiles of optimism by displaying expectations as a function of age. Recall that we adjusted some of the expectation variables to reflect cleaner measures of optimism than the original answers. First, we inverted the answers to the economic depression and job loss questions so that higher values reflect more optimistic expectations. Second, we discarded the sunny day answers of respondents who had moved to another location since their previous interview. Third, we replaced the answer to the question about survival to age A with the difference between the survey answer and the probability obtained from life expectancy tables. All answers were replaced by their deviations from their year-month average.

Figure 9.1 presents the results. In each graph, the dashed line represents the cross-sectional age profile of the original answers, while the solid line reports the age profile constructed from the cumulative slopes of the year-month adjusted answers. The figures show the bootstrap 95 percent confidence intervals around the curves, colored as lighter gray for the cumulative slopes and darker gray for the cross-sectional profiles.[6] With the exception of the survival probability answers, which will be discussed in more detail later, the cross-sectional age profiles blend cohort, time, and selection effects with age effects, while the age profiles from the cumulative year-month adjusted slopes show pure age effects. Each graph includes a horizontal line at the level of the optimism measured at age fifty-one, the normalized starting point for the age profiles.

Age has a negative effect on optimism in five of the six cases, and this effect is statistically significant in the case of the stock market, sunshine, and real income growth expectations. While specific explanations can be constructed for some of the figures (aging may lead to lower real income), it is harder to do so for other figures (the stock market or the sunny day). Therefore, there may be a general negative effect of age on optimism in the domains represented by the three figures.

The solid-line profiles based on cumulative slopes can be thought of as robustness checks for the dashed cross-sectional profiles that remove the potential effects of birth cohort and selection. With the exception of survival expectations, the solid lines are not statistically significantly different from the dashed lines. Most importantly, whenever the dashed cross-sectional

---

6. The boostrap procedure involved constructing entire histories of answers of households (spouses together) and repeating the entire estimation procedure within each bootstrap draw. We expect confidence intervals to be wider for the profiles of cumulative age-adjusted differences because the role of measurement error and other time-varying idiosyncratic variations in the answers is magnified by taking differences.

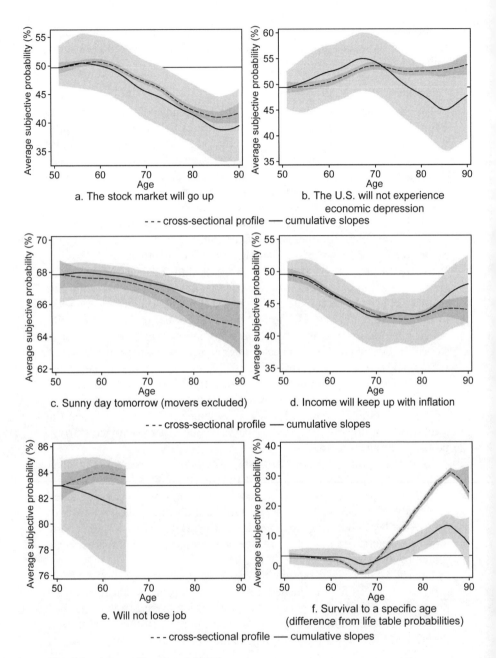

Fig. 9.1   Age profiles of optimism

age profiles are negative, the solid profiles are also significant and negative. Although it is not statistically significant, the divergence between the cross-sectional profiles of the cleaner age profiles of job loss expectations is consistent with selection, as this question is only asked of employed individuals, and individuals with higher expectations are more likely to stay employed than those with lower expectations.

In contrast to the other five variables, the cross-sectional profiles of survival expectations already take selection and cohort effects into account and thus represent the true age effects. Recall that we transformed the answers to the survival question by determining the difference between the respondent's answer and the probability implied by life expectancy tables. Those life table probabilities are already conditioned on cohort (as they are calculated separately for each year) and selection (as they show the probability of survival conditional on being alive for every year of age). In contrast, the profile built up from cumulative differences is biased in this case because it is conditional on survival to the next survey wave. In that way, for each year of age this method selects people with above average survival probabilities. Because these respondents had higher than average probabilities to begin with, the change in their probability is smaller. Because mortality and therefore selection accelerates with age, the divergence between the two lines increases with age.

The increase in optimism about life expectancy for those over age seventy shown by the dashed line in figure 9.1f. is consistent with the findings of Hudomiet and Willis (2013) for HRS and Hurd, Rohwedder, and Winter (2005) using SHARE data from Europe. This phenomenon is not driven by 50 percent answers.[7] We can only speculate about the causes of this increase. This increase may be specific to survival: the true probability of survival declines rapidly, and an individual's expectations may not keep up with that decline. This pattern is also consistent with Carstensen's (2006) theory that the elderly increasingly focus on emotionally rewarding short-term goals. For example, their optimistic survival beliefs may allow them to focus on planning a trip or anticipating the birth of a grandchild without worrying about the possibility that they may not live to experience that pleasurable event. From an economic perspective, in the absence of full annuitization, it is rational for an individual to maintain a buffer of wealth as a precaution against outliving one's assets. Optimism about life expectancy could represent a short-hand way of dealing with uncertainty about the length of life by signaling a need to maintain more wealth than would be required based on the more realistic expectations contained in life tables.

---

7. While 50 percent is close to the "right" answer, based on life table to the survival question on average at younger ages, the right answer becomes substantially smaller at older ages. If people's propensity to say 50 percent increased with age as a result of increased uncertainty, that would show up as increased optimism. However, the increase in optimism remains strong when the 50 percent answers are discarded altogether, as found earlier by Hurd and Rohwedder (2006).

9.2.2 Age Profiles of Uncertainty

We now present the age profiles of our measures of uncertainty. Figure 9.2 shows our preferred measure, the fraction of "don't know" and 50 percent answers, while figure 9.3 shows the fraction of "don't know" answers only. Similarly to the optimism measures, these are adjusted by the year-month of the interview according to formula (2). Also, similarly to the optimism measures, we discarded the sunny day answers of movers. However, in contrast to the optimism measures, we did not adjust survival expectations to life table probabilities here to retain the 50 percent answers.

The cross-sectional age profile of uncertainty is positive in four cases, zero for job loss expectations, and nonmonotonic for survival expectations. Whenever the cross-sectional profile of uncertainty is monotonically increasing, the cleaner age profile is also increasing. While the increase in the cleaner age profiles is statistically significant in only one of those four cases, it is jointly significant for the other three as well. The least precise estimated increase is for job loss expectations, which is only reported until age sixty-five.

When uncertainty is measured by the fraction of "don't know" answers only, uncertainty in survival expectations declines more strongly. Taken together, these results suggest that there is a general increase in people's propensity to give 50 percent and "don't know" answers with age, but the tendency to answer "don't know" as opposed to 50 percent increases significantly with age.

Survival expectations do not exhibit a positive effect: uncertainty does not change significantly until age seventy, and after that point it decreases. This pattern is largely driven by the 50 percent answers, which are responsible in part for the mirroring age profile of survival optimism. When uncertainty is measured by the fraction of "don't know" answers only, uncertainty in survival expectations increases significantly with age, similarly to the other expectations measured here.

Taken together, these results suggest that aging may have a generally negative effect on optimism and a generally positive effect on uncertainty, although these effects are not universal. In the remainder of the chapter we investigate the role of cognitive decline in explaining these general age effects.

9.3 Cognitive Decline

Cognitive functioning declines with age over the age range of our sample. Fluid aspects of intelligence—the ability to think and reason—peak in early adulthood and decline afterward, while more crystallized aspects—acquired knowledge—may continue to improve throughout much of old age and only begin to decline later (Horn and Cattell 1967; Horn and McArdle 2007; McArdle and Willis 2011). The decline in fluid cognitive functioning is a normal phenomenon over the age range of our sample, but some people

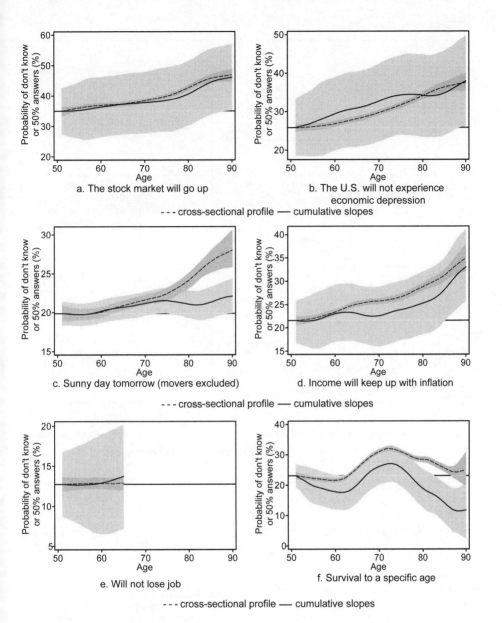

Fig. 9.2 Age profiles of uncertainty

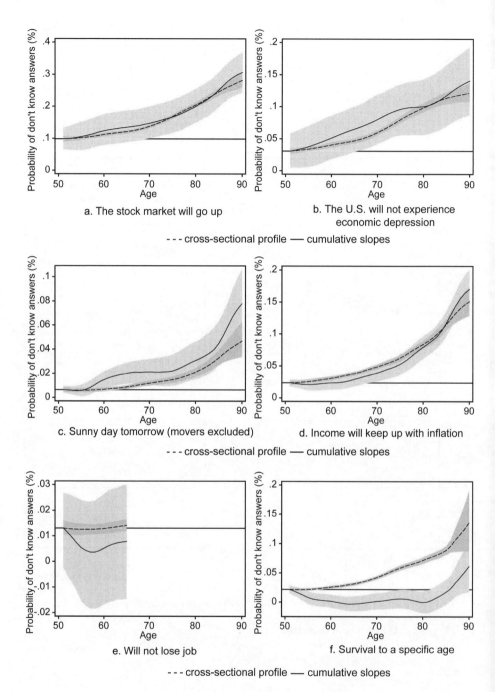

Fig. 9.3   Age profiles of the fraction of "don't know" answers

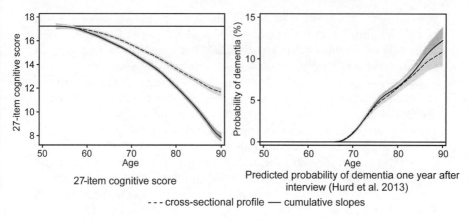

27-item cognitive score

Predicted probability of dementia one year after interview (Hurd et al. 2013)

- - - cross-sectional profile — cumulative slopes

Fig. 9.4   Age profiles of cognitive decline

experience abnormally strong declines due to dementia. Most people do not experience dementia, but even among those who experience normal declines, the rate of cognitive decline can vary considerably.

Short-term memory and awareness follow age patterns that are very similar to fluid aspects of intelligence (McArdle et al. 2002.) Our twenty-seven-score measure of cognitive functioning is a combined measure of short-term memory, awareness, and numerical reasoning. Therefore, this measure should exhibit age patterns similar to those of fluid intelligence: apart from the onset of dementia, the measure should show a steady and relatively stable decline. Agarwal et al. (2009) show that three out of the four HRS tests that we use exhibit this age pattern.

Figure 9.4 shows the age profile of the twenty-seven-score measure of cognitive functioning and the probability of dementia. For each measure, we show both the cross-sectional profiles and the age profile built from cumulative slopes (as defined in equation [1]). The left panel is analogous to the graphs presented by Agarwal et al. (2009) in their figure 4, but we use slightly different samples, a combined measure, and also show confidence intervals. Despite these differences, the left panel of the figure presents a very similar picture to those presented by Agarwal et al. (2009). The cognitive score exhibits a steady decline with age, the cross-sectional profile is above the pure age profile, and the divergence between the two is greater after age seventy-five. These results suggest a strong and steady cognitive decline on average, as well as positive selection based on cognitive capacity that becomes stronger with age. These figures are also consistent with increasing fluid cognitive scores across birth cohorts, known in the psychology literature as the "Flynn effect" (Flynn 1987).

The right panel of figure 9.4 presents an analogous graph featuring the estimated probability of dementia. The age profile of the predicted probability of dementia shows a steady and strong increase after age sixty-seven (the probability is zero earlier). Similarly to the cognitive score, the cross-sectional profiles show a flatter profile indicating positive selection or positive cohort effects, but this difference is not statistically significant.

The age pattern of cognitive decline and the general age patterns of expectations exhibit some symmetries: cognitive functioning and optimism (in most domains) decline with age, while uncertainty appears to increase with age. These symmetries may suggest direct relationships. However, the theoretical arguments for these relationships are not conclusive. On the one hand, this relationship seems natural as forming expectations is a cognitive exercise. On the other hand, one important cognitive aspect of expectations is people's knowledge about the domain of the phenomena. Knowledge is a crystallized form of intelligence, and crystallized intelligence does not decrease together with fluid cognitive functioning (Horn and Cattell 1967). Theoretical arguments by cognitive psychologists and economists (McArdle and Willis 2011) as well as neuroscientists (Reuter-Lorenz and Park 2010) suggest that crystallized intelligence may remain high even if fluid intelligence experiences a steady decline and, in addition, may help compensate for this decline. Moreover, aging may also affect preferences (see, e.g., Carstensen 2006) that can influence the incentives to acquire and process information and knowledge that shape expectations. Therefore, the effect of aging on expectations may operate through mechanisms that are not directly related to the decline in cognitive functioning.

We investigate this question making use of individual heterogeneity in the rate of cognitive decline. If cognitive decline leads to changes in optimism and uncertainty, people who experience stronger declines in cognitive functioning should experience more pronounced changes in optimism and uncertainty.

9.3.1 Measurement Issues and the Risk of Spurious Relationships

Unfortunately, if heterogeneity in cognitive decline and changes in expectations are measured in the same survey, their measured relationship may be spurious. Heterogeneity in measured changes of cognitive functioning includes variations due to short-term idiosyncratic factors and to pure measurement errors, in addition to true variations in the rate of cognitive decline. For example, as we will demonstrate, the wave-to-wave change in the cognitive score is often positive due to short-term variations as opposed to genuine improvements in cognitive abilities. Similar idiosyncratic variations are likely to influence survey answers to expectation questions. Therefore, it may be problematic to perform a joint analysis of these variations. In this section we document the extent of the problem and propose a measurement strategy that minimizes the problem.

To facilitate this discussion, we label all additional variation as the "noise" and true variation in cognitive decline as the "signal." Noise may distort the measured relationship between cognitive decline and expectations measured by the same survey in two ways. First, if noise in cognitive decline is independent of potential measurement error in the optimism and uncertainty measures, a regression with cognitive decline on the right-hand side will produce slope coefficients that are biased toward zero. This is a classical measurement error situation. However, noise in cognitive decline and noise in the optimism and uncertainty measures may be correlated. Variations in the effort required to answer survey questions from interview to interview for the same individual might lead to such a correlation. An interview with a lower input of effort by the respondent may result in lower scores for the cognitive tests and a higher propensity to answer "don't know" or "50 percent" to the expectation questions. This may lead to a spurious relationship between measured cognitive decline and measured uncertainty. Whether the noise is classical or correlated, the magnitude of the bias is larger if the noise-to-signal ratio is larger.

Note that these arguments may be relevant for the relationships among changes in other variables measured in the same survey if they are also subject to considerable noise. The issue is not whether the relationships are causal but whether the relationships measured by survey data correspond to relationships between the phenomena themselves as opposed to pure survey noise. There is no foolproof way to address survey noise. Our strategy in this chapter is to construct measures of age-related changes that are least affected by survey noise and to search for circumstantial evidence indicating whether the measured relationships could be driven by noise.

A natural analysis would relate wave-to-wave changes in measured expectations to wave-to-wave changes in cognitive scores. However, those first-differenced measures are also the most affected by survey noise. To mitigate the bias, we carried out our analysis on individual slopes. For each individual, we regressed the cognitive score on the individual's age at the time of the interview (measured to monthly precision) and saved the coefficients from that regression. For each individual, the slope of cognitive decline is the slope coefficient from this regression. Then, we performed similar individual regressions for each expectation measure after adjustments to the year-month of the interview and the other adjustments described earlier.[8] We restricted the individual regressions to individuals with three or more observations. The maximum number of observations is seven for the cognitive score and smaller for the measures that are not available in every survey wave.

Regressions of the slopes of expectations on the slopes of cognitive decline identify the relationship based only on between-individual heterogeneity. The slopes of cognitive decline are characterized by a lower noise-to-signal

---

8. These include flipping of negative events, defining survival optimism as the difference from life tables, and restricting sunshine data to those who do not change residence.

Table 9.3   Summary statistics of the age-adjusted first difference in cognitive score
                   and the age-adjusted slope of cognitive score

	First difference[a] (1)	Slope measure[b] (2)
Mean	−0.22	−0.22
Standard deviation	1.85	0.52

[a] Wave-to-wave change in the cognitive score divided by wave-to-wave change in the age of the respondent.
[b] Estimated individual slopes of the cognitive score from individual-specific regressions on age at the time of the interview.

ratio than the wave-to-wave changes in the cognitive score (see the following evidence). Therefore, regressions on the slope measures produce estimates that are less biased than the results of regressions on the first differences. The bias is reduced further if the sample is restricted to individuals with a relatively large number of observations used in the individual regressions that estimate the slope measures. Individual slopes are analyzed in the spirit of the latent growth modeling technique used by McArdle et al. (2002).

Table 9.3 presents summary statistics of the age-adjusted first difference of the cognitive score variable (the wave-to-wave difference of the cognitive score divided by wave-to-wave difference in age) and the age-adjusted slope measure of the cognitive score (the slope coefficients of the individual regressions of cognitive score on age). The mean of the cognitive change measures remains the same. Aging one year is associated with an approximately 0.2 percent decline in the cognitive score. At the same time, the variance of the first difference measure is substantially higher than the variance of the slope measure.

Figure 9.5 shows histograms of the first-differenced measure of cognitive decline and the individual slope measures. The graph of the slope measures includes the histogram of all slope estimates as well as the histogram of the slope estimates from the subsample of individuals with the maximum number of observations, which is seven. Within each histogram, lighter colors indicate positive measured changes in cognitive functioning. Positive changes are unlikely to reflect true long-term changes in cognitive functioning because the cognitive measure assesses fluid aspects of cognitive functioning, which typically do not improve with age in this age range.

The histograms show the wide dispersion of the first-differenced measure and the narrower dispersion of the slope measure. The distribution of the slope measure is even more concentrated if it is restricted to the subsample of respondents with the maximum number of observations. There is some excess mass around zero for the first-differenced measure, which is an artifact of normalizing the change in the cognitive measure. As this measure is a small integer, noninteger changes in age do not change the cognitive

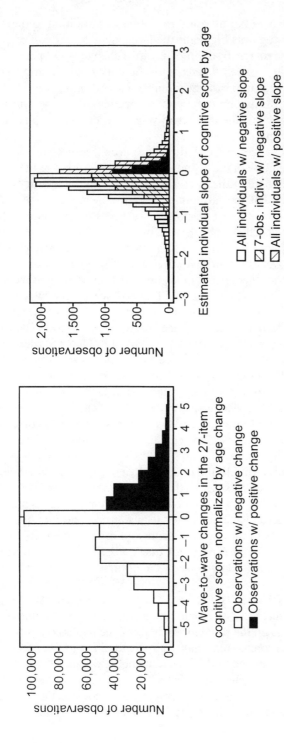

Fig. 9.5 Distributions of the individual measures of cognitive decline

score but lead to a spread of all nonzero changes. In addition to the wide distribution, the histograms highlight the nonnegligible fraction of positive measured changes. The fraction of positive changes is 39 percent for the first-differenced measure, 29 percent for the slope measure, and 25 percent for the slope measure in the maximum-observation subsample. The histograms support the assumption that the slope measures have considerably lower noise-to-signal ratios, especially when restricted to the maximum-observations subsample.

We can examine changes in the method of data collection to provide further evidence of the noise in the cognitive measures. We analyze the effects of wave-to-wave changes in the interview mode and in the identity of the interviewer at the level of the variation in cognitive measures. In the HRS, the baseline interview with each respondent is a personal interview; these occurred in 1992, 1998, 2004, and 2010. Before 2006, subsequent interviews were normally conducted by telephone for respondents under age eighty and in person for those over age eighty. However, a small number of respondents request a change from the normal mode and HRS honors these requests. In 2006, the HRS initiated an "enhanced face-to-face" interview to collect biomarkers and physical performance data. A random half of the longitudinal sample was selected for the enhanced personal interview in 2006 with the other half receiving a personal interview in 2008. The half selected for enhanced interviews in 2006 received second enhanced interviews in 2010. The interview mode changes between two interviews almost half of the time, and these changes are roughly equally split between changes from telephone to personal and vice versa. In 70 percent of cases, the interviewer also changes from wave to wave. These two changes are weakly correlated: a change in the interviewer is 12 percentage points more likely when the interview mode changes.

Changes in the survey mode and in the interviewer may increase noise in measures for a variety of reasons. Both the interview mode and the match between interviewers and respondents can affect the noise in survey answers. Effects on the effort that respondents exert in answering the survey questions may lead to variations in the cognitive score and in the propensity to provide uncertain answers to the expectation questions. Effects on the attitudes of the respondents may lead to noise in the optimism of the expectation answers.

Table 9.4 presents the results. The first column shows the results of regressions on the first difference of the cognitive score. The second column shows results of regressions on the squared residuals of the regression in the first column. Each regression has four main right-hand-side variables capturing whether there was a change in the interview mode, whether the interview mode was personal and unchanged, whether the mode of interview changed from personal to telephone, and whether it changed from telephone to personal. The regressions control for a full set of year-of-age dummies and

Table 9.4   **Changes of interviewers, changes of survey modes, and the mean and variance of changes in the cognitive score**

	First-differenced cognitive score	Squared residual from the regression on the first-differenced cognitive score
Change of interviewer	−0.03	0.3***
	(0.01)*	(0.1)
Interview mode unchanged	0.03	−0.7***
Personal	(0.02)	(0.1)
Interview mode change	0.12	0.3***
Personal to phone	(0.02)***	(0.1)
Interview mode change	−0.02	0.1
Phone to personal	(0.02)	(0.1)
Year of age fixed effects	YES	YES
Year-month fixed effects	YES	YES
R-squared	0.006	0.014
Number of observations	83,673	83,673

Note: Standard errors clustered at the household level in parentheses.
***Significant at the 1 percent level.
**Significant at the 5 percent level.
*Significant at the 10 percent level.

year-month dummies to capture age effects and time effects that may be correlated with changes in the interviewer and the survey mode.

The most important results of table 9.4 are in column (2): wave-to-wave changes in the interviewer and some changes in survey mode are associated with a significant increase in the variance of the measured change of the cognitive score. Compared to individuals with phone interviews with the same interviewer in both waves, the variance of the change in the cognitive score is lower for individuals with personal interviews in both waves, and it is higher for individuals whose interview mode changes from personal to telephone. A change in the interviewer is also associated with a greater variance. Column (1) shows that the decline in the cognitive score is less negative for individuals whose interviews change from personal to telephone and that a change in the interviewer is weakly associated with a stronger decline of 0.03. While some of the associations with the first-differenced score may indicate causality from cognitive decline to changes in data collection, the association of these changes with a higher variance is consistent with some of the variance resulting from survey noise.

We have estimated similar regressions for changes in optimism and uncertainty. The results of those regressions indicate that the associations with changes in survey mode are mixed, but that a significant association exists between the change in the interviewer and the variance of the first-differenced measures of optimism and uncertainty for many expectation questions. Together with the results of table 9.4, these indicate the association between expectation measures and cognitive decline measured by regressions estimated by first differences may be identified in part based on variations in noise. As noise in first-differenced cognitive scores is correlated with noise in first-differenced dependent variables, coefficients in such regressions are likely to be biased away from zero. The results of those regressions indicate strong negative associations between the change in the cognitive score and changes in optimism and positive associations between the change in the cognitive score and changes in uncertainty. However, the potentially spurious nature of those associations is supported by the fact that the estimated relationships are very similar if they are identified solely from positive changes in the cognitive score, where the variation is likely to be dominated by noise.

9.3.2 Expectations and Cognitive Decline

Our preferred specification for estimating the association of changes in expectations with cognitive decline uses individual slope estimates instead of first differences. Because of their lower noise-to-signal ratio, using the individual slope estimates in regressions of expectations on cognitive score are likely to result in a lower bias. Tables 9.5 and 9.6 show the results of the regressions in which the left-hand-side variables are the individual slope estimates of optimism and uncertainty, respectively, for the six probability questions analyzed here.

In each regression, the main right-hand-side variable is the slope of the cognitive score, which we multiplied by negative one to represent cognitive decline. A positive coefficient would imply that cognitive decline is associated with an increase in our measures of optimism or uncertainty. This coefficient is identified from variations in the average rate of cognitive decline across individuals. That rate of decline is estimated from separate regressions for each individual with three to seven observations. The bias of the coefficient on this variable should be smaller for individuals with seven observations than for individuals with fewer observations, a fact that we will take advantage of when conducting robustness checks.

The individual slopes of left-hand-side variables and the cognitive score are calculated from individual regressions with age on the right-hand side, measured to monthly precision. We adjusted each optimism and uncertainty measure to deviations from year-month fixed effects before estimating the individual slopes. The rest of the right-hand-side variables consist of the age of the individual at baseline (the first observation of the cognitive score) normalized to zero at age fifty-one; the dependent variable at baseline as predicted from the individual slope regressions (normalized to have a mean of zero); and the cognitive score at baseline as predicted from the individual slope regressions (normalized to have a mean of zero).

The constants of the regressions show the changes in the left-hand-side

Table 9.5   Cognitive decline and trends in optimism: Estimates from the regressions on individual slopes with respect to age

	Stock market[a]	Economic depression[a]	Sunny day[a]	Income growth[a]	Job loss[a]	Survival (adjusted)[a]
Decline in the cognitive score[b]	-0.62	-1.32	-0.58	-0.36	-0.47	0.04
	(0.17)***	(0.23)***	(0.24)**	(0.23)	(0.23)**	(0.13)
Age at baseline[c]	-0.05	0.03	0.01	0.00	0.03	0.08
	(0.01)***	(0.01)***	(0.01)	(0.02)	(0.02)	(0.01)***
Dependent variable at baseline[d]	-0.14	-0.17	-0.25	-0.10	-0.14	-0.07
	(0.00)***	(0.00)***	(0.00)***	(0.00)***	(0.00)***	(0.00)***
Cognitive score at baseline[e]	0.13	0.20	0.19	0.10	0.12	-0.01
	(0.02)***	(0.03)***	(0.03)***	(0.02)***	(0.03)***	(0.02)
Constant	0.17	-0.18	-0.23	-0.14	-0.36	-0.49
	(0.08)**	(0.14)	(0.16)	(0.12)	(0.11)***	(0.07)***
R-squared	0.43	0.30	0.53	0.32	0.38	0.23
Number of observations	12311	10980	9841	13997	4225	14080

Notes: Bootstrap standard errors clustered at the household level in parentheses.

[a] Estimated individual slopes of the probability answers in percentage terms (from individual-specific regressions on age; the probability answers are adjusted to deviations from year-month fixed effects). The survival probability answers are taken as the differences from the probabilities calculated from the life expectancy tables for people of the same age and gender.

[b] Negative of the estimated individual slopes of cognitive score (from individual-specific regressions on age).

[c] Age measured at the first observation of cognitive score, normalized to age fifty-one.

[d] The dependent variable at its first observation, predicted from the individual regressions, normalized to have a mean of zero.

[e] The cognitive score at the first observation, predicted from the individual regressions, normalized to have a mean of zero.

***Significant at the 1 percent level.

**Significant at the 5 percent level.

*Significant at the 10 percent level.

variables that correspond to aging by one year, measured at age fifty-one, if the dependent variable and the cognitive score are at their average baseline values and if cognitive decline has a slope of zero. Associations with age beyond age fifty-one are allowed to be nonlinear. The coefficient of the age at baseline variable corresponds to that nonlinearity, indicating how the age-related change in the left-hand-side variables changes with age. The coefficient of the dependent variable at baseline shows the relationship between the individual slopes of the left-hand-side variables and their initial values (holding the other variables constant), where the initial value is predicted from the individual-specific regressions. Mean reversion, whether due to noise or to other idiosyncratic variations in the left-hand-side variables, would imply a negative coefficient. The coefficient of the cognitive score at baseline variable shows the correlation between the average change in the left-hand-side variable and the cognitive score at the first observation (holding the slope of the cognitive score and the other variables constant), where the value at the first observation is again predicted from the individual regressions. Here, mean reversion is captured by whether this coefficient has the same sign as the coefficient of the cognitive decline variable because the decline variable is the negative of the average change of the cognitive score.

The results show a modest but often statistically significant association between the rate of cognitive decline and the average change in expectations for all probability questions except for survival. To understand the magnitudes of the coefficients, note that the average rate of decline in the cognitive score for every additional year of age is 0.2 (this is also the 55th percentile of the distribution). Individuals with a 0.1 point higher rate would be at the 70th percentile of the distribution of measured cognitive decline. The coefficients of the cognitive decline variable suggest that individuals with a 0.1 point higher rate of cognitive decline experience, on average, a 0.04 to 0.13 percentage point decline in their answers for every additional year of age. This accounts for 1 to 2 percent of the standard deviation in the slope measures of the left-hand-side variables. Calculated for the twelve-year horizon that the data span, individuals with a cognitive decline at the 70th percentile would experience a 0.5 to 1.5 percentage point decline in their probability answers, which is a small but nonnegligible change. Note that the magnitudes are difficult to appreciate because these coefficients may still be biased in unknown directions. The robust negative coefficients of the dependent variable at baseline suggest strong mean reversion, highlighting the importance of noise in the left-hand-side variables.

The exception to the negative association with optimism is the survival expectation: people with higher rates of cognitive decline do not experience any difference in the changes in their survival expectations from individuals with lower rates of cognitive decline.

The coefficient of the baseline level of cognitive decline is positive in five of the six cases and zero for survival expectations. When positive, these partial correlations show that people with higher levels of cognitive functioning have lower rates of decline in optimism, holding the rate of decline and age constant. The coefficient estimates are positive whenever the coefficient of the cognitive decline is negative, providing additional support for the positive relationship between cognitive functioning and optimism. Note that our finding of mean reversion due to noise in the cognitive decline variable would result in the same sign of the coefficients of level and decline variables because the decline variable is the negative of the change. The fact that we do not find the same sign suggests that the noise in cognitive decline is not strong enough to produce such a mean reversion. Taken together, the coefficients of the cognitive decline variable and the cognitive score at baseline suggest a robust statistically significant relationship between cognitive decline and decreased optimism in five out of the six expectations we analyze.

The constants and coefficients of age in the optimism regressions provide a heterogeneous picture. Optimism about income growth and sunshine do not show significant dependence on age when cognitive decline and baseline cognitive functioning are held constant. Optimism about the stock market shows a weak positive relationship with age starting at age fifty-one that very quickly becomes negative, reaching a strong negative slope of negative one percent by age seventy, even when the rate of cognitive decline and the baseline level of cognitive functioning are held constant (at least as they are measured in our data). Optimism about job loss shows a negative relationship with age at age fifty-one that may or may not lessen with age, as the coefficient of age is positive but insignificant. The age profile of optimism about economic depression is flat at age fifty-one when the level and the change in cognitive functioning are held constant, but it exhibits a small but statistically significant increase at later ages, reaching a slope of 0.7 at age eighty. The estimated age profile of survival expectations is not affected by either the decline or the level of cognitive functioning, and thus it presents the same picture as figure 9.1: survival optimism decreases initially but then increases at around age sixty-five.

Taken at face value, the estimates suggest that cognitive decline is associated with declining optimism in domains of private economic conditions, aggregate economic conditions, and sunny weather. While deteriorating private economic conditions may be affected by declining cognitive functioning for fundamental reasons, declining optimism in the more general domains is more likely to reflect some more general association between age-induced decline in fluid cognitive functioning and less optimistic thinking in general. An increase in optimism about survival expectations with age is an important exception to this phenomenon. As discussed earlier, one reason for this may be based in the psychological tendency for older people to focus on emotional sources of future satisfaction without worrying about whether they will be alive to enjoy them. Another reason is that optimism about the chance of survival may serve as a heuristic device to help people maintain sufficient wealth to enable them to maintain their living standards should they survive to an exceptionally old age.

Some of the variation in observed cognitive decline is because some people suffer from dementia. Recall that we do not observe the expectations of the demented respondents, as they are not asked the probability questions. Instead, we use the predicted individual probability of the onset of dementia one year after the interview as estimated by Hurd et al. (2013). Unfortunately, a joint analysis of the decline in the cognitive score and the potential increase in the probability of dementia is not possible due to the strong correlation between these two characteristics and to the fact that a large portion of the variation in dementia probability is concentrated in the relatively small sample of individuals above seventy-five years of age. To determine whether the estimates in table 9.5 reflect associations with the onset of dementia, we reestimated all regressions on the subsample of respondents whose estimated probability of dementia remained below 5 percent in all survey waves. These results are very similar to those presented in table 9.5, with the exception of sunny day optimism, where the association with cognitive decline is not significant.

We performed several robustness checks. First, we restricted the sample to individuals with the maximum number of observations used in the slope regressions, which is seven for the cognitive score. As suggested by the right panel of figure 9.4, the noise in the slope estimates is substantially smaller in this subsample. The coefficients of the cognitive decline variable are very similar to, and in most cases stronger than, those presented in table 9.5. This suggests that the coefficients in table 9.5 represent genuine associations.

Second, we controlled for symptoms of clinical depression in both the first and last observations of each individual. This robustness check was motivated by the fact that cognitive decline is associated with deteriorating health conditions and that deteriorating health conditions may be responsible for the observed decline in the levels of expectations. That worry should be strongest for the survival expectations, and we do not see any association with cognitive decline despite this concern. However, some subtle changes may operate through depressive symptoms for all other expectations. Controlling for depressive symptoms should lead to weaker coefficients if that concern is warranted, but no such decrease is observed. Whether the estimate is performed for the whole sample, the sample with the maximum number of observations or individuals with low probabilities of dementia across all interviews, controlling for depressive symptoms does not change the results.

Finally, we reestimated all regressions on separate subsamples with declining and increasing slope estimates for the cognitive score. As we have argued, positive slopes are more likely to reflect idiosyncratic positive changes in the measured cognitive score variable than genuine long-run improvements in cognitive functioning. Therefore, if the association between cognitive decline and declining optimism is genuine, it should be strong in the subsample of declining cognitive scores and weak in the subsample of increasing cognitive scores. These results are in line with these general expectations. In most cases, the coefficient estimates of the cognitive decline variable are stronger in the subsample of declining slopes than in the entire sample, and none of these estimates are statistically significant for the subsample with increasing slopes. The results of these robustness checks provide strong support for the relationship between cognitive decline and age-related decline in optimism for five out of the six expectation questions analyzed here. Expectations about survival remain an important exception.

After establishing some fairly general associations between cognitive decline and age-related changes in optimism, we turn to age-related changes in uncertainty. Table 9.6 presents results with a similar structure to table 9.5.

In contrast with the statistically significant results for optimism, the estimated association of the rate of cognitive decline with the rate of increase in uncertainty is not significantly different from zero in four out of the six cases examined here. In the two significant cases the sign is opposite: higher rates of cognitive decline seem to be associated with lower increases in the propensity to provide uncertain answers to the stock market question but with higher increases in the propensity to provide uncertain answers to the sunny day question. In cases where the coefficient of the cognitive decline variable is not significant, the coefficient of the baseline level of cognitive functioning is not significant either. In the other two cases, the coefficients of the levels strengthen the coefficients of the decline: a higher initial level of cognitive functioning is associated with a stronger increase in uncertainty about the stock market but a weaker increase in uncertainty about sunshine. These results suggest that there is no general tendency for age-related changes in uncertainty to be associated with cognitive decline, although cognitive decline may be associated with uncertainty with respect to specific events in specific ways.

The lack of a general association between cognitive decline and increasing uncertainty is confirmed by our robustness checks. The results are similar or even weaker when restricted to individuals with seven observations for the cognitive score or with low probabilities of dementia, and when the results are controlled for depressive symptoms. As an additional robustness check, we reestimated all regressions by measuring uncertainty as the propensity to answer "don't know" (ignoring the 50 percent answers). These results are even weaker, with no association observed between cognitive decline and uncertainty, even in the case of sunshine expectations.

Table 9.6   Cognitive decline and trends in uncertainty: Estimates from the regressions on individual slopes with respect to age

	Stock market[a]	Economic depression[a]	Sunny day[a]	Income growth[a]	Job loss[a]	Survival (unadjusted)[a]
Decline in the cognitive score[b]	-1.05	0.02	1.38	0.19	0.31	0.15
	(0.38)***	(0.45)	(0.47)***	(0.26)	(0.38)	(0.27)
Age at baseline[c]	-0.02	-0.01	-0.04	0.00	-0.03	-0.04
	(0.01)	(0.02)	(0.02)*	(0.01)	(0.03)	(0.01)***
Dependent variable at baseline[d]	-0.00	0.06	0.09	0.00	0.08	0.00
	(0.00)	(0.00)***	(0.01)***	(0.00)*	(0.01)***	(0.00)
Cognitive score at baseline[e]	0.09	-0.03	-0.14	0.01	-0.04	0.03
	(0.04)**	(0.05)	(0.05)***	(0.02)	(0.04)	(0.03)
Constant	0.39	0.41	0.37	0.11	0.20	0.16
	(0.18)**	(0.23)*	(0.31)	(0.14)	(0.18)	(0.13)
R-squared	0.00	0.02	0.03	0.00	0.08	0.00
Number of observations	12,311	10,980	9,841	13,997	4,225	15,718

Notes: Bootstrap standard errors clustered at the household level are in parentheses.

[a] Estimated individual slopes of the percent of missing or 50 percent answers (from individual-specific regressions on age; the uncertainty measures are adjusted to deviations from year-month fixed effects).

[b] See notes for table 9.5.

[c] See notes for table 9.5.

[d] See notes for table 9.5.

[e] See notes for table 9.5.

***Significant at the 1 percent level.

**Significant at the 5 percent level.

*Significant at the 10 percent level.

9.4 Conclusion

This is an exploratory study of the relationship between expectations, aging, and cognitive decline. We used data from seven waves of the Health and Retirement Study (HRS) to establish age patterns in optimism and uncertainty of expectations in six different domains: stock market returns one year in the future, the chance of a future economic depression, whether tomorrow will be a sunny day, whether one's income will keep up with inflation, job loss, and survival to a specific age. Respondents were asked to state their expected probabilities for the events in question. We measure optimism as higher subjective probabilities of positive events and uncertainty as a higher propensity to answer "don't know" or "50 percent."

We find that optimism decreases and uncertainty increases with age in three of the six domains, controlling for time, cohort, and selection effects. We also find that cognitive decline plays a modest but statistically significant role in explaining the decline of optimism in most domains. The important exception to both the effect of age and the role of cognitive decline is survival expectations: optimism about survival increases significantly with age, uncertainty appears to decrease, and cognitive decline plays no role in those effects. Somewhat surprisingly, cognitive decline does not seem to play a role in accounting for the increase in uncertainty in any of the domains that we investigate. We argue that the joint analyses of cognitive decline and changes in expectations that use person-specific slopes provide less scope for finding spurious relationships that would be more problematic in alternative models, and we provide several robustness checks to substantiate our findings on the association between cognitive decline and declining optimism.

Our finding of a general pattern of decreasing optimism and increasing uncertainty about sunshine, growth in real income, job loss, gains in the stock market, and economic depression is consistent with a pattern of cognitive decline that makes it more difficult for people to acquire and process knowledge and information about events in the world. To the extent that these patterns in the survey responses reflect beliefs that people act on in making decisions, we would expect to find that people act with greater caution and take fewer risks as they grow older. Agarwal et al. (2009) argue that declining cognitive capacity causes older people to make more mistakes in decision making. Our results on expectations suggest that older people may reduce the damage from mistaken decisions by attempting to avoid them altogether. For example, avoiding the purchase of a financial product that one does not understand may reduce the risk of being victimized by a scam, but that reduced risk must be balanced against the potential benefits that could be obtained if it is a good product. Increased pessimism and uncertainty would tilt this calculation in favor of avoiding the purchase.

Our finding of increased optimism about survival as people age may be an exception to the aforementioned analysis due to people's inability to adjust their expectations to the acceleration in risk of mortality at later ages. In a somewhat more speculative vain, our results can be interpreted as consistent with Carstensen's (2006) socioemotional selectivity theory of aging that posits that people become increasingly selective, investing greater resources in emotionally meaningful goals and activities because of an ever shorter time horizon before death. We speculate that optimism about survival allows the elderly individual to focus on emotionally rewarding short-term goals such as planning a trip or anticipating the birth of a grandchild without worrying about the possibility that they may not live to experience the pleasurable event. Optimism about survival may also serve an economic purpose as a heuristic that helps people to maintain a buffer of wealth as a precaution against outliving one's assets by giving greater subjective weight to the chance of an unusually long life.

It is important to stress that the findings in this chapter are exploratory and that our interpretation of those findings is speculative. We do believe that greater understanding of the ways in which probability beliefs are influenced by aging and cognition is a promising line of research. One priority for future research will be to link changes in beliefs to behaviors and decisions.

Appendix

Table 9A.1 Cognitive decline and trends in uncertainty (measured as the fraction of "don't know" answers): Estimates from the regressions on individual slopes with respect to age

	Survival (unadjusted)[a]	Sunny day[a]	Income growth[a]	Job loss[a]	Stock market[a]	Economic depression[a]
Decline in the cognitive score[b]	0.20	0.01	0.40	0.08	-0.04	-0.04
	(0.05)***	(0.00)**	(0.08)***	(0.06)	(0.10)	(0.02)*
Age at baseline[c]	0.01	-0.00	0.01	0.00	-0.02	0.00
	(0.00)**	(0.00)*	(0.00)***	(0.00)	(0.01)***	(0.00)
Dependent variable at baseline[d]	0.00	-0.00	0.00	0.00	-0.00	-0.00
	(0.00)***	(0.00)	(0.00)	(0.00)	(0.00)	(0.00)**
Cognitive score at baseline[e]	-0.03	-0.00	-0.03	-0.01	-0.01	0.02
	(0.01)***	(0.00)***	(0.01)***	(0.01)	(0.01)	(0.00)***
Constant	-0.07	0.06	-0.01	0.00	0.43	0.17
	(0.03)**	(0.00)***	(0.04)	(0.04)	(0.07)***	(0.02)***
R-squared	0.01	0.00	0.01	0.00	0.00	0.00
Number of observations	15,718	9,841	13,997	4,225	12,311	10,980

Note: Standard errors clustered at the household level are in parentheses.

[a] Estimated individual slopes of the percent of missing or 50 percent answers (from individual-specific regressions on age; the uncertainty measures are adjusted to deviations from year-month fixed effects).

[b] See notes to table 9.5.

[c] See notes to table 9.5.

[d] See notes to table 9.5.

[e] See notes to table 9.5.

***Significant at the 1 percent level.

**Significant at the 5 percent level.

*Significant at the 10 percent level.

Table 9A.2 Cognitive decline and trends in uncertainty (measured as the fraction of "don't know" answers): Estimates from the regressions on individual slopes with respect to age

	Survival (unadjusted)[a]	Sunny day[a]	Income growth[a]	Job loss[a]	Stock market[a]	Economic depression[a]
Decline in the cognitive score[b]	0.09	0.01	0.05	0.15	0.13	-0.22
	(0.14)	(0.01)	(0.15)	(0.14)	(0.21)	(0.10)**
Age at baseline[c]	-0.01	-0.00	0.01	-0.00	0.01	0.01
	(0.00)**	(0.00)	(0.01)*	(0.01)	(0.01)	(0.00)***
Dependent variable at baseline[d]	0.00	-0.00	0.00	-0.00	-0.00	-0.00
	(0.00)**	(0.00)	(0.00)	(0.00)	(0.00)	(0.00)**
Cognitive score at baseline[e]	-0.00	-0.00	-0.01	-0.02	-0.01	0.04
	(0.01)	(0.00)**	(0.01)	(0.02)	(0.02)	(0.01)***
Constant	0.05	0.06	-0.02	0.01	0.04	0.05
	(0.04)	(0.00)***	(0.05)	(0.07)	(0.09)	(0.05)
R-squared	0.01	0.00	0.00	-0.00	0.00	0.01
Number of observations	7,743	6,346	7,751	2,322	6,919	6,724

Notes: Sample restricted to individuals with the maximum number of observations. Standard errors clustered at the household level are in parentheses.

[a] Estimated individual slopes of the percent of missing or 50 percent answers (from individual-specific regressions on age; the uncertainty measures are adjusted to deviations from year-month fixed effects).

[b] See notes to table 9.5.

[c] See notes to table 9.5.

[d] See notes to table 9.5.

[e] See notes to table 9.5.

***Significant at the 1 percent level.

**Significant at the 5 percent level.

*Significant at the 10 percent level.

References

Agarwal, Sumit, John C. Driscoll, Xavier Gabaix, and David I. Laibson. 2009. "The Age of Reason: Financial Decisions over the Life-Cycle with Implications for Regulation." *Brookings Papers on Economic Activity* Fall (2009): 51–117.

Bassett, William F., and Robin L. Lumsdaine. 1999. "Outlook, Outcomes, and Optimism." Brown University. Unpublished manuscript.

Carstensen, Laura L. 2006. "The Influence of a Sense of Time on Human Development." *Science* 312:1913.

Crimmins, E. M., J. K. Kim, Kenneth M. Langa, and David Weir. 2011. "Assessment of Cognition Using Surveys and Neuropsychological Assessment: The Health and Retirement Study and the Aging, Demographics, and Memory Study." *Journals of Gerontology Series B-Psychological Sciences and Social Sciences* 66:162–71.

Fisher, Gwenith, Halimah Hassan, Willard L. Rodgers, and David R. Weir. 2012. "Health and Retirement Study—Imputation of Cognitive Functioning Measures: 1992—2010 Early Release." http://hrsonline.isr.umich.edu/modules/meta/xyear/cogimp/desc/COGIMPdd.pdf.

Flynn, J. R. 1987. "Massive IQ Gains in 14 nations: What IQ Tests Really Measure." *Psychological Bulletin* 101:171–91.

Horn, J. L., and R. B. Cattell. 1967. "Age Differences in Fluid and Crystallized Intelligence." *Acta Psychologica* 26:107–29.

Horn, J. L., and J. J. McArdle. 2007. "Understanding Human Intelligence since Spearman." In *Factor Analysis at 100. Historical Developments and Future Directions*, edited by Robert Cudeck and Robert C. MacCallum, 206–44. Mahwah, NJ: LEA Publishers.

Hudomiet, P., and Robert J. Willis. 2013. "Estimating Second Order Probability Beliefs from Subjective Survival Data." *Decision Analysis* June (10): 152–70.

Hurd, Michael D. 2009. "Subjective Probabilities in Household Surveys." *Annual Review of Economics* 2009 (1): 543–62.

Hurd, Michael D., Paco Martorell, Adeline Delavande, Kathleen J. Mullen, and Kenneth M. Langa. 2013. "Monetary Costs of Dementia in the United States." *New England Journal of Medicine* 368 (14): 1326–34.

Hurd, Michael D., S. Rohwedder, and S. Winter. 2005. "Subjective Probabilities of Survival: An International Comparison." RAND. Unpublished manuscript.

Kézdi, G., and R. Willis. 2012. "Household Stock Market Beliefs and Learning." NBER Working Paper no. 17614, Cambridge, MA.

Manski, Charles F. 2004. "Measuring Expectations." *Econometrica* 72:1329–76.

McArdle, John J., E. Ferrer-Caja, F. Hamagami, and R. Woodcock. 2002. "Comparative Longitudinal Structural Analyses of the Growth and Decline of Multiple Intellectual Abilities over the Life Span." Developmental Psychology 38 (1): 115–42.

McArdle, John J., and Robert J. Willis. 2011. "Cognitive Aging and Human Capital." In *Grounding Social Sciences in Cognitive Sciences*, edited by Ron Sun, 354–84. Cambridge: MIT Press.

Plassman, B., K. Langa, G. Fisher, S. Heeringa, D. Weir, M. Ofstedal, J. Burke et al. 2007. "Prevalence of Dementia in the United States: The Aging, Demographics, and Memory Study." *Neuroepidemiology* 29 (1–2): 125–32.

Reuter-Lorenz, P. A., and D. C. Park. 2010. "Human Neuroscience and the Aging Mind: A New Look at Old Problems." *Journal of Gerontology: Psychological Sciences* 65B (4): 405–15.

Comment   John B. Shoven

I found this chapter to be thought provoking and stimulating, mostly in the questions that it raised. I think that there is real value in taking a preliminary empirical look at the consequences of declining cognitive abilities among the elderly in terms of their optimism and in terms of their willingness to answer questions about probabilistic expectations. That said, the results of this chapter are limited by the questions available in the HRS data set and they are not very clear. It does appear that the average person becomes somewhat less optimistic as they age, although the magnitude of the effect is modest. The results on their willingness to answer a probabilistic expectations question are even less impressive. When you ask whether those who have suffered a particularly sharp decline in cognition show less willingness to offer an answer to expectations questions, the answer appears to be "no."

The chapter reviews the way cognition is conventionally measured using the HRS. Certainly, the gradual decline in cognition throughout the age range of the HRS with an acceleration in the rate of decline starting at roughly seventy-five is well known and the expected result. A more interesting question, at least to me, would be whether age-specific cognition has been improving along with age-specific health and age-specific mortality. I take it that the mortality improvements, which have been pretty dramatic, indicate that on average most human organs are in better shape at a particular age than in the past. For instance, the mortality of sixty-five-year-old males has dropped from 3.5 percent in the 1950s to 1.5 percent today. This has been accompanied on average by healthier hearts and lungs, for instance. What about the brain? Is the cognition of sixty-five-year-olds today better than it was sixty years ago? The HRS, which has been in the field for just over twenty years, could begin to offer some clues. The authors go to some length to obtain the pure age effect on cognition and I guess what I am saying is that the pure cohort effect would be of interest as well. I was intrigued by the significant and large divergence between the cross-sectional profile of cognition and the profile using cumulative slopes in figure 9.3. The actual cross-sectional evidence shows a much more gradual deterioration in cognitive ability. Part of this may be due to the fact that those with high initial cognition have better mortality and therefore are more likely to be in the sample at later ages. Is this all that is going on or is there more to the story?

The optimism and uncertainty results in the chapter are based on six questions in the HRS. I summarize the questions here: (a) chance of surviving to age A, (b) probability of a sunny day tomorrow, (c) chance that

John B. Shoven is the Trione Director of the Stanford Institute for Economic Policy Research, the Charles R. Schwab Professor of Economics at Stanford University, and a research associate of the National Bureau of Economic Research.

For acknowledgments, sources of research support, and disclosure of the author's material financial relationships, if any, please see http://www.nber.org/chapters/c12981.ack.

your income will keep up with inflation over the next five years, (d) chance of losing your job in the next twelve months, (e) chance of a mutual fund invested in Dow Jones Industrial–type stocks being higher in a year, and (f) chance of a major economic depression in the next ten years. These are not great questions for this study. Here are just some of the problems: Question (b), how will the respondent answer if the actual weather is "partly cloudy"? Question (c), as people leave the labor force between ages fifty and seventy, the actual chance of keeping up with inflation may go down—reducing your answer as you age may not reflect increasing pessimism; it may reflect reality. Question (d) has a similar problem in that the chance of losing a job conditional on having one now is probably a function of age—saying that it is more likely as you age, again, may not be increasing pessimism, simply reality. Question (e), my guess is that most people don't know what the Dow Jones Industrial Average is—most are not in the stock market and have little reason to keep informed about it. And question (f), what is the definition of "major economic depression"? Even prime-age professional economists such as National Bureau of Economic Research (NBER) research associates would have difficulty answering this question. It is possible that people with excellent cognition will be smart enough to answer "don't know," whereas people with reduced cognition will offer a guess of an answer.

The one result that stands out in Kézdi and Willis's chapter is that on average people become more optimistic about their survival probabilities, relative to a life table, as they age. For the other five questions they become slightly more pessimistic about the weather and somewhat more pessimistic about the stock market. I hesitate to reach conclusions about the real income question and the job loss question because the "right" answer may be a negative function of age.

The authors define uncertainty as a "don't know" answer or in some cases as a "50 percent" answer. They find that people are more likely to answer "don't know" or "50 percent" for four of the questions—the stock market question, the economic depression question, the sunny day question, and the inflation protection question as they age. Interestingly, they do not have more difficulty answering the survival question as they get older.

When the authors investigate whether those with particularly severe cognitive decline become more pessimistic and/or more uncertain, they come up with mixed results. On the optimism/pessimism front, they do find that those with more severe cognitive deterioration tend to become more pessimistic, particularly about the chances of an economic depression and the chances of a stock market increase. The other coefficients also reflect increasing pessimism, but the magnitude of the coefficients is modest. On the uncertainty question, or the willingness to offer an answer to these questions, it appears that cognitive decline has little to do with it. The coefficient on cognitive decline is insignificant for four of the six questions and of the opposite sign for the other two. So, this is a puzzling result if one thought that forming expectations is a quantitative calculation that would become more challenging with reduced cognition. The evidence does not support this theory.

As I said at the outset, I found this chapter stimulating; not for the answers that it came up with, but the questions that it asked and the thoughts that it stimulated. I came away thinking that on average people do get slightly more pessimistic as they age and as their cognitive abilities deteriorate. The one question that I would like more evidence on is whether cognition is more associated with age or more associated with mortality risk. Over time, age-specific mortality risk has changed dramatically. I wish I knew more about age-specific average cognitive ability and that may be an additional interesting project for these authors or others.

IV

**Interventions to Improve
Health and Well-Being**

10

Nutrition, Iron Deficiency Anemia, and the Demand for Iron-Fortified Salt
Evidence from an Experiment in Rural Bihar

Abhijit Banerjee, Sharon Barnhardt, and Esther Duflo

10.1 Introduction

According to the World Health Organization (WHO) Global Database on Anemia, 24.8 percent of the world's population is anemic (de Benoist et al. 2008). Iron deficiency, along with other nutritional deficiencies, disease (malaria) and infections (parasites), is one of the leading causes of anemia. The consequences of iron deficiency anemia (IDA) depend on age. For children, IDA is associated with slower physical and cognitive development (Lozoff 2007) with potentially long-lasting effects (Lozoff et al. 2006). For working age adults, IDA may lower productivity, as feeling weak is the most common symptom of the disorder (Haas and Brownlie 2001). Severe anemia during pregnancy can lead to low birth weight and child mortality (Stoltzfus 2001). For older adults who have passed their most physically productive years, high rates of anemia are generally observed, and lower hemoglobin levels are associated with cognitive decline (Peters et al. 2008) and lower physical performance (Penninx et al. 2004).

Abhijit Banerjee is the Ford Foundation International Professor of Economics at the Massachusetts Institute of Technology and a research associate of the National Bureau of Economic Research. Sharon Barnhardt is assistant professor at the Indian Institute of Management, Ahmedabad. Esther Duflo is the Abdul Latif Jameel Professor of Poverty Alleviation and Development Economics and director of the Abdul Latif Jameel Poverty Action Lab at the Massachusetts Institute of Technology and a research associate of the National Bureau of Economic Research.

For financial support, we thank the International Initiative for Impact Evaluation, the UK Department for International Development, and the US National Institutes of Health. For energetic research support, we are grateful to Urmi Battacharya, Anna George, Dwijo Goswami, Radhika Jain, Seema Kacker, Bastien Michel, Achill Rudolph, and Srinivasan Vasudevan. All errors are our own. For acknowledgments, sources of research support, and disclosure of the authors' material financial relationships, if any, please see http://www.nber.org/chapters/c12984.ack.

Reduced productivity caused by IDA and its potential impact on earnings have become an area of focus for health research in developing countries, where large sections of the population provide physical labor in agriculture, construction, and manufacturing. To address iron deficiency anemia, health policies normally focus on providing mineral supplements or fortifying foods. Surprisingly, few evaluations have looked at the impact of treating IDA in any form on actual output. While Basta et al. (1979) found a large effect of iron supplementation on sugar tree tappers in Indonesia (though their study suffered from attrition), Li et al. (1994) and Edgerton et al. (1979) found a much smaller effect on productivity. Thomas et al. (2003) found a large effect of an iron supplementation program on the labor supply and earnings of males who were anemic at baseline, but only for those who were self-employed.

Providing supplements to a large population, particularly pregnant women, is a standard policy in many countries.[1] However, it faces two problems. The first is that it relies on public health infrastructure and local providers, whom the government struggles to monitor (Banerjee, Deaton, and Duflo 2004; Chaudhury et al. 2006). The second is that individuals often do not comply with the protocol, perhaps because potential gains are not easily measurable while potential side effects (such as constipation) are evident (Allen et al. 2006). In our study area, which is covered by a supplementation policy aimed at pregnant women, we found 60 percent of pregnant females to be anemic using the standard 12 g/dL cutoff.

The second approach to prevent widespread anemia is to add iron to foods that are a regular part of the local diet. Fortification is a compelling solution in locations where households regularly purchase packaged foods that can be fortified centrally during mass production. For example, in the United States, all enriched grain products are fortified with folic acid to help prevent neural tube defects in newborns, toothpaste is fortified with fluoride to prevent cavities, salt is fortified with iodine to prevent goiter, and milk is fortified with vitamin D to prevent rickets. Several states in India now have iron fortification subsidies for flour, which is then purchased on the open market.

These channels do not effectively reach low-income populations in remote locations, however, because such populations do not buy as much processed grain. Village-level fortification, which we examined in a prior study (Banerjee, Duflo, and Glennerster 2011) had a very low rate of take-up, which suggests that this is not a sustainable alternative. The study found no impact on anemia after one year, as most households stopped fortifying after six

---

1. Under the National Rural Health Mission in India, large iron supplements are to be provided to pregnant women and adolescent girls, at a cost of INR 105 per 1,000 tablets. This is less than USD 2 for enough supplements for ten women. When cases of severe anemia (a pregnant woman with a hemoglobin level of less than 8 g/dL) are identified they may be addressed with intravenous iron sucrose.

months. This suggests that the need for continued household effort, in particular taking the grain to a mill that is equipped for fortification (and monitoring that the miller actually fortifies the food), is a barrier to long-term take-up.

This project will study the feasibility and the impact of an alternative approach, which is to fortify salt with iron. There are currently two accepted formulas for double-fortified salt (DFS) in India, one produced by the National Institute of Nutrition (Hyderabad) and the other by the Micronutrient Initiative. There is evidence from clinical trials in several countries (including India) that iron-fortified salt has the potential to improve hemoglobin status and reduce anemia among young adults and lactating women (Nadiger et al. 1980; Sivakumar et al. 2001) and children (Nair et al. 1998; Brahmam et al. 2000; Andersson et al. 2008).

These studies, however, involve very small samples in carefully controlled environments, often ensuring consumption by adding the salt to food consumed by the participants, or distributing it at home for free. Thus, there have so far been no large-scale studies of the effect of making DFS available, potentially at a discounted rate, on usage and eventual health, let alone productivity. DFS is a promising technology, for at least three reasons. First, it can be fortified centrally and stored for up to one year due to technology that slows iron and iodine degradation (Ranganathan and Sesikeran 2008). Second, all local diets include salt, whereas some regions eat more rice than flour-based rotis. Third, even in remote villages, households purchase salt throughout the year rather than produce it.

Unless we directly study take-up and impact, however, one cannot assume that DFS will be part of the answer to the anemia problem among the poorest. Furthermore, to the extent a government is willing to subsidize the fight against anemia, it can do so by subsidizing DFS; but without evidence on the willingness to pay for DFS at various prices, how should the subsidy level be set? It may take more than a nudge to shift consumption to DFS, since the benefits may not be obvious. Perhaps the price of DFS needs to be below high-quality iodized salt to change consumer behavior.

Our broader project fills this gap by implementing a large-scale randomized controlled trial in 400 villages in Bihar, including 200 where DFS produced by Tata Chemicals will be made available at a price subsidized by the UK Department for International Development. In this chapter, we report findings from the baseline survey that strongly suggest potential returns to intervention to fight anemia. We find 53 percent of women age 15–49 have hemoglobin levels under 12 g/dL and 21 percent of men have a hemoglobin level under 13, the rough cutoffs for anemia. A large majority of households (94 percent) purchase iodized salt, which makes an intervention with DFS potentially promising.

This chapter also presents the results of a small-scale experiment to assess willingness to pay for double-fortified salt using randomly assigned discount vouchers. We find that the take-up of DFS falls quickly with price. At a price point of 45 percent of the retail price of DFS sold in major Indian metros, the take-up of DFS is 30 percent in private stores.[2] We also assess the impact on purchase behavior of three separate information campaigns: a basic campaign limited to written promotional materials, the basic campaign plus a street play, or all of the above plus a door-to-door public health campaign conducted by incentivized volunteers referred to as ASHAs (accredited social health workers). We find no differential impact of information campaign type among households who were given vouchers to purchase DFS.

10.2 Setting and Background on Double-Fortified Salt

10.2.1 Setting for Baseline Survey and Pricing Experiment

Our pricing experiment and baseline survey for the larger impact assessment were conducted in the state of Bihar. With a population of 104 million (Registrar General of India 2011), a state Human Development Indicator that puts it in 21st place out of 23 ranked states (Planning Commission and IAMR 2011), and an underweight prevalence rate of 56.1 percent for children under age five (Menon, Deolalikar, and Bhaskar 2009), Bihar is large, poor, and undernourished. Anemia rates are also high in the state, as 68 percent of ever-married women fifteen to forty-nine years old and 88 percent of children under age three are anemic according to official sources (International Institute for Population Sciences 2007). Our study takes place in Bhojpur, a district with approximately forty-four doctors for a population of 2.2 million (District Health Society Bhojpur 2011). From our survey, we estimate there are 912 girls for every 1,000 boys under the age of five in the district.

10.2.2 DFS Formulation and Evidence from Studies in Controlled Conditions

The DFS used in the pricing experiments reported here (and for the larger project of which this is part) is manufactured by Tata Chemicals, Ltd., a leading private manufacturer of salt, based in Mumbai. Tata Chemicals uses the National Institute of Nutrition formulation for DFS, which is fortified with 1 mg of iron and 30 to 40 μg of iodine per gram of salt. When consumed regularly at 10 g/day (roughly the consumption of an adult), this formulation is estimated to provide 10 mg of iron and 150 μg of iodine (Ranganathan and Sesikeran 2008), or 56–125 percent of the RDA of iron and 100 percent of the RDA of iodine. This formulation has been endorsed by a committee set up by the Indian Council for Medical Research (ICMR). The maximum

---

2. A rate of 20 to 30 percent of households purchasing DFS was estimated as the requirement to observe an average increase in hemoglobin of 0.7 g/dL, which is meaningful.

retail prices in major urban markets where DFS was introduced under the brand name "Tata Plus" is INR 20 per kg.[3]

10.3 Baseline Survey

10.3.1 Data Collection

The survey was conducted across the fourteen blocks (subdistrict administrative units) of Bhojpur District between May 2011 and March 2012. We excluded villages with fewer than fifty households from the District Rural Development Agency (DRDA) household and village listing for Bhojpur, stratified by block, and randomly selected twenty-eight or twenty-nine villages from each block to include in the study. In total, 400 villages were included. We then randomly selected fifteen households per village to participate in our surveys, which are managed by research associates from the South Asia office of the Abdul Latif Jameel Poverty Action Lab (J-PAL).

Our baseline survey collected information on both households and individual household members. The household module collected information on the economic status of the household: consumption, savings, assets, and so forth. The background modules collected data on time use, food consumption, education, and pregnancy. The health modules collected anthropometric measurements, hemoglobin counts, objective measures of physical fitness, and subjective measures of illness and general health. Finally, the cognition modules involved several tests assessing respondents' memory, attention, and mental awareness. In total, 39,606 individuals in 5,970 households have complete objective health survey data and are reported here.

10.3.2 Education, Income Generation, Assets, and Consumption

Table 10.1 presents a snapshot of the households interviewed for the baseline. There are slightly more women in the sample (20,330 females versus 19,276 males), reportedly due to seasonal migration of adult males for income generation. Households are also young, with nearly 40 percent of the sample under the age of fifteen years. In this area, there is a fairly high percentage of families belonging to Scheduled Castes (19 percent) and other Backward castes (14 percent), but almost no Scheduled Tribes.

Literacy rates, based on reading a paragraph presented by the surveyor, are under 50 percent for women, and much lower for women over age fifty (as may be predicted by historical rates of schooling). Approximately 88 percent of girls under the age of fifteen are presently enrolled in school. Literacy rates are much higher for males in our sample, with 85 percent of males age fifteen to forty-nine and 73 percent of males age fifty and older

---

3. At the time of editing this chapter for publication, the exchange rate was approximately INR 61 per USD.

Table 10.1 Demographics of baseline survey sample

	Age 0–4	Age 5–14	Age 15–49	Age 50+	Total
Households (number)					5,970
Scheduled caste (proportion of heads)					0.19
Scheduled tribe (proportion of heads)					0.004
Other backward caste (proportion of heads)					0.14
General category (proportion of heads)					0.67
Females					
Number	2,462	5,003	9,387	3,478	20,330
Can read paragraph easily or with difficulties (proportion)	—	0.47	0.49	0.17	
Enrolled in school (proportion)	—	.88	.13	—	
Number who are working	—	—	3,651	1,703	
Primary income generating activity is agricultural fieldwork (proportion)	—	—	0.26	0.23	
Primary income generating activity is animal husbandry	—	—	0.60	0.68	
Primary income generating activity is textiles & handicrafts	—	—	0.04	0.01	
Primary income generating activity is shop, business, etc.	—	—	0.03	0.04	
Primary income generating activity is other	—	—	0.08	0.05	
Males					
Number	2,557	5,468	7,658	3,593	19,276
Can read paragraph easily or with difficulties (proportion)	—	0.55	0.85	0.73	
Enrolled in school (proportion)	—	0.91	0.24	—	
Number who are working	—	—	5,826	2,796	
Primary income generating activity is agricultural fieldwork (proportion)	—	—	0.30	0.35	
Primary income generating activity is animal husbandry	—	—	0.37	0.48	
Primary income generating activity is mining, construction, physical work	—	—	0.11	0.05	
Primary income generating activity is shop, business, etc.	—	—	0.13	0.07	
Primary income generating activity is other	—	—	0.09	0.04	

Notes: A dash indicates question not asked for this age group.

Table 10.2   **Household assets and consumption (baseline survey)**

Bicycle (proportion owning)	0.63
Motorcycle or scooter	0.14
Kerosene stove	0.34
Mobile phone	0.77
CD/DVD player or radio	0.25
Television	0.23
Number rooms in house (excluding bathroom)	4.1
Number cows	0.7
Number buffaloes	0.9
Number goats	1.7
Number chickens	0.5
Number pigs	0.03
Total animals	2.7
Monthly per capita consumption (INR)	1,694
Household dietary diversity score (out of 12)	6.8
Last salt purchased was iodized (proportion yes)	0.94

Notes: Household dietary diversity score (HDDS) is the number of food types out of twelve consumed on the previous day. It is a composite measure of food access and socioeconomic status. N = 5,970 households.

able to read the short paragraph easily or with some difficulties. For boys age five to fourteen school enrollment is 91 percent.

Most women in our sample do not earn an income. Those who do are principally engaged in animal husbandry or agricultural fieldwork. For men, the most common income-generating activities are also animal husbandry and agricultural fieldwork, followed by work in shops or in the mining sector.

To approximate relative wealth levels, we asked households a series of questions about the assets they own (table 10.2). More than half of households own a bicycle (63 percent) and 14 percent own a motorcycle or a scooter. Mobile phones can be found in 77 percent of households. Only one-third have a kerosene stove, 25 percent own a radio, and 23 percent have a television.

Houses have approximately four rooms on average (including the kitchen), with a household size of six to seven persons. The average household owns about three animals, the most popular being goats and buffaloes.

We measure consumption with a series of questions about the amount consumed of various categories over the previous thirty days (food broken down into nine types, paan/tobacco/alcohol, fuels, personal and house care, entertainment and media, gambling, travel, phones, other) over the previous year (clothing, shoes, schooling, festivals and ceremonies, health care, and eight types of durable goods). These figures were then converted into an estimated monthly expenditure divided by the number of household members. Monthly per capita consumption is high at just over INR 1,694 (table 10.2), reflecting the value of articles produced as well as purchased in the market.

This is higher than monthly per capita expenditure of INR 1,054 in rural areas in 2009 to 2010 estimated by the National Sample Survey Office (2011).

We also asked individuals which types of foods anyone in the household consumed the day before the survey and counted the number of food groups eaten out of the 12 used to estimate dietary diversity.[4] Unsurprisingly, less than 2 percent of households consumed meat the previous day, about 4 percent consumed eggs, and only about 6 percent consumed fish.[5]

Dietary diversity is a useful proxy for a diet associated with caloric and protein sufficiency, better birth weight, improved child anthropometric status, and higher hemoglobin (Swindale and Bilinsky 2006). As our measurement combines answers for foods consumed by anyone in the household about which the respondent knows, it may be an overestimation of diversity for individual members. Nonetheless, the average household consumed 6.8 out of 12 food groups the previous day. This result is in line with Bhagowalia, Headey, and Kadiyala (2012), who find dietary diversity at the household level to be around 7 in India. Comparatively, Swindale and Bilinsky (2006) recommend setting dietary diversity targets in such a sample using the score for the highest income tercile or the highest diversity tercile in the population. For our sample, the dietary diversity score for the highest diversity tercile is approximately 8.5.

Finally, we also asked about the type of salt that the household normally consumes. In this sample, 94 percent of households reported buying iodized salt the last time they purchased salt.

10.3.3 Health of Children

We turn next to the results of extensive health and physical measurements in our baseline survey. Our full sample of children age fourteen and younger includes 7,465 girls and 8,025 boys. Rates of anemia in young girls and boys are high, at around 50 percent for "any" anemia (see appendix table 10A.1 for thresholds) and around 25 percent for moderate or severe anemia in the age group of six months to under five years (see table 10.3). The gender gap in anemia rates is evident in older children, with 40 percent of girls age five to fourteen years testing as having any anemia (22 percent are moderately or severely anemic) and 29 percent of boys measured as having any anemia (15 percent are moderately or severely anemic).

The vast majority of children eat at least three meals a day. For children there is no standard of thinness related to body mass index (BMI), but in our villages the average BMI among children is around 14.6 to 15.1. According

4. We excluded responses for people who had attended a festival or other special event the previous day.
5. The third National Family Health Survey (NFHS-3) found 7 percent of adults in India eat chicken, meat, or fish daily (Arnold et al. 2009). In Bihar, 18.3 percent of women eat animal protein at least once per week and 20.5 percent eat eggs at least weekly (IIPS and Macro International 2008).

Table 10.3   Individual nutrition and health—children (baseline survey)

Age (yrs)	Girls		Boys	
	0–4	5–14	0–4	5–14
Number	2,462	5,003	2,557	5,468
Hemoglobin (g/dL)	10.70	11.78	10.81	12.18
Anemic (proportion yes)	0.54	0.40	0.49	0.29
Moderately or severely anemic (proportion yes)	0.27	0.22	0.23	0.15
Eats less than 3 meals daily	0.01	0.02	0.02	0.03
BMI	14.63	15.05	15.07	14.86
Mid-upper-arm circumference (cm)	14.07	18.02	14.30	17.50
Mid-upper-arm circumference indicates undernourished (proportion yes)	0.08	—	0.04	—
Completed Queens College Step Test (proportion)	—	0.54	—	0.74
Completed all 3 balance tests (proportion)	—	0.89	—	0.92
Seconds taken to walk 4 meters	—	3.18	—	2.82
Seconds taken to stand up & sit 5 times	—	8.89	—	7.95
Reported health is good or very good (proportion)	0.89	0.94	0.87	0.95
Number illnesses over last 30 days (out of 10 asked)	2.12	1.79	2.26	1.80
Had any illness "all the time" over the last 30 days (proportion)	0.05	0.04	0.06	0.03
Missed school in last 30 days due to illness or excessive fatigue (proportion)	—	0.40	—	0.40
Missed work in last 30 days due to illness or excessive fatigue (proportion)	—	0.26	—	0.24
Depression index (6–18, higher more depressed)	—	7.27	—	7.21

Notes: Hemoglobin and anemia are only for children above the age of six months. For hemoglobin, $N = 1,803$ girls and 1,907 boys age six months to five years old. There is no established MUAC cutoff for people age five to nineteen. Physical tests were administered to individuals age ten and older. For physical tests, $N = 1,785$ girls and 1,851 boys. Balance, walk, and sit/stand only tested if QCST could not be attempted. Disease symptoms asked about were blood loss, bad sight, night blindness, tuberculosis, malaria, pain in joints, worms, bloody stool/urine. The Adapted CES-D Depression Index in this sample has a mean of 8.6 with a standard deviation of 2.73. The median is 8. A dash indicates test not done for the age group.

to mid-upper-arm circumference (MUAC) benchmarks, about 8 percent of young girls and 4 percent of young boys in our sample are undernourished.

We also conducted four objective tests of physical fitness among children age ten and older. The Queens College Step Test (QCST) is a variation of the Harvard Step Test, which has been previously used with Indian populations to create a physical fitness index (Chatterjee et al. 2004, 2005). The QCST is performed using a 16.25-inch-high step. All respondents are asked to follow the same protocol, which required them to step on and off the step to the beat of an electric metronome. All male respondents were asked to follow a ninety-six beats per minute rhythm, while women and children (ten to fourteen years), were asked to follow eighty-eight beats per minute, in accordance to the guidelines established by Chatterjee et al. (2004).

Of the 2,051 girls who attempted the QCST, 54 percent were able to complete it. Of the 2,263 boys who attempted it, 74 percent finished. If a respondent fell out of sync with the beat of the QCST for more than fifteen seconds, he or she was asked to stop and perform the other basic fitness tests.

Second, for the balance tests, respondents were asked to stand in three positions for at least ten seconds (feet side by side, semitandem, full tandem). For those who could not finish or would not attempt the QCST, 89 percent of girls finished all three balance tests and 94 percent of boys finished all three. For the walk test, individuals were asked to walk a distance of four meters in a fast walking pace twice. On average, girls covered this distance in 3.2 seconds and boys covered it in 2.8 seconds. For the fourth test, subjects were asked to sit on and stand up from a stool five consecutive times. Girls did this in 8.9 seconds on average and boys finished in 8.0 seconds.

In addition to objective measures, we also covered subjective health. The surveyors began by asking the respondents to rank their overall health on a scale from 1 ("very good") to 4 ("very bad"). For very young children, a parent was asked the question about the child's health. Self-reported health is good or very good for the vast majority of all ages of children.

Next, respondents were asked to indicate the number of occurrences of short-term sicknesses in the last thirty days as well as more severe disease symptoms in the last six months from two respective lists. Very few children (3 percent to 6 percent) report chronic illness over the past thirty days, though about 40 percent of girls and boys have missed school due to illness or excessive fatigue in the same time period. About one quarter of the older children have also missed work for the same reasons. The most common sicknesses reported for children, adults, and the elderly are cold, fever, fatigue, and diarrhea.

Last, the survey also measured perceived mental health. Respondents were asked to indicate how frequently each mental state from the following list is experienced: (a) I felt sad; (b) I felt like crying; (c) I felt scared; (d) I felt lonely, like I did not have any friends; (e) I felt like people I know were not friendly or did not even want to be with me; and (f) I did not feel like eating or was not hungry. For each mental state the respondent indicates how intensely/often she felt that way in the last week: (a) not at all, (b) a little, or (c) a lot.

Our depression index is formed by summing the intensity values (1–3) for all six feelings. Someone who does not feel any of these negative states over the previous week will, therefore, score a 6. This test is modeled after the CES-D depression index (Radloff 1977).[6] Children scored very low on this index and with no difference between girls (7.3) and boys (7.2), indicating on average they felt one of the negative states a little during the previous week.

10.3.4 Health of Adults

In order to assess the health of adults and older adults, we used a similar set of objective tests and self-reports. They are reported in table 10.4 In this sample, the average woman is anemic, with hemoglobin under 12 g/dL. Among adult women, 52 percent are anemic by all definitions, and 25 percent are moderately or severely anemic. These percentages increase with age: 68 percent of women age seventy and older are anemic by any definition, 39 percent moderately or severely. The situation is only relatively better for adult males for whom the rate of any anemia is 22 percent for the fifteen to forty-nine age group. The gender gap in any anemia goes away in this sample, as the proportion of anemic men increases to 55 percent for men in their sixties and to 67 percent for men over the age of seventy. However, men do have lower rates of moderate and severe anemia in all age groups. Figure 10.1 illustrates the relationship between hemoglobin and age in our sample.

Many adult females and adult males eat fewer than three meals per day, but this is particularly high among men in their sixties (43 percent) and seventies (49 percent). Over 85 percent of women across all age groups never eat meals outside. For adult males under fifty this proportion is only 58 percent, but it rises to 82 percent for men in their seventies. Nonetheless, the percentage of meals taken outside is extremely low for all adults at 6 percent or less, indicating that iron-fortified salt will reach this group if it is in food cooked and consumed at home.

In terms of weight for height, the average adult is within the healthy range for BMI. However, a fairly high proportion of adults have a BMI that would be classified as moderate or severe thinness. This is true for 12 percent of women between the ages of twenty and forty-nine, and increases to 29 percent for women in their seventies. Approximately 10 percent of men age twenty to forty-nine are moderately or severely thin, and this increases to 22 percent among men in their seventies. Figure 10.2 shows the relationship between BMI and age is strong and is not mediated by a measure of wealth. The thinner lines indicate individuals whose household

---

6. The number of feelings and coding of answers of this survey differs from the standard ten-item CES-D index.

Table 10.4   Individual nutrition and health—adults (baseline survey)

Age (yrs)	Female				Male			
	15–49	50–59	60–69	70+	15–49	50–59	60–69	70+
Number	9,387	1,424	1,241	813	7,657	1,123	1,408	1,062
Hemoglobin (g/dL)	11.7	11.7	11.5	11.2	14.0	13.3	12.6	11.9
Anemic (proportion yes)	0.52	0.55	0.59	0.68	0.22	0.39	0.55	0.67
Moderately or severely anemic (proportion yes)	0.25	0.25	0.30	0.39	0.03	0.09	0.16	0.28
Eats less than 3 meals daily	0.19	0.35	0.38	0.39	0.20	0.36	0.43	0.49
Never eats meals outside home (proportion yes)	0.87	0.89	0.87	0.90	0.58	0.64	0.70	0.82
Share of meals taken outside	0.01	0.01	0.01	0.01	0.06	0.04	0.03	0.02
BMI (kg/m^2)	20.34	20.75	20.52	19.39	20.01	20.73	20.04	19.48
BMI indicates moderate or severe thinness (over age 20)	0.12	0.17	0.21	0.29	0.10	0.11	0.17	0.22
Mid-upper-arm circumference (cm)	24.65	24.98	24.39	23.19	25.65	26.18	25.25	24.16
Mid-upper-arm circumference indicates undernourished (proportion yes)	0.17	0.19	0.25	0.41	0.10	0.12	0.22	0.35
Completed Queens College Step Test	0.25	—	—	—	0.73	—	—	—
Completed all 3 balance tests (proportion)	0.88	0.81	0.71	0.53	0.90	0.88	0.82	0.65
Seconds taken to walk 4 meters	3.98	4.03	4.45	5.68	3.26	3.48	3.50	4.30
Seconds taken to stand up & sit 5 times	11.44	12.75	13.66	15.49	10.36	10.86	11.77	13.68
Number of ADL that can be done (out of 6)	3.40	2.57	2.01	1.14	3.95	3.69	3.22	2.20

Self-reported health is good or very good (proportion)	0.79	0.65	0.6	0.56	0.90	0.82	0.75	0.67
Number illnesses over last 30 days (out of 10 asked)	2.95	3.47	3.57	3.75	2.08	2.45	2.62	2.91
Had any illness "all the time" over the last 30 days	0.19	0.30	0.38	0.46	0.10	0.17	0.27	0.41
Missed school in last 30 days due to illness or excessive fatigue	0.31	—	—	—	0.24	—	—	—
Missed work in last 30 days due to illness or excessive fatigue	0.26	0.32	0.33	0.29	0.28	0.31	0.31	0.28
Depression index (6–18, higher more depressed)	9.15	10.09	10.29	10.53	8.11	8.51	8.78	8.98

Notes: Anemia thresholds are adjusted for pregnancy and smoking. Thinness thresholds adjusted for pregnancy. MUAC cutoff for undernourishment for adults is 20. This is a conservative estimate. The QCST was administered to individuals between the ages of ten and forty-nine. Activities of daily living (ADL) asked about were standing up, filling a bucket, walking 0.5 kilometers, walking 5 kilometers, carrying 5 kilograms, and sowing rice for one day. "Can Do" ADL includes "can easily do" and "can do with some difficulty." Disease symptoms asked about were blood loss, bad sight, night blindness, tuberculosis, malaria, pain in joints, worms, bloody stool/urine. A dash indicates question not asked or test not done for the age group.

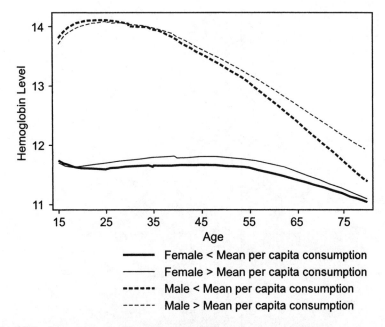

Fig. 10.1   Lowess graph of hemoglobin level by sex and consumption

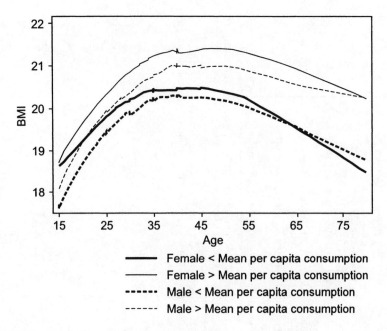

Fig. 10.2   Lowess graph of body mass index by sex and consumption

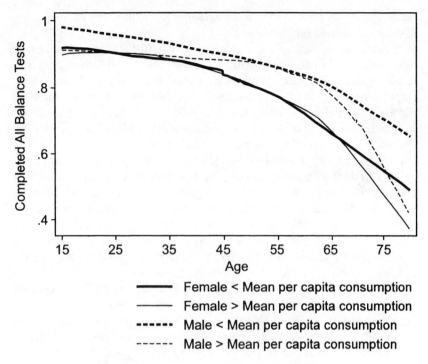

Fig. 10.3   Lowess graph of balance tests by sex and consumption

consumption per person places them in the upper half of the consumption distribution.

Undernourishment among adults is corroborated using a conservative benchmark of a 20 cm MUAC for adults. By this measure, approximately 14 percent of adults under the age of fifty are undernourished. The MUAC is roughly stable until individuals reach their seventies.

For adults, the Queen's College Step Test was limited to people under age fifty; 25 percent of women and 73 percent of men who attempted the test could complete it. Most women under age fifty could, however, complete the three balance tests, as could men of the same age. For both sexes, balance declines as the decades pass. Figure 10.3 highlights the decline, which is greater for women.

Time taken to walk four meters starts at about 4 seconds for adult women and 3.3 seconds for adult men. Both sexes are slower at older ages, but the difference is greater for women. The average man over age seventy covers the distance in the same amount of time as a woman in her sixties. Next, table 10.4 shows us that the time taken to stand up and sit down five times is quite a bit longer for adults than for children. It takes adult women over eleven seconds and adult men need over ten seconds to complete the task. Men are faster than women on this test at all ages, but particularly when comparing women and men in their seventies.

A more direct way to capture physical health through self-reported information is to ask respondents about their ability to perform activities involving different degrees of physical stress. In the survey, adult and elderly respondents were asked to report the level of difficulty they experience during the following seven common activities of daily living (ADL): stand up from sitting on the floor, fill a bucket with water, use a hand pump, walk 0.5 km, walk 5 km, carry 5 kg weight, and sow rice for one day.

For each activity, the respondent indicated whether he or she can do it easily, can do it with some difficulty, finds it very difficult to do, or cannot perform the activity. We report the number of activities that can be done easily or with some difficulty as "can be done." The average working-age woman can complete 3.4 of these activities and the average male can complete 4.0. Older people can do fewer tasks; women in their seventies can only compete one task, while men in their seventies can complete two on average.

Next, we look at reports of subjective health. Nearly 80 percent of working-age women and 90 percent of working-age men report that their health is good or very good. With each decade of age, reports of good health are lower. But, remarkably, 56 percent of women and 67 percent of men in their seventies report that their health is good or very good. This, of course, could be the result of sicker people dropping out of the population.

As in other surveys, we find high rates of self-reported diseases (an "ocean of diseases"). The average number of illnesses reported over the past thirty days is higher for adults of all ages than for children. This potentially reflects the relative difficulty parents had remembering children's illnesses versus their own. Prime-age adult women report 2.95 symptoms of disease over the last thirty days, and 19 percent say they had an illness "all the time" over the last thirty days. This jumps to 3.47 diseases for women in their fifties, 30 percent of who feel ill "all the time," and keeps increasing with age. The same pattern is present for men, though at all ages they report fewer illnesses than women. As in many other studies, we find higher self-reported status among men and women, and self-reported health status declines with age. Remarkably, 26 percent of prime-age women, and 28 percent of prime-age men report having missed some days of work due to illness or excessive fatigue over the last thirty days, which suggests that poor health status may in fact have an impact on productivity.

Finally, we report the results for adults on the depression index in table 10.4 Women under fifty score an average of 9.2 on the test while men score 8.1. This is slightly higher than for children (scoring just over 7). The score is higher with greater age; women in their seventies score 10.5, and men in the same age group score 9.0 on average.

10.3.5 Cognitive Health

An interesting feature of this survey is the combination of the rich demographic and economic data (and the experiment) with a detailed cognitive assessment for both children and adults. The test instruments are based on internationally or locally validated measures, and are described in detail in the appendix. Cognitive health was measured by four age groupings: 0 to 30 months, 5 to 14 years, 15 to 49 years, and 50 years and older.

For infants, the Lucknow Development Screen measures psychomotor skills by asking parents if the infant can complete age-appropriate activities, such as recognizing his or her mother, turning his or her head toward a sound, and walking with help or alone (Bhave, Bhargava, and Kumar 2010). Children in our population score below the expected range of the test: table 10.5 shows approximately 47 percent of infants (both boys and girls) can accomplish all of their age-appropriate tasks. This is also slightly less than the clinical sample in Lucknow used to validate the test for India (142 children age six to twenty-four months), where 49.3 percent of children could complete all age-appropriate tasks. This suggests low levels of cognitive development among infants.

For children between the ages of five and fourteen, we used two tests. The Digit Span Test from the PGI Memory Scale (Pershad and Wig 1988) asks the child to repeat four sequences of numbers, three to eight numbers in length forward and two to eight long backward. The maximum number of digits in a row a child can repeat, forward and backward separately, are the child's scores. Table 10.5 shows children in our sample scored on average from 2.1 to 4.2 on the forward test and from 0.3 to 2.5 on the backward span, depending on age and sex.[7]

The block-tapping test from the National Institute of Mental Health and Neurosciences (Rao, Subbakrishna, and Gopukumar 2004) firsts asks children to tap the top of four matchboxes in the same order they just saw a surveyor tap. The child is next asked to repeat the tap in reverse order. Each correct answer on five forward and five reverse tapping tests earns the child one point. The maximum possible is ten points. Well-nourished children in a Bangalore school were measured at 5.6 taps for ages five to seven, and 7.6 taps for ages eight to ten (Kar et al. 2008).

Our youngest respondents score under these means. The average scores increase with age and are higher for boys than for girls. At the age of five to seven years the gender gap is 0.7 points, with girls earning a total of 3.9 points on average and boys earning 4.6. In the eight- to ten-year group, girls earned 7.8 points and boys 9.5 points. For the oldest children, age eleven to

---

7. In a sample of Italian children age four to ten years, the mean (backward and forward) digit span is approximately 4.5 for both boys and girls (Orsini et al. 1987).

Table 10.5   **Cognitive capacity (baseline survey)**

A. Infants 0–30 months

	Female	Male
Lucknow Development Screen (proportion completed all)	0.47	0.47
Number	952	1,083

B. Children

Age (yrs)	Female			Male		
	5–7	8–10	11–14	5–7	8–10	11–14
Forward digit span (maximum out of 8)	2.08	3.35	3.92	2.30	3.60	4.23
Backward digit span (maximum out of 8)	0.34	1.15	1.87	0.48	1.62	2.49
NIMHANS Visuospatial Working Memory (out of 10)	1.97	3.79	4.48	2.29	4.57	5.74
Number	1,342	1,454	1,623	1,560	1,648	1685

C. Adults 15–49 yrs old

	Female	Male
Number	8,087	6,365
Forward digit span (maximum out of 8)	3.34	4.17

	Female	Male
Backward digit span (maximum out of 8)	1.16	2.27
Word recall (out of 10)	6.29	7.04
Sentence reproduction (out of 12)	7.89	8.66
Word pairs (out of 20)	8.46	11.99
Verbal cognition (out of 42)	22.69	27.71

D. 50 yrs old and older

	Female			Male		
Age	50–59	60–69	70+	50–59	60–69	70+
Number	1,290	1,102	666	1,017	1,284	942
Overall cognition (out of 36)	20.63	19.04	16.86	25.35	24.13	22.29

Notes: The Lucknow Development Screen shows the percentage of infants that can do all age-appropriate actions. Age-appropriate actions can be done by 97 percent of children at a given age. There are no validated cognitive tests for thirty months to fifty-nine months. Elderly cognition is the sum of eleven individual tests.

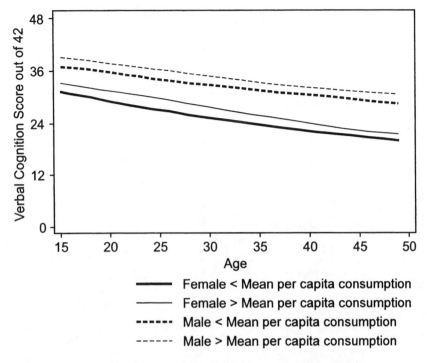

Fig. 10.4   Lowess graph of adult verbal cognition by sex and consumption

fourteen, the gap is widest, with girls earning 10.1 points and boys earning 12.7 on average. Overall, boys performed better than girls by approximately 1.5 points (significant at 99 percent).

For adults (age fifteen to forty-nine), we again used subtests from the PGI Memory Scale. The first test is similar to the children's Digit Span Test with three- to eight-digit forward spans and two- to eight-digit backward spans used. In normative data from Italy, the range for adults age twenty to fifty on the forward span is 6.47 to 6.12 and on the backward span is 5.07 to 4.68 (Monaco et al. 2013). Table 10.5 shows our sample is around two to three digits lower than these on both spans.

The second test asks the individual to listen to a sequence of words read out slowly and then repeat it back after one minute; out of ten possible points, the range of PGI norms for twenty- to fifty-year-olds is 7.6 to 8.3. The third test requires the subject to listen to sentences of increasing length and repeat back phrases from the sentences and can earn the individual twelve points; the range of PGI norms is 7.2 to 7.8. The final test asks the individual to listen to a sequence of word pairs and then to complete the pair when the first word is repeated. The final test is worth twenty points, and the range of PGI norms is 13.8 to 16.6 for the relevant age

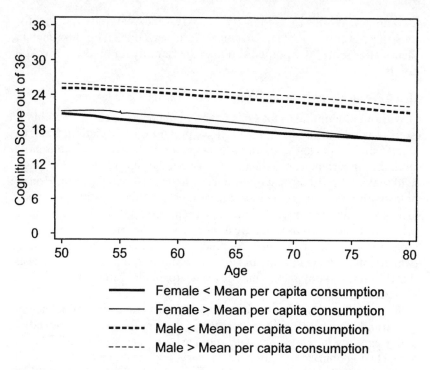

Fig. 10.5 Lowess graph of older adult cognition by sex and consumption

group (Pershad and Wig 1988). This makes the possible total for the final three verbal tests forty-two. The average woman scores twenty-two on this battery of tests, while the average male scores twenty-seven, suggesting the gender gap observed among children persists into adulthood. Figure 10.4 shows that scores are lower for older adults, even in the group under age fifty.

Finally, we measure cognition among adults age fifty and older using the Hindi Mental State Examination (Ganguli et al. 1995), which is based on the Mini-Mental State Examination (MMSE) and validated in India populations. This exam contains eleven different sections involving orientation to time and location, repetition and recall, registration and recognition of objects, figure drawing, and addition (of sevens serially). The maximum score on this battery is 36. In the validation of the test in Ballabargh, a rural setting outside Delhi, with a population over fifty-five years old (mean age 70.7), Ganguli et al. find that the scores varied from 21 among those with no education to 27 among those with some education. Overall, women in our survey age fifty and older score 19.2 points and men score 24. Figure 10.5 shows the decline in women's and men's scores as they age. Table 10.5 shows that women's average scores decline from 20.6 for fifty- to fifty-nine-year-olds to 19 for sixty- to sixty-nine-year-olds and 16.9 for those age seventy and older. Men in their fifties score 25.4 points, men in their sixties score 24.1 points, and men age seventy and older score 22.3 points.

10.3.6 Associations between Anemia and Health Characteristics

Without attempting to make any causal inference (since the causality is likely to run both ways), in table 10.6 we present the associations between anemia and other characteristics separately for each sex. At the household level, there is a significant association between the percentage of the household that is moderately or severely anemic and measures of wealth. Households with more anemic members have slightly lower monthly per capita expenditure and own slightly fewer assets (panel A). Anemia is also more prevalent in households that have a lower level of nutritional variety. This correlation persists (and remains significant) even after controlling for assets (which is strongly significant) and for per capita consumption. This suggests that the prevalence of anemia may be related to quality, rather than quantity, of nutrition.

We also observe many significant associations between individual hemoglobin and other personal characteristics controlling for age, smoking status, and pregnancy in regressions with standard errors clustered at the village level. Hemoglobin is lower for males who never eat meals outside (most adult males are in this category) and is higher among those who eat fewer than three meals daily (most individuals do eat three meals daily—see table 10.4). Interestingly, among females, anemia is not correlated with the number of meals missed.

We also observe a strong pattern of associations between hemoglobin and measures of physical fitness. Higher hemoglobin is associated with higher BMI, higher completion rates for the Queens College Step Test and the balance tests, faster time in walking four meters, faster times standing up and sitting down (for males only), and a higher number of activities of daily living that can be done.

Table 10.4 also shows that higher hemoglobin is associated with better self-reported health, fewer number of illnesses reported, and having an illness "all the time" in the past thirty days. There is, however, no relationship between hemoglobin and the depression index (which was fairly uniformly low among males and females). Table 10.7 shows the relationship between anemia and self-reported health is consistent across all age groups except infants when controlling for BMI, age, sex, consumption, and asset ownership. For respondents over age fifty, anemia is also associated with objective measures of health such as longer times taken to stand and sit five times and being able to do fewer activities of daily living.

We also look at the relationship between anemia status (mild, moderate, and severe) and other measured characteristics. We note that BMI as discussed

Table 10.6   Associations between hemoglobin and personal characteristics (baseline survey)

A. Household level

Association between variable and anemia	Coefficient	SE	N
Monthly per capita consumption (INR 000s)	−0.005***	0.002	5,478
Number assets reported owned (0 to 8)	−0.018***	0.002	5,880
Household dietary diversity score (0 to 12)	−0.013***	0.002	5,200

B. Individual level

	Female			Male		
Association between variable and hemoglobin level	coefficient	SE	N	coefficient	SE	N
Never eats meals outside home (% yes)	−0.02	(0.05)	9,282	−0.22***	(0.04)	9,555
Eats less than 3 meals daily	0.01	(0.04)	15,651	0.25***	(0.05)	16,527
BMI	0.03***	(0.00)	15,282	0.17***	(0.01)	16,170
Completed Queens College Step Test	0.20***	(0.05)	5,072	0.38***	(0.04)	7,598
Completed all 3 balance tests (%)	0.15**	(0.05)	5,984	0.47***	(0.09)	4,102
Time taken to walk 4 meters (seconds)	−0.07***	(0.02)	6,545	−0.11***	(0.03)	4,379
Time taken to sit & stand up 5 times (seconds)	−0.01	(0.01)	6,379	−0.04***	(0.01)	4,287
Number of ADL that can be done (out of 6)	0.05**	(0.02)	9,136	0.18***	(0.02)	9,518
Self-reported health is good or very good (%)	0.19***	(0.03)	15,551	0.60***	(0.06)	16,377
Number illnesses over last 30 days (out of 10 asked)	−0.04***	(0.01)	15,585	−0.13***	(0.01)	16,420
Had any illness "all the time" over the last 30 days	−0.17***	(0.04)	15,590	−0.52***	(0.06)	16,411
Depression index (6–18, higher more depressed)	−0.01	(0.01)	11,387	−0.01	(0.01)	11,846
Lucknow Development Screen—infants	0.35**	(0.11)	699	0.10	0.12	806
Forward digit span—children 5+	0.08***	(0.01)	4,377	0.05***	0.01	4,868
Forward digit span—adults	0.03*	(0.01)	6,076	0.12***	0.02	6,254
HMSE—adults 50+	0.04***	(0.01)	2,963	0.12***	0.02	3,138

Notes: Anemia is defined as percentage of people in the household being moderately or severely anemic. Sixty percent of households have > 0 moderately or severely anemic members. Coefficients reported are from regressions where the outcome variable is hemoglobin level (g/dL) and controls include age, smoker, pregnant. Standard errors clustered by village.

***Significant at the 1 percent level.

**Significant at the 5 percent level.

*Significant at the 10 percent level.

Table 10.7   Anemia and physical health

	(1)	(2)	(3)	(4)	(5)	(6)	(7)
					Time to walk 4 m	Time to stand & sit 5 times	Number ADLs can do
	Self-reported health is good or very good						
Age (yrs)	Under 5	5 to > 15	15 to < 50	50+	50+	50+	50+
Has moderate or severe anemia	0.01	-0.02**	-0.04***	-0.04***	0.07	0.28**	-0.13***
	(0.01)	(0.01)	(0.01)	(0.02)	(0.06)	(0.13)	(0.04)
Age in years	0.04***	0.00**	-0.01***	-0.00***	0.06***	0.13***	-0.05***
	(0.01)	(0.00)	(0.00)	(0.00)	(0.00)	(0.01)	(0.00)
Female	0.03***	-0.01	-0.10***	-0.14***	0.97***	1.85***	-0.81***
	(0.01)	(0.01)	(0.01)	(0.01)	(0.04)	(0.11)	(0.03)
Monthly consumption pp (INR 000s)	-0.01	0	0	0	0	0.01	0
	(0.01)	(0.00)	(0.00)	(0.00)	(0.01)	(0.03)	(0.01)
Number assets owned	0.01**	0.00*	0.01***	0.01***	0	-0.01	0.02**
	(0.00)	(0.00)	(0.00)	(0.00)	(0.01)	(0.03)	(0.01)
BMI	0.01***	0.00*	0	0	0	0.04***	-0.03***
	(0.00)	(0.00)	(0.00)	(0.00)	(0.01)	(0.01)	(0.00)
Constant	0.67***	0.90***	1.01***	1.06***	-0.31	3.22***	8.46***
	(0.04)	(0.02)	(0.02)	(0.06)	(0.23)	(0.51)	(0.15)
Observations	3,561	9,304	14,227	6,111	5,996	5,843	6,066
R-squared	0.022	0.004	0.044	0.035	0.158	0.105	0.204

Notes: Includes controls for percent others in household anemic; household is Scheduled Caste, Scheduled Tribe, or Other Backward Class; and missing consumption or missing assets, which were set to mean levels. Robust standard errors in parentheses.

***Significant at the 1 percent level.

**Significant at the 5 percent level.

*Significant at the 10 percent level.

earlier is in the healthy range on average. Anemia rates seem high in relation to this relatively acceptable physical status. Table 10.8 shows that, unsurprisingly, correlates of anemia include asset ownership, consumption per capita, own BMI, age, and education. Perhaps more interestingly, controlling for everything else, household dietary diversity is correlated with anemia. Along with the fact that this is not a *very* poor population and BMI is acceptable, this suggests that anemia may be due to micronutrient deficiency despite consumption of sufficient calories.

Finally, there are also strong associations between hemoglobin and cognition for all age groups. Higher hemoglobin is associated with slightly higher LDS scores for female infants (the sign is the same, but not significant, for male infants). Higher hemoglobin is also associated with higher cognition for children age five and older and adults of all ages. Though the effect is significant for adults under age fifty, the size is small (0.005 for female and 0.01 for male adults). Table 10.9 shows that lagging infant development and worse memory are also associated with anemia (mild, moderate, and severe) in infants and children, controlling for consumption. These relationships are robust to household fixed effects for children above age five, though they become smaller. Table 10.10 shows a similar pattern for adults and older adults. Anemia is significantly associated with worse memory and cognition after controlling for BMI, age, sex, diet, consumption, and assets—though the association is not robust to household fixed effects.

In summary, the baseline survey paints a picture similar to other surveys of rural populations in India. Anemia is ubiquitous, particularly among women, as are various symptoms of poor health, frequent self-reported diseases, and poor performance on physical fitness tests. What is striking, however, is that this is a population that is neither particularly poor by the standard of rural India (the average per capita consumption is INR 56 per day), and the overall level of nutrition seems to be satisfactory, judging from average BMI (though a substantial fraction of people do not eat three meals a day). There is no proof that anemia is associated with poor nutrition, but it is strongly correlated with dietary diversity among both men and women. There is thus some indication from the baseline that anemia is related to micronutrient availability. In turn, anemia is associated with poor health outcomes and poor cognition outcomes among people of all ages and both genders. Moreover, all households surveyed buy salt, and they frequently buy iodized salt. This suggests that the introduction of salt that is fortified with iodine may be a promising way to fight anemia.

In the second part of this chapter, we report the results of a randomized controlled trial we conducted to determine what the take-up of double-fortified salt would be at various prices, and whether the way information is shared with the villagers would affect this take-up.

Table 10.8   Anemia and household dietary diversity

Dependent variable: Anemic (any) Sex	(1) All	(2) All	(3) Female	(4) Male	(5) All	(6) Female	(7) Male
Household dietary diversity score (/100)	−1.57***	−0.52**	−0.18	−0.89***	−0.47**	−0.17	−0.83***
	(0.18)	(0.21)	(0.29)	(0.29)	(0.21)	(0.30)	(0.29)
Age		0.00***	0.00***	0.00***	0.00***	0.00***	0.01***
		(0.00)	(0.00)	(0.00)	(0.00)	(0.00)	(0.00)
BMI					−0.01***	0	−0.02***
					(0.00)	(0.00)	(0.00)
Female		0.17***			0.18***		
		(0.01)			(0.01)		
Monthly consumption per person (INR 000s)		0	0	0	0	0	0
		(0.00)	(0.01)	(0.01)	(0.00)	(0.01)	(0.01)
Food as percentage of monthly expenditure		0.03	0.06*	0	0.03	0.05	0.02
		(0.02)	(0.03)	(0.03)	(0.02)	(0.03)	(0.03)
Number assets reported own		−0.02***	−0.02***	−0.02***	−0.02***	−0.02***	−0.02***
		(0.00)	(0.00)	(0.00)	(0.00)	(0.00)	(0.00)
Household is SC, ST, or OBC		−0.01**	−0.02**	−0.01	−0.01**	−0.02**	0
		(0.01)	(0.01)	(0.01)	(0.01)	(0.01)	(0.01)
Constant	0.53***	0.34***	0.48***	0.37***	0.45***	0.48***	0.64***
	(0.01)	(0.02)	(0.03)	(0.03)	(0.02)	(0.03)	(0.03)
Observations	34,221	28,540	14,825	13,715	27,949	14,521	13,428
R-squared	0.002	0.061	0.022	0.047	0.063	0.02	0.064

Notes: Columns (2) through (7) include controls for missing assets, missing consumption, and caste, which were set to means.

Robust standard errors in parentheses.

***Significant at the 1 percent level.

**Significant at the 5 percent level.

*Significant at the 10 percent level.

Table 10.9   Anemia and cognition—children

Dependent Variable	(1)	(2)	(3)	(4)	(5)	(6)
	LDS 0 to 30 months		Forward digit span 5 to < 15 yrs		Backward digit span 5 to < 15 yrs	
Any anemia (mild, moderate, or severe)	−0.07**	−0.02	−0.16***	−0.09*	−0.14***	−0.09*
	(0.03)	(0.27)	(0.04)	(0.06)	(0.03)	(0.05)
BMI	0.01**	−0.01	−0.01	−0.03**	0.01	−0.02*
	(0.00)	(0.03)	(0.01)	(0.01)	(0.01)	(0.01)
Age	0	0.06	0.28***	0.29***	0.26***	0.26***
	(0.03)	(0.18)	(0.01)	(0.01)	(0.01)	(0.01)
Female	0.01	−0.05	−0.23***	−0.27***	−0.42***	−0.48***
	(0.03)	(0.22)	(0.03)	(0.05)	(0.03)	(0.04)
Household dietary diversity score (/100)	0.61		4.10***		6.88***	
	(0.95)		(1.35)		(1.16)	
Monthly consumption per person (INR 000s)	0		0.02		0	
	(0.02)		(0.02)		(0.02)	
Number of assets	0.03***		0.11***		0.15***	
	(0.01)		(0.01)		(0.01)	
Household is SC, ST, or OBC	0.02		0.10**		0.16***	
	(0.03)		(0.04)		(0.04)	
Constant	0.20**	0.49	−0.64***	0.48**	−2.67***	−1.05***
	(0.10)	(0.65)	(0.15)	(0.20)	(0.12)	(0.18)
Household fixed effects	No	Yes	No	Yes	No	Yes
Observations	1,340	1,340	9,170	9,170	9,180	9,180
R-squared	0.04	0.92	0.25	0.64	0.31	0.68

Notes: Includes control for currently in school, number animals own, missing school enrollment, missing assets, animals, caste, and HDDS. Robust standard errors in parentheses.

***Significant at the 1 percent level.

**Significant at the 5 percent level.

*Significant at the 10 percent level.

Table 10.10 Anemia and cognition—adults

	(1)	(2)	(3)	(4)	(5)	(6)
Dependent variable	Forward digit span 15 to < 50		Backward digit span 15 to < 50		HMSE score 50+	
Age (yrs)						
Any anemia (mild, moderate, or severe)	−0.06**	−0.05	−0.09***	−0.05	−0.67***	−0.21
	(0.03)	(0.05)	(0.03)	(0.04)	(0.14)	(0.33)
BMI	0.03***	0.02***	0.03***	0.01**	0.11***	0.07
	(0.00)	(0.01)	(0.00)	(0.01)	(0.02)	(0.05)
Age	−0.03***	−0.03***	−0.04***	−0.04***	−0.12***	−0.16***
	(0.00)	(0.00)	(0.00)	(0.00)	(0.01)	(0.02)
Female	−0.80***	−0.84***	−1.06***	−1.12***	−5.01***	−5.36***
	(0.03)	(0.04)	(0.03)	(0.03)	(0.11)	(0.25)
Household dietary diversity score (/100)	4.48***		4.52***		29.98***	
	(1.05)		(1.12)		(4.71)	
Monthly consumption pp (INR 000s)	0.02*		0.01		0.10**	
	(0.01)		(0.01)		(0.04)	
Number of assets	0.15***		0.21***		0.39***	
	(0.01)		(0.01)		(0.04)	
Household is SC, ST, or OBC	0.21***		0.28***		0.63***	
	(0.04)		(0.04)		(0.15)	
Constant	3.38***	4.75***	1.45***	3.29***	25.91***	33.40***
	(0.10)	(0.11)	(0.10)	(0.11)	(0.69)	(1.88)
Household fixed effects	No	Yes	No	Yes	No	Yes
Observations	14,109	14,109	14,097	14,097	5,838	5,838
R-squared	0.16	0.56	0.26	0.62	0.30	0.79

Notes: Also includes control for number animals own, missing assets, animals, caste, and HDDS. Robust standard errors in parentheses.

***Significant at the 1 percent level.

**Significant at the 5 percent level.

*Significant at the 10 percent level.

10.4 Pricing Experiment

10.4.1 Design of Experiment

Double-fortified salt had not been marketed in rural Bihar before this trial. Our pricing experiment, which was conducted in October and November 2011, was designed to assess household willingness to pay for DFS as a first stage in our larger research agenda. As the benefits of iron fortification may not be obvious—even to users—the subsidy to encourage adoption may need to be large enough to make it competitive with iodized salt. Working in one district of Bihar (Bhojpur), we randomly selected forty-three villages in Behea block (an administrative area smaller than the district) and in cooperation with Tata Chemicals we stocked Tata Salt Plus in small private stores (known as kirana shops) and Public Distribution System (PDS) shops. Within these forty-three villages, we randomized assignment of information treatments at the village level and pricing/outlet assignment at the household level. Each village was randomly assigned to receive one of three information campaigns:

1. a basic campaign consisting solely of printed materials displayed at the participating stores;
2. the full Tata campaign, which included street plays and group activities similar to those Tata conducts in other markets, in addition to the basic campaign; or
3. household visits by the government's ASHA health workers, in addition to the basic campaign and the full Tata campaign.

After the campaign was conducted, our team distributed vouchers for DFS purchase to ninety-nine households in each village and conducted a short survey asking about previous salt usage, socioeconomic status, and knowledge of DFS. The net price after discount was INR 12, 11, 10, 9, or 8 per kilogram. Within each of the villages, anyone was free to purchase one-kilogram packets of DFS at the kirana store for INR 17, the price in 2011 without any subsidy. Coupons either showed consumers the full price at local kirana shops and offered them a subsidized price at the government Price Distribution System (PDS) shop, or were valid at the same price (full or various levels of subsidy) at both the PDS shop and the selected kirana(s), in order to assess purchase habits and take-up in both distribution channels. In all, there were eleven types of vouchers (see table 10.11) distributed; all were valid for four weeks.

Our data collection activities included both household survey and administrative data. When the first vouchers were handed out, households were asked to complete a short survey including simple questions about use of PDS and kirana stores and the wealth of the household. The location of these households were also recorded with a handheld GPS device. In addi-

Table 10.11   Pricing experiment vouchers

	Voucher type	PDS price	Kirana price
Lower price only at PDS shops; MRP at kirana	1	8	
	2	9	
	3	10	17
	4	11	
	5	12	
Same price at kirana and PDS shops	6	8	8
	7	9	9
	8	10	10
	9	11	11
	10	12	12
No discount	11	17	17

tion, data were collected on DFS sales and voucher use from the PDS and kiranas, and DFS consumption and satisfaction, as well as possible resale, by households.

Table 10A.2 presents the results of checks of the household-level randomization. Each household characteristic listed was the dependent variable in an ordinary least squares (OLS) regression with ten binary variables indicating voucher type as independent variables along with a covariate for the village. We present the test statistics for the joint test of significance for all of the voucher-type independent variables. This allows us to detect a correlation, if any, between the voucher type assigned to the household and its characteristics. The hypothesis of joint significance can be rejected for all but one of the characteristics: voucher types predict the number of buffaloes a household owns. They cannot, however, predict other measures of economic well-being, such as ownership of land, asset ownership, better construction materials, number of goats owned, or total number of animals owned.

Table 10A.3 presents the results of checks of the village-level randomization of the information campaigns. Again, each row presents the results from a separate regression in which the dependent variable is a household characteristic and the independent dichotomous variables indicate the type of information campaign. Standard errors are clustered at the village level. The fifteen villages that were given the Tata campaign have slightly fewer (−0.22) children per household, are less often constructed of bricks (rather than mud), and own 0.33 fewer animals than households in the fourteen villages that received only the basic information campaign. While 97 percent of households report that they ever buy goods from the PDS, this share is 98 percent for households in the fourteen villages that got all three information campaigns. Since the survey where people were asked about anemia was conducted after the information campaigns, the 5 percentage point increase in ever hearing about anemia in the Basic + Tata + ASHA group likely reflects the success of ASHAs in delivering the health message.

10.4.2 Results of Pricing Experiment

Overall, 4,179 vouchers were distributed, of which 1,237, or 30 percent, were redeemed. Total sales of DFS were 1,808; voucher sales thus comprised 68 percent of total sales. There were 571 purchases of DFS without vouchers (32 percent of total sales). Take-up for those given full-price vouchers was approximately 8 percent.

Table 10.12 presents the results of the pricing experiment. Columns (1) through (5) estimate purchases in both types of stores combined when the amount of the discount offered was from INR 5 to INR 9. At every discount level, total take-up is higher when the discount is available at both outlets than when it is only available at PDS. Offering a discount in the PDS increased total household purchases more than offering it in the private shops (17 pp vs. 14 pp). Each rupee discounted from the price in the PDS increased household purchases by approximate 2.2 pp, while each rupee discount in the private shops increased sales by 2.0 pp. This result is robust to the inclusion of the information campaign in the regressions (column [5]). Column (3) suggests that the impact of the discount is linear over the discount amounts we tested.

The final two columns measure take-up by store type— PDS (column [6]) or kirana (column [7]). These models show that discounting sales simultaneously in both store types increased sales more in private shops than in the PDS shops. When looking at the subset of vouchers that offered the same discount in both PDS and private shops, we can see in figure 10.6 that vouchers are more than twice as likely to be used in the private shops.

Comparing figure 10.6 and figure 10.7 also allows us to see purchase responses at the intensive margin. For example, when a discounted price of INR 8 is available at both types of stores, total take-up is 45 percent; when the same discount is available at only PDS, total take-up falls to 29 percent. At any discount level, the shift from kirana to PDS is incomplete when the discount is constrained to the PDS. Although people are sensitive to price and shift to PDS when the discount is constrained, not all do so. Many households simply do not purchase DFS at all. This is reminiscent of the results from our earlier study (Banerjee et al. 2011), where households were not willing to switch millers permanently to take advantage of the opportunity to fortify grain. Sales appear to be quite sensitive to price, particularly when it falls from INR 10—the price at which regular iodized salt is often sold—to INR 9. When DFS is priced

Table 10.12   Impact of price and information campaign on take-up (price experiment)

Variables	(1) Purchased anywhere	(2) Purchased anywhere	(3) Purchased anywhere	(4) Purchased anywhere	(5) Purchased anywhere	(6) Purchased at PDS	(7) Purchased at kirana
Discount given at PDS (any)	0.166*** (0.03)						
Discount given at kirana (any)	0.136*** (0.02)						
PDS discount amount (INR 5 to 9)		0.022*** (0.00)	0.031** (0.01)		0.022*** (0.00)	0.022*** (0.00)	−0.001 (0.00)
Kirana discount amount (INR 5 to 9)		0.020*** (0.00)	0.017 (0.01)		0.020*** (0.00)	−0.014*** (0.00)	0.034*** (0.00)
PDS discount squared			−0.001 (0.00)				
Kirana discount amount squared			0 (0.00)				
Info campaign: Basic + Tata				−0.002 (0.05)	−0.002 (0.05)	−0.011 (0.05)	0.009 (0.02)
Info campaign: Basic + Tata & ASHA				0.021 (0.06)	0.02 (0.06)	0.02 (0.05)	0.001 (0.03)
Sales at full price (mean)	0.084 [0.28]					0.047 [0.21]	0.037 [0.19]
Observations	4,179	4,179	4,179	4,179	4,179	4,179	4,179
R-squared	0.042	0.05	0.05	0.001	0.05	0.029	0.126

Notes: Table reports results from OLS regressions, in which purchase is the outcome variable. Robust standard errors in parentheses, clustered at the village level. Standard deviations of means in square brackets. Omitted information campaign category is Basic Campaign.

***Significant at the 1 percent level.

**Significant at the 5 percent level.

*Significant at the 10 percent level.

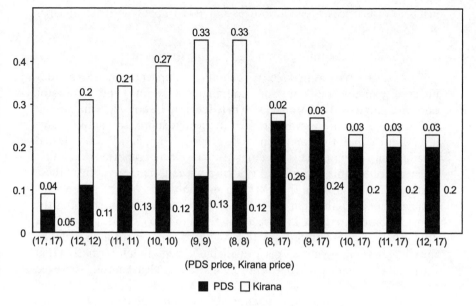

Fig. 10.6   All vouchers: Total take-up by voucher and store type

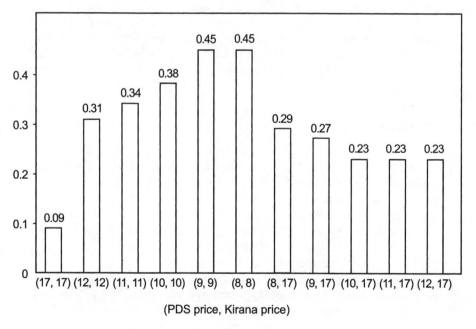

Fig. 10.7   All vouchers: Total take-up by voucher type

just below the price of regular iodized salt, it is probably seen as a cheaper way to buy iodized salt.

10.4.3 Results of the Information Campaign Experiment

The last variable row in table 10.12 shows the impact on take-up of adding a more involved information campaign (led by Tata) and a door-to-door campaign by ASHA workers. There seems to be no effect whatsoever. The estimates are not very precise due to the low sample size at the village level, but the point estimates indicate fairly low impact. We also tested whether information affects price elasticity (results not reported) but found no evidence for this. Additional evidence we collected strengthens these findings. For example, in the ASHA group, only 1 percent of households had heard of DFS through an ASHA. In our first survey, shortly after the information campaigns, 21 percent of the households had heard about Tata salt. They were more likely to have heard about it through a play in the villages where a play was performed, but it seems that information that the product actually existed was not a constraint, at least among surveyed households. Among people who had heard about the salt in the first survey, 35 percent knew it was "healthy," 31 percent knew that it contains iron, and 25 percent knew that it contains iodine. However, only 6 percent reported that it helps fight anemia, and 4 percent that it may help fight common diseases. By the end of the experiment, 68 percent of households knew about DFS, though most still did not know what it stood for or how it differed from regular salt. By and large, it seems that households appear less interested in the specific features of Tata Salt Plus than in the fact that it gives them access to a brand name product at a price that they consider affordable.

10.5 Conclusion

The baseline survey indicated that anemia is prevalent, and may be both caused by and a cause of poverty: households with low expenditure per capita and with low diversity in their diet are more likely to have an anemic member. Anemic individuals are weaker, sicker, and perform worse on cognitive tests than nonanemic individuals. Finding a way to solve this issue on a large scale is important for policy, and would also give us an opportunity for the first time to reliably measure the impact of a plausible instrument to fight IDA on health and economic outcomes.

Double-fortified salt, if priced sufficiently low, seems to have some promise. At a discount of 55 percent, it appears that take-up of DFS was reasonably high, even though households did not quite understand why Tata Plus was more desirable than any other type of salt.

A caveat is that there may have been a Hawthorne effect, since the very fact of distributing a voucher (even for the full price) may have made households aware of the product and may have given them a motive to try it out. Moreover, the sensitivity to a reduction in price through a voucher may be larger than that of a low price offered in the shop if households feel that they have gotten a bargain. In the full-scale experiment, salt was made available at INR 9 per kg, the price that was likely to maximize take-up according to the price experiment. An information campaign similar to the basic campaign was run in every village by a group subcontracted by Tata. We are monitoring take-up, and so far (on a relative small sample) the take-up is only about 10 percent on average, much lower than in the price experiment. This may come from teething problems at the beginning of the program (it took awhile to supply all the shops, and to renew their stocks when they ran low), as well as from poor implementation of the information campaign at this large scale. Tata also reported to us that a take-up of 10 percent is standard for a new product (although this one is discounted).

Appendix

Description of Cognitive Tests

The cognition modules used in the baseline survey drew from a series of tests validated on Indian populations to assess respondents' cognitive ability and awareness. Four different batteries of tests were used to assess these characteristics among respondents of different age groups: infants (1–30 months), children (5–14 years), adults (15–49 years) and elderly (50 years and older). All cognition tests were conducted in isolation with the respondent, or in an isolated area overseen by a guardian, in order to maximize concentration. These tests were also conducted in the local language, Bhojpuri, to facilitate a clear understanding of the exercise.

Infants (1–30 months)

The infant cognition module is entirely based on the Lucknow Development Screen (LDS), a screening tool validated to assess the psychomotor skills of infants. The LDS was adapted from the Bayley Scales for an Indian population in Lucknow, Uttar Pradesh, by Professors Bhave, Bhargava, and Kumar from the CSM Medical University (Bhave, Bhargava, and Kumar 2010). In this test, the mother of the child is asked about the infant's ability to perform a set of tasks (from the infant's capacity to thrust his or her arms and legs forward in play while lying to the infant's ability to walk up stairs and down stairs with help), with the number of tasks asked about depending

Table 10A.1   Thresholds for determining "any" anemia

Age or gender group	Hemoglobin threshold (g/dL)	Smokers (g/dL)
Children (0–4 yrs)	11.0	—
Children (5–11 yrs)	11.5	—
Children (12–14 yrs)	12.0	12.3
Pregnant females	11.0	11.3
Nonpregnant females (15 yrs & older)	12.0	12.3
Adult males	13.0	13.3

Notes: Mild anemia refers to hemoglobin between 10 and 11 g/dL for young children and between 11 and 12 g/dL for everyone else. Moderate anemia is defined as hemoglobin between 7 and 10 g/dL for young children and between 8 and 11 g/dL for older children and adults. Severe anemia is 7 g/dL and below for children and 8 g/dL and below for older children and adults. All of these benchmarks are adjusted for smoking and pregnancy (as reflected in the table) when determining if an individual's hemoglobin measurement reflects mild, moderate, or severe anemia. A dash indicates threshold not available for this age group.

Table 10A.2   Household-level balance checks by voucher type assigned

Dependent variable	N	Test: Voucher dummies are jointly significant	
Number adults in household	4,178	2.51	*F*-stat
		(0.12)	*p*-value
Number children in household	4,178	0.86	
		(0.57)	
Children enrolled in school (%)	4,178	0.84	
		(0.59)	
Household has a below poverty line card (any type)	4,178	0.75	
		(0.68)	
Ever shops at public distribution system shop	4,179	0.54	
		(0.86)	
Household owns other land	4,151	1.02	
		(0.42)	
Number assets owned (out of 8 asked about)	4,178	0.73	
		(0.70)	
House construction includes bricks (not only mud)	4,178	0.76	
		(0.67)	
Number buffaloes owned	4,155	3.41	
		(0.00)	
Number goats owned	4,135	1.29	
		(0.23)	
Total number animals owned	4,179	1.41	
		(0.17)	
Ever heard of anemia	4,178	0.21	
		(1.00)	

Notes: Table reports *F*-statistics and *p*-values for a test of joint significance of voucher-type dummies after OLS regressions in which the voucher assignment is used to predict the characteristic on the left. The regressions also include a covariate for the village, as voucher assignment was done within the village. Households were asked if they owned these assets: TV, motorcycle, music player, gas/kerosene stove, mobile phone, bicycle, chair, cots/beds. Total animals includes cows, buffalos, goats, chickens, and pigs.

Table 10A.3   **Village-level balance checks by information campaign**

	Basic campaign (mean)	Basic + Tata (diff. from basic)	Basic + Tata + ASHA (diff. from basic)	Test: Basic = (B + T) + (B + T + A)
Villages in sample	14	15	14	
Households in sample	1356	1455	1368	
Average village population	1945	−441	−53	0.32
(administrative data)	[1349]	(465)	(537)	(0.58)
Number adults in household	4.77	−0.25	−0.09	1.69
	[3.06]	(0.16)	(0.16)	(0.20)
Number children in household	3.5	−0.22*	−0.16	3.99
	[2.66]	(0.13)	(0.10)	(0.05)
Children enrolled in school	0.62	−0.01	0.00	0.01
(%)	[0.39]	(0.03)	(0.02)	(0.94)
Household has a below poverty	0.56	0.06	0.06	2.35
line card (any type)	[0.50]	(0.05)	(0.05)	(0.13)
Ever shops at public	0.97	0.01	0.01*	3.56
distribution system shop	[0.16]	(0.01)	(0.01)	(0.07)
Household owns other land	0.61	−0.04	−0.07	1.13
	[0.49]	(0.07)	(0.06)	(0.29)
Number assets owned (out of	3.59	−0.31	0.01	1.14
8 asked about)	[2.10]	(0.19)	(0.15)	(0.29)
House construction includes	0.77	−0.08**	−0.02	2.51
bricks (not only mud)	[0.42]	(0.04)	(0.04)	(0.12)
Number animals owned	2	−0.33**	−0.12	3.19
	[4.69]	(0.14)	(0.15)	(0.08)
Ever heard of anemia	0.09	0.02	0.05**	3.75
	[0.28]	(0.02)	(0.02)	(0.06)

Notes: Differences shown are the coefficient on "Basic + Tata" or "Basic + Tata + ASHA" from separate OLS regressions using household-level data and standard errors clustered at the village level. Final column shows F-statistic and p-value for test of joint significance following the regression. Households were asked if they owned these assets: TV, motorcycle, music player, gas/kerosene stove, mobile phone, bicycle, chair, cots/beds. Total animals includes cows, buffalos, goats, chickens, and pigs.

Standard deviation of mean in square brackets and standard error of difference in parentheses in difference columns.

***Significant at the 1 percent level.
**Significant at the 5 percent level.
*Significant at the 10 percent level.

on the age of the child. Therefore, this test requires having accurate information on the age of the infant (in months).

The LDS used for the baseline followed the 97 percent screen; that is, it only inquired about tasks that can be expected to be performed by 97 percent of infants of the infant's age group. All the tasks in the LDS and the age up to which this task is applicable for the 97 percent screening are listed later. The metric from this test is the percentage of children who can perform all of their 97 percent screen tasks. (See table 10A.4.)

Table 10A.4   Lucknow Development Screen

Task	Screening age (in months)
Arms and legs thrust in play	1
Lateral head movement	1
Follows moving person	1
Social smile	3
Holds head steady	4
Recognizes mother	4
Laughs aloud	5
Reaches for dangling ring	5
Turns head to sound	6
Turns supine to prone	8
Sits alone steadily	8
Retains two things in two hands	9
Raises self to sitting	10
Playful response to mirror image	10
Says *da-da*, *ma-ma*	10
Waves *ta-ta*	11
Picks up small things	11
Stands by leaning on furniture	11
Inhibits on command	13
Walks with help	13
Stands alone	16
Speaks two words with meaning	18
Stands up	18
Walks alone	18
Gestures for wants	19
Speaks sentences of two words	25
Walks up and down stairs with help	25

Children (5–14 years)

The child cognition module is based on tests taken from two different batteries. First, it uses the digit span tests from the PGI Memory Scale (PGIMS), a memory scale developed for the Indian population by Professors Dwarka Pershad and N. N. Wig from the Post Graduate Institute of Medical Education and Research, Chandigarh. The digit span test involves a respondent repeating a sequence of numbers articulated by the surveyor. The reverse sequence questions expect the respondent to repeat the numbers articulated in reverse order. The forward sequence begins with a sequence of three numbers and goes up to a sequence of eight numbers. The reverse sequence begins with a sequence of two numbers and proceeds up to a sequence of eight. Two scores are awarded for the maximum number of digits that can be recalled.

The second test in this module is the taken from the visuospatial working memory span task (block-tapping test) from the NIMHANS child neuro-

Table 10A.5   **Adult verbal cognition subtests and scoring**

Test	Maximum points
Word recall	10
Sentence reproduction	12
Word pairs	20
Total points	42

psychology tests. This battery of tests was developed by Professors Kar, Rao, Chandramouli, and Thennarau from the National Institute of Mental Health and Neurosciences (NIMHANS) in Bangalore. The box-tapping test involves the surveyor tapping a set of four matchboxes in a particular order that the respondent is expected to replicate. In the reverse tapping test, the respondent is expected to tap the boxes in the reverse order. There are five tests in each direction and a point is awarded for each correct sequence, making ten the total number of possible points.

Adults (15–49 years)

The adult cognition module was based on four subtests taken from the PGIMS module. The first subtest is the digit span test, which is identical to the one used for the child cognition module. The second is a word recall test, which involves two sets of five words each. Each set of words is recited slowly, and the respondent is asked to remember as many words as possible after a one-minute interval. Each correctly remembered word is given one point. The third is a sentence recall test, where three sentences of increasing length are used. Each phrase correctly recalled from a sentence scores one point. Unlike the word test, there is no interval for recalling the sentence. The last subtest involves the use of related and unrelated word pairs. The respondent is verbally told a list of word pairs at the start of the test. The respondent is then expected to recall the pair of each word recited thereafter. Each correctly recalled pair scores a point. These tests and their maximum scores are listed in table 10A.5.

Older Adults (50 years and older)

The older adult cognition module is based entirely on the Hindi Mental State Examination (HMSE), a version of the Mini-Mental State Examination that has been modified for Indian populations. The HMSE was developed by Professors Ganguli and Ratcliffe from the University of Pittsburgh, in collaboration with the Centre of Ageing Research in New Delhi, India. The HMSE is made up of several different subtests. All the subtests check for basic cognitive awareness and alertness. The scoring for these sections is shown in table 10A.6.

Table 10A.6   Older adult cognition subtests and scoring

Question type	Maximum score
Orientation to time	5
Orientation to location	5
Registration of three objects	3
Days of the week (in reverse order)	5
Recall	3
Ability to recognize objects	2
Sentence repetition	1
Following command	1
Three-step command	3
Figure drawing	3
Attention and calculation (serial sevens)	5
Total score	36

References

Allen, L., B. de Benoist, O. Dary, and R. Hurrell. 2006. *Guidelines on Food Fortification with Micronutrients.* World Health Organization, Food and Agriculture Organization of the United Nations.

Andersson, M., P. Thankachan, S. Muthayya, R. B. Goud, A. V. Kurpad, R. F. Hurrell, and M. B. Zimmermann. 2008. "Dual Fortification of Salt with Iodine and Iron: A Randomized, Double-Blind, Controlled Trial of Micronized Ferric Pyrophosphate and Encapsulated Ferrous Fumarate in Southern India." *American Journal of Clinical Nutrition* 88 (5): 1378–87.

Arnold, F., S. Parasuraman, P. Arokiasamy, and M. Kothari. 2009. "Nutrition in India: National Family Health Survey (NFHS-3), India, 2005–06." *International Institute for Population Sciences* 43.

Banerjee, A., A. Deaton, and E. Duflo. 2004. "Health, Health Care, and Economic Development: Wealth, Health, and Health Services in rural Rajasthan." *American Economic Review* 94 (2):326.

Banerjee, A., E. Duflo, and R. Glennerster. 2011. "Is Decentralized Iron Fortification a Feasible Option to Fight Anemia Among the Poorest?" In *Explorations in the Economics of Aging*, edited by David A. Wise, 317–44. Chicago: University of Chicago Press.

Basta, S. S., Soekirman, D. Karyadi, and N. S. Scrimshaw. 1979. "Iron Deficiency Anemia and the Productivity of Adult Males in Indonesia." *American Journal of Clinical Nutrition* 32 (4): 916–25.

Bhagowalia, P., D. Headey, and S. Kadiyala. 2012. "Agriculture, Income, and Nutrition Linkages in India." Technical Report, International Food Policy Research Institute. Discussion Paper 01195.

Bhave, A., R. Bhargava, and R. Kumar. 2010. "Development and Validation of a New Lucknow Development Screen for Indian Children Aged 6 Months to 2 Years." *Journal of Child Neurology* 25 (1): 57–60.

Brahmam, G., K. Nair, A. Laxmaiah, C. Gal Reddy, S. Ranganathan, M. Vishnuvardhana Rao, A. Naidu et al. 2000. "Community Trials with Iron and Iodine Fortified Salt (Double Fortified Salt)." In *Proceedings of the 8th World Salt Symposium*, Volume 2, 955–60. Amsterdam: Elsevier.

Chatterjee, S., P. Chatterjee, and A. Bandyopadhyay. 2005. "Validity of Queen's College Step Test for Estimation of Maximum Oxygen Uptake in Female Students." *Indian Journal of Medical Research* 121 (1): 32–5.

Chatterjee, S., P. Chatterjee, P. Mukherjee, and A. Bandyopadhyay. 2004. "Validity of Queen's College Step Test for Use with Young Indian Men." *British Journal of Sports Medicine* 38 (3): 289–91.

Chaudhury, N., J. Hammer, M. Kremer, K. Muralidharan, and F. H. Rogers. 2006. "Missing in Action: Teacher and Health Worker Absence in Developing Countries." *Journal of Economic Perspectives* 20 (1): 91–116.

de Benoist, B., E. McLean, I. Egli, and M. Cogswell. 2008. "Worldwide Prevalence of Anaemia 1993–2005: WHO Global Database of Anaemia." Technical Report. Geneva: World Health Organization.

District Health Society Bhojpur. 2011. "District Health Action Plan 2011–2012." Technical Report. Government of India, Ministry of Health and Family Welfare.

Edgerton, V., G. Gardner, Y. Ohira, K. Gunawardena, and B. Senewiratne. 1979. "Iron-Deficiency Anaemia and its Effect on Worker Productivity and Activity Patterns." *British Medical Journal* 2 (6204): 1546.

Ganguli, M., G. Ratcliff, V. Chandra, S. Sharma, J. Gilby, R. Pandav, S. Belle et al. 1995. "A Hindi Version of the MMSE: The Development of a Cognitive Screening Instrument for a Largely Illiterate Rural Elderly Population in India." *International Journal of Geriatric Psychiatry* 10 (5): 367–77.

Haas, J. D., and T. Brownlie. 2001. "Iron Deficiency and Reduced Work Capacity: A Critical Review of the Research to Determine a Causal Relationship." *Journal of Nutrition* 131 (2): 676S–690S.

International Institute for Population Sciences (IIPS). 2007. *India National Family Health Survey (NFHS-3), 2005–06*, Volume 1. Mumbai: IIPS.

International Institute for Population Sciences (IIPS) and Macro International. 2008. *National Family Health Survey (NFHS-3), India, 2005–06: Bihar*. Mumbai, IIPS.

Kar, B. R., S. L. Rao, and B. Chandramouli. 2008. "Cognitive Development in Children with Chronic Protein Energy Malnutrition." *Behaviroral and Brain Functions* 4 (31.10): 1186.

Li, R., X. Chen, H. Yan, P. Deurenberg, L. Garby, and J. Hautvast. 1994. "Functional Consequences of Iron Supplementation in Iron-Deficient Female Cotton Mill Workers in Beijing, China." *American Journal of Clinical Nutrition* 59 (4): 908–13.

Lozoff, B. 2007. "Iron Deficiency and Child Development." *Food & Nutrition Bulletin* 28 (Supplement 4): 560S–571S.

Lozoff, B., J. Beard, J. Connor, B. Felt, M. Georgieff, and T. Schallert. 2006. "Long-Lasting Neural and Behavioral Effects of Iron Deficiency in Infancy." *Nutrition Reviews* 64 (s2): S34–S43.

Menon, P., A. B. Deolalikar, and A. Bhaskar. 2009. *India State Hunger Index: Comparisons of Hunger Across States*. International Food Policy Research Institute.

Monaco, M., A. Costa, C. Caltagirone, and G. A. Carlesimo. 2013. "Forward and Backward Span for Verbal and Visuo-Spatial Data: Standardization and Normative Data from an Italian Adult Population." *Neurological Sciences* 34 (5): 749–54.

Nadiger, H., K. Krishnamachari, A. N. Naidu, B. Rao, and S. Srikantia. 1980. "The Use of Common Salt (Sodium Chloride) Fortified with Iron to Control Anaemia: Results of a Preliminary Study." *British Journal of Nutrition* 43 (1): 45–51.

Nair, K., G. Brahmam, S. Ranganathan, K. Vijayaraghavan, B. Sivakumar, and K. Krishnaswamy et al. 1998. "Impact Evaluation of Iron & Iodine Fortified Salt." *Indian Journal of Medical Research* 108:203–11.

National Sample Survey Office. 2011. *Key Indicators of Household Consumer Expenditure in India 2009–2010 (NSS 66th Round)*. India: Ministry of Statistics and Programme and Implementation.

Orsini, A., D. Grossi, E. Capitani, M. Laiacona, C. Papagno, and G. Vallar. 1987. "Verbal and Spatial Immediate Memory Span: Normative Data from 1355 Adults and 1112 Children." *Italian Journal of Neurological Sciences* 8 (6): 537–48.

Penninx, B. W., M. Pahor, M. Cesari, A. M. Corsi, R. C. Woodman, S. Bandinelli, J. M. Guralnik, and L. Ferrucci. 2004. "Anemia is Associated with Disability and Decreased Physical Performance and Muscle Strength in the Elderly." *Journal of the American Geriatrics Society* 52 (5): 719–24.

Pershad, D., and N. Wig. 1988. *Handbook for PGI Memory Scale Clinical Test*. Agra, Uttar Pradesh, India: National Psychological Corporation.

Peters, R., L. Burch, J. Warner, N. Beckett, R. Poulter, and C. Bulpitt. 2008. "Haemoglobin, Anaemia, Dementia and Cognitive Decline in the Elderly, a Systematic Review." *BMC Geriatrics* 8 (1): 18.

Planning Commission and IAMR. 2011. *India Human Development Report 2011 Towards Social Inclusion*. OUP India.

Radloff, L. S. 1977. "The CES-D Scale: A Self-Report Depression Scale for Research in the General Population." *Applied Psychological Measurement* 1 (3): 385–401.

Ranganathan, S., and B. Sesikeran. 2008. "Development of the Double-Fortified Salt from the National Institute of Nutrition." In *Symposium on Food Technology for Better Nutrition*. Institute of Food Technologists.

Rao, S., D. Subbakrishna, and K. Gopukumar. 2004. *NIMHANS Neuropsychology Battery*. Bangalore, India: National Institute of Mental Health and Neuro Sciences (NIMHANS) Publications.

Registrar General of India. 2011. Census of India, 2011. *India, Provisional Population Totals, Paper 1*.

Sivakumar, B., G. Brahmam, K. M. Nair, S. Ranganathan, M. V. Rao, K. Vijayaraghavan, and K. Krishnaswamy. 2001. "Prospects of Fortification of Salt with Iron and Iodine." *British Journal of Nutrition* 85 (S2): S167–S173.

Stoltzfus, R. J. 2001. "Defining Iron-Deficiency Anemia in Public Health Terms: A Time for Reflection. *Journal of Nutrition* 131 (2): 565S–567S.

Swindale, A., and P. Bilinsky. 2006. "Household Dietary Diversity Score (HDDS) for Measurement of Household Food Access: Indicator Guide." Washington, DC: Food and Nutrition Technical Assistance Project.

Thomas, D., E. Frankenberg, J. Friedman, J. P. Habicht, M. Hakimi, N. J. Jaswadi, and G. Pelto et al. 2003. "Iron Deficiency and the Well-Being of Older Adults: Early Results from a Randomized Nutrition Intervention." In *Population Association of America Annual Meetings*, Minneapolis.

Comment   Amitabh Chandra

This chapter forces us to think about a number of issues that are central to economics and public health, and is far more general than the specific question that is answered in the chapter. More generally, I think of the chapter

Amitabh Chandra is professor of public policy and director of health policy research at the Kennedy School of Government at Harvard University and a research associate of the National Bureau of Economic Research.

For acknowledgments, sources of research support, and disclosure of the author's material financial relationships, if any, please see http://www.nber.org/chapters/c12985.ack.

as encouraging us to ask—why do people not always make decisions that are in their best economic interests?

To set the stage for a broader discussion, consider the key findings from the experiment: Anemia is widely prevalent (over 50 percent of adult women in the sample are anemic) and is correlated with lower physical and cognitive functioning. This is a puzzle because consumption per capita is not low, and average BMI is not extremely low. So simple explanations that emphasize the effect of poverty on material resources are unlikely to be the dominant explanations for the presence of anemia in Bihar. Second, the experiment finds that subsidizing the price of double-fortified salt, which includes iron and iodine, by 55 percent led to a 20 percent increase in take-up. One may cheer that demand curves slope down and that economics is alive, but another view is that even a fairly substantial subsidy does not dramatically increase an activity that is fundamentally good for people. Third, we learn that the informational campaigns that were tried (written promotional materials, a door-to-door campaign) did not increase take-up. And so we learn that imperfect information is not a first-order impediment to low take-up, either. To summarize, while poverty, prices, and information surely matter, they are not by themselves the principal drivers to anemia and low take-up of double-fortified salt.

Similar finding of low take-up of beneficial things are found in a variety of contexts. The Austrian physician Ignaz Semmelweis demonstrated that maternal mortality from puerperal fever (an infection of the genital tract after giving birth) could be reduced from 12.2 percent to 2.4 percent by making physicians wash their hands with chlorinated lime between autopsy and obstetrical rotations. But physicians, even physicians in Boston hospitals in 2013, have been to slow to adopt hand washing. Beta-blockers and aspirin, which showed spectacular results in clinical trials that were conducted in the era of the Apollo landing, had not diffused through American hospitals in the era of iPods. Patients who have suffered heart attacks, and are arguably among the most activated patients as a consequence of what they have confronted, demonstrate remarkably poor adherence with life-saving drugs. There are many examples from outside healthcare, too. Zvi Griliches showed us that hybrid corn was slow to be adopted. David Laibson and Brigitte Madrian have shown us that employees do not avail of the opportunity to maximize wealth by using savings opportunities that are offered to them.

These are behaviors that are hard for simple maximizing models to reconcile. The current approach in economics to explain aberrant, "nonmaximizing" behavior by agents who face the right incentives, is to appeal to behavioral economics and invoke the attendant machinery of discount rates and prospect theory. There is a complementary set of explanations that may be equally powerful. Heterogeneity in the net benefits of adoption, be it adoption of beta-blockers, 401(k)s, or double-fortified salt, may prove to be a worthwhile alternative to consider. I will distinguish between three types of heterogeneity:

Type 1. Heterogeneity in time and hassle costs
Type 2. Heterogeneity in side effects
Type 3. Heterogeneity in benefits, conditional on side effects

Time and hassle costs are incurred by many patients and there is likely to be heterogeneity in these costs across individuals in a way that goes well beyond differences in income and education. Hassle costs, by distracting and exhausting agents, may dissuade people with complex lives from adopting a particular treatment or behavior. Stress and complexity increase the hassle costs and will likely result in an overemphasis on symptom relief.

Heterogeneity in side effects does not make sense for interventions such as 401(k) participation or hand washing, but may be key to the adoption of medical treatments. Individuals know their preferences better than their providers do and it is possible that some of the variation in adherence with their doctor's orders reflects private knowledge of side effects. For iron supplementation for iron deficiency anemia, the CDC notes that the side effects include gastrointestinal side effects such as nausea, vomiting, constipation, diarrhea, dark colored stools, and/or abdominal distress (CDC 1998). That such side effects are likely is not disputed. But their frequency is not known. Even if it is relative to the benefits of supplementation, the presence of hassle costs may focus the mind on short-term reward (avoid side effects) over long-term gain.

This simple framework suggests a number of lessons for public policy. Heterogeneity in hassle costs, without heterogeneity in side effects or heterogeneity in benefits, justifies the case for mandates. Mandates were used to fluoridate water, fight smallpox, and introduce iodized salt. A productive research program would document the absence (or relative absence of) of type 2 and 3 heterogeneity in order for mandates to be used for public health concerns. The presence of type 2 or 3 heterogeneity may be addressed by using user fees (such a copayments). Such fees should discourage use by patients with side effects or low benefits. But in the presence of type 1 heterogeneity (hassle costs), such user fees will almost definitely fire, by reducing demand from agents whose demand will be tempered by the user fees.

In my discussion, I have not focused on the explanations that rely on information (or lack thereof) for behavior. The empirical findings in this chapter, which find that informational campaigns did not increase take-up, support this view. It is also my view that lack of information often may come from the presence of hassle or search costs (type 1 heterogeneity), or that there is substantial type 2 and type 3 heterogeneity (which would predict that people adopt things because they understand the benefits, not because they don't know what's good for them).

The present analysis is not designed to shed light on the particular form of heterogeneity that is responsible for the broad adoption of double-fortified salt. But in principle, uncovering the nature of this latent heterogeneity is something that can be accomplished with a rich set of baseline data. I look forward to seeing the next set of results from this exciting research program.

References

Centers for Disease Control and Prevention (CDC). 1998. "CDC Recommendations to Prevent and Control Iron Deficiency in the United States." *MMWR Recommendations and Reports* 47:1–29.

The Diffusion of New Medical Technology
The Case of Drug-Eluting Stents

Amitabh Chandra, David Malenka,
and Jonathan Skinner

11.1 Introduction

There are large and persistent productivity differences across health care providers and regions—variations in both inputs (utilization) and risk-adjusted outcomes (see Chandra et al. 2013; Baicker, Chandra, and Skinner 2012; Skinner 2012). These studies were largely limited to cross-sectional analysis, and generally tell us little about the dynamic process by which these variations arise. A few studies have examined the role of diffusion for highly effective treatments such as aspirin and beta-blockers for heart attack patients in explaining such productivity differences (e.g., Skinner and Staiger 2009), but these have been limited to a narrow set of technologies with little impact on expenditures. Outside of health economics, however, the idea that the diffusion process of new technologies can explain productivity differences at a point in time is well accepted; for example, in studies of steam engine adoption across countries (Comin and Hobijn 2004). Parente and Prescott (1994) have pointed to modest differences in rates of adoption

Amitabh Chandra is professor of public policy and director of health policy research at the Kennedy School of Government at Harvard University and a research associate of the National Bureau of Economic Research. David Malenka is professor of medicine and of community and family medicine at the Geisel School of Medicine and the Dartmouth Institute for Health Policy and Clinical Practice at Dartmouth College. Jonathan Skinner is the James O. Freedman Presidential Professor of Economics at Dartmouth College, professor of family and community medicine at the Geisel School of Medicine and the Dartmouth Institute for Health Policy and Clinical Practice, and a research associate of the National Bureau of Economic Research.

We are grateful to Douglas Staiger for helpful comments and to Jay Bhattacharya for an insightful discussion of our chapter. This research was funded by the National Institute on Aging through PO1-AG19783 and P01-AG005842. For acknowledgments, sources of research support, and disclosure of the authors' material financial relationships, if any, please see http://www.nber.org/chapters/c12974.ack.

and diffusion across countries as a key factor in why income and growth differ so much across countries. In developing economics, the process and ease of technology diffusion has long been recognized as central to successful income growth (World Bank 2008).

In this chapter, we consider a medical innovation: drug-eluting stents, a commonly used approach to treating the narrowing of coronary arteries, but one with a larger impact on health care cost growth. Until 2003, only bare-metal stents were available to cardiologists seeking to perform revascularization for blockages in the heart. These cylindrical wire meshes were designed to keep arteries from narrowing, and thereby ensure patency (i.e., keeping the blood flowing). Yet bare-metal stents were also subject to restenosis, or a renarrowing of the artery, leading to restricted blood flow. In April of 2003, the Food and Drug Administration (FDA) approved the use of coated antiproliferative drug-eluting stents, designed to further reduce restenosis. In the same month, Medicare allowed for a higher reimbursement for drug-eluting stents, largely to cover their higher cost. Adoption was rapid; by December 2003 more than 65 percent of all stent placements in the Medicare population were drug eluting rather than bare-metal stents. Yet different hospitals exhibited very different diffusion rates; in the bottom quintile of diffusion, drug-eluting stents comprised just 33 percent of total stents for the year following FDA approval, while in the top quintile the equivalent was 83 percent.

We ask why did some hospitals adopt drug-eluting stents earlier than others? In the literature, there are a variety of suggested factors that can lead to more rapid adoption. The classic Griliches (1957) study of hybrid corn hypothesized that profitability was the major incentive to adopting. We define profitability broadly to include both any pure benefit of billing for drug-eluting stents in excess of their costs, as well as placing the specific hospital at an advantage with regard to competition in its market with other hospitals. In other words, drug-eluting stents may not by themselves be profitable, but they could confer a competitive advantage to hospitals seeking to charge insurance companies and employers higher prices for high-quality care.

An alternative explanation relies on physician expertise at the hospital. Higher quality hospitals are the first to adopt drug-eluting stents because they have better knowledge about the benefits or lower costs of adopting them; for example, if they had already been involved with the ongoing randomized trials prior to FDA approval. This explanation is more in line with rural sociologists who, in a debate with Griliches, stressed differences across individuals in their willingness to adopt and/or diffuse the new technology, with those having adopted in the past more likely to adopt the newest technologies (Babcock 1962; Brandner and Strauss 1959).[1]

---

1. Rates of diffusion at the hospital level may include both the adoption of drug-eluting stents by individual physicians, and the diffusion of drug-eluting stents to a wider range of patients by physicians already using the drug-eluting stent.

A third hypothesis, which is complementary to those mentioned previously, stresses knowledge spillovers; diffusion depends on area norms, but correlated behaviors across providers may reflect mimicry (copycat behavior) or true knowledge spillovers. We distinguish between these two hypotheses by testing whether these spillover effects have real incremental effects on patient outcomes; if they do, then the diffusion is productive and reflects learning. If there is no productive effect from diffusion, the evidence is more consistent with mimicry of the new technology, and models of competition in the form of a "medical arms race."

Our final hypothesis is that diffusion occurs by allocating drug-eluting stents to those hospitals most expert in ensuring that they would be used for patients with the greatest *incremental* benefit. The benefit of a drug-eluting stent is directly related to the risk of target lesion restenosis, which in turn is related to patient characteristics and lesion characteristics. If stent manufacturers were rationing their initial supply and acted as "social planners," we would expect to see the greatest incremental health benefit from the early adopters. While such a model seems hypothetical at best, it still provides a reasonable gold standard to judge the real health effects of the uneven diffusion of drug-eluting stents.

11.2 Drug-Eluting Stents: Clinical and Data Issues

Since the 1980s percutaneous coronary interventions (PCIs) have become the preferred strategy for treating patients with blockage(s) of one or more coronary arteries because of atherosclerotic plaque in patients who fail medical management. The original technology used a balloon-tipped catheter to fracture the plaque and stretch the blood vessel. The Achilles' heel of this approach was that as much as half the time the blockage would recur within six to twelve months. This problem stimulated the development of coronary stents: slotted tubes that could be placed across an area of blockage to buttress open the vessel and prevent restenosis. These devices reduced the risk of restenosis but did not eliminate it as the inflammatory and proliferative mechanisms of the vessels response to injury could lead to the ingrowth of smooth muscle through the cells of the stent and restenosis.

In response, the device industry developed drug-eluting stents (DES) which, in contrast to the existing bare-metal stents (BMS), were coated with a drug(s) designed to prevent the overexuberant healing response associated with restenosis. The drug-eluting stent worked, reducing the rate of restenosis from 10–20 percent with bare-metal stents to fewer than 5 percent with a drug-eluting stent. While several studies showed quite different results, the consensus view has converged to one in which the drug-eluting stent confers no advantage in terms of survival or rates of myocardial infarction, but a pronounced decline in the rate of restenosis (and subsequent revascularization).

Based on a premarket experience with 673 patients, the FDA approved the first drug-eluting stent in the United States, the Cordis/Johnson and Johnson CYPHER sirolimus-coated stent, for general use on April 23, 2003. In March of 2004, eleven months later, a second DES stent, the Boston Scientific TAXUS paclitaxel-coated stent, was approved by the FDA.

During the first five months of general distribution of the CYPHER, more than 260,000 stents were shipped. However, during this time the FDA, via Johnson and Johnson, began receiving reports of subacute thrombosis (blood clots forming in the stents causing heart attacks) following placement of the stents. By October 2003 the FDA recognized a significant increase in the number of reported cases of subacute thrombosis compared with what it had been receiving before the DES was introduced. On October 29, 2003, the agency posted a public health notification to physicians describing the receipt, through the voluntary medical device reporting system, of more than 290 reports of subacute thrombosis and sixty deaths associated with use of the CYPHER stent.[2] The notification became a major news item and prompted a flurry of calls from apprehensive patients to physicians asking what they should do. The physician community was left trying to put the FDA's concern in context, and patients were left to deal with their anxiety about having a coronary event. It was unclear at the time whether this flurry of reported cases represented a true increase in the rate of subacute thrombosis over that seen with BMS or a lower threshold for reporting this complication, driven by the high profile of the new device. Over the next several years it was determined that there is a small increased risk of this adverse event but one that can be mitigated by the use of dual antiplatelet agents. Since 2006, there has been a general decline in the use of drug-eluting stents relative to bare-metal stents.

11.2.1 Data

We used a 100 percent national sample of all Medicare Part A hospital claims during 2002–2005 for enrollees age sixty-five and older enrolled in traditional, fee-for-service Medicare programs.[3] The claims data includes unique identifiers for the hospital and patient, the dates of admission and discharge, an admitting diagnosis, procedures performed, and additional diagnoses representing comorbid conditions. The patient's zip code is also reported, which allows us to link him or her to a hospital referral region (HRR), of which there are 306 in the Dartmouth Atlas database. These regions were created to reflect where Medicare enrollees seek tertiary care, such as stents or bypass surgery.

Patients undergoing a percutaneous coronary intervention (PCI) with

2. http://www.fda.gov/MedicalDevices/Safety/AlertsandNotices/PublicHealthNotifications/ucm064527.htm.
3. This section draws heavily from Malenka et al. 2008.

stent placement were identified by the presence of a hospital claim for a bare-metal stent (BMS, ICD-9-CM code 36.06) and/or a drug-eluting stent (DES, ICD-9-CM code 36.07). Patients coded as having placement of both types of stents during their first PCI hospitalization were classified as DES patients.

In this analysis, we used exclusion criteria based on the Stent Anticoagulation Restenosis Trial Study (STARS) (Cutlip et al. 1999). Thus, we excluded patients (a) with an emergency admission, (b) with a diagnosis code for myocardial infarction (MI, ICD-9-CM codes 410–410.6, 410.8–410.9, 5th digit 0 or 1), (c) admitted within seven days of discharge from a prior hospitalization, (d) within one year of coronary artery bypass surgery (CABG, ICD-9-CM 36.1–36.19) or a prior PCI (ICD-9-CM 36.0–36.09), and (e) exhibiting evidence of bypass graft disease on their index claim (ICD-9-CM codes 414.02–414.05, 996.72; to eliminate patients who might have had an intervention on a bypass graft rather than on a native coronary artery). In subsequent work, we hope to also consider patients receiving a stent (either bare-metal or drug-eluting) but who would not have been admitted to the STARS trial.

11.2.2 Comorbid Conditions

The claims data includes up to ten medical diagnoses. Using information from the index admission, we identified the following comorbid conditions as defined by Romano, Roos, and Jollis (1993): history of MI, congestive heart failure, peripheral vascular disease, pulmonary disease, diabetes without complications, diabetes with complications, mild liver disease, moderate or severe liver disease, dementia, renal disease, nonmetastatic cancer, and metastatic solid tumor.

11.2.3 Outcomes

We report two sets of regressions. The first is simply whether the hospital in question experienced a rapid or slow diffusion rate. To do this, we dropped April 2003 (when the drug-eluting stent was first allowed), and considered the ratio of drug-eluting to total stents during the subsequent year: May 2003–April 2004, by hospital.

We also considered health outcome measures to judge the impact of diffusion on actual health outcomes. We used three measures. The first is a serious adverse event: during the year following the stent placement, either death or an ST-elevated myocardial infarction (STEMI) that plausibly arises from restenosis.[4] The second measure is death alone, again during a one-year horizon. The final measure is the rate of repeat coronary revascularization, defined as any PCI, whether it comprises a stent (ICD-9-CM codes 36.0–

---

4. Death was from the denominator file; ST-elevation MI was based on the presence of specific codes on a Part A claim (ICD-9-CM codes 410–410.6, 410.8–410.9, 5th digit 0 or 1).

36.09), or alternatively, a crossover to bypass surgery (CABG ICD-9-CM codes 36.1–36.19).[5]

11.3 Model

In this section we formalize four hypotheses for the diffusion of drug-eluting stents and present candidate variables to test each hypothesis. The first is the classic Griliches (1957) hypothesis that hospitals with the greatest potential financial gains from the new innovation will be the one to adopt it. This may include either hospitals that yield a greater return from using drug-eluting stents either because the markup exceeds the actual cost the hospital pays the stent manufacturer, or because using drug-eluting stents confers a competitive advantage for a hospital in a more crowded market.

To fully test this hypothesis, we would ideally want to know not just Medicare reimbursement rates that may differ across hospitals, but also rates that private insurance pays for the under-sixty-five population. In the absence of such detailed information, we consider instead different types of hospitals, with different levels of financial alignment for adoption decisions. For example, for-profit hospitals should be more likely to adopt new and more profitable technology quickly relative to not-for-profit hospitals, and not-for-profit hospitals would have stronger financial incentives to adopt than government hospitals. And it could well be that the profit-maximizing decision is to not adopt (leading to a negative coefficient for the for-profit dummy variable), since drug-eluting stents were known to reduce the need for revascularization, and thus could cut into volume and hence profits in a dynamic setting.

We can also test for the effect of competition in local markets. We define two variables, one for whether there is another hospital also performing PCI with stenting in the hospital service area (HSA), and if so, how many other hospitals are in the HSA.[6] A positive coefficient for either variable in explaining rates of diffusion would be consistent with a model in which competition leads to more rapid adoption of the newest technology, in this case drug-eluting stents.

Our second hypothesis suggests that the diffusion of stents is driven by expertise of physicians at the hospitals that adopt first. Better places adopt stents first, because they know about the benefit or have a lower cost of adopting them. We test this by considering to what extent rapid diffusion of drug-eluting stents is explained by teaching status of the hospital, the

5. To avoid including patients who experienced an adverse outcome secondary to subacute thrombosis, only patients who survived for at least one day following their procedure were included in the analysis. We also excluded patients with a STEMI coded on their index admission, since we could not determine whether the STEMI was a procedural outcome or the indication for the procedure.

6. There are more than 3,000 hospital service areas, as defined by the Dartmouth Atlas; these were drawn to reflect migration patterns of Medicare patients in 1992–1993. Alternative market measures are also those such as circles with specified radii around each hospital.

log total number of hospital beds, and the log of the volume of bare-metal stents performed during April 2002–March 2003, prior to the introduction of drug-eluting stents. An additional measure is the hospital level of risk-adjusted adverse events during the year prior to the introduction of drug-eluting stents (April 2002–March 2003), where the risk adjusters include age, sex, race, and comorbidities (described in more detail later.)

Both mimicry and knowledge spillovers can explain our third hypothesis: that the probability of adoption in hospital i is an increasing function of adoption in other hospitals in the hospital referral region (HRR).[7] But knowledge spillovers also predict that outcomes at hospital i are an increasing function of adoption in other hospitals in HRR. Thus we consider whether spillovers can explain the adoption of drug-eluting stents; this is a hypothesis consistent with either mimicry or knowledge spillovers. We further test whether spillovers can explain differences in health outcomes—if it does, then the knowledge spillover hypothesis is supported; if not, the mimicry hypothesis gains support.

To explore the fourth hypothesis, the extent to which the distribution of drug-eluting stents is consistent with a first-best allocation as determined by the social planner, we focus on whether the early adopters experienced greater or less incremental gains whether with respect to adverse outcomes (where, on average, there were no benefits), or with regard to a reduction in rates of PCI following the initial placement of the stent(s).

We first estimate hospital-level regressions, where the dependent variable is the hospital-level diffusion rate (drug-eluting stents relative to total stents in the year following FDA approval), and key covariates were noted earlier. To further test the implications of our model for health *outcomes*, we consider patient-level tests of our three outcome measures: an adverse outcome, death, or a subsequent PCI. In this regression analysis, we use a full set of risk-adjustment measures: a secular trend variable, by month; age-sex (five-year categories, by sex); and comorbidities such as past myocardial infarction, vascular disease, pulmonary disease, dementia, diabetes, liver disease, renal disease, and any cancer.

11.4 Results

Table 11.1 presents summary statistics for both the entire sample, and broken out by quintile of diffusion. First, while the average use of drug-eluting stents was 62 percent, there were dramatic differences in the ratio of drug-eluting stents between the highest quintile regions (83 percent) and the lowest quintile regions (33 percent). A graph of the diffusion rates is shown in figure 11.1; as can be seen, most of the gap in diffusion is apparent in the

---

7. There are 306 hospital referral regions (HRRs) in the Dartmouth Atlas; these in turn are built up from the hospital service areas.

Table 11.1   Summary statistics by quintile of diffusion for drug-eluting stents

	Total	Quintile 1	Quintile 2	Quintile 3	Quintile 4	Quintile 5
Fraction drug-eluting stents	0.620	0.327	0.543	0.658	0.743	0.830
Age	74.71	74.78	74.70	74.63	74.44	74.68
Female	0.411	0.432	0.418	0.409	0.406	0.390
African American	0.043	0.046	0.043	0.043	0.048	0.036
Death or STEMI (1 yr)	0.057	0.064	0.058	0.057	0.054	0.050
PCI (1 yr)	0.140	0.138	0.135	0.138	0.145	0.144
For-profit hospital	0.138	0.189	0.196	0.088	0.132	0.082
Government hospital	0.070	0.100	0.044	0.109	0.059	0.036
Teaching hospital	0.247	0.091	0.178	0.218	0.338	0.417
Adult hospital beds	243	176	222	239	284	298

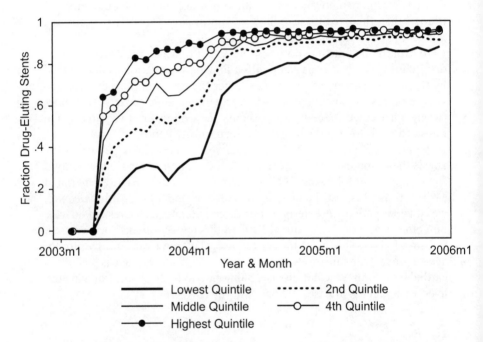

Fig. 11.1   Diffusion pattern of drug-eluting stents, by quintile of hospital, 2003–2004

first year, but by mid-2005 rates of use for drug-eluting stents were well over 80 percent across all quintiles.

The regional variability in the diffusion of drug-eluting stents can also be seen in figure 11.2, which shows the fraction of drug-eluting stents relative to total stents by HRR across the United States. While a few of the regions experienced fewer than 100 observations (and thus might exhibit statistical noise), there is still a remarkable degree of variation in adoption rates that

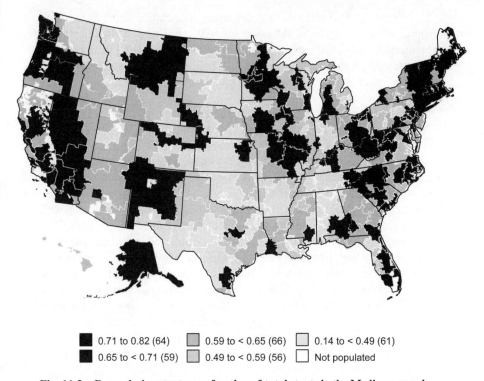

| ■ | 0.71 to 0.82 (64) | ▨ | 0.59 to < 0.65 (66) | ▢ | 0.14 to < 0.49 (61) |
| ■ | 0.65 to < 0.71 (59) | ▨ | 0.49 to < 0.59 (56) | □ | Not populated |

Fig. 11.2   Drug-eluting stents as a fraction of total stents in the Medicare popula-tion by HRR, May 2003–April 2004

are not uniform across regions, and suggest the importance of spatial auto-correlation or spillover effects for individual hospitals.

Returning to table 11.1, there were no differences in age of patients being stented across the groups, nor were there large differences in racial composition, except for the smaller fraction of African Americans in the highest-diffusion quintile. Women were less likely to be stented in the highest-diffusion group, perhaps owing to a lack of appropriate stents in this group.

There are large differences in rates of adverse events across the quintiles of adoption, ranging from 6.4 percent of patients in the lowest-diffusion quintile to only 5.0 percent in the highest-diffusion quintile. One might be tempted to attribute this pattern to the greater effectiveness of the drug-eluting stents over bare-metal stents—as one might do in studies that use distance from the hospital as the "instrument"—but in fact these patterns are present for stent patients both before and after April 2003 when drug-eluting stents were introduced. As we show later, hospitals with greater (risk-adjusted) quality of stenting (as measured by lower adverse event rates) were more likely to adopt, but exhibited no incremental improvement (or any improvement, for that matter) in adverse events.

Finally, while table 11.1 shows a very strong association between teaching hospital status and rates of diffusion (as well as the size of the hospital as measured by beds), there was no consistent pattern of association between for-profit or government hospitals and diffusion of drug-eluting stents. We next turn to a more formal regression analysis that considers these factors in light of our model.

Table 11.2 reports coefficients from a regression of the hospital-level diffusion rate of drug-eluting stents on a variety of different variables as noted previously in section 3. In equation (1), the more parsimonious specification, hospitals with larger shares of African Americans and females are substantially less likely to adopt drug-eluting stents. For example, a hospital with a 10 percent higher fraction of women would exhibit a 3.4 percentage point lower fraction of drug-eluting stents. Teaching hospitals are strongly associated with higher diffusion of drug-eluting stents (10 percent) while for-profit hospitals are almost 5.0 percentage points less likely to adopt. The hypothesis that hospitals adopt in competitive markets is not supported by this regression because we do not see the number of hospitals in an area predict the diffusion of DES.

The fuller specification in table 11.2 includes additional measures hypothesized earlier. (Hospitals in HRRs without other hospitals performing stents are dropped, as there is no plausible spillover effect.) The apparent importance of for-profit hospitals (from equation [1]) disappears when other factors are included. Both the size of the hospital and the cumulative stent volume are significant and positively associated with diffusion rates, although the magnitudes are not large relative to observed differences in the data.

The spillover level—the rate of diffusion of other hospitals in the HRR during the same period—is highly significant with a coefficient of 0.077, consistent with the HRR-level map in figure 11.2. The coefficient on teaching hospital status is still large and significant, as is the pre-drug-eluting stent quality measures. Recall that we used only the pre–April 2003 stenting outcomes data to estimate risk-adjusted rates of adverse events by hospital as a measure of "expertise." These were then used to create quintiles of hospital expertise, with quintile 1 the lowest quality and quintile 5 (the excluded quintile) the best quality. As can be seen from table 11.2, the lowest-quality hospitals (quintile 1) were almost 8 percentage points less likely to adopt drug-eluting stents.[8]

The regressions in table 11.2 therefore are supportive of an expertise model of adoption—given the strong importance of quality-adjusted outcomes and the teaching hospital coefficient—as well as the presence of some

8. This pattern is also consistent with an otherwise puzzling finding presented in an earlier JAMA letter, and reproduced in appendix figure 11A.1. This shows the rate of two-year adverse complications for patients treated with drug-eluting stents (post–April 2003) and those treated with bare-metal stents. While the drop in adverse outcomes for the drug-eluting stent patients may appear to be consistent with greater benefit for these treatments, the sudden jump in complication rates for those with bare-metal stents makes much less sense—except in a world where there is selection bias, not so much because of patient unmeasured confounding, but because of hospital unmeasured confounding—higher quality hospitals adopted drug-eluting stents first.

Table 11.2   **Explaining diffusion at the hospital level**

Variable	Equation 1 (N = 950)	Equation 2 (N = 776)
Share African American patients	−0.171	−0.179
	(1.69)	(1.74)
Share other racial/ethnic patients	0.055	0.102
	(0.60)	(1.04)
Average age	−0.002	−0.011
	(0.44)	(1.53)
Fraction female	−0.339	−0.242
	(3.91)	(2.51)
For-profit hospital	−0.047	0.0068
	(2.72)	(0.34)
Government hospital	−0.028	0.021
	(1.20)	(0.82)
Teaching hospital	0.101	0.076
	(7.21)	(4.76)
Two or more hospitals in the HSA (1 = yes)	0.019	0.019
	(1.19)	(1.07)
Number of hospitals in the HSA	−0.000	−0.000
	(0.849)	(0.21)
Spillover (rate of diffusion in other hospitals in HRR)		0.073
		(2.75)
Log(beds)		0.013
		(1.00)
Log(stent volume) during April 2002– March 2003		0.040
		(6.01)
Q1 (risk-adj. outcomes)		−0.076
		(3.83)
Q2 (risk-adj. outcomes)		−0.033
		(1.66)
Q3 (risk-adj. outcomes)		−0.021
		(1.07)
Q4 (risk-adj. outcomes)		−0.012
		(1.01)
Q5 (reference quintile)		–
R^2	0.11	0.19

Notes: Dependent variable is the rate at which a hospital uses DES. The OLS regression is at the hospital level, with hospitals weighted according to their patient populations. Absolute value of z-statistic in parentheses.

kind of spillover effect (or a geographically correlated unobservable). We next turn to health outcome regressions (at the patient level) to further distinguish between a "mimic" versus a "knowledge spillover" effect, and the hypothesis that hospitals that diffused most rapidly also got the greatest incremental benefits from drug-eluting stents.

Table 11.3 shows these outcome variables using logistics models, so the null hypothesis of no effect corresponds to a coefficient of 1.00. First note

Table 11.3   Logistic analysis predicting health outcomes

Dependent variable	Death or STEMI ($N = 127{,}072$)	1-year mortality	Subsequent PCI
For-profit hospital	1.05	1.04	0.96
	(1.48)	(1.05)	(1.13)
Government hospital	1.126	1.11	0.997
	(2.56)	(2.07)	(0.34)
Teaching hospital	1.017	1.03	1.07
	(0.34)	(0.79)	(4.67)
HRR spillover	1.04	1.03	1.16
	(0.77)	(0.65)	(0.93)
Log (stent volume) pre–April 2003	0.97	0.98	1.14
	(2.90)	(2.42)	(12.79)
Log (beds)	1.02	1.011	0.88
	(1.20)	(0.66)	(6.32)
Diffusion Q1	1.194	1.14	0.97
	(3.15)	(1.96)	(0.77)
Diffusion Q2	1.035	1.04	0.97
	(0.59)	(0.65)	(0.84)
Diffusion Q3	1.129	1.10	0.96
	(2.05)	(1.18)	(0.28)
Diffusion Q4	1.011	0.996	1.04
	(0.33)	(0.11)	(0.74)
Q1 * post-DES	0.983	1.03	1.04
	(0.47)	(0.39)	(0.91)
Q2 * post-DES	1.035	1.04	0.82
	(0.66)	(0.69)	(3.75)
Q3 * post-DES	0.965	1.02	0.89
	(0.59)	(0.37)	(2.27)
Q4 * post-DES	0.988	1.02	0.88
	(0.14)	(0.27)	(2.67)
Q5 * post-DES	0.908	0.93	0.842
	(1.19)	(0.66)	(3.14)
Pseudo R^2	0.044	0.057	0.006

Notes: Dependent variable is the presence of an adverse event, death, or subsequent PCI. Logistic regression (reporting odds ratios) regression is at the patient level Additional variables include month trend, age-sex (five-year categories, by sex), race, comorbidities (past myocardial infarction, vascular disease, pulmonary disease, dementia, diabetes, liver disease, renal disease, any cancer). Absolute value of z-statistic in parentheses.

that the HRR spillover variable is never large in magnitude nor is it significant. This may not be so surprising for health outcomes, where we would not expect large effects of increased drug-eluting stents on adverse events (death or STEMI), but it is more surprising that we do not find such effects on subsequent PCIs, where we would expect a decline if there was "learning by doing." Thus we are led towards a mimic model of adoption rather than one involving knowledge spillovers.

It may appear also from these results that subsequent PCI is not entirely a hard variable, but that higher rates (conditional on other factors and health status) may be observed in teaching hospitals and in hospitals that perform a high rate of stents (conditional on hospital bed size). That is, the likelihood of a second PCI may depend not solely on clinical factors, but also reflect physician opinions about appropriateness for revascularization.

Finally, we can use these logistic regressions to consider the hypothesis that hospitals with the most rapid diffusion also experienced the best health outcomes. While one cannot reject the null that the interaction effects (the quintiles of diffusion times the post-DES dummy variable) are jointly different from zero, one can detect a general pattern; the most rapidly diffusing hospitals appeared to exhibit the greatest relative decline in rates of revascularization (no improvement for the lowest diffusion quintile, versus a significant drop of more than 10 percent for the highest diffusion quintile). In sum, while the results for adverse events are not significant, it does appear that the rapidly adopting hospitals were most effective in reducing rates of restenosis.

One might be concerned with the interpretation of these outcome data if the introduction of drug-eluting stents was also associated with an increase in the overall number of stenting, thus potentially confounding the introduction of stents with an expansion of patients with potentially less (or more) unmeasured confounding factors. However, as shown in Malenka et al. (2008), the total number of stents in this population, on a monthly basis, did not vary appreciably over the time period.

11.5 Conclusion

In April of 2003, the FDA approved the use of drug-eluting stents, designed to reduce renarrowing of the artery at the location of the original stent. Using Medicare claims data, we found remarkable variations in the rates of diffusion of these drugs across hospitals and regions of the United States. We further tested several models of diffusion, and found the most empirical support for models of expertise (better-quality hospitals adopt quicker) and spillover models with correlated diffusion behavior within regions. There is suggestive evidence that hospitals that gained the greatest incremental benefit from drug-eluting stents diffused more rapidly, but there is no support for models of competition, knowledge spillovers, or profit maximization.

Our finding that the quality of the provider is highly predictive of the diffusion of the new technology has implications for studies that use (for example) distance from a catheterization laboratory as an instrument for the specific technology. As McClellan, McNeil, and Newhouse (1994) noted at the time, the risk is that the estimated benefits of the new technology become conflated with the quality of the provider. For this reason, the use of panel studies, rather than cross-sectional analysis, that seek to measure the impact of new technology on health outcomes may be particularly valuable.

There are several limitations to the study. Drug-eluting stents are quite similar to bare-metal stents from the view of the interventional cardiologist. Thus the potential implementation barriers present for, for example, hybrid corn, or the capacity issues associated with the presence of backup catheterization laboratories, are not present for this study as they were for many previous technological advances. Nonetheless, we believe that there are a sufficient number of new drugs and devices with similar characteristics to make these results generalizable.

Drug-eluting stents were also different because they were subsequently found to have more risks than previously understood in the early months of their introduction. A fuller analysis would include not simply the rapid expansion, but also the more gradual "exnovation" of such treatments among those least appropriate for drug-eluting stents. Still, a better understanding of the welfare implications for the uneven diffusion of new technology appears to be a worthwhile goal.

In sum, the diffusion of drug-eluting stents appeared to have been driven by expertise and perhaps even productivity considerations, and so there does not appear to be large welfare costs associated with the uneven diffusion rates.

Appendix

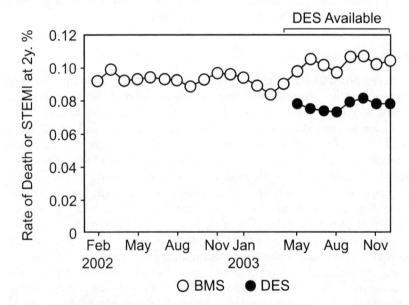

Fig. 11A.1   Mortality and ST-elevation myocardial infarction rates for patients receiving bare-metal stents versus drug-eluting stents

Source: Malenka et al (2008).

Note: BMS indicates bare-metal stents; DES, drug-eluting stents; and STEMI, ST-elevation myocardial infarction.

References

Babcock, Jarvis M. 1962. "Adoption of Hybrid Corn: A Comment." *Rural Sociology* 27:332–8.

Baicker, K., A. Chandra, and J. Skinner. 2012. "Saving Money or Just Saving Lives? Improving the Productivity of the U.S. Health Care Spending." *Annual Review of Economics* 4:33–56.

Brandner, L., and M. A. Strauss. 1959. "Congruence Versus Profitabilty in the Diffusion of Hybrid Sorghum." *Rural Sociology* 24:381–3.

Chandra, A., A. Finkelstein, A. Sacarny, and C. Syverson. 2013. "Productivity and Allocation in the U.S. Healthcare Sector." NBER Working Paper no. 19200, Cambridge, MA.

Comin, D., and B. Hobijn. 2004. "Cross-Country Technology Adoption: Making the Theories Face the Facts." *Journal of Monetary Economics* 51: 39–83.

Cutlip, D. E., M. B. Leon, K. K. L. Ho, P. C. Gordon, A. Giambartolomei, D. J. Diver, D. M. Lasorda, D. O. Williams, M. M. Fitzpatrick, A. Desjardin, J. J. Popma, R. E. Kuntz, D. S. Baim. 1999. "Acute and Nine-Month Clinical Outcomes after "Suboptimal" Coronary Stenting: Results from the STent Anti-Thrombotic Regimen Study (STARS) Registry." *Journal of the American College of Cardiology* 34 (3): 698–706. doi:10.1016/S0735-1097(99)00271-5.

Griliches, Zvi, 1957. "Hybrid Corn: An Exploration in the Economics of Technological Change." *Econometrica* 25 (October): 501–22.

Malenka, D. J., A. V. Kaplan, L. Lucas, S. M. Sharp, and J. S. Skinner. 2008. "Outcomes Following Coronary Stenting in the Era of Bare Metal versus the Era of Drug Eluting Stents." *Journal of the American Medical Association* 299 (24): 2868–76.

McClellan, M., B. McNeil, and J. Newhouse. 1994. "Does More Intensive Treatment of Acute Myocardial Infarction Reduce Mortality?" *Journal of the American Medical Association* 272 (11): 859–66.

Parente, Stephen L., and Edward C. Prescott. 1994. "Barriers to Technology Adoption and Development." *Journal of Political Economy* 102 (April): 298–321.

Romano, P. S., L. L. Roos, J. G. Jollis. 1993. "Adapting a Clinical Comorbidity Index for Use with ICD-9-CM Administrative Data: Differing Perspectives." *Journal of Clinical Epidemiology* 46 (10):1075–79.

Skinner, Jonathan. 2012. "Causes and Consequences of Geographic Variation in Health Care." In *Handbook of Health Economics*, volume 2, edited by T. McGuire, M. Pauly, and P. Pita Baros. Oxford: North Holland.

Skinner, Jonathan, and Douglas Staiger. 2009. "Technology Diffusion and Productivity Growth in Health Care." NBER Working Paper no. 14865, Cambridge, MA.

World Bank. 2008. *Global Economic Prospects: Technology Diffusion in the Developing World 2008*. Global Economic Prospects and the Developing Countries (GEP). Washington, DC: World Bank. Available at http://documents.worldbank.org/curated/en/2008/01/9013126/global-economic-prospects-technology-diffusion-developing-world-2008.

Comment   Jay Bhattacharya

The US Patent Office issued the first patent for a drug-eluting stenting (DES) device in 1997. By 2004, the new technology had transformed the way that patients with coronary artery disease were managed in the United States and elsewhere. The new technology built on an existing technology—coronary artery catheterization and stenting. The DES are now a commonly applied technology, with over a half million patients having a DES placed each year (Roger et al. 2012). In this chapter, Chandra, Malenka, and Skinner ask an important series of questions—which providers were most likely to adopt drug-eluting stents, what motive best explains adoption, and how did the diffusion process affect the welfare of patients? These are important questions because the diffusion of new medical technology plays such a pivotal role in explaining both why American health care is so expensive and why it is broadly seen as providing cutting edge care.

Medical Background

To understand the economics underlying the diffusion of DES devices, a bit of background medicine is necessary. The heart is a muscle, and like any muscle, requires a steady supply of oxygenated blood to survive. The heart muscle is supplied by multiple coronary arteries to perform this function. With each heartbeat, healthy coronary arteries guarantee that the heart receives the oxygen it needs to keep beating.

Unfortunately, the coronary arteries are prone to becoming clogged with atherosclerotic plaques. These plaques impede the flow of blood into the heart muscle and promote the development of blood clots that further reduce blood flow. If these plaques and clots entirely obstruct blood flow within a coronary artery, the muscle tissue normally supplied by that artery is deprived of oxygen and starts to die. A heart attack (or acute myocardial infarction) is what happens when part of the heart muscle dies due to constricted blood flow from the coronary arteries. Coronary artery disease is one of the most common causes of death in the United States.

The prevention and treatment of heart disease follows from this basic biology. Daily low-dose aspirin, for instance, prevents clot formation and hence reduces heart disease risk. A healthy diet reduces the substrates that promote atherosclerotic plaque formation. For patients with substantial blockage of one or more coronary arteries, treatment is focused on restoring clear blood flow to heart muscles. Coronary artery bypass grafts (CABG), for instance, involve open heart surgery to directly replace diseased coronary arteries with vessels that have no plaque. A less invasive procedure, coronary

Jay Bhattacharya is associate professor at the Stanford University School of Medicine and a research associate of the National Bureau of Economic Research.

For acknowledgments, sources of research support, and disclosure of the author's material financial relationships, if any, please see http://www.nber.org/chapters/c12975.ack.

angioplasty, involves inserting a catheter (or long narrow tube) into the coronary artery and taking action to clear the plaque from within the artery itself.

A major problem with both CABG and coronary angioplasty is that the coronary arteries tend not to stay clear of atherosclerotic plaque forever. Restenosis is the process of the cleared coronary arteries becoming blocked again, placing a patient at risk of a heart attack. If restenosis is detected, patients may need to undergo a repeat CABG or angioplasty.

Stents are small metal tubes, placed during angioplasty at the site of the blocked artery, to prevent restenosis. While bare-metal stents can be effective in reducing restenosis rates, even with such stents, restenosis can happen. One reason for this is that the cell lining of coronary arteries (called endothelium) plays a key role in the development of atherosclerotic plaques and in restenosis. Healthy endothelial cells prevent atherosclerotic plaque formation, while diseased cells—and scar tissue caused by stent placement—promote restenosis.

Drug-eluting stents (DES) prevent restenosis by incorporating powerful immunosuppressive drugs (like sirolimus or everolimus) or chemotherapeutic agents (like paclitaxel) into the stent. These drugs, which are delivered over time to coronary artery endothelial cells, for various reasons, prevent or slow the process of the coronary arteries becoming blocked again. At the same time, the process of placing a DES can itself cause damage to the endothelial lining and promote clot formation, so DES patients often need to take powerful anticlotting drugs for years after stent placement.

A Brief Timeline

Given this medical background, the rapid adoption of DES into medical practice should not be surprising. The following is a brief timeline of events that are crucial to understanding the dissemination of DES into practice in the United States.[1] The key events involve clinical science and regulatory action. Crucially, between 2002 and 2008, Medicare paid the same fee for patients undergoing DES placement in multiple coronary arteries as it paid for patients undergoing DES placement in one coronary artery.

- 1997: First patent filed for sirolimus-eluting stents.
- 2001–2002: First randomized evidence shows that DES could reduce restenosis rates relative to coronary angiography using bare-metal stents (BMS) (e.g., Morice et al. 2002).
- 2002: The Center for Medicare and Medicaid Services (CMS) authorizes higher reimbursement for angioplasty with drug-eluting stents; no separate codes, though, for multivessel DES placement.
- 2003: The Food and Drug Administration approves sirolimus DES for use by American physicians.

---

1. This timeline is based in part on Stefanini and Holmes's (2013) review of the literature on DES.

- 2004: The FDA approves paclitaxel DES.
- 2006–2007: New evidence emerges that sirolimus and paclitaxel stents increase the rate of clot formation at the site of the stent (e.g., Daemen et al. 2007); physicians start putting DES patients on long-term anticlotting agents.
- 2007: The FDA approves zotarolimus-eluting stents. Physicians switch away from sirolimus stents.
- 2008: CMS introduces new billing codes to reimburse providers a higher amount for multivessel stenting.
- 2012: More than 500,000 DES placed in American patients with coronary artery disease per year.

Theories of Technological Diffusion

Chandra, Malenka, and Skinner offer three different, though not mutually exclusive, possible mechanisms for the spread of DES technology into practice. Their delineation of the possible mechanisms provides a helpful way to think about the ways in which the process of technological dissemination in medicine is helpful and harmful to patients, both from a medical and from an economic point of view. They also test the four mechanisms against Medicare data to measure the empirical importance of them. They rely on data from 2003 to 2004, a period of time when DES technology was popular but had not yet matured into practice. This is a particularly interesting period to study for technology diffusion because it focuses attention on early adopters. Though none of their empirical tests are definitive, they are all interesting and point toward ways to generate better information.

The first mechanism Chandra, Malenka, and Skinner explore is the profit motive. The idea is simple: health care providers will adopt a new technology if an only if doing so improves the bottom line. There is undoubtedly a lot of truth to this idea; health care providers, whatever their charitable instincts, cannot afford to stay in business indefinitely losing money, and there is a wealth of evidence in the health economics literature in supporting. In Italy, for instance, Grilli, Guastaroba, and Taroni (2007) argue that private hospitals with highly profitable open heart surgical suites have little incentive to provide DES to patients in lieu of a CABG, while the opposite is true in public hospitals. Accordingly, they find that public hospitals in Italy were much quicker to adopt DES than private hospitals.

Chandra, Malenka, and Skinner employ a similar empirical strategy in the American context—they compare the adoption rate of DES by for-profit hospitals against the adoption rate by nonprofit hospitals. Unlike the Italian context, however, it is not true that the placement of DES during this period was always profitable. DES placement for Medicare patients with multivessel coronary artery disease, for instance, was most likely unprofitable for hospitals, since Medicare's billing codes during that period did not distinguish multivessel and single-vessel DES placement. And in fact, the point estimates from the Chandra, Malenka, and Skinner regressions suggest that for-profit hospitals adopted DES at a slower rate than nonprofit hospitals.

The second mechanism that Chandra, Malenka, and Skinner explore is also simple and persuasive: hospitals that were most likely to have experience with DES during its development and testing periods before FDA approval in 2003 are also the ones most likely to adopt the technology quickly. They test this idea by comparing the adoption rates of teaching hospitals against nonteaching hospitals. They reason correctly that the former were more likely to have prior experience with DES placement. The adoption data do in fact confirm that teaching hospitals adopted DES faster than nonteaching hospitals. Perhaps a future analysis could directly measure which teaching hospitals participated in the testing of DES on patients in the pre–2003 era, and compare their uptake against teaching hospitals that did not.

The third mechanism is one of knowledge spillovers—a hospital is more likely to adopt DES technology if doctors in a nearby hospital adopt DES technology. In principle, this could happen for many reasons. For instance, some doctors have admitting privileges to several hospitals. This would induce a mechanical correlation between the hospital-level adoption rates of DES, as long as doctors practice the same way at every hospital. Another possibility is that providers adopt the technology to gain a competitive advantage over the other providers in a market. Or finally, perhaps there is direct transfer of knowledge and expertise from doctor to doctor within a community about the use of the new technology. All of these stories are consistent with Chandra, Malenka, and Skinner's finding of a correlation between a hospital's adoption rate of DES and the adoption rate of other hospitals in a market.

Allocation of New Technologies to Patients

In a separate analysis, Chandra, Malenka, and Skinner study the effects of rapid diffusion of DES on patient outcomes. This complements a prominent earlier study involving two of the three authors, which found that the spread of DES technology decreased restenosis rates in the Medicare population (Malenka et al. 2008). Here, Chandra, Malenka, and Skinner study whether hospitals located in places where DES diffusion was slow had worse outcomes than those located in places where diffusion was fast. This is an important question because, like many new medical technologies, supplies of drug-eluting stents were limited in the 2002–2003 period when they were first introduced. A rational allocation process would send those limited supplies to areas where there are patients who stand to benefit the most from the new technology.

Chandra et al. divide up their sample into quintiles based on the rate of adoption of DES. Table 11C.1 reorganizes the point estimates from the

Table 11C.1   Odds ratios from patient-level regression of repeat coronary angiography

	Pre-DES	Post-DES
Q1 (low diffusion)	0.971	1.014
Q2	0.97	0.812
Q3	0.99	0.891
Q4	1.026	0.909
Q5 (high diffusion)	1	0.866

Table 11C.2   Odds ratios from patient-level regression of death or heart attack

	Pre-DES	Post-DES
Q1 (low diffusion)	1.199	1.161
Q2	1.034	1.081
Q3	1.121	1.075
Q4	1.018	1.008
Q5 (high diffusion)	1	0.918

Note: Technically, Chandra, Malenka, and Skinner study ST-elevation myocardial infarctions.

Chandra et al. logistic regression analyzing the probability of a repeat angioplasty procedure for hospitals in the various diffusion quintiles. The table reports odds ratios of a repeat angiography relative to a hospital in a rapid adoption quintile. Table 11C.2 does the same for the probability of patient death or heart attack following coronary angioplasty.

There are two striking findings. First, *even before the introduction of DES*, patients treated at hospitals that ultimately were slow to adopt DES had lower odds of a repeat coronary angiography, but higher odds of death or a heart attack. Second, the fastest adopting hospitals had the largest improvements in patient outcomes. Together, these findings suggest that the allocation process of new technologies appropriately started with the best-prepared providers.

This is an optimistic take-home message about the American health care system, but this optimism should be tempered when considering the welfare of the early adopting patients. In 2003, when DES diffused into medical practice, there was much that was not known about how best to manage patients with drug-eluting stents. For instance, the fact that many patients should be placed on anticlotting drugs for an extended period after the DES placement was not known. Further, the drug used (sirolumus) has subsequently been replaced by other immunosuppressive agents that apparently produce better outcomes. Any comprehensive welfare analysis of technological spread should account for the fact that early adopters serve as test subjects for the development of the technology, even after it has been approved for use by the various regulatory authorities.

References

Daemen, J., P. Wenaweser, K. Tsuchida, L. Abrecht, S. Vaina, C. Morger, N. Kukreja et al. 2007. "Early and Late Coronary Stent Thrombosis of Sirolimus-Eluting and Paclitaxel-Eluting Stents in Routine Clinical Practice: Data from a Large Two-Institutional Cohort Study." *Lancet* 369:667–78.

Grilli, R., P. Guastaroba, and F. Taroni. 2007. "Effect of Hospital Ownership Status and Payment Structure on the Adoption and Use of Drug-Eluting Stents for Percutaneous Coronary Interventions." *Canadian Medical Association Journal* 176 (2): 185–90.

Malenka, D. J., A. V. Kaplan, F. L. Lucas, S. M. Sharp, and J. S. Skinner. 2008. "Outcomes Following Coronary Stenting in the Era of Bare-Metal Versus the Era of Drug-Eluting Stents." *Journal of the American Medical Association* 299 (24): 2868–76.

Morice, M. C., P. W. Serruys, J. E. Sousa, J. Fajadet, E. Ban Hayashi, M. Perin, A. Colombo et al. 2002. "A Randomized Comparison of a Sirolimus-Eluting Stent with a Standard Stent for Coronary Revascularization." *New England Journal of Medicine* 346:1773–80.

Roger, V. L., A. S. Go, D. M. Lloyd-Jones, E. J. Benjamin, J. D. Berry, W. B. Borden, D. M. Bravata et al. 2012. "Heart Disease and Stroke Statistics—2012 Update: A Report from the American Heart Association." *Circulation* 125:e2–e220.

Stefanini, G. G., and D. R. Holmes, Jr. 2013. "Drug-Eluting Coronary-Artery Stents." *New England Journal of Medicine* 368:254–65.

12

Who Uses the Roth 401(k), and How Do They Use It?

John Beshears, James J. Choi, David Laibson, and Brigitte C. Madrian

The Economic Growth and Tax Relief Reconciliation Act of 2001 allowed plan sponsors to add a Roth 401(k) option to defined contribution savings plans starting on January 1, 2006. Like contributions to a Roth IRA, employee contributions to a Roth 401(k) or 403(b) are not deductible from current taxable income, but withdrawals of principal, interest, and capital gains in retirement are tax free. The Plan Sponsor Council of America (2012) reports that 49 percent of 401(k) plans offered a Roth option in 2011.

In this chapter, we describe the characteristics of employees who utilize the Roth 401(k). We also describe how employees use the Roth 401(k). Roth contributions are advantageous to households whose current marginal tax

John Beshears is assistant professor of business administration at the Harvard Business School and a faculty research fellow of the National Bureau of Economic Research. James J. Choi is associate professor of finance at the Yale School of Management and a faculty research fellow of the National Bureau of Economic Research. David Laibson is the Robert I. Goldman Professor of Economics at Harvard University and a research associate of the National Bureau of Economic Research. Brigitte C. Madrian is the Aetna Professor of Public Policy and Corporate Management at the Kennedy School of Government at Harvard University and codirector of the Household Finance Working Group and a research associate at the National Bureau of Economic Research.

We thank Jim Poterba for insightful comments and Luca Maini, Brendan Price, and Michael Puempel for excellent research assistance. We acknowledge financial support from the National Institute on Aging (grants R01-AG021650 and P01AG005842) and the Social Security Administration (grant FLR09010202-02 through RAND's Financial Literacy Center and grant #5 RRC08098400-04-00 to the National Bureau of Economic Research as part of the SSA Retirement Research Consortium). The opinions and conclusions expressed are solely those of the authors and do not represent the opinions or policies of the NIA, the SSA, any agency of the federal government, or the NBER. The authors have, at various times in the last three years, been compensated to present academic research at events hosted by financial institutions that administer retirement savings plans. See the authors' websites for a complete list of outside activities. For acknowledgments, sources of research support, and disclosure of the authors' material financial relationships, if any, please see http://www.nber.org/chapters/c12978.ack.

rate is lower than their marginal tax rate in retirement. If households understand this fact, then we would expect younger employees to be more likely to allocate contributions to the Roth. Employees with transitorily low income would also be expected to utilize the Roth 401(k). If households are uncertain about whether their marginal tax rate will be higher or lower in retirement, they may wish to hedge this risk by contributing to both Roth and before-tax accounts in their 401(k).

We use administrative 401(k) plan data from twelve companies that introduced a Roth 401(k) option between 2006 and 2010. We find that approximately one year after the Roth has been introduced, 8.6 percent of all 401(k) participants have a positive balance in their Roth account. Roth balances make up only 1.8 percent of total 401(k) balances at these companies on average, a small proportion that partially reflects the short amount of time Roth contributions have been possible relative to other contributions. Looking at flows instead of stocks, Roth contributions constitute 5.4 percent of employee contributions. Roth contributions are much more significant for those who choose to make them. Conditional on having a positive Roth contribution rate, 65.8 percent of employee contributions go to the Roth. Consistent with the existence of a tax diversification motive, 54.8 percent of employees who contribute to the Roth also contribute to another 401(k) account.

Samuelson and Zeckhauser (1988), Choi et al. (2002, 2004), and Beshears et al. (2008) document that many employees are passive in their retirement savings accounts. The low usage of the Roth 401(k) may reflect an active preference against the Roth, but it can also be partially explained if employees who enrolled in the 401(k) when the Roth was unavailable fail to update their 401(k) elections in response to the introduction of the Roth. Supporting the importance of the passivity channel, we find that 19.0 percent of 401(k) participants who were hired after the Roth's introduction have a positive balance in the Roth approximately one year after its introduction. This percentage is much higher than the 7.9 percent of 401(k) participants hired before the Roth's introduction who have a positive balance in the Roth.

Turning to the demographic covariates of Roth usage within the 401(k) participant population, we find that those with positive Roth balances are younger and more likely to be male. Higher-salary workers are less likely to have a positive Roth balance among 401(k) participants who are post-Roth hires, but more likely among 401(k) participants who are pre-Roth hires. The negative correlation among post-Roth hires is consistent with the Roth being more attractive to workers in temporarily low current tax brackets. However, once age is controlled for, salary has at best a weak association with Roth usage in this group. The positive correlation among pre-Roth hires may be explained by a negative correlation between income and passivity, which would cause higher-income employees to be more likely to update their 401(k) elections in response to the Roth's introduction. There is likely also a positive correlation between income and financial literacy, including knowledge of the rules that govern the Roth 401(k). At a given point in calendar time, those with higher tenure at the company are less likely to use the Roth among pre-Roth hires, although the association is small once other variables are controlled for.

Conditional on the employee having a positive 401(k) contribution rate, the Roth contribution rate as a fraction of income is initially declining with age but rises again starting in middle age. Men contribute more to the Roth than women, and participants with higher tenure contribute less. Among pre-Roth hires, higher salaries are associated with a small increase in the Roth contribution rate. The demographic patterns are similar for the Roth contribution rate as a fraction of the total employee contribution rate (before-tax plus after-tax plus Roth). Conditional on contributing to the Roth, being middle aged and female are associated with also contributing to another account in the 401(k). Among pre-Roth hires, low salary and high tenure are associated with mixing contributions.

The remainder of the chapter proceeds as follows. In section 12.1, we summarize some of the institutional rules of the Roth 401(k). Section 12.2 describes our data. Section 12.3 discusses summary statistics on how employees use the Roth 401(k) and the characteristics of Roth users. Section 12.4 investigates the correlates of Roth usage in a multivariate regression framework. Section 12.5 concludes.

12.1 The Rules and Economics of the Roth 401(k)

We begin by describing the tax treatment of three different types of 401(k) contributions: Roth contributions, before-tax contributions, and after-tax contributions. Roth contributions to a 401(k) are not deductible from current-year taxable income, but principal, interest, and capital gains may be withdrawn tax free if the withdrawal is considered "qualified" because (a) the account has been held for at least five years, and (b) the account owner is either older than 59.5, disabled, or deceased. Therefore, the marginal dollar of pretax income can purchase $(1 - \tau_0)(1 + r)$ of future consumption if a Roth account is used as the savings vehicle and the balance is accessed through a qualified withdrawal, where τ_0 is the household's marginal ordinary income tax rate plus the marginal reduction in means-tested benefits (such as the Earned Income Tax Credit) due to the additional dollar of taxable income in the year of the contribution, and r is the return earned on the contribution between the contribution and withdrawal dates. Put another way, each dollar contributed to a Roth account buys $1 + r$ of future consumption. For nonqualified withdrawals, the withdrawn principal is not taxed, but the interest and capital gains are subject to ordinary income tax and may reduce means-tested benefits and increase taxation of Social Security benefits received in the year of the withdrawal. If the account owner is younger than 59.5, the withdrawn earnings are also assessed a 10 percent tax penalty under most circumstances.

In contrast, before-tax 401(k) contributions are deductible from current-year income, but the principal, interest, and capital gains are taxed at the ordinary income tax rate upon withdrawal. Hence, the marginal dollar of pretax income buys $(1 + r)(1—\tau_1)$ of future consumption if it is contributed to a before-tax account, where τ_1 is the household's marginal ordinary income tax rate in the year of the withdrawal plus an adjustment if the withdrawal generates a marginal increase in taxation of Social Security benefits or a reduction in means-tested benefits. An additional 10 percent tax penalty applies to both the principal and earnings withdrawn if the account owner is younger than 59.5.

After-tax 401(k) contributions are not deductible from current taxable income. At withdrawal, principal is not taxed but interest and capital gains are taxed at the ordinary income tax rate, and this interest and capital gains income may affect means-tested benefits and taxation of Social Security benefits. The marginal dollar of pretax income can buy $(1—\tau_0)[1 + (1—\tau_1)r]$ of future consumption if an after-tax 401(k) account is used as the savings vehicle. Equivalently, each dollar contributed to an after-tax account buys $1 + (1—\tau_1)r$ of future consumption. An additional 10 percent tax penalty applies to earnings that are withdrawn by account owners younger than 59.5.

If there are no employer-matching contributions in the 401(k) and withdrawals occur late enough to be considered qualified by the Roth criteria, then saving the next pretax dollar in the Roth is a better financial deal than saving it before tax, if and only if $\tau_0 < \tau_1$. In a progressive tax system whose rules stay fixed over time, τ_1 will typically be less than τ_0 because non-401(k) income in retirement will typically be lower than current income, causing most before-tax 401(k) withdrawal dollars to be taxed at a lower rate than the last dollar of income today. McQuarrie (2008) uses this observation to argue that the Roth 401(k) is inferior to a before-tax 401(k) for many households whose current income pushes them above the lowest marginal tax bracket.[1]

The relative appeal of the Roth increases with the probability of withdrawal before age 59.5, since Roth principal is exempt from the 10 percent early withdrawal penalty but before-tax principal is not. Roth contributions are always a better deal than after-tax contributions if the money is held in the 401(k) long enough to meet the Roth qualifying withdrawal criteria and investment earnings are positive. However, after-tax contributions are some-

---

1. McQuarrie (2008) also considers how tax laws may change in his analysis. Burman, Gale, and Weiner (1998) find that between 1980 and 1995, changes in tax laws had a much larger effect on individuals' marginal tax rates than variation induced by lifecycle income patterns. See Ahern et al. (2005) and Kotlikoff, Marx, and Rapson (2008) for other analyses of the relative merits of the Roth 401(k).

times more liquid before age 59.5, since some 401(k) plans allow younger employees to make withdrawals from after-tax balances while still employed by the company without demonstrating financial hardship.

Although employers can structure their savings plans to allow Roth, before-tax, and after-tax employee contributions, employer matching contributions must be made using before-tax dollars, meaning that the entire principal and earnings of the match balance are subject to ordinary income tax upon withdrawal. A company might not match certain types of employee contributions (e.g., after-tax contributions), but among the types of contributions it does match, the match formula typically does not vary by the type of contribution. This invariance reduces the attractiveness of Roth and after-tax contributions if the employee's marginal 401(k) contribution dollar is being matched. To see this, let m be the rate at which employee contributions are matched. The marginal pretax dollar can earn m match dollars if it is saved using a before-tax account, but only $(1-\tau_0)m$ match dollars if it is saved using a Roth or after-tax account (since τ_0 dollars must be paid in taxes and given up in benefits, thereby preventing the entire dollar from being contributed to the savings plan). The condition under which employees who have no probability of making a nonqualified withdrawal are better off contributing to the Roth rather than the before-tax account is now more restrictive; with an employer match, the Roth is a better financial deal than contributing before tax if and only if

(1) $$(1-\tau_0)[1 + m(1-\tau_1)] > (1-\tau_1)(1 + m).$$

Another factor affecting the attractiveness of Roth versus regular before-tax contributions is whether employees are constrained by the contribution limits on 401(k) plans. Internal Revenue Service regulations stipulate that the combined before-tax plus Roth contributions in a calendar year cannot exceed a certain limit that is adjusted each year. For people younger than fifty, this limit was $14,000 in 2005 (the last year before Roth contributions were allowed); it has been raised several times since then and stands at $17,500 in 2013. The dollar values for each year in the interim are listed in table 12.1. People age fifty and older are allowed an additional "catch-up" contribution; this additional amount was $4,000 in 2005 and has since been increased to its 2013 level of $5,500. In addition to the limits on employee contributions, there is a limit on the combined employer plus employee contribution to 401(k) accounts. This aggregate limit was set at $42,000 in 2005 and has since been raised to $51,000 in 2013 for people under the age of fifty. Because a dollar of Roth balances buys (weakly) more retirement consumption than a dollar of before-tax balances, people who are constrained by the before-tax plus Roth contribution ceiling could find it advantageous to make Roth contributions instead of before-tax contributions in order to extend the 401(k) tax shelter over more effective dollars.

Table 12.1   401(k) contribution limits

| | Employee before-tax plus Roth contribution limit | | Employer plus employee contribution limit | |
	Age < 50 ($)	Additional catch-up contribution limit if age ≥ 50 ($)	Age < 50 ($)	Age ≥ 50 ($)
2005	14,000	4,000	42,000	46,000
2006	15,000	5,000	44,000	49,000
2007	15,500	5,000	45,000	50,000
2008	15,500	5,000	46,000	51,000
2009	16,500	5,500	49,000	54,500
2010	16,500	5,500	49,000	54,500
2011	16,500	5,500	49,000	54,500
2012	17,000	5,500	50,000	55,500
2013	17,500	5,500	51,000	56,500

12.2 Data Description

To analyze the utilization of Roth accounts, we use 401(k) administrative data from Aon Hewitt, a firm with a large US benefits administration and consulting business. We selected twelve companies that introduced a Roth option to their 401(k) plan between 2006 and 2010. The data are repeated cross-sectional snapshots of all employees at each calendar-year-end. Each snapshot contains individual-level data on every employee's current plan participation status, plan enrollment date, monthly contribution rates, plan balances, birth date, hire date, salary (for nine of the twelve companies), and gender. We restrict our sample to employees between the ages of twenty and sixty-nine.

Table 12.2 shows the characteristics of each company as of year-end 2010. In order to preserve these companies' anonymity, we refer to each company by the letters A through L and only disclose approximate employee counts. The companies are all large, ranging from approximately 10,000 employees to 100,000 employees. Eight of the twelve companies are in the financial services industry, and average salaries exceed $100,000 for companies A, E, F, and I. Hence, the employees at these firms are likely to be more financially sophisticated than the typical US employee. Average age ranges from thirty-five to forty-eight years; average tenure at the company ranges from five years to sixteen years; and male percentage ranges from 33 percent to 76 percent.

Table 12.3 summarizes the features of the 401(k) plan at each company as of 2010. Five companies introduced the Roth option in 2006, one in 2007, three in 2008, one in 2009, and two in 2010. Five companies automatically enroll their employees in the 401(k) at before-tax contribution rates of between 2 percent and 6 percent of income. The automatic enrollment companies have an average participation rate of 88 percent, which is higher

Table 12.2   Company characteristics as of 2010

Company	Industry	Total employees	Average age	Median salary ($)	Average salary ($)	Average tenure (yrs)	Percent male (%)
A	Pharmaceutical	~50,000	43.1	95,100	106,089	10.6	54
B	Financial services	~10,000	46.4	77,079	84,285	11.9	42
C	Financial services	~25,000	44.9	75,049	86,705	13.4	54
D	Financial services	~25,000	43.7	54,687	73,679	9.6	46
E	Financial services	~50,000	35.0	140,598	295,206	4.9	61
F	Financial services	~25,000	44.0	80,304	148,184	8.4	60
G	Financial services	~10,000	47.5	N/A	N/A	12.2	53
H	Financial services	~25,000	40.7	N/A	N/A	8.9	33
I	Business services	~25,000	36.4	83,900	109,856	6.6	62
J	Manufacturing	~25,000	46.6	59,218	74,808	16.0	65
K	Manufacturing	~100,000	45.7	67,694	77,694	13.4	76
L	Financial services	~10,000	42.3	N/A	N/A	8.1	35

Table 12.3   401(k) characteristics as of 2010

Company	Participation rate (%)	Enrollment default	Employer match structure	Max contribution allowed (% of salary)	Roth 401(k) introduction date
A	84	3% before-tax contribution rate	75% match on first 6% of income contributed after 1 year of tenure	50	1/1/2008
B	98	3% before-tax contribution rate	70% match on first 6% of income contributed	20	9/1/2006
C	96	3% before-tax contribution rate	100% match on first 6% of income contributed; employees with < 5 years of tenure matched at 80%	100	1/1/2008
D	82	Nonenrollment	133% match on first 3% of income contributed after 1 year of tenure	45	1/1/2006
E	49	Nonenrollment	No match	50	2/1/2006
F	75	Nonenrollment	100% match on first 6% of income contributed after 1 year of tenure	100	1/1/2007
G	88	Nonenrollment	No match	20	1/1/2006
H	74	Nonenrollment	115% match on first 6% of income contributed after 1 year of tenure	20	1/1/2008
I	86	Nonenrollment	No match	50	1/1/2006
J	90	6% before-tax contribution rate	Either 70% or 100% match on first 6% of income contributed	35	1/1/2009
K	74	2% before-tax contribution rate	100% match on the first 2% of income contributed, 50% match on the next 2% of income contributed, and 25% match on the next 4% of income contributed	75	1/1/2010
L	85	Nonenrollment	50% match on the first 6% of income contributed	100	7/1/2010

than the average participation rate of 77 percent among the companies that have opt-in enrollment schemes. Nine companies match employee contributions up to a threshold between 3 percent and 8 percent of income at rates between 25 percent and 133 percent. The maximum percent of a paycheck that can be contributed to the 401(k) ranges from 20 percent to 100 percent. These maximums are subject to IRS restrictions described earlier on the total dollars that can be contributed within a calendar year.

12.3 Summary Statistics on Roth Usage and Roth Users

In this section, we present basic summary statistics on how employees use the Roth 401(k) and the characteristics of employees who use the Roth. We report these statistics for each company as of the end of the first calendar year in which the Roth 401(k) was available for at least eleven months. Thus, for the nine companies that introduced the Roth in a January, the numbers in table 12.4 reflect usage exactly twelve months after Roth introduction. For company E, which introduced the Roth on February 1, 2006, the numbers come from the eleventh month after Roth introduction. For companies B (which introduced the Roth on September 1, 2006) and L (which introduced the Roth on July 1, 2010), we report numbers from sixteen months and eighteen months, respectively, after Roth introduction.

The first column of table 12.4 shows that the Roth is used by only a small minority of 401(k) participants. Only between 3.9 percent and 16.0 percent of 401(k) participants have a positive balance in the Roth; averaging across the sample (weighting each company by its 401(k) participants), 8.6 percent of participants have used the Roth. The sample-wide average is affected by the five companies that automatically enroll their employees with default contribution elections that allocate nothing to the Roth (and everything to the before-tax account). However, if we restrict the sample to companies without automatic enrollment, the fraction of participants with positive Roth balances rises only to 11.5 percent. Plan Sponsor Council of America (2012) reports that a higher proportion of their sample (17.4 percent) contributes to the Roth, but this number is not directly comparable to ours. Their sample comes entirely from 2011, whereas our sample comes from years ranging between 2006 and 2011. Their sample includes companies that have offered a Roth option for many years, whereas we capture the state of Roth participation approximately one year after the Roth's introduction. Nevertheless, our sample may have a lower inherent propensity to contribute to the Roth than the PSCA sample. Aon Hewitt (2012) reports that during 2011, 8.1 percent of 401(k) participants in the companies in their database with a Roth option contributed to the Roth, which is similar to the 8.6 percent figure we calculate for the fraction that have positive Roth balances.

The fraction of employee contribution balances held in the Roth is considerably lower than the fraction of employees with positive Roth balances,

Table 12.4 Roth 401(k) utilization after Roth introduction

Company	The % of 401(k) participants with positive balance in Roth	Average % of 401(k) employee contribution balances in Roth	Average % of 401(k) total balances in Roth	Average % of employee contributions going to Roth at year-end	Average % of employee contributions going to Roth at year-end, conditional on positive Roth contribution rate	The % of employees contributing to both Roth and another 401(k) account at year-end, conditional on positive Roth contribution rate
A	7.6	1.3	1.1	4.1	58.8	64.0
B	5.6	1.3	0.6	2.7	53.8	71.7
C	8.5	2.0	1.2	4.3	55.6	66.4
D	11.4	3.7	2.9	6.7	64.6	59.4
E	8.4	3.4	3.1	7.7	99.9	0.1
F	12.0	5.2	4.1	10.3	77.3	37.7
G	11.0	3.1	2.2	8.8	76.7	39.6
H	9.2	3.6	2.6	5.9	68.7	54.0
I	16.0	6.5	5.1	12.2	74.1	46.0
J	3.9	0.4	0.2	2.0	54.3	70.7
K	6.8	1.2	0.7	3.6	56.4	65.7
L	5.9	3.0	1.6	5.3	77.9	40.6
All	8.6	2.4	1.8	5.4	65.8	54.8
All without autoenrollment	11.5	4.3	3.4	8.5	73.6	45.2

Note: The variables in this table are measured as of the end of the first calendar year in which Roth was available for at least eleven months. All averages are equal weighted by person. Nonbalance variables are measured using the 401(k) elections in effect on the measurement date.

ranging from 0.4 percent to 6.5 percent. The average is 2.4 percent among all companies, and 4.3 percent among companies without automatic enrollment. Roth balances as a percent of total 401(k) balances, which also include balances from the employer match and profit-sharing contributions, are even lower, averaging 1.8 percent across all companies and 3.4 percent among companies without automatic enrollment. The small size of Roth balances partially reflects the fact that the numbers in table 12.4 are calculated shortly after Roth introduction (eleven to eighteen months). Examining just contribution flows, a somewhat larger fraction of employee contributions during the last pay period of the calendar year is going to the Roth: 5.4 percent on average across all companies (8.5 percent excluding automatic enrollment companies), with individual companies ranging from 2.0 percent to 12.2 percent.

Although Roth usage is relatively rare, conditional on being used, Roth contributions constitute the majority of an employee's contributions. On average, Roth contributors at year-end are putting 65.8 percent of their employee contributions in the Roth account. At the individual company level, this conditional average is no lower than 53.8 percent, and it is as high as 99.9 percent at company E, which does not allow employees to contribute to both the Roth account and the before-tax account.[2]

Recall that employer matches are required to be made in before-tax dollars, so any Roth contributor at a company with a match is necessarily engaging in some tax diversification. If employees are unaware that their match is in before-tax dollars, this tax diversification is unwitting. However, a majority of Roth users (54.8 percent) are actively engaging in tax diversification by simultaneously making *employee* contributions to both the Roth and another 401(k) account. This average is diminished by company E, which does not allow tax diversification of employee contributions and also does not have a match. Much of the diversification we observe is not consistent with employees following a naïve 50-50 rule; conditional on having a positive Roth contribution rate, only 15.0 percent has a Roth contribution rate that is equal to the before-tax contribution rate (not shown in tables), which is far below the 54.8 percent engaging in active tax diversification.[3]

Samuelson and Zeckhauser (1988), Choi et al. (2002, 2004), and Beshears et al. (2008) document that many employees are passive in their retirement savings accounts. Therefore, the low usage of the Roth may partially reflect a sluggish response to its introduction rather than an active preference against the Roth. To explore the role of inertia, we examine how Roth participation differs between 401(k) participants who were hired before Roth introduction and participants who were hired after Roth introduction. Inertia can be gener-

2. There is only one person in our company E data who anomalously has both a positive before-tax contribution rate and a positive Roth contribution rate.
3. The fraction that has a Roth contribution rate equal to the sum of the before-tax and after-tax contribution rates, conditional on having a positive Roth contribution rate, is 13.6 percent.

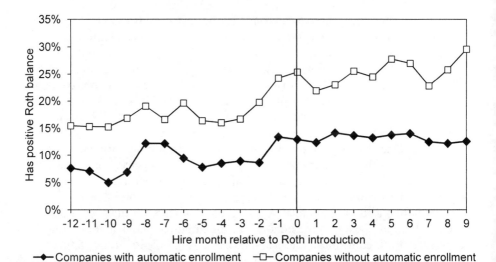

Fig. 12.1   Percent of 401(k) participants with positive Roth balances, by hire month relative to Roth introduction

ated both by the (possibly time-inconsistent) desire to delay incurring action costs (Carroll et al. 2009) and inattention (Cadena and Schoar 2011; Choi et al. 2012). Attention to 401(k) plan features is likely to be especially high at the point employees join the company. Therefore, employees who were hired after Roth introduction are more likely to be aware of the Roth's presence than employees who were hired before the Roth was an option in the plan. At companies without automatic enrollment, the marginal action cost to contribute to the Roth conditional on being a 401(k) participant is also lower for post-Roth hires than for pre-Roth hires. This is because for a 401(k) participant hired after Roth adoption, the Roth option can be chosen while the employee is actively enrolling and has already paid the cost of finding the human resources website or phone number, his password, and so forth. For a 401(k) participant hired before Roth introduction who enrolled before the Roth was available, the marginal cost of contributing to the Roth includes the cost of regaining access to his 401(k) elections through a website or phone number.

Figure 12.1 plots the fraction of 401(k) participants with a positive Roth balance at the end of the first calendar year in which the Roth 401(k) was available for at least eleven months. The horizontal axis is the participant's hire month relative to the Roth introduction month. In both companies with and without automatic enrollment, Roth usage is lower among participants who are pre-Roth hires than participants who are post-Roth hires. Higher Roth usage begins with participants hired in the month prior to Roth introduction, perhaps reflecting when the 401(k) plan literature was revised to show the Roth option. The increase in Roth usage is about 8 percentage points in companies without automatic enrollment and 5 percentage points in companies with automatic enrollment.

Tables 12.5 and 12.6 expand the figure's sample to include all pre- or post-Roth hires, not just those hired in a narrow window around Roth introduction. Table 12.5 shows that among 401(k) participants who were hired after the Roth's introduction, 19.0 percent have a positive balance in the Roth, 13.5 percent of employee contribution balances and 11.4 percent of total 401(k) balances are held in the Roth, and 14.3 percent of employee contribution flows are going to the Roth at year end. These numbers are much higher than the corresponding numbers in table 12.6 for 401(k) participants who were hired before the Roth: 7.9 percent have a positive Roth balance, 1.7 percent of employee contribution balances and 1.1 percent of total 401(k) balances are held in the Roth, and 4.7 percent of employee contribution flows are going to the Roth at year end.

Conditional on using the Roth, post-Roth hires allocate a greater fraction of their contributions (75.8 percent) to the Roth than pre-Roth hires (63.9 percent). This gap narrows considerably when we exclude companies with automatic enrollment from the average; conditional on using the Roth, post-Roth hires in this subsample make 77.4 percent of their contributions to the Roth versus 72.8 percent for pre-Roth hires. Among all of the firms in our study, post-Roth hires are less likely than pre-Roth hires to mix their Roth contributions with other contributions—41.4 percent versus 57.3 percent. This difference is smaller when we study only companies without automatic enrollment—39.6 percent versus 46.5 percent.

In light of the differences in Roth usage between pre- and post-Roth hires, our analysis going forward will analyze these two populations separately.

Table 12.7 shows the average age, average salary, and gender composition of 401(k) participants among post-Roth hires who do and do not have positive Roth balances. Relative to non-Roth users, Roth users are on average younger by 3.4 years and have a salary that is $11,500 lower, but gender composition is similar across the two groups. Excluding companies with automatic enrollment does not qualitatively change the results of these comparisons. Since Roth contributions are advantageous for households whose current marginal tax rate is lower than their marginal tax rate in retirement, the finding that younger, lower-income households are more likely to contribute to the Roth could indicate that households are responding in the correct direction to the tax incentives created by the Roth. The young are more likely to have higher income in retirement than they do currently, and lower-income individuals are more likely to be among the 47 percent of tax units that have no current income tax liability (Williams 2009), so their marginal tax rate in retirement is more likely to be weakly greater than it is today.

The picture changes somewhat for 401(k) participants among pre-Roth hires (table 12.8). Roth users are still younger than non-Roth users, but Roth users have a higher average income and are more likely to be male. Roth

Table 12.5 Roth 401(k) utilization among post-Roth hires

Company	The % of 401(k) participants with positive balance in Roth	Average % of 401(k) employee contribution balances in Roth	Average % of 401(k) total balances in Roth	Average % of employee contributions going to Roth at year-end	Average % of employee contributions going to Roth at year-end, conditional on positive Roth contribution rate	The % of employees contributing to both Roth and another 401(k) account at year-end, conditional on positive Roth contribution rate
A	13.6	7.7	7.7	8.7	66.1	53.9
B	12.2	6.9	3.5	7.5	65.3	53.8
C	23.3	15.3	9.0	16.3	72.5	46.4
D	27.5	17.7	17.5	18.3	71.9	47.5
E	12.4	10.2	10.2	12.4	100.0	0.0
F	22.9	16.9	16.9	18.0	81.7	31.1
G	27.3	19.6	19.6	22.3	79.9	34.7
H	33.3	22.9	22.9	23.2	72.4	48.8
I	28.4	20.5	19.7	21.6	76.4	42.7
J	9.5	8.2	3.0	7.8	71.9	45.7
K	10.6	8.1	3.8	8.5	77.4	37.7
L	6.1	5.4	3.7	5.7	80.9	39.1
All	19.0	13.5	11.4	14.3	75.8	41.4
All without autoenrollment	25.0	17.8	17.4	19.0	77.4	39.6

Note: The variables in this table are measured as of the end of the first calendar year in which Roth was available for at least eleven months. All averages are equal weighted by person. Nonbalance variables are measured using the 401(k) elections in effect on the measurement date.

Table 12.6   **Roth 401(k) utilization among pre-Roth hires**

Company	The % of 401(k) participants with positive balance in Roth	Average % of 401(k) employee contribution balances in Roth	Average % of 401(k) total balances in Roth	Average % of employee contributions going to Roth at year-end	Average % of employee contributions going to Roth at year-end, conditional on positive Roth contribution rate	The % of employees contributing to both Roth and another 401(k) account at year-end, conditional on positive Roth contribution rate
A	7.2	0.9	0.7	3.8	57.9	65.3
B	4.9	0.7	0.3	2.2	50.4	76.9
C	7.6	1.1	0.7	3.4	51.8	71.0
D	10.1	2.5	1.7	5.7	62.8	62.3
E	8.0	2.8	2.4	7.2	99.8	0.2
F	10.6	3.4	2.4	9.1	76.0	39.6
G	10.0	2.0	1.2	7.9	76.1	40.5
H	8.1	2.7	1.7	5.1	67.9	55.1
I	14.3	4.5	3.1	10.8	73.4	47.0
J	3.8	0.3	0.2	1.9	53.3	71.9
K	6.6	0.8	0.5	3.3	54.0	68.9
L	5.9	2.7	1.4	5.2	77.6	40.7
All	7.9	1.7	1.1	4.7	63.9	57.3
All without autoenrollment	10.2	3.0	2.1	7.4	72.8	46.5

Note: The variables in this table are measured as of the end of the first calendar year in which Roth was available for at least eleven months. All averages are equal weighted by person. Nonbalance variables are measured using the 401(k) elections in effect on the measurement date.

Table 12.7   Characteristics of Roth users and nonusers among post-Roth hires

Company	Age		Salary ($000s)		% male		N
	Roth users	Nonusers	Roth users	Nonusers	Roth users	Nonusers	
A	33.9	35.8	69.5	76.8	54.6	47.8	2,323
B	35.2	38.0	64.4	65.0	52.2	42.8	756
C	32.9	35.6	61.8	64.8	59.9	59.2	1,189
D	35.0	38.3	20.5	25.0	51.0	48.3	2,175
E	27.9	31.3	121.5	194.5	72.6	64.3	1,000
F	34.6	39.1	55.7	62.1	67.4	57.2	2,075
G	33.0	38.4	N/A	N/A	53.9	49.0	801
H	34.0	36.6	N/A	N/A	46.1	48.2	958
I	30.9	35.5	62.6	79.2	60.0	60.3	2,978
J	33.7	37.7	63.8	51.3	65.3	65.2	514
K	35.6	37.7	65.0	58.1	78.1	73.5	5,466
L	34.2	36.0	N/A	N/A	53.8	45.4	427
All	33.5	36.9	57.3	68.8	60.5	59.6	20,662
All without autoenrollment	33.0	36.7	52.3	77.3	57.6	55.1	10,414

Note: The variables in this table are measured as of the end of the first calendar year in which Roth was available for at least eleven months. We exclude people with zero 401(k) balances.

Table 12.8 **Characteristics of Roth users and nonusers among pre-Roth hires**

Company	Age		Salary ($000s)		% male		Tenure (years)	
	Roth users	Nonusers	Roth users	Nonusers	Roth users	Nonusers	Roth users	Nonusers
A	40.3	43.6	94.2	94.9	59.1	51.7	9.2	10.8
B	42.5	46.2	74.1	74.4	41.2	41.3	10.7	12.1
C	41.4	45.6	79.3	73.7	59.6	52.0	11.4	14.7
D	39.9	44.4	77.8	78.4	59.6	44.4	8.6	11.6
E	36.2	36.2	313.6	289.5	71.4	61.4	9.7	7.6
F	40.7	44.6	199.4	155.1	70.8	56.7	7.2	8.8
G	41.7	45.5	N/A	N/A	71.0	53.7	8.9	10.2
H	36.5	43.1	N/A	N/A	43.5	32.1	6.9	11.4
I	31.8	37.2	83.2	109.6	64.8	58.3	5.2	7.0
J	43.4	46.7	71.7	70.6	70.4	64.8	14.1	16.6
K	43.4	47.1	82.1	79.8	76.3	73.2	12.6	15.1
L	40.6	44.8	N/A	N/A	48.3	35.8	7.8	11.1
All	39.8	44.6	103.8	96.8	65.3	58.1	9.5	12.5
All without autoenrollment	37.3	42.2	130.4	136.6	62.3	48.8	7.3	9.7

Note: The variables in this table are measured as of the end of the first calendar year in which Roth was available for at least eleven months. We exclude people with zero 401(k) balances.

users also have lower average tenure at the company. Restricting the sample to companies without automatic enrollment causes the salary relationship to flip sign, however, so that Roth users have a lower salary than non-Roth users, as in the post-Roth hire population.

The instability of the salary effect is somewhat surprising, but the patterns can be rationalized. In principle, the Roth should appeal to taxpayers with *temporarily* low income, not permanently low income. If our income variable is highly correlated with *permanent* income, we should not expect to see a robust relationship between Roth usage and income. In fact, there are even countervailing effects. Workers with high observed income are likely to be more financially literate, leading them to use the Roth account with *greater* frequency, since relatively literate households are more likely to know about and understand the Roth accounts and to act upon preferences to contribute to a Roth.

12.4. Regression Analysis of Correlates of Roth Usage

In this section, we analyze the correlates of Roth usage in a multivariate regression framework. The dependent variables vary, but all of them are measured as of the end of the first calendar year in which the Roth was available for at least eleven months. The explanatory variables are measured as of the same date and do not change across regressions: age in excess of twenty years, age in excess of twenty years squared, a male dummy, log salary (when available), and log tenure. The two age terms are often divided by 100 or 10,000 so that more significant digits appear in the table. The top rows of the tables show results for regressions that are run separately by company, but the last two rows show coefficients from regressions that pool either all companies with complete data on employee characteristics, or all companies with complete data on employee characteristics that do not have automatic enrollment. Regressions that contain more than one company also control for company dummies. Our discussion will mostly focus on the pooled company regressions with the most comprehensive set of companies.

Table 12.9 shows coefficients from regressing a dummy for having positive Roth balances on the control variables. Among both post- and pre-Roth hires, older 401(k) participants are less likely to use the Roth. The second derivative with respect to age is positive, but Roth usage with respect to age does not reach its minimum until age fifty-two among post-Roth hires and age fifty-nine among pre-Roth hires, when the probability of Roth usage is 18.2 percentage points and 12.9 percentage points lower, respectively, than for twenty-year-olds. Men are 2 to 3 percentage points more likely to use the Roth. Salary has at best a weak relationship with Roth usage. There is no significant salary relationship among post-Roth hires, indicating that the negative correlation between Roth usage and salary in table 12.7 is driven by Roth users being younger than non-Roth users. In companies without automatic enrollment, the salary coefficient is in fact negative and significant, although small in magnitude—a 10 percent increase in salary decreases the probability of Roth usage by only 0.1 percentage points. The salary coefficient is significantly positive but small in magnitude for pre-Roth hires—a 10 percent increase in salary increases the probability of Roth usage by 0.1 percentage points. Unlike for the univariate comparison of means in table 12.8, the positive pre-Roth hire relationship with salary in the regression holds even when the sample excludes automatic enrollment companies. Tenure has no correlation with Roth usage in the post-Roth hire cohort, and a significant but small negative correlation with Roth usage in the pre-Roth hire cohort. In the latter group, a 10 percent increase in tenure decreases the probability of Roth usage by 0.1 percentage points.

In table 12.10, we examine the demographic correlates of the Roth contribution rate as a fraction of income, conditional on having a positive total 401(k) balance. Roth contributions initially fall with age before rising. Among post-Roth hires, the Roth contribution rate falls by 1.5 percent of income from age twenty to forty-five and then rises. At age sixty-nine, the Roth contribution rate is only 0.12 percent of income lower than at age twenty. Among pre-Roth hires, the Roth contribution rate falls by 1.0 percent of income from age twenty to fifty-three and then rises, but at age sixty-nine, the Roth contribution rate is still 0.8 percent of income lower than at age twenty. Men contribute 0.5 percent of income more than women to the Roth in the post-Roth hire cohort, and 0.2 percent of income more than women in the pre-Roth hire cohort. Salary is uncorrelated with the Roth contribution rate among post-Roth hires, but is positively correlated with the Roth contribution rate among pre-Roth hires. In the latter group, a 10 percent increase in salary is associated with a 0.03 percent of income increase in the Roth contribution rate. Tenure is negatively correlated with the Roth contribution rate; a 10 percent increase in tenure is associated with a 0.02 percent of income decrease in the Roth contribution rate among post-Roth hires and a 0.002 percent of income decrease among pre-Roth hires.

The Roth contribution rate reflects both the desired overall savings rate in the 401(k) and the desired fraction of 401(k) balances in the Roth. In table 12.11, we isolate the latter by using as the dependent variable the Roth contribution rate as a fraction of the total employee contribution rate (i.e., the before-tax plus after-tax plus Roth contribution rate). Among post-Roth hires, the fraction is initially decreasing with age but bottoms out at age forty-eight, when participants allocate 18.8 percentage points less to the Roth than twenty-year-olds. At age sixty-nine, participants allocate 9.0 percentage points less to the Roth than twenty-year-olds. For pre-Roth hires, the fraction also decreases with age until fifty-four, when participants allocate 10.3 percentage points less to the Roth. Men allocate 3.0 percentage points more to the Roth if hired after Roth introduction and 1.7 percentage points more if hired before Roth introduction. Salary has a minor

Table 12.9   Demographic correlates of having positive Roth balance

A. Post-Roth hires

Company	(Age − 20) / 100	(Age − 20)² / 10,000	Male	log(salary)	log(tenure)	N
A	−1.00***	1.99**	0.05***	−0.02	−0.01	2,085
	(0.32)	(0.82)	(0.02)	(0.02)	(0.01)	
B	−0.43	0.34	0.03	0.02	−0.00	756
	(0.45)	(1.06)	(0.03)	(0.02)	(0.02)	
C	−1.25***	1.94*	0.01	0.02	−0.02	1,188
	(0.46)	(1.17)	(0.02)	(0.03)	(0.02)	
D	−2.00***	3.54***	0.02	−0.00	0.01	2,175
	(0.34)	(0.81)	(0.02)	(0.01)	(0.02)	
E	−2.86***	7.29***	0.06***	−0.02	0.02	1,000
	(0.49)	(1.41)	(0.02)	(0.02)	(0.02)	
F	−1.13***	1.32*	0.08***	−0.00	−0.05**	2,075
	(0.31)	(0.69)	(0.02)	(0.02)	(0.03)	
G	−1.79***	2.37*	0.04	N/A	−0.05	801
	(0.53)	(1.29)	(0.03)		(0.03)	
H	−1.27**	1.98	−0.01	N/A	0.02	958
	(0.53)	(1.31)	(0.03)		(0.04)	
I	−2.10***	3.56***	0.03*	−0.09***	−0.01	2,978
	(0.31)	(0.80)	(0.02)	(0.02)	(0.01)	
J	−0.71	0.96	0.00	0.06***	0.05***	514
	(0.46)	(1.17)	(0.03)	(0.02)	(0.02)	
K	−0.34**	0.26	0.02*	0.06***	0.03***	5,466
	(0.14)	(0.32)	(0.01)	(0.01)	(0.01)	
L	−0.26	0.41	0.02	N/A	−0.01	427
	(0.40)	(0.96)	(0.02)		(0.02)	
All with complete data	−1.15***	1.82***	0.03***	0.01	0.00	18,237
	(0.10)	(0.24)	(0.01)	(0.00)	(0.00)	
All with complete data and without autoenrollment	−1.94***	3.20***	0.04***	−0.01**	−0.00	8,228
	(0.16)	(0.40)	(0.01)	(0.01)	(0.01)	

B. Pre-Roth hires

Company	(Age − 20)/ 100	(Age − 20)² / 10,000	Male	log(salary)	log(tenure)
A	−0.76***	1.07***	0.02***	0.02***	−0.00
	(0.07)	(0.15)	(0.00)	(0.00)	(0.00)
B	−0.25**	0.14	−0.00	0.01*	0.00
	(0.12)	(0.24)	(0.01)	(0.00)	(0.00)
C	−0.40***	0.28	0.01***	0.03***	−0.01***
	(0.09)	(0.18)	(0.00)	(0.00)	(0.00)
D	−0.67***	−0.76***	0.05***	0.00**	−0.02***
	(0.09)	(0.17)	(0.00)	(0.00)	(0.00)
E	−1.91***	4.65***	0.03***	0.01***	0.01***
	(0.12)	(0.27)	(0.01)	(0.00)	(0.00)
F	−0.58***	0.50***	0.03***	0.03***	−0.01***
	(0.09)	(0.18)	(0.01)	(0.00)	(0.00)
G	−0.22**	−0.11	0.07***	N/A	−0.01***
	(0.10)	(0.19)	(0.01)		(0.00)
H	−0.77***	1.11***	0.02***	N/A	−0.03***
	(0.07)	(0.15)	(0.00)		(0.00)
I	−1.90***	2.95***	0.04***	−0.01**	−0.01***
	(0.11)	(0.25)	(0.00)	(0.01)	(0.00)
J	−0.32***	0.38***	0.01***	0.01***	−0.00
	(0.06)	(0.11)	(0.00)	(0.00)	(0.00)
K	−0.30***	0.23***	0.01***	0.03***	−0.01***
	(0.03)	(0.07)	(0.00)	(0.00)	(0.00)
L	−0.17	0.10	0.03***	N/A	−0.02***
	(0.15)	(0.30)	(0.01)		(0.00)
All with complete data	−0.67***	0.87***	0.02***	0.01***	−0.01***
	(0.02)	(0.05)	(0.00)	(0.00)	(0.00)
All with complete data and without autoenrollment	−1.14***	1.66***	0.04***	0.01***	−0.01***
	(0.05)	(0.10)	(0.00)	(0.00)	(0.00)

Notes: Each row of this table reports coefficients from a separate ordinary least squares regression where the dependent variable is a dummy for having a positive Roth balance at the end of the first calendar year in which Roth was available for at least eleven months. We exclude people with zero 401(k) balances. The regressions include a constant. Regressions with multiple companies in them also control for company dummies. Standard errors are in parentheses. To preserve the anonymity of the companies, sample sizes are not listed in panel B.

***Significant at the 1 percent level.

**Significant at the 5 percent level.

*Significant at the 10 percent level.

Table 12.10   Demographic correlates of Roth contribution rate

A. Post-Roth hires

Company	(Age − 20)	(Age − 20)² / 100	Male	log(salary)	log(tenure)	N
A	-0.13*** (0.03)	0.26*** (0.08)	0.54*** (0.14)	0.01 (0.19)	-0.16 (0.13)	2,085
B	-0.06** (0.03)	0.10 (0.07)	0.36** (0.15)	0.14 (0.14)	-0.01 (0.11)	756
C	-0.15*** (0.04)	0.34*** (0.10)	0.28 (0.22)	0.35 (0.24)	-0.24 (0.18)	1,188
D	-0.13*** (0.03)	0.32*** (0.08)	0.44** (0.18)	0.09 (0.10)	-0.15 (0.18)	2,175
E	-0.45*** (0.10)	1.29*** (0.29)	0.66 (0.45)	0.17 (0.36)	-0.27 (0.51)	1,000
F	-0.06 (0.10)	0.06 (0.22)	2.12*** (0.62)	-0.27 (0.49)	-1.51* (0.84)	2,075
G	-0.14** (0.06)	0.27* (0.15)	0.86** (0.37)	N/A	0.01 (0.35)	801
H	-0.09** (0.03)	0.20** (0.08)	0.21 (0.20)	N/A	-0.24 (0.24)	958
I	-0.29*** (0.04)	0.56*** (0.10)	0.30 (0.21)	-0.12 (0.25)	-0.26 (0.18)	2,978
J	-0.04 (0.03)	0.08 (0.08)	-0.08 (0.18)	0.19 (0.15)	0.27** (0.12)	514
K	-0.05*** (0.01)	0.10*** (0.03)	0.10 (0.08)	0.42*** (0.06)	0.16*** (0.05)	5,466
L	-0.00 (0.02)	-0.00 (0.05)	-0.03 (0.13)	N/A	0.05 (0.10)	427
All with complete data	-0.12*** (0.01)	0.24*** (0.04)	0.52*** (0.09)	0.01 (0.06)	-0.19*** (0.07)	18,237
All with complete data and no autoenrollment	-0.19*** (0.03)	0.37*** (0.08)	0.81*** (0.18)	-0.10 (0.12)	-0.47*** (0.18)	8,228

B. Pre-Roth hires

Company	(Age − 20)	(Age − 20)² / 100	Male	log(salary)	log(tenure)
A	-0.05***	0.07***	0.15***	0.21***	-0.03
	(0.01)	(0.01)	(0.03)	(0.04)	(0.02)
B	-0.02***	0.02	-0.02	0.04**	0.04**
	(0.01)	(0.01)	(0.03)	(0.02)	(0.02)
C	-0.04***	0.05***	0.08**	0.24***	-0.04
	(0.01)	(0.02)	(0.04)	(0.03)	(0.02)
D	-0.02***	0.02	0.28***	0.03	-0.12***
	(0.01)	(0.01)	(0.03)	(0.02)	(0.02)
E	-0.14***	0.27***	0.40***	0.48***	0.01
	(0.03)	(0.06)	(0.12)	(0.07)	(0.08)
F	-0.09***	0.12*	0.78***	1.02***	0.06
	(0.03)	(0.06)	(0.19)	(0.10)	(0.10)
G	-0.01	-0.01	0.64***	N/A	0.00
	(0.01)	(0.02)	(0.07)		(0.04)
H	-0.03***	0.05***	0.19***	N/A	-0.14***
	(0.00)	(0.01)	(0.02)		(0.01)
I	-0.17***	0.28***	0.26***	0.06	0.04
	(0.01)	(0.03)	(0.05)	(0.06)	(0.04)
J	-0.02***	0.02*	0.02	0.10***	0.00
	(0.00)	(0.01)	(0.02)	(0.02)	(0.01)
K	-0.03***	0.05***	0.04**	0.20***	-0.03***
	(0.00)	(0.01)	(0.02)	(0.02)	(0.01)
L	-0.00	0.01	0.25***	N/A	-0.13***
	(0.02)	(0.03)	(0.08)		(0.05)
All with complete data	-0.06***	0.09***	0.18***	0.31***	-0.02**
	(0.00)	(0.01)	(0.02)	(0.01)	(0.01)
All with complete data and no autoenrollment	-0.11***	0.18***	0.42***	0.46***	-0.05*
	(0.01)	(0.02)	(0.05)	(0.03)	(0.03)

Notes: Each row of this table reports coefficients from a separate ordinary least squares regression where the dependent variable is the Roth contribution rate at the end of the first calendar year in which Roth was available for at least eleven months. A 1 percent contribution rate corresponds to a dependent variable value of 1, not 0.01. We exclude people with zero 401(k) balances. The regressions include a constant. Regressions with multiple companies in them also control for company dummies. Standard errors are in parentheses. To preserve the anonymity of the companies, sample sizes are not listed in panel B.

***Significant at the 1 percent level.

**Significant at the 5 percent level.

*Significant at the 10 percent level.

Table 12.11 Demographic correlates of Roth contribution as a percent of total employee 401(k) contribution

A. Post-Roth hires

Company	(Age – 20)	(Age – 20)² / 100	Male	log(salary)	log(tenure)	N
A	-1.19***	2.35***	4.26***	-1.06	-1.67	2,005
	(0.24)	(0.61)	(1.16)	(1.53)	(1.02)	
B	-0.98***	1.56*	2.91	0.90	-0.89	695
	(0.33)	(0.80)	(1.87)	(1.72)	(1.51)	
C	-1.73***	3.22***	-0.29	1.28	-1.82	1,159
	(0.37)	(0.93)	(1.99)	(2.20)	(1.62)	
D	-1.86***	3.49***	4.37***	-0.28	0.58	2,063
	(0.27)	(0.65)	(1.52)	(0.85)	(1.53)	
E	-2.84***	7.35***	4.98**	-2.14	2.17	877
	(0.52)	(1.48)	(2.31)	(1.90)	(2.59)	
F	-1.18***	1.68***	8.14***	0.38	-6.69***	2,029
	(0.27)	(0.60)	(1.72)	(1.36)	(2.35)	
G	-2.11***	3.48***	5.08*	N/A	-3.58	762
	(0.47)	(1.16)	(2.75)		(2.59)	
H	-1.31***	2.00*	1.23	N/A	1.80	877
	(0.44)	(1.09)	(2.55)		(3.03)	
I	-2.49***	4.69***	2.55*	-7.78***	-0.33	2,815
	(0.26)	(0.68)	(1.45)	(1.72)	(1.20)	
J	-0.83*	1.58	1.11	1.58	2.26	425
	(0.43)	(1.10)	(2.54)	(2.08)	(1.98)	
K	-0.43***	0.49*	1.62*	4.53***	0.20	4,994
	(0.12)	(0.29)	(0.85)	(0.58)	(0.61)	
L	-0.10	0.02	1.66	N/A	3.17*	325
	(0.41)	(0.99)	(2.51)		(1.82)	
All with complete data	-1.32***	2.32***	3.03***	0.36	-1.13***	17,062
	(0.08)	(0.20)	(0.50)	(0.36)	(0.42)	
All with complete data and no autoenrollment	-2.03***	3.64***	4.28***	-1.48***	-0.30	7,784
	(0.14)	(0.34)	(0.82)	(0.57)	(0.81)	

B. Pre-Roth hires

Company	(Age − 20)	(Age − 20)² / 100	Male	log(salary)	log(tenure)
A	-0.59***	0.89***	1.65***	1.85***	-0.41***
	(0.05)	(0.10)	(0.20)	(0.25)	(0.14)
B	-0.38***	0.52***	-0.27	0.38**	0.09
	(0.07)	(0.14)	(0.32)	(0.16)	(0.19)
C	-0.49***	0.66***	0.72***	1.63***	-0.80***
	(0.06)	(0.11)	(0.24)	(0.24)	(0.17)
D	-0.47***	0.58***	3.67***	-0.15	-1.45***
	(0.06)	(0.12)	(0.27)	(0.17)	(0.17)
E	-1.22***	2.42***	3.62***	1.24***	-0.43
	(0.13)	(0.32)	(0.60)	(0.38)	(0.42)
F	-0.74***	0.89***	3.26***	2.72***	-1.79***
	(0.09)	(0.18)	(0.53)	(0.28)	(0.27)
G	-0.49***	0.45***	6.03***	N/A	-1.02***
	(0.10)	(0.18)	(0.47)		(0.32)
H	-0.77***	1.30***	1.46***	N/A	-2.43***
	(0.06)	(0.12)	(0.31)		(0.19)
I	-1.83***	3.06***	3.67***	-1.05**	-0.91***
	(0.10)	(0.22)	(0.42)	(0.46)	(0.30)
J	-0.28***	0.37***	0.43***	0.73***	-0.02
	(0.04)	(0.07)	(0.16)	(0.15)	(0.09)
K	-0.30***	0.37***	0.62***	1.44***	-0.38***
	(0.02)	(0.04)	(0.13)	(0.12)	(0.07)
L	-0.40**	0.47	0.87	N/A	-2.25***
	(0.17)	(0.32)	(0.80)		(0.53)
All with complete data	-0.61***	0.90***	1.72***	0.89***	-0.57***
	(0.02)	(0.03)	(0.08)	(0.07)	(0.05)
All with complete data and no autoenrollment	-1.06***	1.59***	3.65***	0.79***	-1.44***
	(0.04)	(0.08)	(0.21)	(0.14)	(0.13)

Notes: Each row of this table reports coefficients from a separate ordinary least squares regression where the dependent variable is the Roth contribution rate as a percent of the total employee 401(k) contribution rate at the end of the first calendar year in which Roth was available for at least eleven months. A dependent variable value of 1 corresponds to 1 percent, not 100 percent. We exclude people with zero 401(k) balances. The regressions include a constant. Regressions with multiple companies in them also control for company dummies. Standard errors are in parentheses. To preserve the anonymity of the companies, sample sizes are not listed in panel B.

***Significant at the 1 percent level.

**Significant at the 5 percent level.

*Significant at the 10 percent level.

effect, being insignificant for post-Roth hires (unless automatic enrollment companies are excluded, in which case a 10 percent increase in salary is associated with a 0.1 percentage point decrease in the Roth fraction) and a significant but economically small effect among pre-Roth hires, where a 10 percent increase in salary increases the Roth fraction by 0.09 percentage points. Higher tenure decreases the Roth fraction for both post-Roth hires (0.1 percentage points per 10 percent increase in tenure) and pre-Roth hires (0.06 percentage points per 10 percent increase in tenure).

Because matching contributions are required to be in before-tax dollars, the fraction of employee contributions going to the Roth is greater than the fraction of total 401(k) contributions going to the Roth in companies that match contributions. However, we find in untabulated results that the demographic patterns do not change materially when we use the fraction of total 401(k) contributions going to Roth as our dependent variable instead of the fraction of employee contributions going to the Roth.

Finally, in table 12.12, we examine the demographic correlates of having a positive non-Roth employee contribution rate conditional on having a positive Roth contribution rate, which is a sign of a deliberate tax diversification strategy. Among post-Roth hires, contributing to both accounts increases with age until age forty-three, when employees are 42.1 percentage points more likely than twenty-year-olds to do so, and then decreases to the point where at age sixty-nine, employees are 8.5 percentage points less likely to contribute to both accounts than twenty-year-olds. Contributing to both accounts is 5 percentage points less likely for males, but there is no relationship with salary or tenure. Among pre-Roth hires, contributing to both accounts also increases with age until age forty-seven, when employees are 32.1 percentage points more likely to do so than twenty-year-olds, but even sixty-nine-year-olds are 10.3 percentage points more likely to contribute to both accounts than twenty-year-olds. As with post-Roth hires, pre-Roth men are 6 percentage points less likely to contribute to both accounts, but unlike post-Roth hires, pre-Roth employees with low salaries and high tenure are more likely to contribute to both, although the effect sizes are economically small and salary is not significant when automatic enrollment companies are excluded.

12.5 Conclusion

Roth 401(k) usage is relatively uncommon in our sample of firms; approximately one year after the Roth is introduced, only 8.6 percent of 401(k) participants have positive Roth balances. But among those who do contribute to the Roth, Roth contributions constitute a large fraction of their total contributions. The young are more likely to use the Roth and to allocate a larger fraction of their contributions to it. This correlation could be consistent with a rational response to the Roth's tax incentives, since Roth contributions

Table 12.12   Demographic correlates of having a positive non-Roth employee contribution conditional on having a positive Roth contribution

A. Post-Roth hires

Company	(Age − 20) / 100	(Age − 20)² / 10,000	Male	log(salary)	log(tenure)	N
A	4.02*** (1.19)	−8.51** (3.33)	−0.12** (0.06)	−0.09 (0.09)	0.06 (0.05)	279
B	3.15 (1.99)	−4.94 (5.50)	−0.22* (0.11)	0.13 (0.15)	−0.11 (0.09)	80
C	3.86** (1.14)	−8.13** (3.17)	0.03 (0.06)	0.06 (0.08)	0.01 (0.05)	261
D	3.35*** (0.74)	−7.38*** (1.82)	−0.07 (0.04)	0.04 (0.03)	−0.05 (0.05)	526
E	—	—	—	—	—	—
F	3.04*** (0.75)	−6.68*** (1.85)	−0.11** (0.05)	−0.03 (0.04)	0.10 (0.06)	447
G	1.73 (1.13)	−2.88 (2.94)	−0.09 (0.07)	N/A	−0.03 (0.06)	213
H	2.18** (1.04)	−3.63 (2.62)	−0.08 (0.06)	N/A	−0.05 (0.08)	281
I	4.46*** (0.65)	−10.00*** (1.86)	−0.02 (0.04)	0.07 (0.05)	−0.05 (0.03)	797
J	2.36 (3.06)	−6.96 (8.65)	−0.00 (0.16)	0.24 (0.15)	−0.11 (0.17)	46
K	2.82*** (0.76)	−5.35*** (1.90)	−0.02 (0.05)	−0.10** (0.05)	0.07** (0.03)	551
L	−7.69* (4.41)	17.92 (10.67)	0.01 (0.24)	N/A	0.06 (0.17)	23
All with complete data	3.60*** (0.31)	−7.70*** (0.82)	−0.05*** (0.02)	0.00 (0.01)	0.01 (0.02)	2,987
All with complete data and no autoenrollment	3.77*** (0.39)	−8.34*** (1.03)	−0.06** (0.02)	0.03 (0.02)	−0.03 (0.02)	1,770

Table 12.12 (continued)

B. Pre-Roth hires

Company	(Age − 20) / 100	(Age − 20)² / 10,000	Male	log(salary)	log(tenure)
A	2.65***	−4.79***	−0.08***	−0.17***	0.03*
	(0.47)	(1.03)	(0.02)	(0.03)	(0.01)
B	4.81***	−9.09***	−0.00	−0.05	−0.01
	(1.08)	(2.35)	(0.05)	(0.03)	(0.04)
C	3.26***	−6.15***	−0.04	−0.09***	0.06***
	(0.59)	(1.24)	(0.03)	(0.03)	(0.02)
D	0.68	−1.29	−0.10***	0.04***	0.08***
	(0.43)	(0.94)	(0.02)	(0.01)	(0.01)
E	—	—	—	—	—
F	2.00***	−3.51***	0.01	−0.05***	0.03**
	(0.48)	(0.99)	(0.03)	(0.02)	(0.01)
G	2.44***	−5.11***	−0.10***	N/A	−0.02
	(0.56)	(1.14)	(0.03)		(0.02)
H	3.37***	−7.88***	−0.07***	N/A	0.09***
	(0.50)	(1.15)	(0.03)		(0.02)
I	4.20***	−8.68***	−0.07***	−0.12***	−0.00
	(0.50)	(1.34)	(0.02)	(0.03)	(0.02)
J	2.81***	−5.27***	−0.02	−0.15***	0.03*
	(0.70)	(1.45)	(0.03)	(0.03)	(0.02)
K	2.83***	−5.17***	−0.05***	−0.03*	0.02**
	(0.27)	(0.55)	(0.02)	(0.02)	(0.01)
L	1.96	−4.25	−0.03	N/A	0.05
	(1.63)	(3.54)	(0.07)		(0.05)
All with complete data	2.39***	−4.45***	−0.06***	−0.03***	0.03***
	(0.16)	(0.33)	(0.01)	(0.01)	(0.01)
All with complete data and no autoenrollment	1.92***	−3.53***	−0.07***	−0.00	0.04***
	(0.25)	(0.55)	(0.01)	(0.01)	(0.01)

Notes: Each row of this table reports coefficients from a separate ordinary least squares regression where the dependent variable is a dummy for having both positive Roth and positive non-Roth employee contribution rates at the end of the first calendar year in which Roth was available for at least eleven months. The sample is restricted to employees who have a positive Roth contribution rate on this date. The regressions include a constant. Regressions with multiple companies in them also control for company dummies. Standard errors are in parentheses. To preserve the anonymity of the companies, sample sizes are not listed in panel B.

***Significant at the 1 percent level.

**Significant at the 5 percent level.

*Significant at the 10 percent level.

are advantageous to those whose current marginal tax rate is lower than the marginal tax rate at which those contributions will later be withdrawn.

Roth participation is more than twice as high among 401(k) participants who were hired after the Roth introduction relative to 401(k) participants who were hired before the Roth introduction. Because of passivity or inattention, 401(k) participants do not react quickly to the Roth option when it is introduced after they have already joined the 401(k) plan.

References

Ahern, Michael, John Ameriks, Joel Dickson, Robert Nestor, and Stephen Utkus. 2005. "Tax Diversification and the Roth 401(k)." Vanguard Center for Retirement Research (18). https://advisors.vanguard.com/iwe/pdf/CRR_Roth_401k_IWE.pdf.

Aon Hewitt. 2012. "2012 Universe Benchmarks: Measuring Employee Savings and Investing Behavior in Defined Contribution Plans." http://www.aon.com/human-capital-consulting/thought-leadership/retirement/reports-2012_universe_benchmarks.jsp.

Beshears, John, James J. Choi, David Laibson, and Brigitte C. Madrian. 2008. "The Importance of Default Options for Retirement Savings Outcomes: Evidence from the United States." In *Lessons from Pension Reform in the Americas*, edited by Stephen J. Kay and Tapen Sinha, 59–87. Oxford: Oxford University Press.

Burman, Leonard E., William G. Gale, and David Weiner. 1998. "Six Tax Laws Later: How Individuals' Marginal Federal Income Tax Rates Changed Between 1980 and 1995." *National Tax Journal* 51:637–652.

Cadena, Ximena, and Antoinette Schoar. 2011. "Remembering to Pay? Reminders vs. Financial Incentives for Loan Payments." NBER Working Paper no. 17020, Cambridge, MA.

Carroll, Gabriel D., James J. Choi, David Laibson, Brigitte C. Madrian, and Andrew Metrick. 2009. "Optimal Defaults and Active Decisions." *Quarterly Journal of Economics* 124:1639–74.

Choi, James J., Emily Haisley, Jennifer Kurkoski, and Cade Massey. 2012. "Small Cues Change Savings Choices." NBER Working Paper no. 17843, Cambridge, MA.

Choi, James J., David Laibson, Brigitte C. Madrian, and Andrew Metrick. 2002. "Defined Contribution Pensions: Plan Rules, Participant Decisions, and the Path of Least Resistance." In *Tax Policy and the Economy* (vol. 16), edited by James Poterba, 67–114. Cambridge, MA: MIT Press.

———. 2004. "For Better or For Worse: Default Effects and 401(k) Savings Behavior." In *Perspectives on the Economics of Aging*, edited by David A. Wise, 81–121. Chicago: University of Chicago Press.

Kotlikoff, Laurence J., Ben Marx, and David Rapson. 2008. "To Roth or Not?—That Is the Question." NBER Working Paper no. 13763, Cambridge, MA.

McQuarrie, Edward F. 2008. "Thinking About a Roth 401(k)? Think Again." *Journal of Financial Planning* (July):38–48.

Plan Sponsor Council of America. 2012. "PSCA's Annual Survey Shows Company Contributions Are Bouncing Back." Press release. October 11. http://www.psca

.org/psca-s-annual-survey-shows-company-contributions-are-bouncing-back. (accessed March 29, 2013).

Samuelson, William, and Richard Zeckhauser, 1988. "Status Quo Bias in Decision Making." *Journal of Risk and Uncertainty* 1:7–59.

Williams, Roberton. 2009. "Who Pays No Income Tax?" Washington DC: Tax Policy Center, Urban Institute and Brookings Institution.

Comment   James M. Poterba

This is an interesting chapter that offers empirical evidence on the role of Roth 401(k) plans in the saving decisions of US workers. Roth 401(k)s first became available in 2001, but uncertainty about whether the legislation that created them would expire in 2010 initially slowed their diffusion. In 2006, tax legislation made them permanent. This chapter explores the experience of a small group of large firms that adopted Roth 401(k) plans between 2006 and 2010. The notable findings include: the take-up rate for Roth 401(k)s has been quite slow; age and income have modest predictive power in explaining Roth 401(k) participation, but much remains unexplained; and inertia appears to play an important role in the choice between regular and Roth 401(k) plans. Each of these findings is informative and is likely to stimulate follow-on research.

The chapter begins by discussing the choice problem facing an individual who has access to both a regular and a Roth 401(k). The problem is an extended version of the standard asset location problem, in which an individual must choose between saving in a taxable and a tax-deferred account. When both a Roth and a regular 401(k) are available, the individual must choose how much to save in each tax-deferred account. Corner solutions are possible—contributing to only one type of account—as are solutions that involve some "diversification" through contributions to both accounts. The chapter explains that even when an individual chooses to direct all of her contributions to a Roth 401(k), any employer-matching contributions must be placed in a regular 401(k). This means that anyone choosing the "Roth only" strategy at a firm with matching contributions is de facto diversified. There is an upper limit on the amount that can be contributed to either a Roth or a regular 401(k). That limit is $17,500 in 2013, and it is the same for both regular and Roth 401(k)s.

James M. Poterba is the Mitsui Professor of Economics at the Massachusetts Institute of Technology and president and chief executive officer of the National Bureau of Economic Research.

For acknowledgments, sources of research support, and disclosure of the author's material financial relationships, if any, please see http://www.nber.org/chapters/c12979.ack.

The authors describe the standard "Roth versus regular" argument that is found in the financial advice press, which focuses on the relationship between a potential contributor's current marginal tax rate and her expected marginal tax rate in retirement. If a potential contributor believes that her tax rate will be higher in the future than today, then contributing to a Roth 401(k) dominates contributing to a regular 401(k) because paying tax on the contributed income today rather than on the account withdrawals in the future will probably result in a higher net-of-tax payout when the account is drawn down in retirement. While theoretically correct, in practice it may be difficult for an individual to reliably predict her future tax rates.

Several factors contribute to this difficulty, particularly for those who are several decades from retirement. First, there are individual-specific uncertainties associated with the lifetime income trajectory. This includes both uncertainties about the amount that will be earned from wages and potentially from investments at different ages, and uncertainty about the age of retirement at which drawdown of retirement accounts is likely to begin. Most individuals experience substantial variation from year to year in their earnings. This translates into variation in marginal income tax rates, although given the relatively broad income classes that map into marginal tax rates in the US tax code, there is less variation in tax rates than in earnings.

Second, complex tax provisions that affect an individual's tax rate both while working and while retired can make the tax rate comparison quite difficult. While working, for example, whether an individual qualifies for the Earned Income Credit (EIC) can have a substantial effect on her marginal income tax rate. Contributions to a regular 401(k) plan are excluded from the income measure that determines EIC eligibility, while contributions to a Roth 401(k) are not. The choice of plan could therefore affect EIC benefits for some low and moderate income taxpayers. In 2013, a married couple with two children could receive some benefit from the EIC until their wage income exceeded \$48,378. Thus, for example, a married individual with wages of \$49,000 could contribute \$2,000 to a regular 401(k) and receive a tax benefit from the EIC as a result.

There are also complex tax provisions that may apply when the taxpayer is taking withdrawals from a 401(k) account. One example involves the rules that determine the tax treatment of Social Security benefits. The share of a taxpayer's Social Security benefits that is included in taxable income depends on modified adjusted gross income (MAGI), which is the sum of various income flows. Depending on the taxpayer's circumstances, receiving an additional dollar of non–Social Security income can expose fifty or eighty-five cents of Social Security income to taxation, or it may not affect the tax treatment of Social Security income at all. For taxpayers who are in the 15 percent marginal income tax bracket, the potential taxation of a larger share of their Social Security benefits when they receive additional non–Social Security income can generate an effective marginal tax rate of 22.5 percent (1.5 * 15), 27.75 percent (1.85 * 15), or 15 percent. For many taxpayers who are still years or decades from retirement, predicting whether their postretirement income will subject them to these higher marginal tax rates is very difficult. The choice between a Roth and a regular 401(k) can also affect the tax regime that a retiree faces. Roth 401(k) payouts are not included in modified AGI, while regular 401(k) payouts are.

Finally, tax reform creates another source of uncertainty about future tax rates. The United States experienced substantial tax reforms in 1981, 1986, 1993, 2001, and 2013. Significant reforms can have substantial impacts on marginal tax rates. Burman, Gale, and Weiner (1998) calculate the change in marginal tax rates on labor income for households between 1980 and 1995. Primarily as a result of the tax reforms of 1981 and 1986, more than half of all taxpayers experienced marginal tax rate reductions of more than 10 percentage points, and over 70 percent experienced declines of at least 5 percentage points. The uncertainty created by tax reform supports the argument that taxpayers may wish to pursue a diversified strategy with respect to their use of Roth and regular 401(k)s.

The difficulty that a taxpayer faces in predicting her future tax rate, in the face of potential legislative changes, can be illustrated by reflecting on current tax reform discussions. Reports by organizations such as the Congressional Budget Office regularly point to a long-term fiscal gap facing the United States: revenues are projected to fall short of expenditures over horizons of fifty and seventy-five years. One might conclude that this implies a substantial likelihood of higher tax rates in the future, which would enhance the value of a Roth 401(k) relative to a regular 401(k). But that presumes both that the fiscal gap is closed by raising revenue rather than cutting spending, and that the additional revenue is raised via higher tax rates. There are other ways to raise revenue. One possibility is broadening the tax base while keeping marginal rates constant or even reducing them. This scenario might make a regular 401(k) more attractive ex post than a Roth 401(k). Another option might be a shift toward a value added tax (VAT). If a VAT were adopted at a high enough rate to make it possible to lower existing income tax rates, then the regular 401(k) would once again look more attractive ex post than the Roth 401(k) since the taxes are paid at withdrawal, when income tax rates might be lower than they are today. A Roth 401(k) contributor, in contrast, would have paid tax on the amount contributed to the account at high current tax rates, and would then pay VAT—just as a regular 401(k) contributor would—when the funds were withdrawn.

There are aspects of the choice between Roth and regular 401(k)s that are difficult to integrate with the comparison of current and future tax rates. A particularly important one is that Roth 401(k) holders are exempt from the required minimum distribution rules that apply to regular 401(k)s. This makes it possible for Roth account holders to accumulate for longer in a tax-deferred setting than their regular 401(k) counterparts. Recent proposals for limits on the total value of an individual's qualified plan assets might also make Roth 401(k)s more attractive than regular 401(k)s, because the taxes have already been paid on the former and this permits a higher level of retirement consumption to be supported by a given account balance.

A very interesting finding is that those who contribute to Roth 401(k)s are also likely to contribute to a regular 401(k). This appears to be "tax regime diversification," just what many financial planners recommend. The finding is likely due in part, but not completely, to the fact that employer-matching contributions to a Roth 401(k) are deposited into a regular 401(k). But assuming, as the authors conclude, that at least some of those who are contributing to both Roth and regular 401(k)s are doing so by design, one might consider two potential interpretations of this pattern. The first is that it reflects a rational decision to spread one's retirement income across tax regimes, thereby purchasing some insurance against adverse movements in future tax rates. The second is that it is the result of naïve participant behavior. There is some evidence, for example in Benartzi and Thaler (2007), that some workers use a $1/N$ heuristic in choosing investment options in 401(k) plans. In the context of plans that offer both Roth and regular 401(k)s, this could appear as diversification.

One direction that the authors might explore in future work concerns the behavior of limit contributors. Consider the choice between a Roth 401(k) and a regular 401(k) for an individual who wishes to fund the highest possible level of retirement consumption using tax-deferred accounts. This individual would be comparing a limit contribution to a Roth 401(k) and a limit contribution to a regular 401(k). While both account types face a \$17,500 limit in 2013, the taxes have already been paid on the amount in the Roth account. In T years, the amount of net-of-tax spending that can be supported by a \$17,500 contribution to a regular 401(k) is $(1 + r)^T *$ $(1 - t_T) * 17500$, where t_T is the marginal tax rate that applies to withdrawals. In contrast, a limit contribution to a Roth 401(k) will support future consumption of $(1 + r)^T * 17500$. Thus the Roth limit contribution effectively delivers $(1 + r)^T * t_T * 17500$ of *additional* retirement consumption. The retirement consumption maximizer who can afford the taxes and contributions associated with a Roth limit contribution would therefore choose a Roth account, even if her tax rate was expected to remain constant or even to drop slightly in retirement. The behavior of limit contributors may provide another opportunity to distinguish between alternative models of 401(k) contributor decision making.

References

Benartzi, Shlomo, and Richard Thaler. 2007. "Heuristics and Biases in Retirement Saving Behavior." *Journal of Economic Perspectives* 21:81–104.
Burman, Leonard, William Gale, and David Weiner. 1998. "Six Tax Laws Later: How Individuals' Marginal Federal Income Tax Rates Changed Between 1980 and 1995." *National Tax Journal* 51:637–52.

Contributors

Abhijit Banerjee
Department of Economics
Massachusetts Institute of Technology
50 Memorial Drive
Cambridge, MA 02142-1347

James Banks
Arthur Lewis Building-3.020
School of Social Sciences
The University of Manchester
Manchester M13 9PL England

Sharon Barnhardt
Indian Institute of Management -
  Ahmedabad
Vastrapur
Ahmedabad 380 015 India

John Beshears
Harvard Business School
Baker Library 439
Soldiers Field
Boston, MA 02163

Jay Bhattacharya
Center for Primary Care and Outcomes
  Research
Stanford University School of
  Medicine
117 Encina Commons
Stanford, CA 94305-6019

Axel Börsch-Supan
Munich Center for the Economics of
  Aging (MEA)
Amalienstrasse 33
D-80799 Munich, Germany

Amitabh Chandra
John F. Kennedy School of
  Government
Harvard University
79 JFK Street
Cambridge, MA 02138

James J. Choi
Yale School of Management
135 Prospect Street
P.O. Box 208200
New Haven, CT 06520-8200

David M. Cutler
Department of Economics
Harvard University
1805 Cambridge Street
Cambridge, MA 02138

Angus Deaton
361 Wallace Hall
Woodrow Wilson School
Princeton University
Princeton, NJ 08544-1013

Esther Duflo
Department of Economics
Massachusetts Institute of Technology
50 Memorial Drive
Cambridge, MA 02142

Kaushik Ghosh
National Bureau of Economic
    Research
1050 Massachusetts Avenue
Cambridge, MA 02138

Florian Heiss
LS Statistics and Econometrics
University of Düsseldorf
Universitätsstrasse 1, Geb. 24.31
40225 Düsseldorf, Germany

Michael D. Hurd
RAND Corporation
1776 Main Street
Santa Monica, CA 90407

Arie Kapteyn
Center for Economic and Social
    Research
University of Southern California
12015 Waterfront Drive
Playa Vista, CA 90094

Elaine Kelly
Institute for Fiscal Studies
7 Ridgmount Street
London WC1E 7AE England

Gábor Kézdi
Department of Economics
Central European University
9 Nador Street
Budapest, Hungary

David Laibson
Department of Economics
Littauer M-12
Harvard University
Cambridge, MA 02138

Mary Beth Landrum
Department of Health Care Policy
Harvard Medical School
180 Longwood Avenue
Boston, MA 02115-5899

Brigitte C. Madrian
John F. Kennedy School of Government
Harvard University
79 JFK Street
Cambridge, MA 02138

David Malenka, MD
Dartmouth-Hitchcock Medical Center
One Medical Center Drive
Lebanon, NH 03756

Daniel McFadden
Department of Economics
549 Evans Hall #3880
University of California, Berkeley
Berkeley, CA 94720-3880

Erik Meijer
Center for Economic and Social
    Research
University of Southern California
12015 Waterfront Drive
Playa Vista, CA 90094-2536

Pierre-Carl Michaud
Department of Economics
University of Québec at Montréal
Case postale 8888, Succ. Centre-Ville
Montréal, Québec H3C 3P8 Canada

James M. Poterba
Department of Economics E17–214
Massachusetts Institute of Technology
77 Massachusetts Avenue
Cambridge, MA 02139

Susann Rohwedder
RAND Corporation
1776 Main Street
Santa Monica, CA 90407

Morten Schuth
Munich Center for the Economics of
    Aging (MEA)
Amalienstrasse 33
D-80799 Munich, Germany

John B. Shoven
Department of Economics
Stanford University
579 Serra Mall at Galvez Street
Stanford, CA 94305-6015

Jonathan Skinner
Department of Economics
6106 Rockefeller Hall
Dartmouth College
Hanover, NH 03755

James P. Smith
RAND Corporation
1776 Main Street
Santa Monica, CA 90407-2138

Arthur A. Stone
Department of Psychiatry and
  Behavioral Sciences
Putnam Hall
Stony Brook University
Stony Brook, NY 11794-8790

Till Stowasser
Department of Economics
University of Würzburg
Stephanstraße 1
D-97070 Würzburg, Germany

Steven F. Venti
Department of Economics
6106 Rockefeller Center
Dartmouth College
Hanover, NH 03755

Robert J. Willis
3254 ISR
University of Michigan
426 Thompson Street
Ann Arbor, MI 48106

Joachim Winter
Department of Economics
University of Munich
Ludwigs-Maximilians Universität
Ludwigstr. 28 (RG)
D-80539 Munich, Germany

David A. Wise
Harvard University and National
  Bureau of Economic Research
1050 Massachusetts Avenue
Cambridge, MA 02138

Richard Woodbury
National Bureau of Economic
  Research
1050 Massachusetts Avenue
Cambridge, MA 02138

Wei Xie
Department of Economics
University of Southern California
Los Angeles, CA 90089

Author Index

Page numbers followed by the letter *f* or *t* refer to figures or tables, respectively.

Subject Index